the book of
management

the ten essential skills for achieving high performance

Eric Baron, Michael Benoliel, Mike Bourne, Pippa Bourne,
DeeDee Doke, Peter Hobbs, Wei Hua, Johanna Hunsaker,
Phillip L. Hunsaker, Raphael Lapin, James S. O'Rourke, Aileen Pincus

London, New York,
Munich, Melbourne, Delhi

Project Editor: Daniel Mills
Project Designers: Saskia Janssen,
Edward Kinsey, Charlotte Seymour
Managing Editor: Penny Warren
Managing Art Editor: Glenda Fisher
Production Editor: Ben Marcus
Senior Production Controller: Man Fai Lau
Creative Technical Support: Sonia Charbonnier
Publisher: Peggy Vance

First published in Great Britain in 2010 by
Dorling Kindersley Limited
80 Strand, London WC2R 0RL
Penguin Group (UK)

Copyright © 2008–2009, 2010
Dorling Kindersley Limited

10 9 8 7 6 5 4 3 2 1

Material in this publication was previously
published by DK as the following titles in the
Essential Managers series: *Managing People*,
2009; *Motivating People*, 2009; *Project
Management*, 2009; *Achieving High
Performance*, 2009; *Effective Communication*,
2009; *Interviewing People*, 2009; *Presenting*,
2008; *Negotiating*, 2009; *Selling*, 2009;
Working with Difficult People, 2009.

A CIP catalogue record for this book
is available from the British Library

ISBN: 978 1 4053 5899 6

Colour reproduction by Alta Images, London
Printed and bound in China by Starlite

Discover more at
www.dk.com

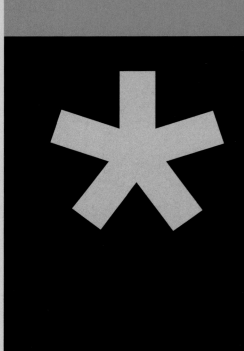

Contents

MANAGING
PEOPLE

Contents

Introduction

Managing other people is perhaps the most challenging task facing any manager. It is a dynamic process that is always evolving to accommodate changes in the diverse and complex workplace. *Managing People* provides the understanding and skills that will help you to develop and manage effective and high-performing teams of satisfied and productive individuals.

Being an effective manager of people starts with self-awareness and self-management. Interpersonal skills are extremely important, in both one-on-one and team situations, as you need to be able to influence others to accomplish their own and the organization's goals. Creating high-performing teams is crucial for any manager today and requires the abilities to set goals, plan and design work, delegate tasks, motivate followers, appraise performance, and solve problems.

As a leader of your team, you need to invest considerable time in helping others to improve their performance and develop their careers. Successful mentoring can contribute to fulfilment of personal, professional, and organizational goals. In helping others to be successful by applying the skills and guidelines presented in *Managing People*, you will not only enhance your effectiveness as a manager, but become a leader that others want to follow.

Chapter 1
Understanding yourself

Knowing yourself will give you valuable insights into your aptitude for managing others. It allows you to understand how you're perceived by others, why they respond to you in the way they do, and how to get the best from them.

Developing self-awareness

Awareness of your emotions, personality, what you enjoy and dislike, what motivates you, and what comes easily or poses challenges is a key precursor to developing effective managerial ability. Quite simply, if you can't manage yourself, you will not be able to manage anyone else.

Keeping moving

The best way to enhance your self-awareness is to learn in a systematic way from your own experiences. Start by reflecting on situations in your working life, your actions in response to them, and the outcomes of these events. Schedule a regular time to do this, either at the beginning or end of a workday, when you are not in the thick of the action. Give yourself space to reflect, and make sure you can be alone and uninterrupted for a significant period of time. Try to gain a better understanding of what happened and think about how you can learn from each situation.

Keeping a journal

Keeping a journal is a good way to help you learn from experience. Journals are similar to diaries, but include entries that address critical aspects of your managerial experiences and reflect on interactions with bosses, employees, and team-mates. Such entries can describe a good (or bad) way someone handled a situation; a problem in the making; the different ways people react to situations; or your thoughts on people in the news, or in books or films. If you want to solicit feedback, post your journal as an online blog.

TIP

MAKE NOTES
Use your journal to "think on paper" about what you have read about management in this or other books, or your experiences in management training programmes.

Analyzing your performance

Assessing your progress towards your goals can help you gain a fuller understanding of your strengths and weaknesses. Whenever you make a key decision or take a key action, write down what you expect will happen. Then, every three or four months, compare the actual results with your expectations. If you practise this method consistently, it will help you discover what you are doing, or failing to do, that deprives you of the full benefits of your strengths, and will demonstrate areas in which you are not particularly competent and cannot perform adequately.

IN FOCUS... FEEDBACK

It is important to find at least one person in your life who will give you honest, gut-level feedback, to help you gain perspective on your experiences and learn from them. This should be someone you trust enough to go to when you have real problems and ask, "Am I off base here? Am I crazy?" This person could be a partner, a mentor, a best friend, a co-worker, a therapist, or a personal coach. Today, many organizations are providing their managers with 360-degree feedback, allowing them to receive insights on their strengths and weaknesses from other members of staff.

Using emotional intelligence

Emotional intelligence (EI) is the ability to monitor and work with your and others' emotions. It is measured in EQ, which is the emotional equivalent of IQ. Daniel Goleman – author of the bestselling *Emotional Intelligence* – and other writers suggest that a technically proficient manager with a high EQ will be more successful than a manager who has only a high IQ.

Understanding EQ

Your EQ is the measure of your ability to understand and interact with others and becomes more important the more people you deal with. EQ does not measure personality traits or cognitive capacity. Emotional intelligence can be developed over time and can be improved through training and therapy. Those with a high EQ will be better able to control their own emotions, while at the same time using them as a basis for action. Working with emotions, rather than being at the mercy of them, makes individuals more successful in dealing with the demands of the environment around them. They are better able to control impulses and deal with stress, and better at problem solving. All of these qualities help the individual to perform more competently at work.

✔ CHECKLIST APPLYING EMOTIONAL INTELLIGENCE

	YES	NO
• Am I aware of my feelings and do I act accordingly?	☐	☐
• Can I share my feelings in a straightforward, composed manner?	☐	☐
• Do I treat others with compassion, sensitivity, and kindness?	☐	☐
• Am I open to the opinions and ideas of others?	☐	☐
• Can I decisively confront problem people?	☐	☐
• Do I maintain a balance between my personal life and work?	☐	☐

Managing emotions

Emotional intelligence has two aspects: one inward facing and one outward facing. The first of these is your emotional self-awareness and your ability to manage your own emotions. The second is your degree of empathy, or awareness of others' emotions, and your ability to productively manage relationships with others. Both inward- and outward-facing aspects of emotional intelligence are made up of a number of skills or competencies.

Using EI at work

To be a successful manager in today's business world, a high EQ may be more important than sheer intellectual or technical ability. A manager who leads a project team of diverse people will need to understand and interact successfully with others. Applying emotional intelligence at work means you are open to the ideas of others and can build and mend relationships with others. You are aware of your feelings and act accordingly, articulating ideas so that others can understand them, developing rapport, building trust, and working towards consensus. Managers who are attuned to their own feelings and the feelings of others use this understanding to enhance personal, team, and organizational performance.

The four competencies of emotional intelligence

SELF-AWARENESS
Emotional self-awareness; accurate self-assessment; self-confidence

SELF-MANAGEMENT
Emotional self-control; trustworthiness; conscientiousness; achievement orientation; adaptability; optimism; initiative

SOCIAL AWARENESS
Empathy; organizational awareness; service orientation

RELATIONSHIP MANAGEMENT
Development of others; inspirational leadership; influence; communication; change catalyst; conflict management; bond building; teamwork and collaboration

Applying assertiveness

An effective manager needs to behave in an active and assertive* manner to get things done. Assertive managers are able to express their feelings and act with appropriate degrees of openness and candour, but still have a regard for the feelings or rights of others.

Understanding personality types

***Assertive** — being able to make clear statements of what you want from others in a given situation, without being abrasive or demeaning.

Assertiveness and the ability to express your feelings to others are skills that people possess to different extents. Some are aggressive, direct, and blunt, and can appear domineering, pushy, or self-centred. Most people tend to be passive, inhibited, and submissive; they bottle up their feelings and fail even to stand up for their legitimate rights. Passive individuals seek to avoid conflicts and tend to sublimate their own needs and feelings in order to satisfy others.

Most people fall between the extremes of passive and aggressive. At these extremes, passive and aggressive behaviours hinder effective managerial relations because neither encourages openness. Effective managers need to be assertive, express their ideas and feelings openly, and stand up for their rights, and all in a way that makes it easier for those they are managing to do the same. The assertive manager is straightforward yet sensitive to the needs of others; he or she does not seek to rule over less assertive people. Seeking dominance may produce short-term results but will not make the best use of the team-members' abilities.

? ASK YOURSELF... AM I ASSERTIVE ENOUGH?

- Does my response accurately reflect how I feel if I'm given a compliment about my work?
- Am I able to speak up when I'm in a group of strangers?
- If others interrupt me when I am talking, can I hold my ground?
- Do I avoid being taken advantage of by other people?
- Am I able to criticize others' work if I think they might react badly?

Becoming more assertive

STATE YOUR CASE
Try beginning your conversations with "I" phrases, such as "I think", "I believe", or "I need".

BE PREPARED
Prepare for tricky encounters: have all the facts to hand, and try to anticipate the other person's replies.

USE OPEN QUESTIONS
If you are finding it hard to get a person to talk to you, use open questions that cannot be answered with a simple "yes" or "no" answer.

VISUALIZE YOURSELF
Try assertive role play with a trusted colleague, to help you to see yourself as an assertive person.

GET PERSPECTIVE
Try to see a situation from the other person's point of view. Most workplace bullies, for example, are hiding their own insecurities or an inability to do the job. Use this knowledge to give you perspective on any feelings of intimidation or offence you experience, and offer the bully help to overcome their problems.

BE PATIENT
You'll need time and practice to become comfortable with the new behaviour. If you are naturally a passive person, recognize that those around you may initially be uncomfortable when you start to become more assertive.

Examining your assumptions

Managers tend to treat their staff according to assumptions they hold about what motivates people. These assumptions create self-fulfilling prophecies in the behaviour of the staff. Managers reward what they expect, and consequently only get what they expect. Challenging your own assumptions is one of the first steps in becoming a better manager.

Contrasting X and Y styles

Prominent management theorist Douglas McGregor distinguished two management styles – X and Y – based on the assumptions held by managers about the motives of their staff. X-style managers believe that workers need to be coerced and directed. They tend to be strict and controlling, giving their workers little latitude and punishing poor performance. They use few rewards and typically give only negative feedback. These managers see little point in workers having autonomy, because they think that the workforce neither expects nor desires cooperation.

X AND Y ASSUMPTIONS

X-STYLE MANAGERS	Y-STYLE MANAGERS
Employees inherently dislike work and will attempt to avoid it.	Employees can enjoy work and can view it as being as natural to them as rest or play.
Employees must be coerced, controlled, or threatened with punishment to achieve goals.	People will exercise self-direction and self-control if they are committed to the objectives behind the tasks they are performing.
Employees will shirk responsibility and seek formal direction.	The average person can learn to accept and seek responsibility.
Most workers place security above all other factors associated with work and will display little ambition.	Most workers place job satisfaction and career fulfilment high on their list of priorities.

Y-style assumptions reflect a much more optimistic view of human nature. Y-style management contends that people will gladly direct themselves towards objectives if their efforts are appropriately rewarded. Managers who hold Y assumptions assume a great deal of confidence in their workers. They are less directive and empower workers, giving them more responsibilities and freedom to accomplish tasks as they deem appropriate. They believe that people have hidden potential and the job of the manager is to find and utilize it.

Shaping the environment

Organizations that are designed based on X-style assumptions are very different to those designed by Y-style managers. For example, because they believe that their workers are motivated to help the organization reach its goals, Y-style managers will decentralize authority and give more control to workers than will X-style managers. A Y-style manager realizes that most people are not resistant to organizational needs by nature, but may have become so as a result of negative experiences, and strives to design structures that involve the employees in executing their work roles, such as participative management and joint goal setting. These approaches allow employees to exercise some self-direction and self-control in their work lives.

In Y-style management, although individuals and groups are still accountable for their activities, the role of the manager is not to exert control but to provide support and advice and to make sure that workers have the resources they need to effectively perform their jobs. By contrast, X-style managers consider their role to be to monitor workers to ensure that they contribute to the production process and do not threaten product quality.

TIP

ANALYZE YOURSELF

Honestly review every decision you make and every task you delegate. In each case, ask yourself what you assumed the staff involved would think, and how you expected them to behave. Remember that positive expectations help to produce positive outcomes.

Clarifying your values

Values are stable and enduring beliefs about what is good, right, and worthwhile and about the behaviour that is desirable for achieving what is worthwhile. To be an effective manager, it is necessary to have a good understanding of what your values are and to act accordingly.

Defining values

Values are formed early in our lives, from the influence of our parents, teachers, friends, religious leaders, and media role-models. Some may change as we go through life and experience different behaviours. Your values manifest themselves in everything you do and the choices that you make. If you are someone who particularly values promptness, for example, you will make sure that you always behave in ways that mean you are on time for appointments. The thought of being late will stimulate feelings of stress in you, and induce a subsequent adrenaline rush as you hurry to be at the appointment on time. As a manager, it is important for you to clarify your values, so that you can determine what your goals are and how you want to manage yourself and others to achieve them.

❓ ASK YOURSELF... ABOUT YOUR INFLUENCES

- Who are the individuals and what are the events that influenced the development of my value system?
- Are these sources of influence still as important to me as recent events and people who influence me now?
- Are my values still appropriate as guides of behaviour in the world I live in today?
- Should I consider changing some of my values to make them more relevant?

Clarifying your personal values

It may sound strange, but one of the best ways to clarify your personal values and gain a clear understanding of what is important to you is to think about how you would like to be remembered in your eulogy. Sit quietly and consider how you want your friends and family to remember you, and what you want your work colleagues to say they thought of you. Also think of your broader contributions – how would you like to be remembered in the communities you are a part of? Make notes, and use the information you write down to identify the values that are most important to you.

Dealing with conflicts

It can be challenging when your personal values conflict with those of your organization, or when there are conflicting values between individuals or sub-groups. Value differences can exist, for example, about how to perform jobs, the nature of reward systems, or the degree of intimacy in work relationships. Having a clear understanding of your own personal value set will help you to manage these conflict situations. If you are clear about your own values, you can act with integrity and practise what you preach regardless of emotional or social pressure. To address a conflict situation, first make sure you are aware of, understand, and are tolerant of the value differences held by the other parties. This will help you to determine whether the value conflict is, in fact, irresolvable and will require personnel changes, or whether compromises and adjustments can be made to accommodate the different perspectives.

IN FOCUS...
TYPES OF VALUE

Values can be classified into two types: terminal and instrumental. Terminal values (your "ends" in life) are desirable ends or goals, such as a comfortable, prosperous life, world peace, great wisdom, or salvation. Instrumental values (the "means" to those ends) are beliefs about what behaviours are appropriate in striving for desired goals and ends. Consider a manager who works extra hours to help deliver a customer's rush order. The attitude displayed is a willingness to help a customer with a problem. The value that serves as the foundation of this attitude might be that of service to others.

Developing your personal mission statement

A personal mission statement provides you with the long-term vision and motivation to manage yourself and others in your team according to your own values. It also allows you to establish your purpose and goals as a manager. Regular evaluation of your performance, based on your mission statement, inspires good self-management.

Defining your future

Your personal mission statement spells out your managerial philosophy. It defines the type of manager you want to be (your character), what you want to accomplish (your contributions), and what principles guide your behaviour (your values). It provides you with the vision and values to direct your managerial life – the basis for setting long- and short-term goals, and how best to deploy your time.

TIP

LEARN FROM SETBACKS

Things will not always work out as you have planned. When you experience setbacks, be honest with yourself about what happened and why, and think carefully about whether you need to re-evaluate your goals.

Setting out your philosophy

Make sure that your personal mission statement is an accurate reflection of your values, goals, and aspirations for success. A personal statement might read: "My career goals are to effectively manage my team to achieve respect and knowledge, to use my talents as a manager to help others, and to play an active role in this organization." Another individual's statement might have a very different focus: "As a manager in this creative firm, I want to establish a fault-free, self-perpetuating learning environment." Re-evaluate your mission statement on a regular basis – annually, at least – to ensure that it still describes your overall vision for your future as a manager.

BE SMART
Set goals that are Specific, Measurable, Attainable, Realistic, and Time-bound. You are much more likely to achieve goals that are well defined and within your reach.

SET YOUR GOALS
Personalize your goals. You will be far more committed to goals that you have set yourself, rather than those that have been set for you by someone else.

SEE THE FUTURE
Develop a vision of what it will be like when you achieve your goals. Your vision of a desirable future can be a powerful motivating force.

Setting and attaining your personal managerial goals

UP

GET SUPPORT
Develop a support group of people who will help you in achieving your goals. Your support group should include those with the resources you need to be successful.

REWARD YOURSELF
Reward yourself for small wins. When you achieve incremental progress towards your goals, treat yourself to a reward, such as a night out or some recreational activity.

EVALUATE PROGRESS
Continually evaluate your performance against your mission statement. When things do not work out, be honest with yourself about why.

Chapter 2

Interacting with others

Your effectiveness as a manager is defined by your ability to interact with other people. A manager needs to guide others through careful communication, teaching, and assessment to work to their full potential, both individually and as a team.

Communicating effectively

It is easy to see investment in communication as a luxury, especially in times of economic adversity. However, good communication is a proven tool for improving commitment in those you are managing, and so for boosting revenue and product quality.

Getting your message across

Communication is the process of sending a message to another person with the intent of evoking an outcome or a change in behaviour. It is more efficient when it uses less time and fewer resources; it is effective when the information is conveyed exactly as you intend. Good communication means balancing the two: for example, explaining a new procedure to each staff member individually may be less efficient than calling a meeting where everyone can hear about it. However, if staff members have very disparate sets of interests, one-to-one coaching may be more effective.

Delivering messages

The components of the communication process are the sender, the receiver, the message, and the channel. First, the message is encoded into a format that will get the idea across. Then it is transmitted through the most appropriate channel. This is chosen on the basis of efficiency and effectiveness, as well as practical factors, such as the need to produce a stable record of the communication; whether the information needs to be kept confidential; speed and cost; and the complexity of the communication.

Channels can be oral (speeches, meetings, phone calls, presentations, or informal discussions); written (letters, memoranda, reports, or manuals); electronic (emails, text messages, podcasts, video conferences, websites, or webcasts); or nonverbal (touch, facial expression, or intonation). Finally, the message must be successfully decoded by the receiver. Many factors may intrude, preventing the receiver from correctly understanding what they are told. These range from semantics or different word interpretations to different frames of reference, cultural attitudes, and mistrust.

Before you send a message, ask yourself how much you understand about it, and what is the level of the recipient's understanding? Will the recipient understand the language and jargon you use, and do they have technology that is compatible with yours?

TIP

REDUCE "NOISE"
Noise is anything that interferes, at any stage, with the communication process. The ultimate success of the communication process depends to a large degree on overcoming noise, so make an effort to keep your messages clear, concise, and to the point.

CASE STUDY

Tom's of Maine
Tom Chappell is the founder of Tom's of Maine, a successful natural toothpaste and health company in the US. Chappell is a strong believer in using face-to-face communication to deal with rumours, morale issues, and other communication problems. Every month, he meets informally with his employees and talks about the company's performance and future plans, and solicits feedback from every member of his staff. He says that the best way to deal with employee communication is to be honest and forthright, share information, and "tell it like it is".

Sending messages

Effective communication with those you are managing requires that you send clear and comprehensible messages that will be understood as you intend them to be. You can transmit messages more effectively by making them clearer and developing your credibility.

TIP

BE CONSISTENT
Ensure that your messages are congruent with your actions. Saying one thing and doing another is confusing and creates distrust.

Getting your point across

To be successful, every manager must develop the ability to send clear, unambiguous messages that efficiently convey the information they want to deliver. Effective messages use multiple channels to get the information across; for example, if you match your facial and body gestures to the intended meaning of a message while drawing a diagram to explain it, you are using three channels. Make sure that you take responsibility for the feelings and evaluations in your messages, using personal pronouns such as "I" and "mine". Make the information in your messages specific, and refer to concrete details, to avoid the possibility of misinterpretation. Keep your language simple, and avoid technical jargon.

Hitting the right tone

"I need the report delivered by 4.30pm on Friday afternoon."

"I need the report delivered as soon as possible."

"I'm not happy when you're late for meetings."

"Everyone feels you're not pulling your weight."

✔ CHECKLIST COMMUNICATING USING EFFECTIVE MESSAGES

	YES	NO
• Do I use multiple channels when sending messages?	☐	☐
• Do I provide all relevant information?	☐	☐
• Am I complete and specific?	☐	☐
• Do I use "I" statements to claim my messages as my own?	☐	☐
• Am I congruent in my verbal and nonverbal messages?	☐	☐
• Do I use language that the receiver can understand?	☐	☐
• Do I obtain feedback to ensure that my message has been understood and not misinterpreted?	☐	☐

Being credible

Sender credibility is reflected in the recipient's belief that the sender is trustworthy. To increase your sender credibility, ensure that you:

• Know what you are talking about: recipients are more attentive when they perceive that senders have expertise.

• Establish mutual trust: owning up to your motives can eliminate the recipient's anxiety about your intentions.

• Share all relevant information: senders are seen as unethical when they intentionally provoke receivers into doing things they would not have done if they had had all of the information.

• Be honest: one of the key things people want in a leader and co-worker is honesty. As a sender, avoid any form of deception, which is the conscious alteration of information to influence another's perceptions.

• Be reliable: if you are dependable, predictable, and consistent, recipients will perceive you as being trustworthy.

• Be warm, friendly, and supportive: this will give you more personal credibility than a posture of hostility, arrogance, or abruptness.

• Be dynamic: being confident, dynamic, and positive in your delivery of information will make you seem more credible than someone who is passive, withdrawn, and unsure.

• Make appropriate self-disclosures: responsibly revealing your feelings, reactions, needs, and desires to others is essential when establishing supportive relationships. It facilitates congruency, builds trust and credibility, and helps recipients of your messages develop empathy and understanding with you.

Listening actively

Many communication problems develop because listening skills are ignored, forgotten, or taken for granted. Active listening is making sense of what you hear. It requires paying attention and interpreting all verbal, visual, and vocal stimuli presented to you.

Understanding the basics

Active listening has four essential ingredients: concentration, empathy, acceptance, and taking responsibility for completely understanding the message. To listen actively, you must concentrate intensely on what the speaker is saying and tune out competing miscellaneous thoughts that create distractions. Try to understand what the speaker

LISTENING WELL

FAST TRACK	OFF TRACK
Keeping an open mind, free from preconceived ideas	Judging the value of the speaker's ideas by appearance and delivery
Giving the speaker your full attention while they are talking	Thinking about what you are going to say while the speaker is talking
Assessing the full meaning behind the words that are being spoken	Listening for specific facts rather than the overall message
Asking questions when you need more information	Interrupting the speaker when you have a better idea
Withholding judgement until the speaker has finished talking	Always trying to have the last word

wants to communicate rather than what you want to understand. Listen objectively and resist the urge to start evaluating what the person is saying, or you may miss the rest of the message. Finally, do whatever is necessary to get the full, intended meaning from the speaker's message – listen for feelings and content, and ask questions to ensure you have understood.

Employing the techniques

Active listening is hard work and starts with your own personal motivation. If you are unwilling to exert the effort to hear and understand, no amount of additional advice is going to improve your listening effectiveness. If you are motivated to become an effective listener, there are a number of specific techniques you can use to improve your skills:
• Make eye contact: this focuses your attention, reduces the likelihood that you will become distracted, and encourages the speaker.
• Show interest: use nonverbal signals, such as head nods, to convey to the speaker that you're listening.
• Avoid distracting actions: looking at your watch or shuffling papers are signs that you aren't fully attentive and might be missing part of the message.
• Take in the whole picture: interpret feelings and emotions as well as factual content.
• Ask questions: seek clarification if you don't understand something. This also reassures the speaker that you're listening to them.
• Paraphrase: restate what the speaker has said in your own words with phrases such as "What I hear you saying is…" or "Do you mean…?"
• Don't interrupt: let speakers complete their thoughts before you try to respond.
• Confront your biases: use information about speakers to improve your understanding of what they are saying, but don't let your biases distort the message.

SET THE CONTEXT
Mentally summarize and integrate what a speaker says, and put each new bit of information into the context of what has preceded it.

Nonverbal communication is made up of visual, vocal, and tactile signals and the use of time, space, and image. As much as 93 per cent of the meaning that is transmitted in face-to-face communication can come from nonverbal channels, so you should be aware of these cues.

Decoding the truth

The visual part of nonverbal communication is often called body language. It includes expressions, eye movement, posture, and gestures. The face is the best communicator of nonverbal messages. By "reading" a person's facial expression, we can detect unvocalized feelings. Appearance is important, too – people do judge a book by its cover, and most of us react favourably to an expected image. In terms of dress, colour can convey meaning (brown can convey trust; dark colours, power), as does style (pure fibres such as wool or silk suggest higher status). Posture is important – a relaxed posture, such as sitting back with legs stretched out and hands behind the head, signals confidence.

If a person says one thing but communicates something different through intonation and body language, tension and distrust can arise; the receiver will typically choose the nonverbal interpretation because it is more reliable than the verbal. For example, if you ask your boss when you will be eligible for a promotion and she looks out of the window, covers a yawn, and says, "I would say you might have a chance in the not-too-distant future", you should not count on being promoted soon.

NERVOUSNESS
Clearing one's throat, covering the mouth while speaking, fidgeting, shifting weight from one foot to the other, tapping fingers, pacing.

BOREDOM OR IMPATIENCE
Drumming fingers, foot swinging, brushing or picking at lint, doodling, or looking at one's watch.

Feelings that can be read from gestures and body language

OPENNESS
Holding hands in an open position, having an unbuttoned coat or collar, removing one's coat, moving closer, leaning slightly forward, and uncrossing arms and legs.

DEFENSIVENESS
Holding body rigid, with arms or legs tightly crossed, eyes glancing sideways, minimal eye contact, lips pursed, fists clenched, and a downcast head.

CONFIDENCE, SUPERIORITY, AND AUTHORITY
Using relaxed and expansive gestures, such as leaning back with fingers laced behind the head and hands together at the back with chin thrust upward.

Teaching skills

As a manager, an important part of your role is to help those you are managing to develop their skills. If you can encourage the development of skills such as self-awareness, communication, and time management, you will be rewarded with a high-performing team.

HOW TO... TEACH NEW SKILLS

Help the learner to form a conceptual understanding of a new skill.

↓

Plan how they can test their understanding of the skill.

↓

Get the learner to apply the new skill in concrete experience.

↓

Observe what happened and discuss ways in which they can improve.

Learning by experience

People learn faster and retain more information if they have to exert some kind of active effort. The famous quote, attributed to Confucius: "I hear and I forget. I see and I remember. I do and I understand" is frequently used to support the value of learning through experience. A major implication of this notion is that new skills can be learned only through experimenting with new behaviours, observing the results, and learning from the experience. The learning of new skills is maximized when learners get the opportunity to combine watching, thinking, and doing. The experiential learning model encompasses four elements: learning new concepts (conceptualizing), planning how to test the ideas (plan to test), actively applying the skill in a new experience (gaining concrete experience), and examination of the consequences of the experience (reflective observation). After reflecting on the experience, the learner uses the lessons they have learned from what happened to create a refined conceptual map of the skill, and the cycle continues.

To use the experiential learning model to teach skills, you need to: ensure that the learner understands the skill both conceptually and behaviourally; give them opportunities to practise it; give feedback on how well they are performing the skill; and encourage them to use the skill often enough so that it becomes integrated into their behavioural repertoire.

EFFECTIVE APPROACHES TO TEACHING SKILLS

APPROACH	WHY IT WORKS
Being prepared Knowing ahead of time what you want the outcome of your skills training to be.	Unless you know where you want things to go, you won't know how to conduct yourself to get there.
Listening Keeping communication lines open and indicating to others that their opinions are important.	The key to effectively teaching a skill is often expressed by the learner, but overlooked by the manager when they fail to hear it.
Using questions Presenting a concept, options for applying it, and the consequences, then asking the learner what they will do.	Asking rather than telling an employee how best to apply a new skill shows respect, and, because it allows them to think it through for themselves, it helps them to learn faster.
Being positive Correcting mistakes in a positive way, not in one that is patronizing or makes others feel worthless and inferior.	Using positive messages, such as "I can see that you want to do well and I think that I can help you learn to do better", will help to motivate the person you are teaching.
Being honest and upfront Making it clear to the learner what is really required of them, and why this is important.	People will be more willing to accept your skill teaching if they trust and respect you because they will believe you are honest and forthright.
Setting performance targets Indicating the acceptable level of performance you expect from those you are teaching, and holding them to it.	In the long run, people will respect you more if you hold them to a standard of performance, as they will know any praise they receive from you is sincere and deserved.

Inspiring others

When you endeavour to teach new skills to others, you are attempting to motivate specific behaviour changes in them. This is more effective if you can convince those you are teaching that, by acting as you suggest, they will gain something that they value. Successful teaching requires you to inspire others to want to cooperate with you. However, different people consider different skills to be more or less valuable to them, so you will also discover that the majority of responsibility for the learning of a new skill rests with the person you are teaching. Learners who really want to improve their skills and are willing to put in the effort will be successful.

Giving feedback

Most managers will enthusiastically give their employees positive feedback but often avoid or delay giving negative feedback, or substantially distort it, for fear of provoking a defensive reaction. However, improving employees' performance depends on balanced and considered feedback.

Valuing feedback

Providing regular feedback to your employees will improve their performance. This is because:
• Feedback can induce a person to set goals, which act as motivators of their performance.
• Feedback tells the person how well they are progressing towards those goals. Positive feedback gives reinforcement, while constructive negative feedback can result in increased effort.
• The content of the feedback will suggest ways that the person can improve their performance.
• Providing feedback demonstrates to a person that you care about how they are doing.

As a rule, positive feedback is usually accepted readily, while negative feedback often meets resistance. When preparing to deliver negative feedback, first make sure you are aware of any conflict that could arise and think about how to deal with it. Ensure that negative feedback comes from a credible source, that it is objective, and that it is supported by hard data such as quantitative performance indicators and specific examples.

TALK ABOUT THE JOB
Keep feedback job-related. Never make personal judgements, such as "You are stupid and incompetent."

GIVE DETAIL
Avoid vague statements such as "You have a bad attitude" or "I'm impressed with the job you did." The recipient needs to understand exactly what they have or haven't done well.

How to provide feedback

USE GOALS
Keep feedback goal-oriented. Its purpose is not to unload your feelings on someone.

BE NON-JUDGEMENTAL
Keep feedback descriptive and fair rather than judgemental.

MAKE IT ATTAINABLE
When delivering negative feedback, make sure you only criticize shortcomings over which the person has some control.

EXPLAIN YOUR REASONS
Explain to the recipient why you are being critical or complimentary about specific aspects of their performance.

ENSURE A GOOD FIT
Tailor the feedback to fit the person. Consider past performance and future potential in designing the frequency, amount, and content of performance feedback.

CHECK UNDERSTANDING
Once you have given your feedback, have the recipient rephrase the content to check that they have fully understood what you have said and are taking away the right message from your feedback session.

Negotiating

Negotiation is a process by which two or more parties exchange goods or services and attempt to agree upon the exchange rate for them. Managers spend a lot of time negotiating, and need to be able to do it well. They have to negotiate salaries for incoming employees, cut deals with superiors, bargain over budgets, work out differences with associates, and resolve conflicts between members of their team.

Understanding approaches

There are two general approaches to negotiation: distributive and integrative bargaining. Distributive bargaining assumes zero-sum conditions, that is: "Any gain I make is at your expense", and vice versa. Integrative bargaining assumes a win–win solution is possible. Each is appropriate in different situations.

Distributive bargaining tactics focus on getting an opponent to agree to a deal that meets your specific goals. Such tactics include persuading opponents of the impossibility of getting their needs met in other ways or the advisability of accepting your offer; arguing that your position is fair, while theirs is not; and trying to get the other party to feel emotionally generous towards you and accept an outcome that meets your goals.

CASE STUDY

A win–win solution

After closing a $15,000 order from a small clothing retailer, sales rep Deb Hansen called in the order to her firm's credit department, and was told that the firm could not approve credit for this customer because of a past slow-pay record. The next day, Deb and the firm's credit supervisor met to discuss the problem. Deb did not want to lose the business; neither did the credit supervisor, but he also didn't want to get stuck with a bad debt. The two openly reviewed their options. After considerable discussion, they agreed on a solution: the credit supervisor would approve the sale, but the clothing store's owner would provide a bank guarantee that would assure payment if the bill was not paid within 60 days.

Finding solutions

Integrative, or win–win, bargaining is generally preferable to distributive bargaining. Distributive bargaining leaves one party a loser, and so it tends to build animosities and deepen divisions between people. On the other hand, integrative bargaining builds long-term relationships and facilitates working together in the future. It bonds negotiators and allows each to leave the bargaining table feeling that he or she has achieved a victory. For integrative bargaining to work, however, both parties must openly share all information, be sensitive to each other's needs, trust each other, and remain flexible.

Negotiating well

Careful attention to a few key guidelines can increase a manager's odds of successful negotiation outcomes. Always start by considering the other party's point of view. Acquire as much information as you can about their interests and goals. Always go into a negotiation with a concrete strategy. Treat negotiations the way expert players treat the game of chess, always knowing ahead of time how they will respond to any given situation.

HOW TO... NEGOTIATE

Begin with a positive overture, and establish rapport and mutual interests.

Make a small concession early on if you can. Concessions tend to be reciprocated and can lead to a quick agreement.

Concentrate on the issues, not on the personal characteristics or personality of your opponent.

If your opponent attacks you or gets emotional, let them blow off steam without taking it personally.

Pay little attention to initial offers, treating them as merely starting points.

Focus on the other person's interests and your own goals and principles while you generate other possibilities.

Emphasize win–win solutions to the negotiation.

Make your decisions based on principles and results, not emotions or pressure.

Managing conflict

Conflict is natural to organizations and can never be completely eliminated. If not managed properly, conflict can be dysfunctional and lead to undesirable consequences, such as hostility, lack of cooperation, and even violence. When managed effectively, conflict can stimulate creativity, innovation, and change.

TIP

PUT YOURSELF IN THEIR SHOES
Empathize with the other parties in the conflict, and try to understand their values, personality, feelings, and resources. Make sure you know what is at stake for them.

Understanding the causes

Conflicts exist whenever an action by one party is perceived as preventing or interfering with the goals, needs, or actions of another party. Conflicts have varying causes but are generally rooted in one of three areas: problems in communication; disagreements over work design, policies, and practices; and personal differences.

Disagreements frequently arise from semantic difficulties, misunderstandings, poor listening, and noise in the communication channels. Communication breakdowns are inevitable in work settings, often causing workers to focus on placing blame on others instead of trying to solve problems.

Conflicts can also result when people or groups disagree over goal priorities, decision alternatives, performance criteria, and resource allocations. The things that people want, such as promotions, pay increases, and office space, are scarce resources that must be divided up. Ambiguous rules, regulations, and performance standards can also create conflicts.

Individual idiosyncrasies and differences in personal value systems originating from different cultural backgrounds, education, experience, and training often lead to conflicts. Stereotyping, prejudice, ignorance, and misunderstanding may cause people who are different to be perceived by some to be untrustworthy adversaries.

Handling conflict

There are five basic approaches managers can use to try to resolve conflicts. Each has strengths and weaknesses, so choose the one most appropriate to your situation:

• Avoidance: not every conflict requires an assertive action. Avoidance works well for trivial conflicts or if emotions are running high and opposing parties need time to cool down.

• Accommodation: if you need to maintain a harmonious relationship, you may choose to concede your position on an issue that is much more important to the other party.

• Competition: satisfying your own needs at the expense of other parties is appropriate when you need a quick resolution on important issues, or where an unpopular action must be taken.

• Compromise: this works well when the parties are equal in power, or when you need a quick solution or a temporary solution to a complex issue.

• Collaboration: use this when the interests of all parties are too important to be ignored. Discuss the issues openly and honestly with all parties, listen actively, and make a careful deliberation over a full range of alternatives.

Approaches to conflict-handling

	UNCOOPERATIVE	COOPERATIVE
ASSERTIVE	**COMPETITION** Using your formal authority to resolve issues the way you want.	**COLLABORATION** Finding a solution that is advantageous to all parties.
	COMPROMISE Each party gives up something to reach a solution that is satisfactory to all.	
UNASSERTIVE	**AVOIDANCE** Withdrawing or postponing the conflict.	**ACCOMMODATION** Yielding to another party's position.

Valuing diversity

Understanding and managing people who are similar to us can be challenging, but understanding and managing those who are dissimilar from us and from each other is tougher. As the workplace becomes more diverse and as business becomes more global, managers must understand how cultural diversity affects the expectations and behaviour of everyone in the organization.

LET EVERYONE KNOW

Make a public commitment to valuing diversity – this will ensure that you are accountable for your actions, and may attract potential employees who prefer to work for someone who values equal opportunities for all.

Understanding the changes

The labour market is dramatically changing. Most countries are experiencing an increase in the age of their workforce, increased immigration, and, in many, a rapid increase in the number of working women. The globalization of business also brings with it a cross-cultural mandate. With more businesses selling and manufacturing products and services abroad, managers increasingly see the need to ensure that their employees can relate to customers from many different cultures. Rich McGinn, of US telecommunications giant Lucent Technologies, said: "We are in a war for talent. And the only way you can meet your business imperatives is to have all people as part of your talent pool." Workers who believe that their differences are not merely tolerated but valued by their employer are more likely to be loyal, productive, and committed.

Capitalizing on diversity

Managers face many challenges capitalizing on diversity, such as: coping with employees' unfamiliarity with native languages, learning which rewards are valued by different ethnic groups, and providing career development programmes that fit the values of different ethnic groups. There are several ways for you to try to capitalize on diversity:

• Communicate your objectives and expectations about diversity to employees through a range of channels, such as vision and mission statements, value statements, slogans, creeds, newsletters, speeches, emails, and everyday conversations.

• Recruit through non-traditional sources. Relying on current employee referrals usually produces a limited range of candidates. Try instead to identify novel sources for recruitment, such as women's job networks, ethnic newspapers, training centres for the disabled, urban job banks, and over-50s clubs.

• Use diverse incentives for motivation. Most studies on motivation are by North American researchers on North American workers. Consequently, these studies are based on beliefs that most people work to promote their own well-being and get ahead. This may be at odds with people from more collectivist countries, such as Venezuela, Singapore, Japan, and Mexico, where individuals are driven by their loyalty to the organization or society, not their own self-interest.

TIP

PRACTISE WHAT YOU PREACH
First look into your heart and mind and root out any prejudice. Then, demonstrate your acceptance in everything that you say and do.

Chapter 3

Managing a team

Teams are the cornerstones of most public and nonprofit organizations. Successful team leaders understand what makes a team effective and what can lead to failure. To be a successful manager, you need to be able to plan and design the work of your team, delegate tasks effectively, monitor progress, and motivate your team to excel.

Setting goals and planning

Planning is a key skill for any manager and starts with having a good understanding of the organization's objectives. It involves establishing a strategy for achieving those goals using the personnel available, and developing the means to integrate and coordinate necessary activities.

Knowing your goals

Planning is concerned with ends (what needs to be done) and means (how those ends are to be achieved). In order to create a plan, managers must first identify the organization's goals – what it is trying to achieve. Goals are the foundation of all other planning activities. They refer to the desired outcomes for the entire organization, for groups and teams within the organization, and for individuals. Goals provide the direction for all management decisions and form the criteria against which actual accomplishments can be measured.

Setting your goals

There are five basic rules that can help you set effective goals. Always make your goals SMART: Specific, Measurable, Aligned, Reachable, and Time-bound.

• **Specific** Goals are meaningful only when they are specific enough to be measured and verified.

• **Measurable** Goals need to have a clear outcome that can be objectively assessed. They also need to have clear benchmarks that can be checked along the way.

• **Aligned** Goals should contribute to the mission, vision, and strategic plan of the organization and be congruent with the values and objectives of the employee implementing them.

• **Reachable** Goals should require you to stretch to reach them, but not be set unrealistically high.

• **Time-bound** Open-ended goals can be neglected because there is no sense of urgency to complete them. Whenever possible, goals should include a specific time limit for accomplishment.

HOW TO... DEVELOP AND IMPLEMENT A PLAN

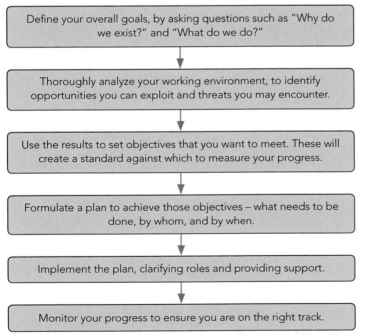

Define your overall goals, by asking questions such as "Why do we exist?" and "What do we do?"

Thoroughly analyze your working environment, to identify opportunities you can exploit and threats you may encounter.

Use the results to set objectives that you want to meet. These will create a standard against which to measure your progress.

Formulate a plan to achieve those objectives – what needs to be done, by whom, and by when.

Implement the plan, clarifying roles and providing support.

Monitor your progress to ensure you are on the right track.

TIP

LOOK TO THE FUTURE

Write down three SMART goals that you want your team to achieve in the next five years, and then plan how you will reach them.

Designing work

Job design refers to the way tasks are combined to form complete jobs. It involves trying to shape the right jobs to conform to the right people, taking into account both the organization's goals and the employees' satisfaction. Well-designed jobs lead to high motivation, high-quality performance, high satisfaction, and low absenteeism and turnover.

TIP

GET THE RIGHT PERSON FOR THE JOB

It is very difficult to completely change how a person performs, so try to match people to jobs that they are good at. This will make them most likely to achieve good results.

Defining jobs

Jobs vary considerably: a lifeguard, for example, will have very different day-to-day responsibilities from an accountant or a builder. However, any job can be described in terms of five core job dimensions:
• Skill variety: the degree to which a job requires a variety of different activities so that the worker can employ a number of different skills and talents.
• Task identity: the degree to which a job requires completion of a whole and identifiable piece of work.
• Task significance: the degree to which a job has an impact on the lives of other people.
• Autonomy: the degree to which a job provides freedom and discretion to the worker in scheduling their tasks and in determining how the work will be carried out.
• Feedback: the degree to which the worker gets direct and clear information about the effectiveness of his or her performance.
As a manager, you can maximize your team's performance by enhancing these five dimensions. Skill variety, task identity, and task significance combine to create meaningful work. Jobs with these characteristics will be perceived as important, valuable, and worthwhile. Jobs that possess autonomy give workers a sense of responsibility for their results. Jobs that provide feedback indicate to the employee how effectively he or she is performing.

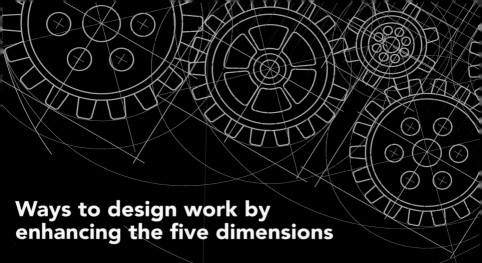

Ways to design work by enhancing the five dimensions

1 COMBINE TASKS
Put existing fragmented tasks together to form larger modules of work. This can help to increase skill variety and task identity.

2 CREATE NATURAL WORK UNITS
Design tasks to form an identifiable whole to increase employee "ownership" and to encourage workers to view their jobs as important.

3 ESTABLISH CLIENT RELATIONSHIPS
Building direct relationships between the worker and the client – the user of the product or the service that the employee works on – increases skill variety.

4 EXPAND JOBS VERTICALLY
Giving employees responsibilities formerly reserved for managers closes the gap between the "doing" and "controlling" aspects of the job and increases autonomy.

5 IMPROVE FEEDBACK CHANNELS
Feedback tells employees how well they are performing, and whether their performance is improving, deteriorating, or remaining constant. Employees should receive feedback directly as they do their jobs.

high-performing teams

As Lee Iacocca, former CEO of Chrysler Corporation, said: "All business operations can be reduced to three words: people, product, and profit. People come first. Unless you've got a good team, you can't do much with the other two." Successful managers are those who create, work with, and manage successful teams.

Defining high-performing teams

A team is two or more people who meet regularly, perceive themselves as a distinct entity distinguishable from others, have complementary skills, and are committed to a common purpose, a set of performance goals, and an approach for which they hold themselves mutually accountable. High-performing teams engage in collective work produced by coordinated joint efforts that result in more than the sum of the individual efforts. Teams of 10 or fewer members find it easiest to interact constructively and reach agreement.

Understanding team performance

WHO ARE WE?
Sharing strengths, weaknesses, work preferences, and values allows the establishment of a set of common beliefs for the team, creating a group identity and a feeling of "what we stand for".

WHERE ARE WE NOW?
Understanding the current position means that a team can reinforce its strengths, improve on its weaknesses, and identify opportunities to capitalize on and threats to be aware of.

WHERE ARE WE GOING?
Teams need to have a vision of the pot of gold at the end of the rainbow. They also need a mission, a purpose, and a set of specific team goals that they are all excited about.

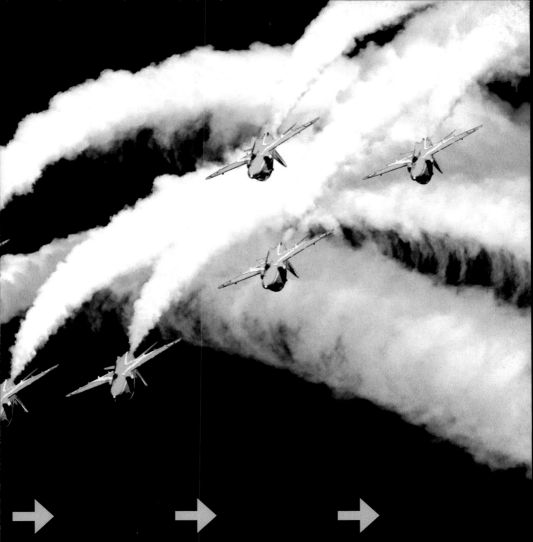

HOW WILL WE GET THERE?
Team members must understand who will do what and when to accomplish team goals, and must be clear about their job description, roles on the team, responsibilities, and areas of authority and accountability.

WHAT SUPPORT DO WE GET/NEED?
Reviewing each member's training and development needs an set the stage for individual training, counselling, and mentoring that will strengthen both the individual and the team.

HOW EFFECTIVE ARE WE?
Regular performance reviews of quantity and quality outputs and the team process – with recognition and reward for success – ensure achievement of team goals and provide members with standards.

IN FOCUS... MUTUAL TRUST

A climate of mutual trust is essential in a high-performing team – each member of the team needs to know they can depend on the others. Successful managers build mutual trust by creating a climate of openness in which employees are free to discuss problems without fear of retaliation. They are approachable, respectful, and listen to team members' ideas, and develop a reputation for being fair, objective, and impartial in their treatment of others. Consistency and honesty are key, so they avoid erratic and unpredictable behaviour and always follow through on any explicit and implied promises they make. Communication is at the heart of building and maintaining mutual inter-dependence between members of a team. Managers of high-performing teams keep team members informed about upper-management decisions and policies and give accurate feedback on their performance. They are also open and candid about their own problems and limitations.

TIP

CHANGE PERSONNEL

If your teams get bogged down in their own inertia or internal fighting, rotate the members. Consider how certain personalities will mesh and re-form your teams in ways that will better complement skills.

Achieving good teamwork

To help your teams perform to the best of their ability, create clear goals. All team members need to have a thorough understanding of the goals of the team and a belief that these goals embody a worthwhile result. This encourages team members to sublimate personal concerns to those of the team. Members need to be committed to the team's goals, know what they are expected to accomplish, and understand how they will work together to achieve these goals.

However, these goals must be attainable; team members can lose morale if it seems that they are not. To avoid this, set smaller interim milestones in the path to your overall goal. As these smaller goals are attained, your team's success is reinforced. Cohesiveness is increased, morale improves, and confidence builds.

As the manager of a team, it is your job to provide the resources and support that the members need to achieve success. Offer skills training where needed, either personally or by calling in specialists within your organization or outside training services.

Steering your team

Team members should all share in the glory when their team succeeds, and they should share in the blame when it fails. However, members need to know that they cannot ride on the backs of others. Identify what each member's individual contribution to the team's work should be and make it a part of his or her overall performance appraisal.

To help monitor performance, select members of the team to act as participant–observers. While a team is working, the role of the participant–observer is to focus on the processes being used: the sequence of actions that takes place between team members to achieve the team's goal. Periodically, the participant–observer should stop the team from working on its task and discuss the process members are engaged in. The objectives of the participant–observer are to continuously improve the team's functioning by discussing the processes being used and creating strategies for improving them.

Setting standards

Create a performance agreement to record the details of what the team is aiming to achieve, what is required and expected of every team member, and what support will be available to them. Setting out the framework for team success clearly helps to ensure that there is a mutual understanding and common vision of the desired results and emphasizes the standards that you expect from every team member.

CHECKLIST CREATING A TEAM PERFORMANCE AGREEMENT

	YES	NO
• Have I identified what is to be done and when?	☐	☐
• Have I specified the boundaries (guiding rules of behaviour) or the means for accomplishing results?	☐	☐
• Have I identified the human, financial, technical, or organizational support available to help achieve the results?	☐	☐
• Have I established the standards of performance and the time intervals for evaluation?	☐	☐
• Have I specified what will happen in performance evaluations and the consequences of not meeting the standards?	☐	☐

Delegating effectively

Managers are responsible for getting things done through other people. You need to accomplish assigned goals by delegating responsibility and authority to others. Empowering others through delegation is one of the most powerful managerial tools for increasing productivity.

Empowering others

Managers delegate by transferring authority and responsibility for work to employees. Delegation empowers employees to achieve goals by allowing them to make their own decisions about how to do a job. Delegation also helps develop employees for promotion opportunities by expanding their knowledge, job capabilities, and decision-making skills. Delegation frequently is depicted as having four key components:

- **Allocation of duties** Before a manager can delegate authority, the tasks and activities that need to be accomplished must be explained.
- **Delegation of authority** Delegation is the process of transferring authority to empower a subordinate to act for you as a manager.
- **Assignment of responsibility** Managers should assign responsibility to the empowered employee for performing the job adequately.
- **Creation of accountability** Managers should hold empowered employees responsible for properly carrying out their duties. This includes taking responsibility for the completion of tasks assigned to them and also being accountable to the manager for the satisfactory performance of that work.

Feeling the benefits

Effective delegation is key for any manager. It will free up your time, allowing you to focus on big-picture strategic activities. It can also lead to better decision-making, because it pushes decisions down the organization, meaning that decision-makers are often closer to the problems. It also helps those you are managing develop their own decision-making skills and prepares them for future promotion opportunities.

Letting go

Managers often have trouble delegating. Some are afraid to give up control, explaining, "I like to do things myself, because then I know it's done and it's done right." Others lack confidence in their employees or fear that they may be criticized for others' mistakes. While you may be capable of doing the tasks you delegate better, faster, or with fewer mistakes, it is not possible to do everything yourself. However, you should expect, and accept, some mistakes by those you delegate to. Mistakes are often good learning experiences. You also should put adequate controls and mechanisms for feedback in place so you will know what is happening.

HOW TO... DELEGATE

CLARIFY THE ASSIGNMENT
Explain what is being delegated, the results you expect, and the timeframe.

↓

SET BOUNDARIES
Ensure that the delegatees understand precisely what the parameters are of the authority you are bestowing on them.

↓

ENCOURAGE PARTICIPATION
Involve delegatees in decisions about what is delegated, how much authority is needed, and standards to be attained.

↓

INFORM OTHERS
Let everyone who may be affected know what has been delegated to whom and how much authority has been granted.

↓

ESTABLISH CONTROLS
Agree on a specific time for completion of the task, and set dates when progress will be checked and problems discussed.

↓

ENCOURAGE DEVELOPMENT
Insist from the beginning that when delegatees come to you with a problem, they also bring a possible solution.

Motivating others

Every day, people make decisions about how much effort to put into their work. Managers have many opportunities to influence these decisions and motivate their team by providing challenging work, recognizing outstanding performance, allowing participation in decisions that affect employees, and showing concern for personal issues.

Understanding needs

As a manager, you need to understand what drives your team to do the best that they can. American psychologist Abraham Maslow proposed that every individual has a five-level hierarchy of needs that they are driven to attempt to satisfy. Once a lower-level need has been largely satisfied, its impact on a person's behaviour diminishes, and they begin to be motivated to gain the next highest level need.

There are two aspects to what makes a person perform well: ability and motivation. Ability is the product of aptitude, training, and resources, while motivation is the product of desire and commitment. All of these elements are required for high performance levels. If someone is not performing

CASE STUDY

Prioritizing needs

Theresa, a successful technical writer and a single parent, had been earning a good salary and benefits that enabled her to provide for her family's physical well-being: ample food, comfortable housing and clothing, and good medical care. Her company then announced that it was downsizing, and she feared being made redundant. This triggered concerns about her safety needs and

meant that she became much less concerned about the higher order needs of belonging to a group or her own self-esteem to perform creative and technically accurate work. Rather, she was motivated to do whatever was necessary to ensure that she kept her job or could find a new one. Once Theresa knew that her job was safe, she changed back to having a higher-order need, energizing her behaviour.

well, the first question you should ask yourself is: "Is their poor performance the result of a lack of ability or a lack of motivation?" Motivational methods can often be very effective for improving performance, but if the problem is lack of ability, no amount of pressure or encouragement will help. What the person needs is training, additional resources, or a different job.

Maslow's hierarchy of needs

SELF-ACTUALIZATION NEEDS
The highest level is to feel that we are achieving life goals. At work, this means being able to exercise creativity and to develop and fully utilize our skills.

ESTEEM NEEDS
Next, we are motivated by the need for self-esteem and esteem from others, such as recognition for accomplishments and promotion.

SOCIAL NEEDS
Once you feel reasonably secure, social needs begin to take over. At work, this means having good relationships with co-workers and participating in company social functions.

SAFETY NEEDS
Once physiological needs are satisfied, safety needs are aroused. These can be satisfied at work by having job security and safe working conditions, and receiving medical benefits.

PHYSIOLOGICAL NEEDS
Our most basic needs are for physical survival, such as to satisfy hunger or thirst. At work, this is receiving enough pay to buy food and clothing and pay the rent.

Appraising performance

As a manager, you must ensure that objectives are met and also that employees learn how to enhance their performance. Providing structured feedback through the formal performance appraisal process can increase productivity and morale and decrease absenteeism and staff turnover.

KEEP YOUR OPTIONS OPEN

When giving your appraisal, avoid absolutes such as "always" and "never" – if the person you are appraising can introduce one exception to your statement, it can destroy the entire statement's validity and damage your credibility.

Assessing progress

Giving feedback in a formal way in performance appraisal interviews conveys to those you are managing that you care about how they are doing. Appraisals allow you to set goals and monitor achievement, helping to motivate your team to perform to a higher level. They allow you to tell each individual how well they're progressing, which can reinforce good behaviour and extinguish dysfunctional behaviour. However, the interview itself should be the final step in the performance appraisal process. Appraisal should be a continuous process, starting with the establishment and communication of performance standards. Continually assess how each individual is performing relative to these standards, and use this information to discuss a person's performance with them in the appraisal interview.

ASK YOURSELF... AM I PREPARED FOR THE APPRAISAL?

- Have I carefully considered the employee's strengths as well as their weaknesses?
- Can I substantiate, with specific examples, all points of praise and criticism?
- Have I thought about any problems that may occur in the appraisal interview?
- Have I considered how I will react to these problems?

Conducting the appraisal interview

Start with the aim of putting the person at ease. Most people don't like to hear their work criticized, so be supportive and understanding and create a helpful and constructive climate. Begin the interview by explaining what will transpire during the appraisal and why. Keep your appraisal goal-oriented, and make sure that your feedback is specific. Vague statements provide little useful information. Where you can, get the person's own perceptions of the problems being addressed – there may be contributing factors that

you are unaware of. Encourage the person to evaluate themselves as much as possible. In a supportive climate, they may acknowledge performance problems independently, thus eliminating your need to raise them. They may also offer viable solutions.

At the end of the interview, ask the recipient to rephrase the content of your appraisal. This will indicate whether or not you have succeeded in communicating your evaluation clearly. Finish by drawing up a future plan of action. Draft a detailed, step-by-step plan for improvement. Include in the plan what needs to be done, by when, and how you will monitor the person's activities.

CONDUCTING APPRAISAL INTERVIEWS

FAST TRACK	OFF TRACK
Focusing only on feedback that relates to the person's job	Sharing your feelings about a person's personality
Providing both positive and negative feedback	Focusing your comments only on bad performance
Sharing first-hand observations as evidence	Including rumours and allegations in your appraisal
Being unafraid to criticize the person constructively	Avoiding offending the other person by sugarcoating your criticism

Chapter 4

Leading others

Leadership is the process of providing direction, influencing and energizing others, and obtaining follower commitment to shared organizational goals. Managers need to lead their team, setting ethical boundaries for them to follow, developing a power base for influencing them to change in positive ways, and helping them improve through coaching and mentoring.

Setting ethical boundaries

Few of us would be likely to steal or cheat, but how principled would you be, or should you be, when faced with routine business situations involving ethical choices? As a leader, you need to have a clear understanding of your ethical principles and set a consistent example for your team.

Understanding ethics

Ethics refer to the rules or principles that define right or wrong conduct. In the workplace, acting ethically is not just an abstraction, it is an everyday occurrence. Consider this dilemma: an employee, after some pressure from you, has found another job. You are relieved because you will not have to fire him; his work has been substandard for some time. But your relief turns to dismay when he asks you for a letter of recommendation. Do you say no and run the risk that he will not leave? Or do you write the letter, knowing that you're influencing someone else to take him on?

Being responsible

Ethics is important for everyone in an organization, particularly as some unethical acts are also illegal. Many organizations want employees to behave ethically because such a reputation is good for business, which in turn can mean larger profits. However, acting ethically is especially crucial for managers. The decisions a manager makes set the standard for those they are managing and help create a tone for the organization. If employees believe all are held to high standards, they are likely to feel better about themselves, their colleagues, and their organization.

Developing ethics

The behaviour of managers is under more scrutiny than that of other members of staff, and misdeeds can become quickly and widely known, destroying the reputation of the organization. It is important for managers to develop their own ethical boundaries – lines that they and their employees should not cross. To do this, you need to:
• Know and understand your organization's policy on ethics.
• Anticipate unethical conduct. Be alert to situations that may promote unethical behaviour. (Under unusual circumstances, even a normally

ethical person may be tempted to act out of character.)
• Consider all consequences. Ask yourself questions such as: "What if my actions were described in detail on a local TV news show, or in the newspaper? What if I get caught doing something unethical? Am I prepared to deal with the consequences?"
• Seek opinions from others. They may have been in a similar situation, or at least can listen and be a sounding board for you.
• Do what you truly believe is right. You have a conscience and are responsible for your behaviour. You need to be true to your own internal ethical standards. Ask yourself the simple question: "Can I live with what I have decided to do?"

? ASK YOURSELF... IS WHAT I'M ABOUT TO DO ETHICAL?

• Why am I doing what I'm about to do?
• What are my true intentions in taking this action?
• Are there any ulterior motives behind my action, such as proving myself to my peers or superiors?
• Will my actions injure someone, physically or emotionally?
• Would I disclose to my boss or my family what I'm about to do?

Ensuring cultural fit

An organization's culture, or personality, refers to the key characteristics that the organization values and that distinguish it from other organizations. Managers need to be aware of organizational culture because they are expected to respond to the dictates of the culture themselves and also to develop an understanding of the culture in those they are managing.

Analyzing organizational culture

The cultural imperatives of an organization are often not written down or even discussed, but all successful managers must learn what to do and what not to do in their organizations. In fact, the better the match between the manager's personal style and the organization's culture, the more successful the manager is likely to be. Founders create culture in three ways. First, they hire and keep employees who think and feel the way they do. Second, founders indoctrinate and socialize these employees to their way of thinking. Third, founders act as role models, and their personality becomes central to the culture of the organization.

Being able to discern an organization's culture is not always a simple task. Many organizations have given little thought to their culture and do not readily display it. To try to find out more about your organization's culture, you might:

• Observe the physical surroundings. Look at signs, pictures, styles of dress, length of hair, the degree of openness among offices, and how those offices are furnished and arranged.

• Listen to the language. For example, do managers use military terms, such as "take no prisoners", and "divide and conquer"? Or do they speak about "intuition", "care", and "our family of customers"?

• Ask different people the same questions and compare their answers. You might ask: how does this company define success? For what are employees most rewarded? Who is on the fast track and what did they do to get there?

Sustaining culture

Managers are responsible for sustaining organizational culture, by helping new employees learn and adapt to it. A new worker, for example, must be taught what behaviours are valued and rewarded by the organization, so that he or she can learn the "system" and gradually assume those behaviours that are appropriate to their role.

CASE STUDY

Keeping culture consistent

At coffee retailer Starbucks, every employee goes through a set of formal classes during their first few weeks on the job. They are taught the history of the firm, coffee-making techniques, and how to explain Starbucks's Italian drink names to baffled customers, and given coffee-tasting classes. The firm's socialization programme turns out employees who are well versed in the company's culture and can represent Starbucks's obsession with "elevating the coffee experience" for its customers.

Solving problems

Managerial success depends on making the right decisions at the right times. However, unless you define a problem and identify its root causes, it is impossible to make appropriate decisions about how to solve it. Effective managers know how to gather and evaluate information that clarifies a problem, develop alternatives, and weigh up the implications of a plan before implementing it.

Spotting problems

A problem exists when a situation is not what is needed or desired. A major responsibility for all managers is to maintain a constant lookout for existing or potential problems, and to spot them early before they escalate into serious situations. Managers fulfil this responsibility by keeping channels of communication open, monitoring employees' current performance, and examining deviations from present plans as well as from past experience. Four situations can alert managers to possible problems:
- A deviation from past experience
- A deviation from a set plan
- When other people communicate problems to you
- When competitors start to outperform your team or organization.

The problem-solving process

1 IDENTIFYING
Being conscious of what is going on around you, so you can spot problems early.

2 DEFINING
Making a careful analysis of the problem to be solved, in order to define it as clearly as possible.

Finding solutions

Problem solving involves closing the gap between what is actually taking place and a desired outcome. Once you have identified a problem that needs to be addressed, start by analyzing the problem and defining it as clearly as you can. This is a key step: the definition you generate will have a major impact on all remaining steps in the process. If you get the definition wrong, all remaining steps will be distorted, because you will base them on insufficient or erroneous information. Definition is important even if the solution to the problem appears to be obvious – without a full assessment you may miss an alternative resolution that is more advantageous.

Gather as much information about the situation as you can. Try to understand the goals of all of the parties involved, and clarify any aspects of the problem you are unclear about.

Once you are satisfied that you have a full understanding of the issues, develop courses of action that could provide a resolution to the problem. There is often more than one way to solve a problem, so it is critical to consider all possible solutions and arrive at several alternatives from which to choose.

Your decision will provide you with an action plan. However, this will be of little value unless it is implemented effectively. Defining how, when, and by whom the action plan is to be implemented and communicating this to those involved is what connects the decision with reality.

Your involvement should not end at implementation, however. Establish criteria for measuring success, then track progress and take corrective actions when necessary. Try to develop and maintain positive attitudes in everyone involved in the implementation process.

4 IMPLEMENTING
Setting your action plan in motion, by creating a schedule and assigning tasks and responsibilities.

MAKING THE DECISION
Evaluating the alternatives and choosing a course of action that will improve the situation in a significant way.

5 FOLLOWING THROUGH
Monitoring progress, to ensure that the desired outcome is achieved.

Building power

Power is the capacity to influence an individual or group to behave in ways they would not have on their own. Learning how to acquire power and exercise it effectively will help you manage and influence others and develop your managerial career.

Developing power bases

Managerial positions come with the authority to issue directives and allocate rewards and punishments – for example, to assign favourable or unfavourable work assignments, hold performance reviews, and make salary adjustments. However, you can also build power in other ways:
• Expertise: organizations are often dependent on experts with special skills, such as in technology.
• Charisma: when others admire you and identify with you, you have referent power over them.
• Access to information: having information that only you have access to but others need gives you power.
• Association power: having confidantes in powerful positions can increase your power.
• Impression management: shaping the image you project to others in order to favourably influence how others see and evaluate you can give you power. For example, it might be used when lobbying your boss for a pay rise or a promotion.
• Politicking: you don't always win just by being a competent performer. Politicking is taking actions to influence, or attempt to influence, the distribution of advantages and disadvantages within your organization. It involves using strategies to influence decision outcomes in your favour.

REASONING
Use facts and data to make a logical or rational presentation of ideas. This is most effective when others are trustworthy, open and logical.

HIGHER AUTHORITY
Gain the support of those above you to back your requests. This is only effective in bureaucratic organizations where there is great respect for authority.

COALITIONS
Develop support in the organization for what you want to happen. This is most effective where final decisions rely on the quantity not the quality of support.

BARGAINING
Exchange benefits or favours to negotiate outcomes acceptable to both parties. This works best when organizational culture promotes give-and-take cooperation.

FRIENDLINESS
Use flattery, create goodwill, act humbly, and be supportive prior to making a request. This works best when you are well liked.

Ways to use managerial power to obtain desired outcomes

SANCTIONS
Use organizationally derived rewards and punishments to obtain desired outcomes. This approach is only for influencing subordinates, and may be seen as manipulative.

ASSERTIVENESS
Be direct and forceful when indicating what you want from others. This strategy is most effective when the balance of power is clearly in your favour.

Managing change

Individuals, managers, teams, and organizations that do not adapt to change in timely ways are unlikely to survive in our increasingly turbulent world environment. Managers that anticipate change, learn to adapt to change, and manage change will be the most successful.

Overcoming resistance

Change is the process of moving from a present state to a more desired state in response to internal and external factors. To successfully implement change, you need to possess the skills to convince others of the need for change, identify gaps between the current situation and desired conditions, and create visions for desirable outcomes.

Experienced managers are aware that efforts to change often face resistance. This can be for a variety of reasons, including fear, vested interests, misunderstanding, lack of trust, differing perceptions of a situation, and limited resources. You need to be able to counter this resistance to change through education, participation, and negotiation.

IN FOCUS... PHASES OF CHANGE

Planned change progresses through three phases:

• **Unfreezing** This involves helping people see that a change is needed because the existing situation is undesirable. Existing attitudes and behaviours need to be altered during this phase to reduce resistance, by explaining how the change can help increase productivity, for example. Your goal in this phase is to help the participants see the need for change and to increase their willingness to make the change a success.

• **Changing** This involves making the actual change and requires you to help participants let go of old ways of doing things and develop new ones.

• **Refreezing** The final phase involves reinforcing the changes made so that the new ways of behaving become stabilized. If people perceive the change to be working in their favour, positive results will serve as reinforcement, but if not, it may be necessary to use external reinforcements, which can be positive or negative.

Promoting change

Major change does not happen easily. Effective managers are able to establish a sense of urgency that the change is needed. If an organization is obviously facing a threat to its survival, this kind of crisis usually gets people's attention. Dramatically declining profits and stock prices are examples. In other cases, when no current crisis is obvious, but managers have identified potential problems by scanning the external environment, the manager needs to find ways to communicate the information broadly and dramatically to make others aware of the need for change. Managers also have to develop and articulate a compelling vision and strategy that people will aspire to, that will guide the change effort. The vision of what it will be like when the change is achieved should illuminate core principles and values that pull followers together. Lastly, institutionalizing changes in the organizational culture will refreeze the change. New values and beliefs will become instilled in the culture so that employees view the changes as normal and integral to the operations of the organization.

TURN TO THE POSITIVE

Try to use any resistance to your proposed change for your benefit, by making it a stimulus for dialogue and a deeper, more thoughtful analysis of the alternatives.

Helping others to improve

Helping employees become more competent is an important part of any manager's job. It contributes to a three-way win for the organization, the manager, and the employees themselves. By helping others resolve personal problems and develop skill competencies – and so help them improve their performance – you will motivate your team to achieve better results for themselves and for the organization.

Diagnosing problems

If you can reduce unsatisfactory performance in the people you are managing, you ultimately make your job easier because you will be increasingly able to delegate responsibilities to them. Unsatisfactory performance often has multiple causes. Some causes are within the control of the person experiencing the difficulties, while others are not.

✔ CHECKLIST DETERMINING THE CAUSE OF UNSATISFACTORY PERFORMANCE

	YES	NO
• Is the person unaware that their performance is unsatisfactory? If yes, provide feedback.	☐	☐
• Is the person performing poorly because they are not aware of what is expected of them? If yes, provide clear expectations.	☐	☐
• Is performance hampered by obstacles beyond the person's control? If yes, determine how to remove the obstacles.	☐	☐
• Is the person struggling because they don't know how to perform a key task? If yes, provide coaching or training.	☐	☐
• Is good performance followed by negative consequences? If yes, determine how to eliminate the negative consequences.	☐	☐
• Is poor performance being rewarded by positive consequences? If yes, determine how to eliminate the positive reinforcement.	☐	☐

Ways to help others improve

- Ask questions to help discover sources of problems.
- Accept mistakes and use them as learning opportunities.
- Help develop action plans for improvement.
- Seek to educate rather than to assist.
- Provide meaningful feedback for learning.
- Encourage continual improvement.
- Demonstrate unconditional positive regard by suspending judgement and evaluation.
- Recognize and reward even small improvements.
- Actively listen to employees and show genuine interest.
- Model the behaviours you desire.

Demonstrating positive regard

The relationship between you and the person you are helping is critical to the success of the coaching, mentoring, or counselling you undertake with them. For a helping relationship to be successful it is important to hold the person being helped in "unconditional positive regard". This means that you accept and exhibit warm regard for the person needing help as a person of unconditional self-worth – a person of value no matter what the conditions, problems, or feelings. If you can communicate positive regard, it provides a climate of warmth and safety because the person feels liked and prized as a person. This is a necessary condition for developing the trust that is crucial in a helping relationship.

Conducting a helping session

Before you speak to someone about how to help them improve their performance, make sure you have acquired all the facts about the situation. Take time to think about what type of help the situation requires and consider how the person might react and how they might feel about what you are going to discuss. During the helping session:
• Start by discussing the purpose of the session.
• Try to make the person feel comfortable and at ease.
• Establish a non-defensive climate, characterized by open communication and trust.
• Before you discuss the problem you have identified, raise and discuss positive aspects of the person's performance.
• Mutually define the problem (performance or attitude).
• Mutually determine the causes. Do not interpret or psychoanalyze behaviour; instead, ask questions such as, "What's causing the lack of motivation you describe?"
• Help the other person establish an action plan that includes specific goals and dates.
• Make sure expectations are clearly understood.
• Summarize what has been agreed upon.
• Affirm your confidence in the person's ability to make needed changes based on his or her strengths or past history.
After the session, make sure that you follow up to see how the person is progressing, and modify the action plan if necessary.

 IN FOCUS... FEEDBACK

People need feedback about the consequences of their actions if they are to learn what works and what doesn't and then change their actions to become more effective. Carefully thought-out feedback can increase performance and positive personal development. Applying feedback in the helping process involves:
• Describing observed behaviours and the results and consequences of those behaviours.
• Assessing the impact of the observed behaviours in terms of organizational vision and goals.
• Predicting the personal consequences for the person involved if no changes take place.
• Recommending changes the person could make to improve their behaviour.
    This sequence of actions applies whether the type of help being given to the person is coaching, mentoring, or counselling.

Counselling others

Counselling is the discussion of emotional problems in order to resolve them or to help the person better cope. Problems that might require counselling include divorce, serious illness, financial problems, interpersonal conflicts, drug and alcohol abuse, and frustration over a lack of career progress. Although most managers are not qualified as psychologists, there are several things managers can do in a counselling role before referring someone to a professional therapist.

Confidentiality is of paramount importance when counselling others. To open up and share the reasons for many personal problems, people must feel that they can trust you and that there is no threat to their self-esteem or their reputation with others. Emphasize that you will treat in confidence everything that the other person says regarding personal matters.

TIP

BE SUPPORTIVE
Reassure those you are counselling that their problems have solutions and that they have the ability to improve their situation.

Dealing with personal problems

Getting a person to recognize that they have a problem is often the first step in helping them deal with it. You can then follow up by helping them gain insights into their feelings and behaviours, and by exploring the alternatives open to them.

Sometimes people just need a sounding board for releasing tension, which can become a prelude to clarifying the problem, identifying possible solutions, and taking corrective action. Talking things through in a counselling session can help people sort out their feelings into more logical and coherent thoughts.

Above all, be supportive and provide reassurance. People need to know that their problems have solutions. If problems are beyond a person's capability to solve, explain how professional treatment can be obtained, through Employee Assistance Programmes, for example, or health plans.

Coaching and mentoring

Coaching is the process of helping people improve performance. A coach analyzes performance, provides insight on how to improve, and offers the leadership, motivation, and supportive climate to help achieve that improvement. In mentoring relationships, a more experienced person formally pairs up with a less experienced one to help show them "the ropes" and to provide emotional support and encouragement.

HOW TO... COACH A PROCESS

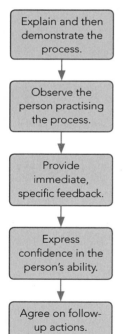

Explain and then demonstrate the process.

Observe the person practising the process.

Provide immediate, specific feedback.

Express confidence in the person's ability.

Agree on follow-up actions.

Helping others develop

As a coach, a manager's job is to help members of their team develop skills and improve. This involves providing instruction, guidance, advice, and encouragement. Effective coaches first establish a supportive climate that promotes development. It is particularly important that you remain non-judgemental and understanding throughout the process, try to solve problems jointly, and educate those you are coaching about how to solve their own problems in the future. As you learn more about the person you are coaching, try to determine the sources of any problems they are having, and provide meaningful feedback.

Mentoring is a broader role. The goal of a mentor is to help a less experienced person achieve his or her career goals. Mentors perform as both coaches and counsellors as they guide their less experienced associates towards improved performance. Mentoring can help new organization members gain a better understanding of the organization's goals, culture, and advancement criteria. It can also help them become more politically savvy and avoid potential career traps. As a mentor, try to help others reduce the stress caused by uncertainty about how to do things and deal with challenging assignments. Be a source of comfort when newer, less experienced people just need to let off steam or discuss career dilemmas.

Three key skills for successful coaching

1
FINDING WAYS TO IMPROVE PERFORMANCE

3
CREATING A SUPPORTIVE CLIMATE

Help others improve by observing what they do, asking questions, listening, and crafting unique improvement strategies.

Use active listening, empower others to implement appropriate ideas, and be available for assistance, guidance, and advice.

2
INFLUENCING OTHERS TO CHANGE THEIR BEHAVIOUR

Monitor people's progress and development, and recognize and reward even small improvements.

Be a role model for the qualities that you expect from others, such as openness, commitment, and responsibility.

Involve others in decision-making processes – this helps to encourage people to be responsive to change.

Break large, complex projects into series of simpler tasks – this can boost confidence as the simpler tasks are achieved.

Managing careers

In today's rapidly changing business landscape, managers need to actively manage their careers and provide career guidance to those they are managing. To determine where and how you can best contribute, you need to know yourself, continually develop yourself, and be able to ascertain when and how to change the work you do.

Charting your own career path

Self-assessment is an ongoing process in career management. Successful careers develop when people are prepared for opportunities because they know their strengths, their methods of work, and their values. Self-directed career management is a process by which individuals guide, direct, and influence the course of their careers. This requires exploration and awareness of not only yourself, but also your environment. Individuals who are proactive and collect relevant information about personal needs, values, interests, talents, and lifestyle preferences are more likely to be satisfied and productive when searching for job opportunities, to develop successful career plans, and to be productive in their jobs and careers.

IN FOCUS... CAREER STAGES

Individuals just beginning their careers are usually more concerned with identifying organizations that have the potential to satisfy their career goals and match their values. After settling into a job, focus shifts to achieving initial successes, gaining credibility, learning to get along with their boss, and managing image.

Managers in the middle of their careers are more concerned with career reappraisal, overcoming obsolescence owing to technological advances, and becoming more of a generalist. In the later stages of their careers, managers focus more on teaching others and leaving a contribution before retirement.

Driving forward

The first step in self-directed career management is planning. Taking your strengths, limitations, and values into account, start searching the environment for matching opportunities. Use the information you gather to establish realistic career goals and then develop a strategy to achieve them. As you progress through your career plan, regularly undertake performance appraisals to make sure that you are remaining on track and that your goals haven't changed.

Directing others

The most important thing you can do to contribute to the career development of others is to instil in them the need to take responsibility for managing their own careers. Then you can provide support that will enable those you are managing to add to their skills, abilities, and knowledge, in order to maintain their employability within the organization. To help those you are managing develop their careers:

• Keep your team updated about the organization's goals and future strategies so that they will know where the organization is headed and be better able to develop a personal career development plan to share in that future.
• Create growth opportunities for your team, to give them new, interesting, and professionally challenging work experiences.
• Offer financial assistance, such as tuition reimbursement for college courses or skills training.
• Allow paid time off from work for off-the-job training, and ensure that those you are managing have reasonable workloads so that they are not precluded from having time to develop new skills, abilities, and knowledge.

MOTIVATING PEOPLE

Contents

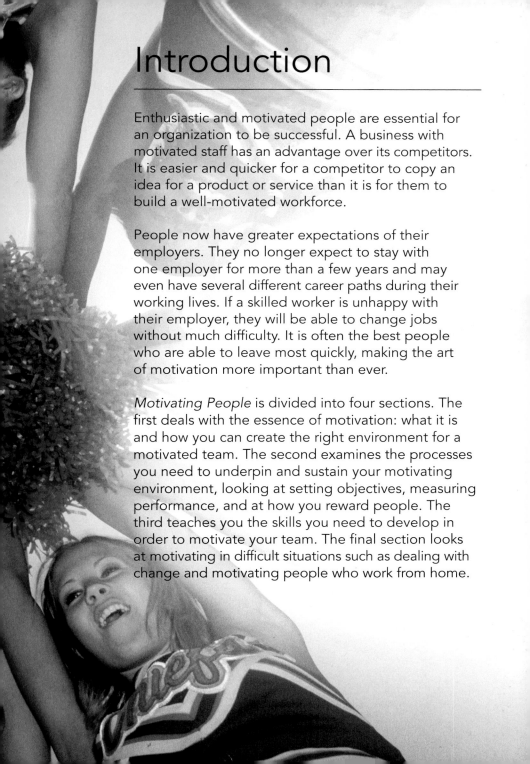

Introduction

Enthusiastic and motivated people are essential for an organization to be successful. A business with motivated staff has an advantage over its competitors. It is easier and quicker for a competitor to copy an idea for a product or service than it is for them to build a well-motivated workforce.

People now have greater expectations of their employers. They no longer expect to stay with one employer for more than a few years and may even have several different career paths during their working lives. If a skilled worker is unhappy with their employer, they will be able to change jobs without much difficulty. It is often the best people who are able to leave most quickly, making the art of motivation more important than ever.

Motivating People is divided into four sections. The first deals with the essence of motivation: what it is and how you can create the right environment for a motivated team. The second examines the processes you need to underpin and sustain your motivating environment, looking at setting objectives, measuring performance, and at how you reward people. The third teaches you the skills you need to develop in order to motivate your team. The final section looks at motivating in difficult situations such as dealing with change and motivating people who work from home.

Chapter 1
Creating a motivating environment

The context of motivation is important, as it is an essential element in the mix that delivers high performance. As a manager you will need to understand the principles of motivation to create the right environment in your organization.

Supporting performance

Motivation is a major driver of individual, team, and organizational success. But having motivated people isn't sufficient to guarantee high performance. There are other factors that must be considered, including having the ability and opportunity to do well.

TIP

MOTIVATE EVERYONE

In every team, some members demand more attention than others. Make sure you motivate all team members, even the quiet ones.

Directing efforts

Motivation is the will to do something. It comes from inside us, and herein lies the challenge for management: how do you motivate your people to achieve the organization's goals? Motivation is more than enthusiasm – it is about directing people's efforts. If you are a manager, your performance will depend on the efforts of your employees. Set clear goals for them and keep thinking about how you can support and motivate them. This is essential for the organization's and your own success.

Achieving success

A motivated person or group also requires the opportunity and ability to boost their performance. Opportunity covers two aspects – ensuring that your people have the tools and resources needed to do the job, and allowing them the space to do the job well without restrictions. A person's ability is a crucial factor that is often overlooked. It is created by combining an individual's innate skill or talent with experience.

ASK YOURSELF... IS MY TEAM ABLE TO PERFORM?

- Do my team members know what their goals are?
- What aspects of the work and environment demotivate them?
- Which tools are constraining the output?
- Do my team members have the basic ability and training to do their jobs?
- How can I improve the abilities of my team?

Maximizing performance

PERFORMANCE

Set clear goals, create enthusiasm

Provide proper tools, remove constraints

Develop skills, provide experience

MOTIVATION

OPPORTUNITY

ABILITY

Principles of motivation

There are three accepted theories of motivation: Maslow's hierarchy of needs, Herzberg's motivation and hygiene factors, and expectancy theory. How you use these, coupled with your own beliefs, will influence how you manage and motivate people.

TIP

GET FAMILIAR WITH YOUR STAFF
Remember everybody is an individual. To motivate someone you need to get to know them well and understand their own personal motivators and demotivators.

Maslow's motivation theory

American psychologist Abraham Maslow, one of the founding fathers of motivation theory, suggested that people have a hierarchy of needs. The basic needs should be satisfied first, and once these are met, you must appeal to the higher level of needs if you are to continue to motivate someone. Maslow's work suggests that people have different needs at different times. Some of these needs will be satisfied at work, and others through life outside work. But if you want to motivate your staff you need to get to know them, their interests, and their aspirations so you can adapt the organization's as well as your own approach to their changing situation.

IN FOCUS... MASLOW'S HIERARCHY OF NEEDS THEORY

Maslow's hierarchy of needs starts with the physiological needs of life: being able to breathe, being fed, and staying warm. The next level is concerned with security: being safe and secure. The third level relates to social needs: love and membership of wider social groups. The fourth level is esteem: the need for respect and a feeling of worth. The final level is self-actualization, where the desire is to be happy through achieving ambitions and fulfilling your potential. Maslow believed that once a lower level need was satisfied, its motivational impact declined and was replaced by higher level needs.

Expectancy theory

Expectancy theory was developed by Professor Victor Vroom in the 1960s. It proposes that people are motivated by being involved in setting their own goals, by receiving feedback along the way, and by recognition for what they achieve. Feedback is important, since it is very motivating to know how well you are progressing towards the target.

Herzberg's theory

TIP

LOOK BEYOND SALARY

Focus on the other benefits you can use to motivate people including recognition, advancement, and development.

The psychologist Frederick Herzberg divided sources of motivation into "motivators" and "hygiene factors". Hygiene factors don't motivate, but if they are not dealt with, they can turn people off. Having a dirty office is irritating, but having the cleanest office in the world isn't motivational. Herzberg believed salary is often a hygiene factor. If people are paid fairly, they are satisfied, but paying above the norm doesn't motivate people.

Herzberg's motivators and hygiene factors

MOTIVATION

HERZBERG'S HYGIENE FACTORS

HERZBERG'S MOTIVATORS

Hygiene Factors	Motivators
Salary	Recognition
Supervision	Progression
Company policy	Achievement
Working conditions	Responsibility
Personal relationships	The work itself

Your beliefs about human nature affect how you manage people. Douglas McGregor, author of *The Human Side of Enterprise*, created two extreme management approaches which he called theory X and theory Y. Theory X is based on the structuring of work precisely and at a detailed level, directing and controlling what people do, and motivating them through rewards and punishment. Theory Y suggests appealing to people's higher-level needs through communicating and negotiating goals and outcomes. If managers in your organization act as if they believe in theory X, employees are likely to be demotivated. You can set rules to protect the organization from lazy and uncommitted employees.

Theory X beliefs
- People are lazy.
- People lack ambition, dislike responsibility, and need to be told what to do.
- People are unconcerned by the organization's goals and need to be driven to perform.

Theory Y beliefs
- Most people are not naturally lazy, and work is a source of satisfaction.
- Most people learn to accept responsibility.
- Most people will work towards objectives to which they are committed.

UNDERSTAND YOUR STAFF

Be clear about your beliefs on how people behave at work. Keep asking yourself what you can start doing differently each day to keep your staff motivated.

GIVE CREDIT
Most people appreciate external recognition of their achievements so publicize their success and good work.

OFFER FEEDBACK
Keep talking and discussing with your staff – people need to receive regular feedback on progress in order to continue to perform well.

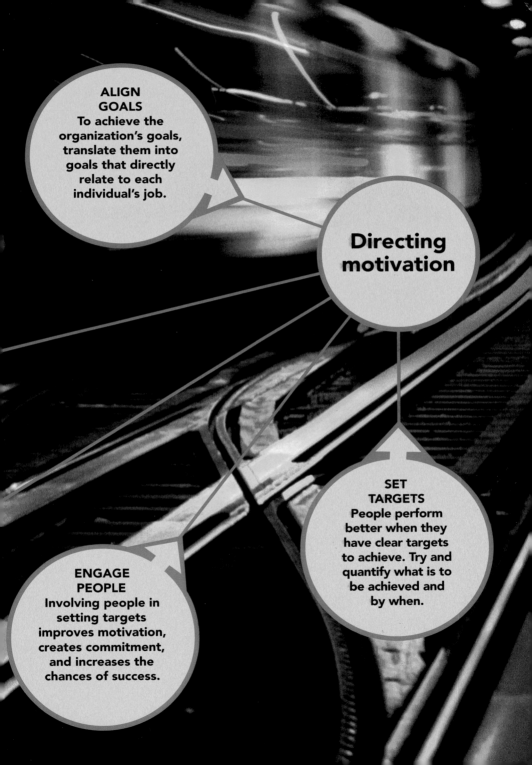

Creating the right conditions

Broadly speaking, elements of motivation can be divided into two groups: tangible elements, such as the physical working environment, and intangible elements, such as status. Tangible elements are known as "hygiene factors", which are the basic work needs. Intangible elements are known as "motivators". Some, such as pay, straddle both groups; for example, money pays your bills, but higher pay rates can also be a form of recognition.

KEEP YOUR EARS OPEN

Pay attention to the general office chatter to find out what frustrates people.

Recognizing basic needs

Although it may seem odd, working in smart surroundings is not the greatest motivator. It is very pleasant and can signal a certain status, but it's not essential. The majority of people want to do a good job. They want to work to the best of their ability. It will almost certainly take them longer to do something if they don't have the proper tools to do it. Basic work needs in an average office to include:

• Good light and ventilation
• A comfortable temperature
• Sufficient desk space
• A comfortable chair
• Reliable equipment and systems such as a computer, printer, photocopier, and telephone
• An area for refreshment
• A separate area to get away from the desk.

Considering intangible motivators

BUILD A REPUTATION

Focus on establishing your organization's credibility – it can take years but will enable you to attract the best employees away from your competitors.

Intangible motivators are more difficult to identify and usually vary from person to person, although there are some that are common to most people. These fall across a spectrum ranging from those that are fairly easily defined, such as job security, flexible working, recognition, and career development, to those that are very personal, such as achievement – the feeling of having done a job well, belonging to a worthwhile organization, or being part of a well-respected team. These motivators are often highly prized and many people would rather work for an organization of which they are proud, or that takes account of their work-life balance, than for one that simply pays well.

✔ CHECKLIST **ARE WORKING CONDITIONS OPTIMUM?**

	YES	NO
• Is the physical working environment satisfactory?	☐	☐
• Are we offering a reasonable rate of pay?	☐	☐
• Does my team have the right tools for the job?	☐	☐
• Am I aware of what their frustrations are?	☐	☐
• Are we able to offer flexible working hours?	☐	☐
• Are our managers well trained?	☐	☐

Creating a high-performance culture

Some organizational cultures motivate people to perform well, while some motivate people to stay within their job description and not take risks. Your management style will create the culture for your team, so your actions are critical to motivation and performance.

Understanding culture

*Blame culture
— culture in which the organization looks to apportion blame rather than resolve problems. It is encapsulated by the question "whose fault is it?"

Culture is defined by an organization's values and behaviour. It is about the way things are done. Supportive cultures create a trusting environment that facilitates motivation. On the other hand, a blame culture* creates a climate of fear. Rather than promoting an environment in which mistakes are not made, it leads to one in which no one will take any risks and where people are more concerned about checking their own work than moving forward and achieving objectives.

CREATING A POSITIVE CULTURE

FAST TRACK

OFF TRACK

FAST TRACK	OFF TRACK
Demonstrating commitment to the organization's values	Lacking confidence in leaders
Focusing on opportunities	Covering up problems
Creating trust between people	Putting the blame on others
Learning from mistakes	Exercising too much control

TIP

BE PERSISTENT

To establish an open culture, always be asking "Why?" If you do not get the answer you need, keep asking until you reach the core of the issue.

Embedding the culture

A culture of openness motivates the whole team to perform. It is created by leaders communicating a clear vision of what they want the values of their organization to be. Many organizations publish their values and display them on their websites and intranet. The organization setting is important, but you should also create your own local team culture. To encourage a culture of openness you will need to respond positively when people present their mistakes or problems. You must use the opportunity to help people learn from their mistakes, rather than to pass judgement or criticize their actions. Believing that most people want to do a good job will help you do this. Over time, your action will create trust, and people will respond to your approach and confide in you. As you resolve their issues, you will motivate the whole team to perform.

Recruiting the right people

Most managers inherit existing teams and have the task of managing people with a given set of experience, skills, and personalities. When you bring in a new person, you can make a considerable difference to the performance and overall motivation of your team.

Introducing a new recruit

Long-established teams usually build good working relationships and have a strong sense of loyalty to the team and the organization, but they can also develop a reluctance to change and make improvements. Individuals may have become bored, and be demotivated as a result. Bringing in a person with new ideas can re-motivate a team. However, if you bring in the wrong person or handle their integration into the team ineptly, you may damage the team spirit. So it is important to consider a new recruit carefully.

Finding the right recruit

There are two key questions to ask when recruiting. The first is: "Does this person have the right experience, knowledge, and skill to do the job?" The second relates to attitude and approach: "How will this person contribute to the team and the organization?" The answers to the first question should be apparent from the individual's CV, and can be checked at the interview. The answers to the second can be sought during the interview process. Spotting self-motivated personnel is a challenging task. You can judge whether the individual is self-motivated by finding out whether they progressed in their previous organization, have learnt from mistakes, and if they have interests outside work.

Ensuring successful recruitment

Recruitment is an expensive process, so when you bring in a new person you want to make sure they stay and are successful in improving team performance. Your role as manager is to ensure that the new recruit has the best possible start. Consider how you will introduce them and integrate them into your existing team. Make sure team members are aware of the person's background and what they will be doing. Brief the individual on their personal objectives and the overall team objectives. If you work in a large organization you may want to appoint a mentor to work closely with the person through the early stages in their new role.

IN FOCUS... DOCTOR BELBIN'S TEAM ROLES

Dr R. Meredith Belbin, a British researcher and management theorist, established a set of team roles, each associated with a particular type of personality. These included implementers, shapers, completer/finishers, plants (people who have original ideas), evaluators, specialists, co-ordinators, team workers, and resource investigators (people who explore new ideas). To succeed, teams need a balance of functional ability (the professional skills and technical backgrounds required for the project) and their team roles. Teams work best when there is a balance of roles so that the team members can motivate and learn from each other.

Measuring motivation

Motivation is not something you can easily sense when you walk into an office. You may spot tangible signs, but often they represent just a snapshot of what is happening at a given time. So it is helpful to try to measure the mood of the workforce. This is best done by means of a survey.

TIP

KEEP ASKING FOR FEEDBACK

Persevere with regular surveys, even if the results of the first one shock you. Over time and with attention, you can improve your results and the motivation of your staff.

Conducting a survey

It is generally accepted that motivated employees perform better, so it is important to establish how your employees are feeling as objectively as you can. The best way to get reliable and anonymous feedback about the mood of the workforce is through a regular staff opinion survey. Markus Buckingham and Curt Coffman, management consultants at the Gallup organization, developed a set of 12 questions to measure the motivation of a workforce. Does your staff:
• know what is expected of them at work?
• have the materials and equipment they need to do their job properly?
• have the opportunity to do their best every day?
• receive recognition or praise for good work? Have they in the last week?
• have a supervisor, or someone at work who cares about them as a person?
• have someone who encourages their development?
• believe their opinions at work appear to count?

• believe the mission of the company is important?
• believe their co-workers are committed to their work?
• have a best friend at work?
• have someone to talk to about their progress?
• have opportunities at work to learn and grow?

They also suggest you should ask how satisfied your employees are with your organization as an employer. Their research showed that responses to the questions can be positively linked to productivity, profitability, customer satisfaction, and staff turnover. Conducting the survey each year will allow you to compare the results over time, and reveal where improvements are being made and where you need to take action.

Providing feedback

If you conduct a survey, it is always important to give feedback. Ideally you should communicate this at team level, but when teams have returned fewer than seven completed surveys, you should not give the results, as anonymity will be undermined. Present and discuss the results openly, focusing on issues raised by the survey and actions that could be taken to avoid problems and improve things in the future. Be careful not to over-promise to avoid creating unrealistic expectations amongst your employees.

TIP

CHECK THE RESPONSE RATE

When conducting a survey, always measure your response rate – the number responding as a percentage of those sent the survey. A low response in an area can be an early indicator of problems.

MEASURING STAFF OPINION

⬆ FAST TRACK	❗ OFF TRACK
Conducting regular staff opinion surveys	Disregarding or being uninterested in staff opinion
Allowing the staff to make their responses anonymous	Discouraging completion of the staff survey
Taking the survey seriously so that a majority of staff complete it	Asking the staff ambiguous or irrelevant questions

Chapter 2

Building processes for motivation

Once you have succeeded in creating an environment to develop a motivated workforce, you need to implement and maintain processes to underpin it. These processes provide a structure that demonstrates "how things are done".

Designing a job role

Jobs roles are changing as a result of the breaking down of hierarchy in organizations. Individuals now have a greater choice of what their job profile should be, so to retain the best employees and motivate them at work, you will need to design their job roles carefully.

BE ENTHUSIASTIC
Give full attention and energy to your own job role, only then will you be able to understand and design a suitable job role for your employees.

Making a job role motivational

You may work in a pleasant environment, but if you see no purpose in your job, you are unlikely to be motivated. This is why it is so important to design a job role that is suitable for each employee. In a well-designed job, the job-holder should be able to use a variety of skills in their job, be involved in the whole activity, and have a meaningful role in which they understand the impact of the work they do. You should give your staff freedom to carry out tasks and provide them with regular feedback on what they are doing well as well as where they need to improve.

Improving a job role

Few managers have the opportunity to design a job role from scratch. Unless you are embarking on a major change programme, any new job will almost certainly have to fit in with the current structure. However, you can make changes that will have a significant effect on motivation in your team. Every individual has different strengths and skills. If you understand what these are, you may be able to allocate the work in your team to play to someone's strengths. Bring your team together and ask them to think about their jobs and how they could be better designed. Be careful, though, because any changes have to be made in the light of the overall effectiveness of the organization. For example, deciding that you will unilaterally agree a policy of flexible working for your team is probably not a good idea for the organization as a whole. An effective way of improving existing jobs is job rotation – moving people around so that they develop a broader range of skills and gain experience of doing other jobs. Job enrichment is a means of giving people greater depth rather than breadth in their roles. It is about giving them more responsibility, autonomy, and discretion. This is often done to add interest where people are in very straightforward jobs.

TIP

ASSESS YOUR OWN ROLE
Think about your role. What do you like about it? What do you not like? Can you change it? Does it give you any pointers as to how your staff perceive their own roles?

ASK YOURSELF... HOW DO I DEFINE A ROLE?

- What is the tangible outcome of the role?
- What would happen if the role did not exist?
- What place does the role have in the structure of the organization?
- Do I know my employees well enough to design a suitable role for them?
- Could the role be broken down and shared amongst existing employees?
- Can I enrich the existing job role?
- How will the results of the post-holder's contribution be measured?

Creating a balance

In motivating people to perform well, you should aim to balance high performance with constructive behaviour as well as balance short-term success with achieving longer-term goals. It is also important to give equal weight to the needs of the organization and the individual.

Balancing performance indicators and behaviour

***Gaming* —**
the behaviour associated with achieving the target numbers by any means and without regard for delivering real performance.

Most measurements of performance don't give a view of the future. Take the sales target as an example. Close to the month end, a salesman may make unrealistic promises to his customers and take orders that will allow him to reach his bonus. This will ensure achievement of the performance target, but his behaviour may upset the customer in the longer term, causing his customer to place their business elsewhere. This behaviour is gaming* the system and as a manager you need to take steps to avoid this.

Balancing short- and long-term needs

TIP

CHOOSE YOUR STYLE

In a crisis, short-term motivational techniques will be most appropriate, but make sure you return to long-term techniques when the crisis is over.

Motivation has short- and long-term elements. In the short term, commitment, direction, and enthusiasm will motivate people. But in the longer term, people need to see that they are being led and that changes are being made to help them do their work. In the longer term, giving people the right tools, creating the right working environment, and giving them the training they need is much more motivational. Short-term success has to be translated into long-term success by changing the way the work is done.

Blake–Mouton management grid

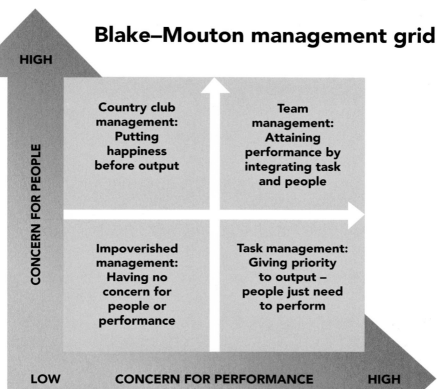

HIGH

CONCERN FOR PEOPLE

Country club management: Putting happiness before output

Team management: Attaining performance by integrating task and people

Impoverished management: Having no concern for people or performance

Task management: Giving priority to output – people just need to perform

LOW CONCERN FOR PERFORMANCE HIGH

Balancing work and individual needs

Ask yourself whether you are people-focused or task-focused – do you devote most of your effort to achieving the goals that have been set for the organization, or do you focus on ensuring that people are content in their jobs? In reality, you should do both. The organization needs to achieve its goals and targets, so these are important.

However, the people who work for the organization have their own needs and these can't be ignored. The key to motivational management is to align your employees' needs closely with those of the organization. Management theorists Robert Blake and Jane Mouton created a grid that reflects four approaches to management. They suggest that managers should aim to be in the top right hand box, showing high concern for both people and performance.

Conducting appraisals

An appraisal is a formal process for setting objectives, measuring progress, and providing feedback to employees on performance. When conducted in an appropriate manner, it can motivate individuals to perform more effectively and progress within the organization.

Benefiting from appraisals

One of the key benefits of the appraisal process is that it provides a structured approach to managing performance. This is important, as personal objectives are essential to guiding motivation. It also forces managers to sit down and have a frank discussion with each team member. It is important not to rely on the appraisals alone to manage your team; you will need to monitor performance regularly and communicate informally as well. However, having an organization-wide mechanism for managing performance and career aspirations is invaluable.

REVIEWING
Assess the individual's performance and discuss their career aspirations.

Focusing on the "how"

Appraisals normally consist of formal meetings between the individual and their immediate manager, focusing on objectives and their progress. Discuss how the objective is being achieved as well as what has been achieved. The "how" is essential for long-term success. If an individual has achieved a high level of output but has poached resources from other teams to achieve this, take this into account while assessing performance.

RECORD KEEPING
Take down detailed notes of issues discussed and action points for the future.

Elements of an appraisal

GOAL SETTING
Review progress against current objectives and set new objectives that are linked to the organization's goals.

ANALYSIS
Consider development needs for the current role and future progression if appropriate.

EXAMINATION
Talk about more intangible issues, such as how objectives have been achieved.

COMMUNICATION
Discuss specific problems, especially those that have prevented your employee from meeting an objective.

Setting objectives

Setting objectives is one of the most difficult tasks a manager faces. If the objectives are too hard, people can become demotivated, but if they are too easy, people coast along. Objective setting takes time and effort, but it is the only real way of directing your staff.

TIP

EVALUATE THE OBJECTIVES

There is a saying "what gets measured gets done", so ensure the goals you set correspond with what you want the individual to deliver.

Setting objectives in context

Everybody in your organization is dependent on the efforts of other people, so, in setting objectives, you need to take account of the context. For example, the sales team is often seen as a department where targets are achieved solely through the efforts of the sales people, but this is not the case. The team that processes the orders is also important, as are those who designed and created a good product. Motivating people to exert higher levels of effort will improve performance, but in many administrative, service, and manufacturing jobs the system has a much greater impact on the level of output than the effort of individual employees. As a manager you will need to keep this in mind while setting goals for your employees to avoid unrealistic expectations from your staff.

Linking objectives to strategy

TIP

SET RELEVANT GOALS

Ensure that you don't set objectives just because they are easily measurable. Always think: does this objective really matter?

People are motivated when their objectives are linked to the overall goals of the organization and they can see how they contribute to the organization's success. Without this line of sight, people can easily lose their sense of purpose at work, which can adversely affect their motivation. Cascade the objectives down through the organization, with each department having a stated aim and a set of goals that must be reached to achieve the overall objective.

Achieving objectives through targets

Break down objectives into individual targets that can be used as measures of performance. For example, the objective might be to improve the quality of customer service in a restaurant, and the targets following from that might be to have all diners seated within five minutes of their arrival, to have orders transmitted to the kitchen within five minutes of being taken, and to clear tables within five minutes of the diners vacating them.

Creating stretch goals

Stretch goals are goals that are demanding, but not impossible to reach – often described as "high but achievable". You will need to be careful when you set these goals to make them work. Here are some tips to help you avoid the pitfalls:
• Understanding past performance will be important – you should know what your employee is capable of if you want to set a stretch goal. Your employee may well be looking to set an easier target, so there is a limit to how much you can rely on their input.
• Targets are usually set in advance for the year, but circumstances can change rapidly in a volatile environment. To keep your people focused and motivated, be prepared to be flexible and reset the targets to maintain the stretch.
• Targets need to be seen as being fair. The degree of difficulty should be the same for all. Often, the targets you set across your team will vary from individual to individual, according to the requirements of the task and the team's overall capabilities. Explain carefully why the targets have been set. If they are perceived as being unequal, they will cause friction and demotivation.

HOW TO... SET TARGETS

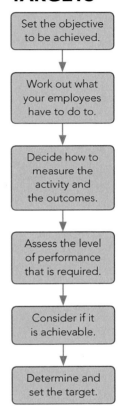

Set the objective to be achieved.

↓

Work out what your employees have to do to.

↓

Decide how to measure the activity and the outcomes.

↓

Assess the level of performance that is required.

↓

Consider if it is achievable.

↓

Determine and set the target.

TIP

EQUIP YOUR STAFF
Consider what people need to do their job. It is frustrating if you can't perform because of lack of equipment.

Creating personal objectives

Not all the objectives you set should be linked to short-term performance outcomes. There must be a balance between the needs of the organization and those of the individual. Training and development may take your staff away from their day-to-day job and may require the organization to spend money, but setting a personal development goal is motivational as it demonstrates the organization is interested in the individual and their long-term career. As part of the appraisal process, discuss the employees' skills and longer term development needs and include these in their personal objectives.

TIP

PULL TOGETHER
Allocate a shared objective to multiple people. The benefits of working as a team outweigh the motivation of individual objectives.

Communicating the objectives

How you set objectives is very important. Set targets face to face with your employees. This will allow you to explain what the targets are and discuss their feasibility and implications. To be motivational, objectives need to be owned, so discuss them with your employees to get feedback. This will help you gauge whether they are prepared to accept the objective. Choose a suitable channel to communicate with them. If you distribute the sales targets for the year by e-mail, it will tell everyone what is required, but does little for motivation. If you manage too many people to see them all individually, consider how to reorganize the reporting relationship to ensure each individual is managed properly.

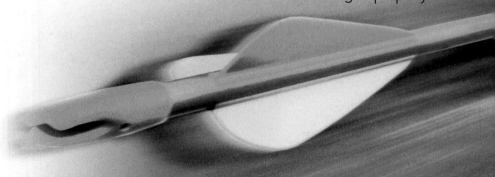

Defining a S.U.S.T.A.I.N.A.B.L.E objective

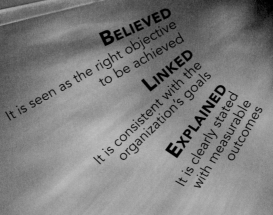

STRETCHING
It requires commitment and effort

UNDERSTOOD
Employees know what has to be achieved, what is required, and why it is important

SUPPORTED
It includes a plan of action that should ensure success

TIME BOUND
Everyone knows what has to be achieved by when

ACHIEVABLE
It is realistic within resource and time constraints

INCLUSIVE
It draws colleagues into achieving the goal

NEGOTIATED
Objectives are agreed upon rather than imposed

ANSWERABLE
Performance outcome, not the activity, is measured

BELIEVED
It is seen as the right objective to be achieved

LINKED
It is consistent with the organization's goals

EXPLAINED
It is clearly stated with measurable outcomes

Measuring progress

Feedback is an important element of motivation. Once objectives have been set it is important that you track and monitor progress and discuss it with your staff. But you also need to know when to intervene and when to leave a situation alone.

Measuring key activities

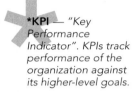

KPI — *"Key Performance Indicator". KPIs track performance of the organization against its higher-level goals.*

The usual way of measuring progress is to plot a graph of KPIs*, such as monthly sales figures, against the target. But not all progress can be tracked so simply – some projects require considerable input before change in the output can be measured. To avoid demotivating your staff, you need to measure progress against each of the activities that contributes to achieving the outcome.

Feeding back results

Measurement provides feedback and feedback should be acted upon. For the measurement to be motivational, make sure that those being measured see the results and understand how they were calculated. If this doesn't happen, they will not know how to improve their performance. Ideally, people need to measure their own performance, so that feedback is instantaneous. This way the individual or team can see quickly how they are progressing, allowing them to act even before management is alerted to a problem – for example, keeping a graph of calls handled or components produced provides feedback in real time. But you can't measure progress on all aspects of your work. Sometimes others have to measure your work for you – many accounting measures fall into this category.

TIP

REGULATE

Measure often, but be aware that if you measure too often, you may not be able to detect any change.

Choosing the right measure

You need to choose the correct indicator to measure your employees' performance. For instance, how would you assess the performance of a maintenance team? Is it good if they are constantly busy and working long hours? Does this show how motivated they are? If they are all sitting down drinking coffee is it because they are lazy and demotivated? In fact, you want your maintenance team to be idle most of the time, as this means that all the equipment is working and your factory is producing. Be careful to choose the correct measure, and not to confuse high levels of activity with performance.

ASK YOURSELF...
AM I MEASURING CORRECTLY?

- Do I have a clear measure of performance?
- Do I have a clear measure of activity?
- Do I know how much effort is required to perform well?
- Do I review performance regularly?
- Do I give feedback regularly?
- Do I use the measures of performance in formal reviews?
- Do I use the measures to take decisions?
- Do I communicate performance indicators to all those involved?
- Do I ensure that all those involved understand what the performance is and how we deliver it?
- Do I understand the external factors that affect the performance being measured?

CASE STUDY

"Andon" way of measuring

Many Japanese car manufacturers use an "Andon" system on their production lines. This system allows a worker to stop the whole production line because he has encountered a problem he can't solve himself. When this process was adopted in a European car plant, the flashing lights triggered by the Andon system brought all the managers down onto the shop floor. They would remain there to provide support and motivation until the plant restarted. As problems reduced and the Andon system was used less frequently, managers stayed away. Though this was a sign of success, the production workers didn't see it as such as they lost touch with their managers making them feel neglected and less inclined to use the system when things went wrong. The company eventually realized their mistake and ensured that management discussed and reviewed progress with the production workers regularly and, most importantly, celebrated success together.

Training and development

Research has shown that employees, particularly young people, value development opportunities. A company that offers training and development is showing commitment to its employees, developing them for the future, and helping them to do a better job in the process.

MATCH TRAINING WITH ABILITY
Some people prefer to learn by "doing" and others are happy to read about a subject or listen to a lecture, so consider what you want the training to achieve, and then establish how the individual learns best.

Making the case for training

Training should be encouraged so that it is woven into the culture of the organization. Having a good training scheme and being aware of development needs are good ways of attracting the best people to join your organization, of motivating them, and also of retaining them. This can give a business a substantial advantage over its competitors. It is essential that the training itself is of a good standard, otherwise it is a waste of time. Though the appraisal meeting provides a formal opportunity for the individual and manager to discuss training, development needs arise throughout the year and should be addressed from time to time to ensure success. You must also ensure the training meets the employee's own development needs to keep them motivated.

Getting the best from training

Any type of training involves spending time or money (and usually both), so it is important to ensure you derive maximum benefit from it. Make sure you seek out underlying needs, suited to the individual's job role. For example, if they are learning a skill, make sure they will be able to practise it. Having established these, you should brief the individual beforehand on what they can expect from the training. Discuss afterwards what they have learnt and how they should use it.

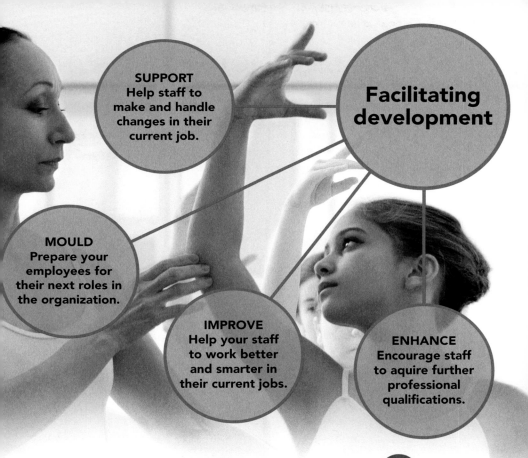

SUPPORT
Help staff to make and handle changes in their current job.

Facilitating development

MOULD
Prepare your employees for their next roles in the organization.

IMPROVE
Help your staff to work better and smarter in their current jobs.

ENHANCE
Encourage staff to aquire further professional qualifications.

Exploring ways of development

Rather than sending employees for external training, you can consider other methods of development:
• **Job rotation** Moving around the organization to learn different jobs and acquire new skills and knowledge in the process.
• **Secondment** Working in another department on a project, to give a broader perspective to their work.
• **Coaching and mentoring** Receiving one-to-one support from a more experienced colleague.
• **Professional qualification** A qualification in marketing or finance can provide a life-time benefit. This requires a lot of of time and effort, so both the individual and the organization must be ready to commit.

TIP

MANAGE EXPECTATIONS

Increase your employees' prospects in the organization after they complete the training by offering them more responsibility, or they might look for a better opportunity somewhere else.

Recognizing performance

Most people think money is the key motivator and reward for good performance. It isn't. It may be motivating to have a pay rise or bonus but the effects are often short-lived. Simple recognition is a very powerful motivator, and can and should occur every day. Just praising someone who is doing something well can make all the difference, and costs nothing.

TIP

USE INGENIOUS WAYS TO PRAISE

Make praise public. For example, print out customer commendations and place them on the notice board for everyone to see.

Giving recognition

Everyone likes to receive a thank you and to get credit for work well done. Identifying when things have been done well and recognizing this formally is an excellent way of motivating on a day-to-day basis.

All organizations should ensure that the basics of recognition, such as saying "thank you", are ingrained in all employees. However, many companies also run formal recognition systems. These tend to reward the teams or individuals with the greatest output, those who have built good relationships with their customers, and those who have supported their colleagues most.

Recognition, whether formal or informal, is a way of ensuring that people, and managers in particular, are on the lookout for good performance, and promote it around the company. Here are some other ways to recognize the efforts of your employees:
- Send them an e-mail thanking them for their support.
- Copy their boss into the thank-you e-mail.
- Take them (or the team) out for a drink after work.
- Buy them and their partner dinner.
- Give them a bunch of flowers or a box of chocolates with a note.
- Explain at the team meeting what they did and why it was so good.
- Create a scheme for "employee of the month".
- Give them a half-day holiday.
- Ensure that your team celebrates success.

Using the personal touch

Informal recognition systems may rely on local management initiative, but they are essential. They require managers to know what is going on and to be able to spot good work and high levels of effort. As a manager, you need to be involved in what your employees are doing and saying. This, in itself, is motivating to your staff, who see that you are interested in their work.

However, be aware that recognition is not as simple as saying "thank you" – people can see when you aren't being sincere. It is important to react spontaneously when you notice their efforts and mean what you say. Tell your boss about employees who perform well – being perceived positively by the senior management will boost their morale. Your staff will also appreciate it if you make a personal effort to recognize good performance by thanking them face-to-face. If appropriate, consider an inexpensive gift such as flowers or chocolates, although if you start doing this, make it a policy for all high-performing employees, to avoid accusations of favouritism.

✔ CHECKLIST RECOGNIZING WORK

	YES	NO
• Do you always say thank you?	☐	☐
• Do you always make a positive comment when work is done well?	☐	☐
• Do you try to catch your staff doing something well every week?	☐	☐
• When you see exceptional performance, do you tell everyone?	☐	☐
• Do you buy a small gift to say thank you when appropriate?	☐	☐
• Do you exploit the formal recognition system for good performance?	☐	☐

Paying for performance

Pay is often used as a motivator. It can take the form of salary increases, commission, or bonuses. Rules can be set in advance for deciding how much is paid using a particular formula, or a judgement can be made at the end of the year as to how much is deserved.

STAY ON TRACK

Always link bonuses back to what the organization is trying to achieve in the long run. If you don't, you will be rewarding behaviour that is not benefiting the organization.

Motivating through pay

The motivational element of pay comes from linking the level of financial return to the performance of an individual or team. The intention is to motivate people to put in more effort because they know they will receive a greater financial reward. Here are some other reasons for linking pay and performance:
• To follow the norm in the industry
• To manage costs – pay is given in proportion to the financial results received.

Linking pay and performance

To link pay and performance, you must be able to objectively measure the element of performance you wish to reward. You need to select the elements you reward with care – if you reward only one element of performance you will need other management approaches to ensure other aspects are not neglected. Fairness is one of the most important factors in linking performance with reward. When the system is seen to be fair, people will be motivated. If people work independently, then reward the individual for his or her performance. If team effort is required, you must reward the team effort. Target setting is the most difficult aspect of linking pay to performance. You will need to collect enough data to be sure that your target is both stretching and attainable.

METHODS OF LINKING PAY AND PERFORMANCE

METHOD	POSITIVE IMPACT	NEGATIVE IMPACT
Directly linking bonus to achieving specific targets	• Makes the reward mechanism very clear • Encourages very specific behaviour	• Can become very rigid and therefore irrelevant if circumstances at the workplace change
Indirectly linking bonus and pay to performance	• Allows managers to exercise their judgement • Allows a more rounded view of performance	• Makes the reward mechanism less clear
Setting targets through consultation	• Motivates people through engagement in the target-setting process	• Can become a negotiation • Will encourage people to set easy targets • Will encourage people to hoard (rather than share) information
Linking size of incentive to goals	• Large incentives will be acted on • Small incentives help communication of goals	• Large incentives may encourage cheating • Small incentives may fail to motivate people
Paying a bonus when a fixed-value target is achieved	• The threshold target becomes specific and is easy to comprehend	• There is no incentive to perform once the target is reached • There is no incentive to perform if the target becomes unattainable • Encourages gaming – the pulling forward and putting back of performance between periods to achieve the bonus
Paying a bonus at each step towards achieving a target	• Creates an incentive to perform over a range of outcomes • Rewards high performers for their work	• Sets a less specific expectation
Linking performance to salary increases	• Reduces costs as increments are usually smaller than bonus payments	• Invariably, such increases are paid for the rest of the employee's time of service
Setting targets afterwards by comparison with others	• Makes targets appropriate in nearly all circumstances	• Makes the link between effort and performance, and performance and reward, less clear

Chapter 3

Developing the skills of motivation

Once you have learnt the principles of motivation and how to create the right environment for it to flourish, you need to develop the skills to motivate your team. It is important to practise these skills continually to increase your capability.

Motivating yourself

As a manager, you are a role model: your staff will notice what you say, how you say it, and how you behave. It is important that you are motivated yourself. Remember that the principles of motivation apply just as much to you as they do to your team.

Understanding what you want

BE PROACTIVE
If you don't like something and you can change it or think it can be changed, take positive action.

It is worth thinking about what you really want. This will help to motivate you and enable you to structure your ambitions and goals. Understanding what you want applies to your personal life as much as to your work life – the two are intertwined. If you really want to spend more time with your family then you are unlikely to be motivated if you are in a job where you are required to spend many hours at work. If you come to the conclusion that you're not in the right job, you are better off moving to a new job that suits your circumstances better.

Knowing what motivates you

Most people are so busy with their day-to-day activities that they don't take time out to reflect on what they enjoy doing. Everyone has to do tasks they don't like, but if you can build several tasks you really enjoy into your day, it will help to keep you motivated. Think about your work – what aspects do you enjoy? Is it contact with people? Writing a report? Creating a new idea? Can you do more of these activities? What do you not enjoy? Can you minimize the time you spend on these tasks in future? Is there a better way of doing them? It is easy to put off tasks you don't enjoy doing, but this is a mistake because the thought of doing them remains on your mind. The trick is to do them, get them out of the way, and start something you really want to do that will motivate you.

Setting your own goals

Set goals for yourself, just as you would for your staff. This gives you something to aim for. Ensure your goals mean something to you, to give you a sense of achievement. Be precise and set a timeframe, so that you can monitor your progress. If the goal is large, break it down into manageable chunks. Don't say "I will increase my personal network of contacts"; say instead, "I will add five new contacts to my personal network from the construction sector by the end of December."

Goals don't have to be totally work-related. In fact, it is a good idea to have some personal goals. For example, you might decide that you need to lose weight or improve your health. In this case one of your goals might be to lose 5kg (11lb) or to participate in some organized runs by a certain date.

To give yourself some extra motivation to achieve your chosen goals, spend some time visualizing what it will be like when you have achieved them.

TIP

THINK LATERALLY
Visualize what a successful person you know would do when faced with the problem you're up against. This can help resolve a problem that you don't know how to handle.

Dealing with problems

From time to time, problems will arise at work. They generally fall into two groups: those you can ease or solve and those you can do nothing about. It is no use worrying about something you cannot change. Recognize this, work around it, and get on as best as you can without brooding. If the problem is beyond your control but is very important to you, speak to your boss. If possible, come up with a solution yourself and suggest it to them.

Learning from mistakes

It is easy to lose motivation when you have made a mistake, but remember that no one is perfect. If you aren't making any mistakes, it probably means you aren't taking any risks and are staying within your "comfort zone". If a mistake occurs, do not make excuses or blame someone else. Accept constructive criticism, learn what you can from it, and move on.

DEALING WITH CRITICISM

FAST TRACK	OFF TRACK
Listening to what is being said	Becoming defensive
Making sure you understand what you are being criticized for	Focusing on failure
Seeking clarification if necessary	Taking it personally
Reflecting on the action to take	Dwelling on past problems

Being positive

If all you do is moan about problems and always appear negative, you will have no hope of motivating your staff. But this does not mean you always have to be cheerful and only see the advantages in everything around you. It is important to be realistic. If you have started a project and you can see problems with it, your first task is to find ways of resolving them. If the problems really can't be resolved, you will probably have to work around them. Let your staff know what the problems are, but also tell them that you will help to work through them. Ensure they know what your expectations are of them.

TIP

STAY POSITIVE
Concentrate on the good things you have done. Build up a store of positive experiences and keep these in your mind.

Balancing work and life

Successful people usually have a wide range of hobbies and interests outside work, together with a broad network of friends and contacts. It is often helpful to share problems with people away from your place of work because they see them in a new light. Even if you thoroughly enjoy your job, do not become a workaholic. If you spend all your time concentrating on your work you will eventually become tired, dissatisfied, and demotivated.

Being a good motivator

Motivation is not just about understanding and applying the theories – it is about how you put them into practice. In essence, being a good motivator is part of being a good leader – someone who people follow. For this to happen, you need the personal characteristics that make people want to follow you.

TIP

BE AWARE

Pay attention to what is going on around you to understand what motivates your staff, but ensure you don't get involved in gossip.

Knowing what makes a good motivator

There is no single "good" management style that will turn you into a good motivator. If you try to adopt a style with which you feel uncomfortable, you will come across as being insincere and you won't be trusted. However, there are some characteristics that all good motivators share. It is worth reflecting on the people you believe are good motivators – what was it about them that spurred you on to achieve? This will give you an insight into your own personal motivation, as well as helping you to consider how you can motivate your team.

✔ CHECKLIST ARE YOU A GOOD MOTIVATOR?

	YES	NO
• Can you be trusted – do what you say you will do?	☐	☐
• Can you build rapport with individuals on the team?	☐	☐
• Are you loyal to your team?	☐	☐
• Are you fair in your dealings with people?	☐	☐
• Do you share credit with the team for achievements?	☐	☐
• Can you see the individual's perspective whilst keeping the organization's goal in mind?	☐	☐

Balancing trust and authority

One of the most important characteristics of good motivators is that they can be trusted. It is only possible to motivate people for a very short time without gaining their trust. To gain the trust of your team, never make promises you can't keep – if you let people down, they will be very wary in the future. If something goes wrong, it is your job as the leader of the team to take responsibility and criticism for it. You have to defend your team in public while investigating in

...be avoided ...fficult balance ..." and being ...e will depend ...ation. Some ...very little ...taff – others ...e in your ...aintained, ...d, making ...ith poor ...however, you ...our team, and ...ou or not.

TIP

EMPATHIZE WITH YOUR STAFF
Understanding your team's problems and empathizing with their position will help you to motivate them better.

HOW TO... MOTIVATE YOUR STAFF

Share the vision with your team.

↓

Make the goals real to your people.

↓

Give regular feedback to your staff.

↓

Recognize performance.

↓

Celebrate success with all those involved.

Focusing on the future

As a manager, you need to organize and take care of detail, but someone who spends all their time on this without seeing the wider context is unlikely to be a good motivator. You need to know how reaching your immediate goal will lead to achieving the ultimate objective. An often-quoted example of this is two bricklayers who are asked what they are doing. "I'm laying bricks," says one. The other says "I'm building a cathedral." A good motivator will paint a picture of the objective to strengthen their team's sense of purpose.

Making people feel valued

If people feel valued by their manager, they will be prepared to make the extra effort that can make the difference between success and failure. However, in facing the day-to-day pressures of meeting deadlines and trying to achieve targets, many managers overlook the relatively small actions that show they value the individuals in their team.

Understanding the benefits

New employees are usually brimming with enthusiasm when they join an organization or begin a new role. But somewhere along the line, it is common for most staff to suffer from demotivation. If the organization fails to value its staff, why should they contribute whole-heartedly to the organization's success? Although "valuing someone" may sound intangible and woolly, research shows that employees who are valued perform better in their job and this, in turn, leads to higher levels of business performance.

REWARD
Not every organization can pay the best wages in the industry but it is important that your staff are rewarded fairly for their work and that they understand the organization's policy and see that it is applied consistently.

Q IN FOCUS... COMMITMENT-BASED HR

Researchers have defined two types of HR practice: commitment based and transaction based. Commitment-based practices focus on developing the long-term relationship between the employer and the employee in an organization. Mentoring, training, and development are all examples of commitment-based practices.

Transaction-based practices focus on the here and now, just paying people for the work they do. A recent study in the UK showed that commitment-based practices increased employee engagement, which led to higher levels of product and service quality, innovation, and better financial performance.

RECOGNITION
Simply saying thank you when people are doing things well and taking the trouble to show that you appreciate them form the first step in valuing people.

PERSONAL TOUCH
Getting to know people as individuals so they feel you are taking an interest in them personally is vitally important. But make sure you extend the same level of interest and flexibility to all members of your team. It is easy to slip into the habit of favouritism.

Techniques for making staff feel valued

POWER OF EXPRESSION
Employees feel valued if their opinions are heard and taken into account during decision making.

TRAINING AND DEVELOPMENT
People feel valued if the organization invests in them and in their future. Organizations that invest in people find that people commit to them, so training and development become essential.

PROMOTION
People who perform well will look to progress in their career. Helping them in that progression demonstrates your commitment to them.

Developing communication

Communication and openness are important tools for motivation. If you don't communicate effectively, people will feel unimportant and undervalued. Ambiguous communication can also lead to the spreading of rumours, which is particularly unhealthy as they play on people's fears.

Sharing information

There is a balance between sharing what you know and worrying people unnecessarily. In some cases it is important first to consider the consequences of sharing information. Unless you are at the stage of consulting people, it is sometimes better to wait until you have some tangible ideas to put forward. Putting forward woolly thoughts rarely leads to people feeling they are being kept informed. They are more likely to think you are hiding something. However, it is better to err on the side of over-communicating than to hold information back.

Communicating well

Communication is a two-way process. It is not just about telling people something – it is also about listening to what is being said. Good motivators are people who think about what they are saying and how they are saying it. They constantly gauge the response from their listeners, and when they have spoken, they keep quiet and listen. In this way they gain insights into how people are feeling and receive new ideas and perspectives. Practise listening: you will be surprised by how much you can learn.

BE A GOOD LISTENER

Look at the speaker, lean forward, and encourage them by nodding your head. Good listeners will also ask questions and seek clarification if they do not understand a point.

Selecting the right channel

How you communicate is just as important as what you communicate, so it is essential to think carefully about which communication channel to use. Everyone is different – some people prefer to read information, others to hear it. If you have something important to say it is a good idea to use several different communication channels to strengthen your message and to appeal to people in different ways. Having a one-to-one meeting is good for dealing with individual problems but can be time consuming, while a team meeting allows discussion of issues and facilitates mutual understanding. The telephone is a convenient way to give information that is easy to understand. E-mails, newsletters, and the intranet are impersonal but provide an instant means of reaching a large number of people.

Managing politics

Politics in the workplace are hard to avoid. Whatever you do, cliques will form, people will jockey for position, and rumours will be spread. In the longer term this leads to energy being diverted away from the business and can even lead to victimization and bullying of individuals. It is important you know what is going on and put a stop to it. Politics can undermine the positive culture of the organization, and damage motivation. Bullying has the same effect, so when you detect this happening, act quickly and prevent it from happening in the future. Plug yourself into your organization's networks so you understand what is going on, but avoid letting it distract you from your own work.

Identifying demotivation

Demotivation in the workplace has a wide variety of causes, from tiredness and overwork to problems at home. Demotivated employees can affect the morale of their colleagues, and whole teams can also become demotivated, so it is essential to be able to spot the signs of demotivation and to act quickly.

Spotting the signs

Everyone has days when they feel demotivated and below par. Demotivation may not always be immediately apparent but there are some signs to watch out for. An employee may be slumped at their desk, gazing into space, or tapping their fingers on the desk. You can also tell how they are feeling from the tone of their voice. A monotonous tone or yawning may be signals that someone is bored or tired. While these are not always signs of serious demotivation and you shouldn't be too quick to jump to conclusions, you should still check them out. Other signs of demotivation include people who normally react well to requests failing to respond or avoiding volunteering for new tasks. Don't let too much time pass before you act. Anyone can have an off day, but if it persists, or there is a regular pattern to their mood swings, then you should talk to the individual concerned. If they feel overworked, see if you can re-allocate some of their work. Saying you appreciate what they have been doing can be enough to raise their spirits and re-motivate them. Even a quick "How are things today?" shows you have noticed and care about how they are feeling.

Dealing with performance issues

One of the most noticeable signs of more serious problems is when someone who is normally a good worker fails to perform. Of course, this may just be a one-off instance. Perhaps the individual has had a particularly difficult task to do or a difficult customer to deal with. But if their work is constantly below their normal standard, there is a problem that you need to tackle. Neither will this type of problem be solved by a quick question about how the person is, nor will it be solved by a military-style inquisition. You will need an in-depth discussion to identify what is wrong and what can be done to put it right. Discuss the problem in a confidential meeting, set targets for improving performance, and agree on a strategy to resolve it.

ACT QUICKLY
If you spot the signs of demotivation in one of your employees, their colleagues will see them too. Don't ignore the signs: take action quickly before the team think you haven't noticed or don't care.

Countering absenteeism

High levels of staff absenteeism are a strong sign of a demotivated team. To deal with this, talk to staff after every absence. Meet with every absent staff member, so that you cannot be accused of singling anyone out, but make the discussion private, so you can adapt your approach depending on how often the individual is absent and the underlying cause. The objective of the meeting is twofold: first, so your staff are aware that you have noted their absence, and second, to ascertain the cause. Finding out why people are absent is the first step to tackling the problem.

Be aware of staff turnover. Even if the figure for your department is below average, make sure you know why people are leaving. New staff bring in new ideas, but high levels of staff turnover unsettle a team and can demotivate those left behind. Your organizations' human resources team should always conduct exit interviews to establish why someone is leaving, and you must ensure the feedback is passed on to you.

Consulting others

Consultation plays an important part in motivation. Jointly setting goals and targets with others communicates what is to be achieved and increases their commitment to achieving them. So consult when you can, but realize that if you have to make a quick decision it is not always possible.

OPEN IT UP

Involve people in decision making whenever you can. Teams often make better decisions than individuals.

Involving people

Think about how you feel when you are told about decisions that directly affect you at work. How would you feel if they were announced with no prior warning or consultation? Sometimes it can be a pleasant surprise, but often you feel bewildered: "Why did they do that? What a stupid decision!" Now think about the decision on which you have been consulted or involved. You know why the decision was taken, and although you may not fully agree with it, you won't think it is stupid. Consulting avoids the immediate negative impact on morale and performance.

BE CLEAR

People need to know when you are giving orders and when you are consulting. Make this absolutely clear or you will cause confusion.

Benefiting from consultation

You will benefit from consulting with others because:
• You can involve others in the process of setting goals and agreeing on actions, drawing them into the process and increasing their commitment to the project.
• You will gain information from other persepectives, on the basis of which you can decide and act.
• You and your team will improve your understanding of what has to be achieved, and why.
• It can help you in setting targets at the right level.
• The whole process can be motivational and help to strengthen bonds within your teams.
• The final agreement strengthens the commitment of the team, ensuring they will perform.

KNOWING WHEN TO CONSULT

CONSULT...	DON'T CONSULT...
• When you have the time to consult.	• When people are expecting to be told what to do.
• When there is still time to influence the decision.	• When decisive action needs to be made quickly.
• When your team's input will improve the decision.	• When the decision has already been made.
• When you need the team to agree on the project's goal for its success.	• When there is an obvious technical expert whose advice you should follow.

Avoiding pitfalls

There are a number of pitfalls of consulting. It is important that people know when they are being consulted and when they are being informed of a decision. Some targets are not negotiable – they have been set high up in the company and allocated to your team. If you are going to consult in this situation you will need to explain that the target is not for negotiation, but you want input on how it is going to be met. Ask yourself whether the consultation is genuine and not a public-relations exercise. If there is little likelihood of the organization taking account of what is being discussed, you must still take feedback from your staff for them to let off steam, but also explain to them that while you will pass their comments on, you don't expect things to change as a result.

CASE STUDY

You don't know what you don't know

An electricity distribution company faced the issue of needing to undertake maintenance on its power lines but having to compensate customers every time the power was cut off. Staff worked quickly on the repairs, but the costs were high. In order to cascade the strategy down the organization, the objective of reducing the cost was delegated to the front-line maintenance team. They came up with the solution of buying a generator so the electric supply could be maintained whilst the repairs were made. When this was proposed to the finance director, his immediate reply was "Do you know what a generator costs?" They didn't, but he didn't know the cost of cutting the supply. The new generator cost $1 million, but by consulting the front-line staff and involving them in the decision-making process, the company rapidly paid off the cost of the generator and made significant savings.

Delegating effectively

Delegating tasks is not only a way to reduce your workload, it can also motivate employees. However, while having a task delegated to you can be a highly motivating experience, it can also result in loss of confidence and demotivation if you are unable to complete the tasks.

Knowing when to delegate

While delegation reduces your workload, it also means letting go of the task and giving it to someone else. This means you should only delegate tasks with a clear structure. Implement a monitoring process so that you can assure yourself that progress is being made and the person is comfortable with the task in hand. Delegate when the task is likely to be repeated, making it worth the time and effort, or when the task itself may be motivating for someone else to do. Avoid delegating if there are time constraints or the individual does not have the skill or experience.

5
SUPPORT
Encourage and guide the individual or team, give feedback regularly, and keep a check on progress.

Deciding how to delegate

How to delegate will depend on the working environment, how well you know the person you are delegating to, their level of experience, and the importance of the task. Delegation takes time to do well. With an experienced team, it can be done over a cup of coffee, but if you have a critical project or you are working with people you don't know well, it is better to be formal. Ideally this should involve a face-to-face meeting supported by an e-mail or document recording what has been agreed. Ensure that you have allocated the time both to hand over the task and to follow up.

1

IDENTIFY
Define the task, check that all the required resources are available, and specify the desired outcomes.

2

DISTRIBUTE
Decide who you are going to assign the task to and allocate the resources in a judicious manner.

Delegating efficiently

3

BRIEF
Communicate and agree the goals with your employees. Try to delegate a whole task rather than part of it.

4

MONITOR
Ensure each employee who has been delegated a specific part of the task is performing.

Coaching successfully

There are many different forms of coaching but, in essence, coaching at work is about having a series of conversations with someone to help them to perform better in their job. It is also a highly effective way of motivating them by focusing on their needs.

Coaching on a daily basis

Many people think of coaching as a special form of training undertaken only by a specialist coach. In many cases it is. However, as a manager you will need to understand the principles of coaching and build them into your day-to-day work. You may want to coach someone for a specific task or to prepare them to take on a more senior role. Coach the individuals in your team so they can handle their own work independently. As well as motivating them, this saves you time by enabling them to take responsibility for their own work.

Being a good coach

Assist your employees throughout the duration of the task and keep giving them feedback.

Make observations on someone's behaviour which they may not have noticed themselves.

Enable your staff to find their own way through a problem and suggest practical solutions.

Encourage individuals or teams to take responsibility for a particular task.

Developing your coaching skills

The fundamental skills of coaching are building trust, listening, and questioning. Put the person at their ease to encourage them to talk. While you need to keep the conversation on track, allow them to speak without interruption as far as possible. Ask questions to help maintain their focus and show you are listening. This will also encourage them to think about better ways of doing things and see issues from a wider perspective. Support them as they try implementing their solutions, and give appropriate feedback.

TIP

STIMULATE VIEWPOINTS

By asking a challenging question, you may help your employees to see the issue from a different perspective.

Giving constructive feedback

Feedback is an important part of the coaching process. But make sure it is well-intentioned and constructive. You should also try to make it objective and, above all, not personally hurtful. Try to ensure you back up what you are saying with some evidence. If the individual has no control over something then there is little point in giving them feedback on it.

GIVING APPROPRIATE FEEDBACK

⬆ FAST TRACK	❗ OFF TRACK
Being precise about the feedback	Rushing through what you have to say
Giving the individual time to respond	Giving negative feedback in public
Being constructive	Being uninterested in the way the individual is responding

Chapter 4

Motivating in difficult situations

The environment, processes, and skills of motivation are all important, but some situations will require you to modify your approach. You will need to maintain motivation during change, and in dispersed teams and difficult people.

Motivating during change

Change creates uncertainty for people; it can make them anxious so that they take their eye off the job in hand. However, change is increasingly a requirement for organizations to survive. Being able to motivate during change is therefore an extremely important skill.

Recognizing change

Change is rarely popular, and even seemingly trivial innovations in the organization can cause outrage among your staff. Often this is because people don't understand what is happening. This can be avoided if you think through the change in advance and ask yourself two questions:
• Who will this change affect?
• How will the change look from their point of view?
You will then be able to consult those concerned and ensure they are aware of the benefits the change will bring. This process will ensure they stay motivated.

Identifying the types of change

Change can be categorized as either "hard" or "soft". Hard changes are usually well defined in advance. People can be told what will happen and what is expected of them. In a "soft" change, the details of the change are unknown, and only the direction of the change is clear. The organization has to search for a solution and everyone will have to work through the change together. Major corporate turnarounds often fit this category, as do large-scale cultural change programmes*. The best way to cope with a soft change is to become involved, so you have a chance to shape both the change itself and the future of your team.

***Cultural Change Programme**
— *programme by which the organization tries to change its values and the behaviour of its employees.*

Being prepared for the change

Be prepared for any kind of response to change and realize that those affected will respond emotionally, and may at times appear irrational. As a manager you can help them to adjust by:
• Accepting the reaction and responding constructively
• Providing information and support
• Creating new roles and objectives
• Giving people a clear vision of the long-term outcomes.

ASK YOURSELF... ARE YOU PREPARED TO MOTIVATE YOUR STAFF THROUGH CHANGE?

• Do I need to introduce different motivational goals for the team?
• Do I need to re-set or re-emphasize motivational goals for individuals?
• Will my team lose incentives such as bonuses?
• How can I maintain motivation in spite of this?
• Will the current recognition and reward system be appropriate after the change?
• If not, what changes in the organization will be required to motivate my team in the new way of working?

TIP

SHOW ENDURANCE
Plan for the downturn in performance associated with change, and absorb some of the frustration and anger.

Recognizing the stages of change

More than half a century ago, the sociologist Kurt Lewin identified three major stages of change. These stages will help you to understand the timing of changes, and can be used as a guide for steering people through the process of change.

• **Unfreezing** In this stage you will prepare for change. People will need to recognize the need for the change, and the way things are done will have to be unfrozen, to allow the change to occur. People will be very uncertain during this process.

• **Moving** You will implement the change in this stage by altering working practices, restructuring jobs, or moving people about. People will find everything very new and will need your support and guidance during this process.

• **Refreezing** In this last stage, new ways of working become embedded in the organization. During this phase, people should be finding their feet and starting to move forward. The idea of refreezing is to prevent the organization reverting to its old ways.

The change rollercoaster

PERFORMANCE AND SELF-ESTEEM

Uncertainty

Denial

Blaming others

Blaming self

Despair

TIME

Managing the change rollercoaster

Different people react to change differently, but during major changes, they go through a series of responses that can be characterized as a "rollercoaster ride". This starts with denial, moves on to blaming others, then themselves, which can lead to despair. Self-esteem and performance plummet. However, people then start to test the new environment and ways of working, build confidence, and move on to achieve success. Quite often, once the change has taken place, it is a matter of settling down to the new way of working. You will have to re-establish the culture, rebuild the team morale, and reassure individuals. When the change means employees are made redundant, make the process as painless as possible. Do everything you can to protect their dignity, and help them to take the next steps in their lives.

Performing well

Growing confidence

Testing new ways of working

TIME

Motivating dispersed workers

Developments in technology now enable many people to work from home or in a dispersed team*. In addition, flatter organizational structures mean that even larger organizations have local offices employing just a few people. These arrangements bring benefits, such as flexible working hours, but there are serious implications for motivation.

Working away from the office

*Dispersed team — *a team based in a small office out of immediate contact with the main body of the organization.*

For many employees, not working in an office is a dream. For the employer it can mean lower office costs and also better productivity, as staff don't have to spend time commuting to work.

However, the reality can be less appealing. If you work from home, you can feel isolated, making it hard to stay motivated. Individuals miss the buzz of the office, the companionship of colleagues, and the sparking of ideas when they meet other people. In an office, for example, when something goes wrong, you can turn to a colleague who will help you put the problem in perspective.

Recruiting the right candidate

If a job role will be dispersed or home-based, you should look for certain characteristics at the recruitment stage. If someone lacks self-discipline, cannot manage their time well, or appears to need close supervision, they are unlikely to be suitable. You will need to instill loyalty to ensure they are motivated and focused on the goals to be achieved. At the interview, ensure the candidate is prepared for the working environment. At home this means having room for equipment and a quiet environment. For a dispersed team member, it is the lack of direct supervision and support.

Keeping home workers motivated

A crucial aspect of motivating home workers is to take proactive steps to ensure they have everything they need to work effectively. Agree on targets and time scales and monitor them regularly to check that they are on track. Organize regular visits to the main office, such as monthly team meetings, and arrange one-to-one meetings to catch up on progress and to spot any problems before they become too serious. Make sure home- and locally based workers are kept up to date with any new developments, and remain in regular contact – not just by e-mail.

EXERCISE TRUST
Trust your home workers or dispersed teams. While you need to know the work is being done, you won't motivate people by checking up on them all the time.

Providing support

To keep your dispersed workers motivated, make sure they feel connected to and supported by the organization as a whole. Arrange a thorough induction at your main office and ensure your home workers meet the people they will be e-mailing and speaking to on the phone. You may also need to arrange briefing sessions on working from home. It is particularly important to ensure dispersed teams have all the equipment they need to work effectively. It may be tempting to provide more senior people in head office with the most reliable and expensive IT equipment, but for remote team members, any breakdown is likely to be highly frustrating and time consuming. A comfortable working environment is just as important when working from home or in a small local office.

Depending on the structure, encourage people working near each other to meet up to discuss work. Include home workers and locally based teams in social activities if possible. Look and listen for any signs of stress. Set out precise procedures on who to contact if things go wrong. Make sure "out of sight" is not "out of mind".

Motivating underperformers

At some stage, you will have to manage someone who is not performing well. For the success of your team and the organization, it is important to deal with their problems, as not only will their performance be affected, but they may also disrupt the motivation of your entire team.

HOW TO... DISCUSS PROBLEMS

Inform the individual in advance what you want to discuss.

↓

State your understanding of the situation.

↓

Let the individual explain how they see the issues.

↓

Get them to accept there is a problem if they have not done so.

↓

Encourage them to come up with some solutions.

↓

Arrange a follow-up meeting.

Identifying problems

Everyone makes mistakes occasionally, and while it is important to respond to them constructively, if you do not deal with underperformance your entire team may lose motivation. Get to know what individual team members are capable of and take action when you notice something is going wrong. Watch out for a change in performance. If someone is making more mistakes than usual, you will need to take some action.

Broaching the subject

How you approach the situation will depend on the circumstances. If someone has made a few silly mistakes you may just need to let them know you have noticed, and ask what happened and how it can be avoided in the future. If problems continue, you will need a more considered meeting. Create the same conditions as you would for a performance appraisal meeting – ensure you have privacy, won't be interrupted, and that the individual is comfortable. Prepare for the meeting, and make sure your facts are correct. Think about the problems and possible reasons for them and, if possible, consider them from the perspective of the individual. Try to remain calm and objective at all times and don't digress by discussing other people or issues that don't affect the individual's own performance.

Finding solutions

There may be deep-seated issues behind the obvious reasons for underperformance, and you need to uncover these – otherwise you will only be applying a temporary patch to the problem. Listen very carefully to what is being said, and then probe gently to get underneath the words. In these situations people often blame others or find excuses. Make sure they take responsibility for their own performance. For example, if they say problems are occurring because they are consistently receiving information they need too late, ask why they have not spoken to the person causing the delay.

TIP

BE QUICK TO TAKE ACTION
Ensure you deal with performance problems as soon as they occur. It is very easy to ignore them, especially when you are busy, but doing this will not make them go away.

AGREEING TO SOLUTIONS

PROBLEM	RELEVANT QUESTIONS	POSSIBLE SOLUTIONS
Cannot carry out tasks to the required level	Do they have the right training? Do they have the support they need? Were they recruited into the wrong job?	Provide training or equipment; set objectives for improvement; move them to another role; agree this is not the job for them.
Sudden decline in performance level; making too many silly mistakes	What is causing the lack of concentration? Is it a situation outside work or a problem with a colleague?	Be sympathetic – if necessary let them take some time off work. Work together to find a solution.
Slow decline in performance level	Are they bored with their role? Do they need more challenge to motivate them? Are they overwhelmed by work?	Check whether their role can be broadened or seconded. Help them to manage their workload better.
Timekeeping is bad	Do they have new commitments at home? Are there any personal issues affecting them?	Give them an option of flexible working hours if it helps. Provide professional help if required.
Relationships with colleagues are poor	Are they overloaded with work? Are they showing signs of stress? Is it because of personality clashes?	Train them in "soft" skills such as emotional intelligence. See if they can be moved to a different team.

Motivating a project team

Cross-departmental project teams are common in many organizations. In this situation, you may well find yourself managing a project involving people who don't report to you. As a project leader, your motivational skills will be critical to the project and your own success.

TIP

ENCOURAGE TEAM SPIRIT

Assist and support other members of the team and do not talk behind their backs.

Maintaining the momentum

Every project goes through stages. At first everyone is keen and excited to be involved. Then the work begins. At some stage, problems and setbacks will arise and individuals will become disillusioned and demotivated. This is a critical stage where you, as the project manager, will have to keep the momentum going and make sure people maintain focus and energy. Bring your team together. Remind them that in every project worth doing there are bound to be some setbacks. Bring to mind their earlier successes, explain why the project is still important, and work together to find solutions to the problems. If you still find that they are not giving their best to the project, carefully suggest that there may be someone better equipped to take their role – they will probably receive your message and change their approach.

Sharing success

Motivating a project team is often one of the most difficult tasks. You may not be the line manager of those involved, so you don't have the usual authority and reward mechanisms at your disposal. You may have been given the opportunity to be the project leader, but you will need to share the success with others. If the other team members see you taking all the credit for the project, they will disengage. You need to manage this balance. If the project is successful, you will get recognized, so be generous with your praise along the way. People like their boss to hear good things about them and it only costs you a little time to copy someone into an e-mail saying thank you. Be careful of individuals who "grand stand" and claim greater responsibility for the success of the project than is justified by their contribution.

TIP

MOTIVATE FOR EVERYONE'S BENEFIT

When motivating your project team, think about what benefits your team can expect from succeeding.

Driving project teams forward

EXUDE ENTHUSIASM
Make the measures of success very explicit and exude your enthusiasm for the project.

GIVE VISIBILITY
Explain that being part of the project will bring people to the notice of their seniors, which can help their careers.

HAVE FUN
Make the project interesting and fun so that people participate and contribute willingly.

USE PEER PRESSURE
Involve the whole team to help you apply pressure on any member who is underperforming.

BE FIRM
Threaten to remove an underperforming team member – and make sure you can back up your threat if necessary.

Motivating teams

Having a group of motivated individuals in your department is a good start, but you won't be really successful unless you have a motivated team. People in teams bounce ideas off each other and work together to achieve better results than individuals working alone.

Painting a picture of the future

One of the most important motivators for a team is having a common goal that each individual has a genuine commitment to achieving. Paint a picture, either graphically or in words, describing what success will look like. Be enthusiastic about achieving it. Talk about your people's role in delivering the success and allude to the benefits of being successful and what success will feel like.

Elements of an effective team

A GOOD LEADER
Having a leader who applies, at team level, all the lessons for motivating each individual on the team.

PEOPLE WHO CAN WORK TOGETHER
Consisting of people who respect fellow team members and are allowed to question and express dissent on occasions.

Creating a sense of belonging

The sense of "belonging" is a very important motivator and, while this does develop naturally when a team has been together over a period of time, a good manager will speed up the process and ensure it is maintained by, for example, celebrating success. Make sure that each member of your team knows how they fit into the working of the whole organization.

Setting benchmarks

At times, seemingly motivated and well-established teams can become complacent. One way of avoiding this is to take your team on benchmarking* visits. Find an organization that does something very well and go and visit them. You will find many organizations are only too happy to do this, particularly if they can "benchmark" with you in return.

*Benchmarking — the systematic process of comparing your performance with others'.

GOOD COMMUNICATION PROCESSES
Establishing free-flowing information within the team and good networks and contacts outside.

OPEN TO ALTERNATIVES
Considering all options and opening the team to external criticism, or ensuring that you have at least one respected critic on the team.

COMMON UNDERSTANDING
Having complete awareness of the team's goals along with an understanding of the role and contribution of each team member.

Bringing it all together

Motivation is part art and part science. You need to understand the theory and apply it in practice with feeling and sincerity. Motivation is like a chain – it is only as strong as its weakest link. It ceases to become effective if any of the links are missing.

TIP

GAIN YOUR STAFF'S TRUST

Take genuine interest in your employees –support them in a professional crisis and look after their long-term career interests to keep them motivated beyond the short term.

Keeping your staff motivated

Motivating people in the short term is relatively easy. But when you have to motivate people over the longer term, enthusiasm alone won't work. To do this you have to create a culture that is conducive to success, balance organizational and personal goals, and ensure people are genuinely interested in the success of the organization. To keep people motivated over the long term, you must be trusted as a leader. You will need to support people by giving them the tools and resources to do the job, helping them overcome obstacles that may get in the way, developing their skills, and rewarding success. Being a good motivator will not only help your organization but will boost your career too.

Making each job worthwhile

All jobs in your organization are important – if not, they should be eliminated immediately. Ensure that every job is done well, from dealing with customers, to producing high quality products and keeping the facilities clean. Achieving this requires all managers and supervisors in the organization to engage, motivate, and direct their staff. As a manager it is your responsibility to make the organization a great place for people to work and to encourage them to contribute to the success of the organization.

Tracking performance

Always ensure that you and your team are developing, learning, and moving on. You will achieve success only when your team has a positive perception of you, and the organizational environment is favourable and supportive. Use the scorecard featured below to track your performance in motivating people. Think about the elements of the scorecard as the links in a chain. Each link has to be strong to give the chain strength, so use the scorecard to guide where you need to focus your attention. It is important that you plan to strengthen any weaknesses that may appear. You could even use the scorecard with trusted team members or colleagues to help you develop your abilities and become a great motivator.

TIP

REVIEW PERFORMANCE

Every six months you should stop and reflect on your team's performance. Ask yourself where you are succeeding, and where you are falling short.

Motivation scorecard

HOW MOTIVATED IS MY STAFF?
Does my team:
• show enthusiasm?
• work well with each other?
• go the extra mile?
• perform well?
• achieve the goals
that are set for them?

HOW WELL AM I PERCEIVED?
Do I:
• have the trust of my staff?
• have a good working
relationship with my team?
• support my colleagues?
• appear approachable?
• motivate people well?

HOW SUPPORTIVE IS THE ENVIRONMENT?
Do we:
• have the opportunity
to do well?
• have the tools to do our job?
• have the support of our
bosses and colleagues?

HOW ARE WE LEARNING?
Have I:
• developed my own
skills and abilities?
• helped someone to learn a
new skill in the last month?
• helped someone get
promoted this year?

PROJECT MANAGEMENT

Contents

Introduction

Project management is the skill of moving from ideas to results and, as such, is applicable to every significant initiative we are given or come up with ourselves. Today, individuals, organizations, and nations need project management skills more than ever in a world that values individual and collective initiative above just about any other attribute.

Project Management outlines a range of practical understandings and skills that will make your projects both successful and satisfying. It will provide you with common-sense solutions to the project management issues you will face as you plan and implement a project, and the tools, tips, and techniques it contains are intended to help you achieve consistent success using minimum resources. The book is written for those taking their first steps in project management, but also offers helpful reminders to those with more experience.

In the final analysis, your success as a project manager is down to you; it will depend on your ability to make your vision of "what can be" more influential in your own and other people's thinking and actions than the reality of "what currently is". If the following pages guide, challenge, and energize you in this quest they will have fulfilled their purpose.

Chapter 1

Thinking "project"

Projects are the mechanism by which organizations and individuals change and adapt to take advantage of new opportunities or counter threats. In a world in which business competitiveness is based on a search for new products and ways to do things, every individual can improve their prospects by always thinking: "Where is the project in my current situation?"

What is a project?

A project is a piece of work that is designed to bring about an agreed beneficial change within a fixed timeframe using specified resources. Projects usually require the coordinated activity of a number of people to achieve that outcome, and often incorporate an element of risk.

What makes a task a project?

Projects are the way in which human creativity is most effectively harnessed to achieve tangible, lasting results. In the past they may have been called something different, but building a pyramid, painting a ceiling, or founding a nation all required vision, planning, and coordinated effort – the essential features of what we now call a project. In practical terms, just about any initiative or piece of work that is too large or unfamiliar to be completed successfully without some measure of preparation and planning can, and usually should, be approached as a project.

Defining a project

At its simplest level, a project is a "one-off" scope of work defined by three parameters – time, cost, and quality. In other words, it is the means by which a particular result is delivered using specified resources within a set timeframe.

For most projects, one of these three parameters is "fixed" (i.e. should not or cannot change), but there is flexibility in at least one of the other two. Where the quality of the product is fixed (bringing a new drug to market, for example), costs have a tendency to rise and deadlines to slip if work is more extensive or complex than was first envisaged. Where the deadline is fixed (as for a tender deadline or a business conference), people either throw more resources at the project to make sure that it is ready on time, or they cull desirable but non-essential features in order to deliver the essential elements of quality within the timeframe available.

Achieving change

Some projects are highly visible – large and prestigious building projects, for example – while for others, no-one except those directly involved has any understanding of, or interest in, what they will deliver.

Whatever the size and nature of a project, the principal aim is always to bring about a change that is viewed as beneficial by the person or people sponsoring it.

CASE STUDY

Setting the standard

When Tim Smit pitched the idea of creating a science-based visitor attraction showcasing 100,000 plants from around the world in a disused clay pit in South West England, few would have expected the Eden Project to have become the icon it is today. Despite the technological challenges of creating the world's largest greenhouses – two giant transparent domes – the main construction phase was complete by March 2001. Since then, it has been visited by more than 10 million people at a rate of over one million a year, and has brought over £850m to the local economy. Just as importantly to Smit, Eden is now a significant contributor to the global debate on sustainable development and environmental issues. As with any high-profile project, commentators offer a variety of explanations for its success: technology made the original design and spectacular scale possible, but Smit's vision, inspirational leadership, and refusal to compromise on quality were undoubtedly central.

The project sequence

The lifecycle of any project consists of six main phases: initiation, definition, planning, control, implementation, and review. At whichever point you, as project manager, enter the project's life, be sure to acquaint yourself as fully as possible with any preceding phases you have missed.

TIP

FOCUS ON DEFINITION
Fully explore the "whats" and "whys" of the project before you start to make practical plans – this will help you avoid the need for costly revisions in later phases.

Defining project phases

The initiation and definition phases involve using tools and approaches to identify the situation to be addressed, the desired end result, and the core team responsible for making it happen. Once these are established, the planning phase focuses on the detail of what has to be produced and how this can be done most effectively with minimum risk. While planning continues throughout the project, there is generally a point at which significant resources are committed, and the control phase sees work begin.

The schedules and budgets that you established while planning will allow you to track progress and make adjustments as needed. As the control phase nears completion, focus switches to preparation for

The six phases of a project:

INITIATION
Identifying the problem to be solved or opportunity to be exploited.

DEFINITION
Refining your understanding of what you want to achieve, by when, and with what resources.

PLANNING
Deciding in detail how to achieve the objective – timescales, resources, responsibilities, and communications.

the moment when the results will "go live". While you should have been considering the needs and expectations of end users at every stage, your primary focus during this implementation phase should be taking steps to ensure that they react positively to the change your project has brought about. Plan your review stage around pre-defined criteria by which the project's success can be measured. These can then be used to declare it complete before moving into a phase where resources are reallocated and lessons learnt.

Maintaining flexibility

While in theory the phases provide a logical sequence, in practice they often overlap, so you need to adopt a rolling process of continuous review during the definition, planning, and control phases. For example, you may need to modify the initial scope* of a project to fit with what proves to be possible once you have produced a first draft of the plan. Similarly, experience gained from work early in the project may lead you to identify flawed assumptions about the duration and complexity of tasks, leading to a re-evaluation of timescales, budgets, and other resources.

*Scope — *a description of the desired end result of a project. For clarity, it often includes reference to the context in which the end result will be delivered, and who the end user will be.*

CONTROL
Doing the work, monitoring progress, and adjusting the plan according to need.

IMPLEMENTATION
Passing what you have created over to those who will be using it, and helping them to adjust to any changes.

REVIEW
Assessing the outcome and looking back to see if there is anything you could have done differently or better.

Defining the team

Role clarity is essential if you are to deliver a successful project. As every project is a new and often unique scope of work, and project teams are often built from scratch, it is vital that each stakeholder* in your project is clear about exactly what their role entails and what they will be expected to deliver.

Understanding key roles

Every project is different, but there are a number of key roles that apply to most projects (see right). The relationship between these roles is functional rather than hierarchical. Although by the nature of the role the sponsor will usually be the most senior member of the project team – and will certainly be more senior than the manager – little else can be assumed about the relative seniority of other team members. Technical specialists, in particular, frequently have skills based on years of experience and are often "senior" to the project manager.

*Stakeholder — *anyone who has influence over, or interest in, the process or outcome of a project.*

Knowing your team

Your project team will generally be made up of people from your organization and contractors – referred to as internal and external team respectively. Clearly these are key stakeholders in the success of your project, so as project manager you must make their motivation and focus a priority. This may take some skill and effort: team members frequently have other work to juggle. In addition, they will be influenced by a second ring of stakeholders over whom you have no direct control (or of whom you have no knowledge), such as their line managers, colleagues, clients, and suppliers.

TIP

BEWARE THE BUYER

Buyers often wield significant power where a project has been procured. Those that also act as the client can sometimes have an adversarial relationship with the project. Handle such clients carefully, using the sponsor where necessary.

Key project roles

SPONSOR
The person who owns the resources needed for success and on whose authority the project takes place.

MANAGER
Has day-to-day executive responsibility for the project. Manager and sponsor must be in complete agreement about what constitutes success with respect to time, cost, and quality.

TECHNICAL SPECIALISTS
In many projects, success depends on the input of a small number of people with expert skills, high levels of access, or personal decision-making authority.

CLIENT (OR SENIOR USER)
Coordinates or represents the interests of the end-user group. If there are multiple end-user groups with differing views, there may be a number of clients.

BUYER
Buyers procure or commission projects on behalf of end users, and are judged primarily on their ability to source suppliers and negotiate competitive rates on contracts.

QUALITY ASSURANCE
In larger projects, a team may be assigned to ensure that all prescribed methodologies are carried out properly. (In smaller projects, the sponsor should do this.)

END USERS
End users are often represented by the client, but there are key moments in most projects when it is helpful to communicate directly with this group.

Being project manager

As a project manager, you will be the central hub around which your project team is formed. Much of your success will depend on your ability to make the project something others want to be involved in or, at the very least, do not want to oppose.

Owning the project

Whether you have been delegated the role of project manager, or you sold an idea upwards to someone capable of sponsoring it, you are likely to have demonstrated personal and managerial competence and commitment to the change under consideration.

"Competence" and "commitment" are the sorts of solid but colourless words often found in management books; however, the last thing a project manager can afford to be is colourless. Indeed, the very best project managers are a paradoxical combination of "larger than life" – self-confident, decisive, creative, and engaging; and self-effacing – down to earth, hands on, and keen to learn from other members of their team and promote their contributions.

Selling the idea

To be fully convincing as a project manager, you must first be convinced of the value of the initiative under consideration yourself. If you do not believe the results are attainable, or are lukewarm about their value, you are unlikely to make the sacrifices or identify the creative solutions required when the going gets tough – as it almost invariably will at some point. Furthermore, you must be able to communicate your enthusiasm to others and have the confidence to stand up to opposition both inside and outside the

✔ CHECKLIST AM I READY TO MANAGE THIS PROJECT?

	YES	NO
• Do I have a clear idea of who the end users are in my project and what the world looks like through their eyes?	☐	☐
• Do I understand what is required of this project and why?	☐	☐
• Do I care about the outcome enough to make personal sacrifices to achieve it?	☐	☐
• Am I confident I can deliver it given the constraints of cost and time?	☐	☐
• Am I prepared to take risks and back my own judgement where necessary?	☐	☐

project team. Conversely, you must be a good listener – able to sift through the opinions of others and take on their ideas whenever they improve the quality of outcome or the likelihood of success.

Taking on responsibility

To be an effective project manager, you must have a balance of task- and people-related skills. While your ultimate aim is to deliver a result, success comes from building diverse individuals into a strong team and motivating them to produce quality results within the requisite timeframes. Often, you will achieve this through personal determination, creativity, and powers of persuasion. At a deeper level, you also need the moral courage and integrity to treat every member of the team the same, irrespective of their seniority and personality. You also need excellent time management and personal organization, so that you can think beyond immediate distractions or crises to provide proactive leadership to other members of the team. While it is important to have at least some understanding of the technical aspects of the project, your management role is to provide the decision-making, planning, and leadership skills outlined in this book.

TIP

PLAY DEVIL'S ADVOCATE

Anticipate opposition by thinking through possible criticisms of your project and coming up with effective counter-arguments so that you are well prepared to tackle negative views.

Working with your sponsor

The relationship between the project manager and the sponsor is the foundation upon which the whole project is built. Both must have the same understanding of what constitutes success and must have established a relationship of trust that enables each to share issues and concerns with the other as soon as they crop up.

TIP

AVOID SURPRISES
Never try to hide things that have gone wrong from your sponsor – even if this means admitting a serious mistake on your part.

Engaging the sponsor

Your sponsor should be the individual (rather than the group, team, or committee) who owns the resources required to make the project successful and will act as the final arbiter of success. This will be based partly on hierarchical seniority and partly on personal authority. Effective sponsorship is one of the key determinants of your success, so a wise project manager invests time and effort, firstly in selecting the right person – if you have a choice; secondly in forging the right relationship; and thirdly in providing the sponsor with the information and arguments he or she needs to defend or champion the project as necessary.

IN FOCUS... CHOOSING YOUR OWN PROJECT SPONSOR

If you are in a position to choose your sponsor, your goal should be to achieve just the right balance between authority and accessibility. While it is generally helpful to have as senior a sponsor as possible, you also need someone for whom the project is significant enough to command their active interest. A sponsor who keeps up to date with your progress and is aware of potential or actual issues will be well placed to make decisions or help you overcome any opposition or obstacle to the project without the need for extensive briefing. You need to be able to consult your sponsor quickly when things go wrong and feel comfortable that you are more than just one commitment among many.

Meeting your sponsor

Your first meeting with the sponsor of your project is a key moment of influence. This meeting should not be just about the detail of the project, but must also establish how you and the sponsor will work together to make the project succeed. Give high priority to agreeing communication channels and escalation procedures – how and when to involve the sponsor when things go wrong. In larger projects, key team members such as a senior user or technical specialist may also be invited to attend this meeting.

Identifying poor sponsorship

Beware the sponsor who cancels or postpones your meetings at short notice, or who fails to get your project on to the agenda of key decision-making meetings. Quickness to apportion blame, or to get unnecessarily embroiled in detail, are other indications that your sponsor has become detached from the aims and progress of your project. Think very carefully about what you should do and who you might speak to if your sponsor's lack of engagement starts to threaten the success of your project.

HOW TO...
FORGE A GOOD SPONSOR–MANAGER RELATIONSHIP

Be clear on your own role: this will give the sponsor confidence that you are the right person for the job.

↓

Express clear expectations of them to ensure you set a worthwhile "contract" upon which to build your relationship.

↓

Take time to establish personal rapport with the sponsor.

↓

Ask about other projects they have sponsored and project managers they have worked with, to establish their style of working and likes and dislikes.

↓

Use examples and scenarios to agree how you should interact when things go wrong.

↓

Find out from them what information they require, when or how frequently they need it, and what format they would like it in.

Documenting progress

Standard documents and agreed circulation and sign-off procedures increase the efficiency of project teams and improve communication, particularly between sponsor and manager. If your organization does not yet have a standard set of project documents, you can enhance your reputation considerably by producing your own.

INVEST TIME EARLY ON

It is often difficult to find the time in a busy schedule to develop and manage project paperwork, but a little time spent considering documentation early on will get your project off on the right foot.

Designing documentation

Having a suite of carefully designed project documents allows information to be carried over from one project milestone to the next – or even from project to project – and helps occasional stakeholders find information quickly within a particular document. Simple formats work best, and should incorporate a cover sheet identifying the document, the project to which it refers, and the key stakeholders involved. Never underestimate presentation: people are quick to judge based on first impressions, and if your paperwork looks professional, they will treat you as such unless you subsequently prove otherwise.

Using document sign-offs

The practice of physically signing off documents is a very useful way to get people to take a project seriously. However, any decision about whether to use it needs to be sensitive to the culture of your organization: if people are generally good at engaging with projects and delivering on promises, then asking for signatures may be seen as unnecessarily aggressive. If this is not the case and a firmer line is required, implementing a policy of signing off documents is most easily achieved if you employ it from the start, with all document formats having space for signatures.

Key project documents

Each of the six phases of your project requires different documentation to record important details. Depending on the size and nature of your project, these may include:

01
INITIATION PHASE
- **Mandate:** agreement of the need for the project and its aims.
- **Brief:** a description of the issue to be resolved or the opportunity to be exploited.

02
DEFINITION PHASE
- **Project Initiation Document (PID):** defines what the project must deliver and why.
- **Business case:** the financial figures behind the opportunity.
- **Risk log:** a record of all risks and approaches to resolution.

03
PLANNING PHASE
- **Schedule and resource plans:** the plan in detail, including completion dates and resource requirements.
- **Quality plan:** what processes will be monitored, and how.

04
CONTROL PHASE
- **Changes to scope:** agreed modifications to the original brief.
- **Milestone reviews:** progress against schedule and budget.
- **Quality reviews:** confirmation that processes are being followed.

05
IMPLEMENTATION PHASE
- **User Acceptance Test (UAT):** reports and sign-offs from end users at all levels.
- **Implementation schedule:** the plan for how the project will be handed over to end users.

06
REVIEW PHASE
- **Post-implementation review:** assesses what the project has delivered.
- **Lessons learnt review:** how things could have been done better.

Chapter 2

Setting up a project

A successful project depends on clear thinking in the preparatory stages. The initiation and definition phases of the project management process build on each other to establish precisely what the project is expected to deliver to the end users, while the planning phase sets out how this is to be achieved.

Initiating the project

The aim of the initiation phase is to set out the reasons for a project and the context in which it will run. As project manager your aim in this phase is to secure the briefing, backing, and resources you need from your sponsor to begin a detailed evaluation of the work to be undertaken.

Agreeing the brief

The first step in the initiation phase is to establish that both you and your sponsor view success in the same terms – both the result to be achieved and the way you will work together to achieve it. Based on these discussions the project mandate and brief can be drawn up. These should document, respectively, the business opportunity or issue to be addressed, and some outline thoughts on how this might best be done. The initiation phase should end with the sponsor signing off the brief and allocating resources that allow you to move into the definition and planning phases of your project.

Getting the right support

The type of support you need from your sponsor during this phase will to a degree be dependent on where the idea for the project came from.

• **Top-down initiation** In most organizations, targets for future development and plans for a variety of initiatives become projects undertaken by operational managers. In this kind of "top-down" initiation, the sponsor delegates the execution of the project to you. This is a critical point for you: do not let nerves or excitement cloud your judgement of what you need at this stage. You can expect strong support from above, but need to secure a very clear brief of what is expected of the project.

• **Bottom-up initiation** Not all the best ideas come from those at the top of an organization; those closest to the customer may be first to spot commercial opportunities. Successful projects initiated from the "bottom up", by people who end up managing them, indicate a very healthy corporate culture. It shows that those at more junior levels are having initiative rewarded with real responsibility – and this represents an opportunity that should be seized. Your advantage in this case is that you will be highly motivated, with a very clear idea of what you want to achieve and how this could be made possible. Your priority is to obtain solid support from a sponsor who is fully behind the project so that you can go on to deliver results that justify his or her confidence in you.

IN FOCUS...
PITCHING YOUR OWN PROJECT

If you identify an opportunity requiring more resources than you personally can muster, your first step should be to target a suitable sponsor and pitch your idea. Your presentation should identify the size of the opportunity and be supported by hard evidence. Think about the questions your sponsor might ask. Prepare well: there are unknowns and risks in any project, so your sponsor's decision will be based as much on your credibility as the strength of the idea. Even if you do not get sponsorship for this idea, you can enhance your prospects of getting future projects sponsored if you have put a well-argued case forward.

Building a project team

One of the most important functions of the project manager is to build and maintain the "team dynamic". By giving your project a strong and positive identity, and making the team a rewarding environment in which to work, you increase the likelihood that people will give you that "extra 10 per cent" that dramatically increases the quality of their contribution and reduces the amount of effort it takes to manage them.

Putting a team together

An effective project manager builds a team with a strong sense of identity. This is often more challenging in a small team than in one with a higher profile and fully dedicated team members. Start by taking time to select the right people, with input from the sponsor. Base your decisions on availability and relevant skills/knowledge/contacts, but also take personality "fit" and motivation into account. Stakeholder analysis (described overleaf) can be a useful tool for assessing potential candidates and finding the best way to manage them. Make a personal approach to each person selected and request their participation. Don't beg; simply explain why you have selected them and the benefits they can expect for being involved.

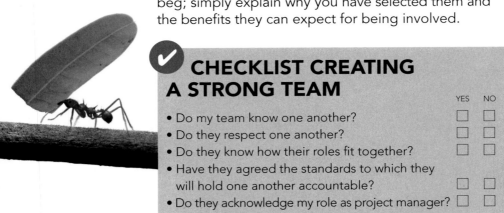

✔ CHECKLIST CREATING A STRONG TEAM

	YES	NO
• Do my team know one another?	☐	☐
• Do they respect one another?	☐	☐
• Do they know how their roles fit together?	☐	☐
• Have they agreed the standards to which they will hold one another accountable?	☐	☐
• Do they acknowledge my role as project manager?	☐	☐

Getting started

Hold an initial meeting with all project team members. It is helpful to have the sponsor present for a proportion of a "kick-off" meeting, but you will enhance your authority as the project manager if you are the one to arrange and chair the meeting. (If you do not have the authority to do this, you may struggle to manage the group through the rest of the project.)

Discuss team roles and ground rules for your project before getting into the detail of the task to be undertaken. People appreciate being asked about their experience of project teamwork, whether there is anything they particularly like or dislike, and what their hopes and concerns are. Talk with the group about how project decisions (particularly in relation to deadlines) will be made; how the team will acknowledge success; what to do if people fail to deliver; and how conflicts will be resolved.

Developing identity

A strong team is built on a strong identity. Give your project a name, but beware of choosing anything too clever – the best names are generally low key, with positive connotations, offering a useful shorthand reference for the project. Create a team location, be it a building, room, desk, or notice board, or a virtual location on the intranet or web. Make it somewhere that information can be displayed and progress checked, and give people reasons to frequent it.

Members of your team will take greater "ownership" of your project if they feel as if they are an important part of it. Involve them in production of the work schedule, risk analysis, and problem solving. Establish "soft" success criteria, relating to teamwork, morale, personal behaviour, and learning, in addition to the hard criteria set out in your project definition.

Analyzing stakeholders

The various stakeholders in your project – from the sponsor to each individual internal team member – all view it from very different perspectives. Analysis of each stakeholder's attitude towards your project, and their degree of influence within it, can be a useful part of the process by which a team is put together and managed.

Identifying key players

All projects have multiple stakeholders. Some will be more important than others, either because of their involvement in delivering elements of the work, or because they are influential in the environment where the work is being produced or will be deployed.

Stakeholder analysis allows you to identify the most important people in your project and decide where to invest time and resources. It should lead to a communication plan aimed initially at canvassing opinion and then providing the right people with timely information throughout the project's lifecycle.

TIP

GET PROOF
Don't ascribe the highest level of attitude towards the project – being wholly committed – to a stakeholder unless you find positive proof in their words and actions that they are both intellectually and emotionally committed.

Performing the analysis

Consider every stakeholder in your project in relation to two scales – influence and attitude. Rate each person or group according to their influence within the project, and whether they can be influenced by you as the project manager. Next, rate them on their attitude towards the project. Use the matrix on the facing page to mark the desired and actual position of stakeholders: draw a circle on the grid where you want them to be and a cross where they currently are. Where circles and crosses are co-located consider what you need to do to maintain their position; where they are separate consider what you need to do to improve the situation.

Influencing stakeholders

As a general rule, you are unlikely to be able to move strongly negative stakeholders to the positive side, but it may be possible to neutralize their opposition. Where there is opposition from an especially powerful stakeholder or group of stakeholders, steps may have to be taken to reduce their influence or the project may have to be abandoned.

Your relationship with the sponsor, and his or her position in your organization, may be very helpful. You need to have the confidence to address senior or challenging stakeholders directly, but also the wisdom to know when this may be counterproductive and a situation is better addressed by involving the sponsor.

STAKEHOLDER ANALYSIS MATRIX

INFLUENCE WITHIN THE PROJECT		Wholly committed	Generally positive	Neutral	Generally opposed	Actively opposed
	Significant influence; cannot always be influenced by you					
	Marginal influence; cannot always be influenced by you	◯ ← X		Technical specialist		
	Influence equal to you			⊗ Quality assurance manager		
	Significant influence; can be influenced by you		◯ ←		X	Internal team member
	Marginal influence; can be influenced by you					

ATTITUDE TOWARDS THE PROJECT

Defining the details

Before committing significant resources, you must have agreement on what your project should produce, by when, and using what resources. While the brief should have identified the rationale and broad strategy behind a project, the next step is to define the scope of the project – precisely what will be handed over to the end users on completion.

Asking for input

In broad terms, defining the scope of your project is done by asking the right people the right questions in the right way, and recording your findings clearly. Consider the most important players in your project, identified in your stakeholder analysis: which of these have key roles in defining what the project must deliver? Time invested discussing the project brief with stakeholders, particularly the client and end users, is rarely wasted. The views of the sponsor are a good starting point – if your project required an initiation phase, you will have already obtained these from the mandate and the brief. Clients and end users should have significant input into the scope of your project, but also consider those with whom they interact, such as anyone who manages the end users or who will support them in areas relating to your project after implementation. It may also be helpful to speak to anyone who will be responsible for maintaining the product, capability, or facility that your project will deliver.

What?
- **What is the problem to be fixed?**
- **What would be the impact of not fixing it?**
- **What exactly is the result required?**
- **What has been tried before?**

Why?
- **Why is this result required?**
- **Why doesn't it exist already?**

Gathering information

Focused and well-structured conversations not only deliver useful information from stakeholders, but can also build your credibility with the client. Generally speaking, it is best to have these discussions face-to-face, as this allows you to assess each person's understanding of, and commitment to, the project. Although your primary purpose is to uncover the information you need to create a clear scope, in-depth questioning often exposes hitherto unexplored aspects of people's work to scrutiny. This can sometimes be resented, so tread carefully, but be courageous enough to continue lines of questioning that are uncovering useful information.

How?
- **How will it be used?**
- **How long will it be in service for?**

Where?
- **Where will it be used? (Physically, and in what context?)**
- **Where is this in our list of priorities?**

Asking the right questions to define the scope

Who?
- **Who are the end users?**
- **Who will support it?**
- **Who will manage it?**

When?
- **When will it be used?**

IN FOCUS... THE FIVE WHYS

A simple but surprisingly powerful technique for establishing the link between a project and your organization's key strategic objectives is to ask the client why they want what the project delivers. Insist that they answer this question beginning with the words "in order to". Then take the answer they give and ask them why *that* is important; again, insist on "in order to". Repeat this process for as many times as it takes to connect your project to your organization's main business strategy. As a rule of thumb, if the sequence of questioning does not lead to one of your organization's strategic goals within five steps, then the project may not be worth pursuing.

TIP

ASK "GREAT QUESTIONS"

Think carefully about the questions you ask your client. If you can get him or her to say "That's a great question!" you will have helped them uncover a new perspective, and transformed your status from supplier to partner.

Understanding your client

Your first aim should be to establish how well your client understands the situation surrounding your project and the benefit they expect it to deliver. Inexperienced project managers sometimes make the mistake of trying to zero in too quickly on what the client sees as the essential and desirable features of the end product. In cases where the client does not know what they want, avoid asking direct questions about the scope, as this is likely to confuse and could lead to frustration, embarrassment, and conflict – not the ideal start to a relationship that should become a central axis of the project team.

TIP

CREATE A BOTTOM LINE

Set a "Fit for Purpose Baseline" – the minimum that your project can deliver and still be deemed a success.

Prioritizing features

In most projects, as you go through the definition process you will identify a number of features required of the end result. Some will be essential, while others are "nice to have". In order to highlight where clashes exist, take each feature in turn and create designs based on that alone; then consider the results with the client and develop a definition that delivers the perfect mix of features to the end user.

Adding creativity

As part of the definition phase of your project, it is always worth taking a moment to think how it could be transformed from delivering a "fit for purpose" solution to being a project that catches the eye for creativity and elegance. This need not take much time; the main thing is to suspend judgement on ideas and have some fun. Then change your mindset and assess what additional perspectives your creative musings have uncovered. Try to identify more than one option – even when there is an obvious solution. Take time to consider at least three possible approaches (one of these might be "do nothing"). Your aim should be to find one way to make your project exciting and different for your end users or for your team.

Recording the scope

The investigations you undertake during the definition phase are to enable you to generate a detailed Project Information Document (PID). This is an expansion of the brief, incorporating all the additional information you have gathered from discussions with stakeholders. The PID is the document on which the sponsor will make a decision on whether to commit significant resources to the project. Once signed off, it becomes a binding agreement between the sponsor, the project manager, and the client, so its format and content are of paramount importance. The information in the PID needs to be easily accessible, so don't include more than is necessary for the size and complexity of your project.

✔ # CHECKLIST UNDERSTANDING THE SCOPE OF YOUR PROJECT

	YES	NO
• Do you have a clear idea of the objective of your project – what it is intended to achieve?	☐	☐
• Do you know why this is important?	☐	☐
• Do you know how and when it will be achieved?	☐	☐
• Have you determined who will be involved?	☐	☐
• Have you identified the deliverables for your project?	☐	☐
• Have you obtained enough information to allow your sponsor to make a decision on whether to proceed?	☐	☐

Developing a business case

Every project will represent an investment in time, effort, and resources, so a key question to address during the definition phase is: "Is this project worth it?" The business case for a project weighs up two factors: the cost of undertaking the project and the benefits it is likely to deliver.

Weighing up costs

When assessing the potential costs of your project, make sure you only take future costs into account – past expenditure is irrelevant in deciding whether to take the project forward. Only include incremental costs in your assessment: those that change as a result of the project being undertaken. For example, if your project requires that you hire two extra staff but is running from company offices, the additional staff costs should be included but the accommodation costs should not.

GETTING THE BUSINESS CASE RIGHT

FAST TRACK

OFF TRACK

FAST TRACK	OFF TRACK
Using the sponsor's financial advisors to put together your business case	Basing your business case on your own gut feelings and untested assumptions
Setting a notional hourly rate for work done by internal team members, especially technical specialists	Considering internal team costs a "free" resource when additional or unplanned work has to be done
Including contingency funds in your cost assessment, to allow for unexpected outlays	Deciding to ignore potential risks and take the chance that nothing will go wrong

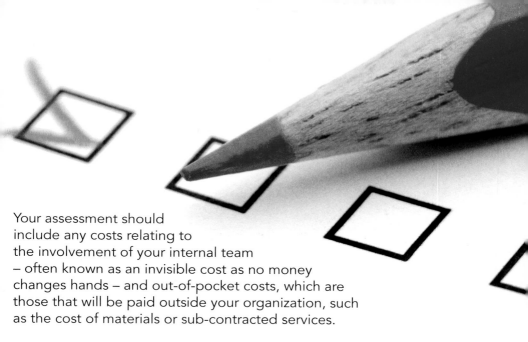

Your assessment should include any costs relating to the involvement of your internal team – often known as an invisible cost as no money changes hands – and out-of-pocket costs, which are those that will be paid outside your organization, such as the cost of materials or sub-contracted services.

Assessing benefits

While it is often easy to identify the "change" your project will deliver, it may be more difficult to quantify the nature, scale, and timing of the benefit. As a rule, the benefits from a project should be aligned with at least one of the organization's strategic goals (such as increasing revenue or reducing costs, for example) if it is to proceed. Consider also the point at which the benefits can be expected. In some cases, a smaller return earlier is preferable to a larger one that will take longer to come in. Projected benefits can rarely be guaranteed and so any complete cost/benefit analysis should contain an assessment of what could go wrong and the effect of this on the overall outcome. While your aim should be to put a percentage figure on the likelihood for the project delivering the intended benefit, this is always a judgement based on incomplete information. In the end it is your sponsor's job to make the decision, but it must be based on accurate information provided by you.

TIP

KNOW YOUR STUFF

Work with experts to put your business case together, but make sure you understand the basis on which they have done this well enough to form a view on what they have produced.

Projects, by their nature, are risky, so it could therefore be argued that your key role as a project manager is to identify, plan for, and manage risk. Risk analysis is undertaken in the definition phase, but should be followed by a continuous cycle of management and analysis throughout the control and implementation phases of your project.

Planning for risk

Initial identification of risk often takes the form of a Risk Workshop – a group of people getting together with the express intention of identifying and evaluating all the risks in a particular project or phase. From that point on every review meeting should contain an agenda item on "open" or "live" risks. As a project manager, the risks you should be most concerned with are those that will have an impact on one of the three project parameters (time, cost, or quality).

Risks need to be evaluated with respect to two criteria: probability (how likely they are to happen) and impact (how serious it would be if they do). Most tasks in your project will contain some element of risk, so you will need to set a threshold at which you are going to begin to plan. For tasks that carry a risk that is above your threshold for probability and impact, identify a response in advance, and monitor progress towards completion more carefully than usual.

In all but the smallest projects, risks should be recorded in a risk log. This document describes each risk, its impact and probability, and countermeasures to deal with it. It can also include the proximity of the risk (when it will need active management) and any early indicators that the probability of the risk has changed. The contents of the risk log should be reviewed throughout the lifecycle of the project.

PREVENT
Terminate the risk by doing things differently. This is not always a realistic possibility.

PLAN CONTINGENCY
Have a Plan B that will achieve the same result by a different route and leave future plans intact.

REDUCE
Take action to reduce either the likelihood or impact of the risk.

Dealing with risk

These are the five ways of dealing with risk, as outlined in the internationally recognized project management standard PRINCE2.

TRANSFER
See if you can spread the risk so that the consequences become less serious (this is the principle on which insurance works).

ACCEPT
There are some risks that are considered acceptable because the cost of dealing with them is greater than the increased benefit one would get from developing countermeasures.

Planning the project

The production of an accurate and detailed plan is one of the project manager's most important responsibilities. However, do not make the mistake of thinking you should do it on your own. By involving the team in the planning process you increase their understanding of what has to be done and generally gain an extra level of commitment to deadlines.

Developing a project plan

The following ten-step Team Planning technique uses sticky notes and a flip chart to produce a project plan. By following the process outlined, you will produce a robust and accurate project plan and maximize buy-in from those who will be instrumental in delivering it. Do the first four steps in this process on your own, getting the team involved once you have some raw material for them to work on. This reduces the cost of planning and makes briefing easier as you have something to show them.

PROJECT OBJECTIVE

BY: (DATE)

DELIVER: (PRODUCT)

TO: (CLIENT/END USER)

IN ORDER TO: (BENEFIT)

PRODUCT
e.g. MANUALS
PRINTED

1 **Restate the objective** Start by reducing the objective of your project – defined in the initiation and definition process – into a single statement of intent that fits on one large sticky note (see left).

2 **Brainstorm the products** The products of a plan are the building blocks that, when added together, deliver that project's end result. Brainstorm between five and 15 products for your project on separate sticky notes, and place them in roughly chronological order down the short side of a piece of A1 flip chart paper.

3 **Brainstorm the tasks** Tasks are activities or actions undertaken by individuals or groups that normally require their presence or participation for the whole duration. Take a pack of sticky notes in a different colour to the one you used to set out the products. Brainstorm the tasks that need to be done by you and other people to deliver each of the products, writing one task on to one sticky note. Draw two fields on the bottom half of the sticky note, so that you can add additional information later.

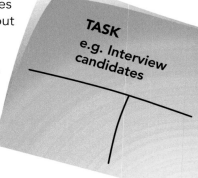

4 **Place the tasks in order** Place the tasks in roughly chronological order across the page, keeping them in line with the product to which they are connected. Where tasks can be done simultaneously, place them below one another, and where they depend on one another or on using the same resources, place them sequentially. Involve the rest of the delivery team in adding to and refining this skeleton plan.

TIP

USE COLOUR
Choose a different colour of sticky note for the objective, the products, and the tasks of your project (here, orange, pink, and yellow, respectively) to give at-a-glance clarity to your plan.

5 **Confirm the tasks** Step back and look at the logic flow of your plan. Involve the implementation team in this step – it can be a useful "reality check" on your logic. When people identify modifications to your plan, listen carefully and incorporate their suggestions, changing or adding sticky notes as necessary.

6 **Draw in dependencies between tasks** A dependency is the relationship between two tasks. The most common type of dependency is end–start (one task ending before the next can start). Dependency can be based either on logic or on resource. Once you have confirmed all tasks are represented and that they are in the right places, take a pen and draw in arrows to represent the dependencies between the tasks required to complete your project.

7 **Allocate times to tasks** Use the experience of your project team to identify what resources and how much effort will be required to complete each task. Note: this is not how long people need to complete the task ("Calendar time"), but how much effort they will need to put in ("Timesheet time"). Write the time needed for each task into the bottom right-hand field on each sticky note. Where possible, use the same unit of time throughout.

8 **Assess and resolve risks** Get input from every member of the project team on what they consider to be risks. Give each member of the team two or three sticky notes of a different colour to the ones you have already used, and get them to place them behind the tasks they consider riskiest. Once everyone has placed their notes, facilitate a discussion around their choices, agreeing what countermeasures to adopt and who will be responsible for them.

Example of a project plan:

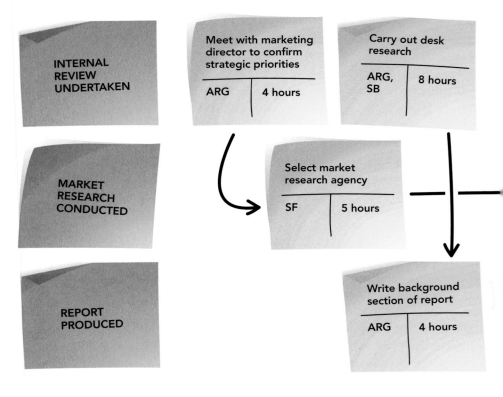

9 **Allocate tasks** Get your team together and allocate who will do what. People who have been allowed to contribute to the plan in the ways described in steps five to eight will generally have already identified the tasks they would like to work on, or at least recognized that they are the best person to do certain tasks even if they don't want to do them. Simply introduce this step by saying to your team: "Right, who's going to do what?" and then wait for a response. You may be greeted with silence at first, but gradually people will begin to volunteer for tasks. Record names or initials in the bottom left-hand box on each sticky note.

10 **Agree milestones and review points** Take sticky notes of the same colour as those that you used for the products of your project, and place one at the end of each line of tasks. Now facilitate a discussion about when people will be able to complete their tasks and write specific dates (and possibly even times) for when you will review progress. If your project is time-critical, begin with the deadline and work back towards the present; if quality or cost are critical, begin at the present and work forward. Make sure that people cross-check their deadlines with other work or life commitments.

Conduct market research	
Agency	2 weeks (lapsed time)

BY: 1ST SEPTEMBER

DELIVER: MARKET ANALYSIS PLUS RECOMMENDATIONS

TO: MARKETING DIRECTOR

IN ORDER TO: ALLOW HER TO DECIDE HOW TO SPEND NEXT YEAR'S BUDGET

Analyze market-research findings and decide on key recommendations	
ARG, SB, SF	6 hours

Write final draft report and prepare presentation	
ARG, SB, SF	6 hours

Present to marketing director	
ARG, SB	1 hour

Estimating time

Being able to estimate the amount of time required for the tasks and activities of a project is a key skill for any project manager. Indeed, in smaller projects that do not have an explicit budget, keeping to time is likely to be one of the measures of your effectiveness as project manager.

HOW TO... ESTIMATE THE TIME REQUIRED

Break down tasks until you know precisely who is doing what.

↓

Involve the person who will be doing the task in deciding how long it will take.

↓

Seek advice from those that have done similar tasks before.

↓

Use a time estimation formula.

Getting schedules right

In most cases, estimating task times with any degree of accuracy requires a combination of experience and common sense. However, this presupposes that you have correctly identified the task. When projects are late, it is often because activities have not been thought through or recorded properly, so what seemed like a very straightforward task (such as getting a decision from the finance department, for example) gets estimated as a single event rather than a number of small but significant and connected steps, each taking time and effort.

Involving the team

In most small projects, and certainly in an environment where there are numerous projects running side by side, the challenge is not so much to estimate how much effort tasks will take, but how much time someone needs to be able to complete a task alongside the many other demands made of him/her. Involve team members who will be performing critical tasks in your decision-making process. Ask each person for their estimation of the amount of time they will need to able to complete a certain task, given their other commitments. Be prepared to challenge these estimates if you disagree, but beware of putting undue pressure on people to reduce them.

Using time estimation formulae

Different organizations, industries, and sectors employ different models or formulae to estimate time. At first sight they always seem mathematical, but in most cases their effectiveness is psychological – either overcoming aversion to estimating, or encouraging more careful thought in those who tend to rush in.

Perhaps the most widely known is the PERT formula (Project Evaluation and Review Technique). To use PERT you need three estimates of the time it could take to complete a task or activity:
• The most likely time required (Tm)
• The most optimistic time assessment (To)
• The most pessimistic time assessment (Tp)

Use the following formula to estimate the most probable duration for that activity (Te):

$$Te = \frac{To + 4Tm + Tp}{6}$$

The formula can be weighted towards pessimism – if the consequences of a late completion of a particular task are severe, for example – by reducing the Tm multiplier and adding a Tp multiplier:

$$Te = \frac{To + 3Tm + 2Tp}{6}$$

Representing the plan

Once created, your project plan should become your main point of reference for managing progress during the control phase of the project. It is a living document, and you should expect that it will be updated through several versions to keep up with changing circumstances and to take account of incorrect estimates of time or cost.

Making a digital record

For most projects, you will want to represent your project using a software package rather than on paper. This gives your plan a more professional look and makes it easier to store and to communicate to others; and it allows you to automatically calculate items such as overall cost, critical path duration, and resource requirements. Using software, a single plan can easily be converted into a number of formats so that different aspects of the project are highlighted. In addition, the impact of changes or variances can more easily be tested, and multiple versions can be held for comparison.

There are many types of software package available, each with their own strengths and weaknesses. Choosing the right one for your needs will depend on the size and complexity of your project, the experience of the project team, and the software to which they all have access. As a general rule, ensure that managing the software you choose will not get in the way of managing the project itself, and that everyone will have first-hand access to the sections of the plan relevant to their work.

? ASK YOURSELF... WHAT ARE MY REQUIREMENTS?

- What aspects of the plan will I need to analyze and when?
- In what circumstances will I need to present or discuss the plan?
- How often will it need updating?
- Who else needs to have access to the plan?
- What representation will be most easily accessible and understood by them?

CHOOSING SOFTWARE

SOFTWARE PACKAGE TYPE	STRENGTHS	WEAKNESSES
Specialist project management software Ideal for a specialist project environment where people are familiar with its use and can read all formats and representations intuitively.	• Allows you to make multiple representations of the plan • Calendar facility allows longer-term scheduling • Shows dependencies between tasks • Integrates schedule, budget, and resource plans • Allows automatic calculation of critical path and resource implications	• "Occasional" project managers may spend more time learning to use the software than actually using it • Over-sophisticated for small projects • Does not readily integrate project work and day-to-day activities
Spreadsheet software Useful for simpler projects and where managing a budget is important.	• Widely available, so most stakeholders will be able to access the plan • Flexible for smaller projects • Allows automatic calculation of durations and costs using formulae • Graphical representation of tasks is possible	• Requires specialist knowledge to represent more complex information • Does not readily integrate project work and day-to-day activities
Graphics packages Useful for communicating the plan to project stakeholders as a presentation, and for highlighting the relationships between tasks.	• Good for making a professional-looking representation of your plan • Has multiple options for representing products, tasks, and responsibilities • Project templates available in many packages	• Not universally available, so some stakeholders may not be able to access the plan • Has no automatic interface with diary or financial packages, so schedules/budgets require manual updating when adjustments are made
Diary and tasklist software Ideal for a multi-project environment or where people have to integrate project work with day-to-day business as usual; and for small projects with no cash budget.	• Easy integration between project and day-to-day work • Good at representing the schedule • Widely available • A familiar format for most project stakeholders	• Not good at representing critical path, resource plans, or budgets • No automatic tie-in with budgeting software • Does not allow you to show the relationships between tasks graphically

Chapter 3
Managing work in progress

Management during the control phase, once a project is under way, requires a sophisticated skill-set that includes team leadership, delegation and communication, budget and schedule management, and high performance under pressure.

Making time for the project

Project management is rarely a full-time role, except in large or specialist organizations. Finding time for your longer-term work is often one of the biggest challenges faced by managers of smaller projects, especially when the planning stage ends and hands-on work begins.

Recognizing your priorities

Most modern approaches to time management address our tendency to prioritize urgency over importance when deciding what to do on a day-to-day basis. While the ability to react to unforeseen problems is essential, being purely "reactive" damages productivity, reduces the quality of results, and not least is stressful for you.

As a project manager your focus has to be further ahead than the immediate; hence the emphasis on definition and planning, on proactive communication with all stakeholders, and on risk analysis.

TIP

Finding your focus

GET ORGANIZED

Plan regular two-hour slots of project time in your diary. Set yourself a specific task to do in that time one week ahead, and then prepare as you would for an exam, gathering the information and resources you need to complete the task successfully.

Finding time to focus on the big picture is the key to integrating your long-term role and responsibilities with the short-term demands of your project.

• Start with a plan: begin every day by spending five to ten minutes getting a handle on your agenda for that day. Identify time already allocated to meetings and other fixed tasks. Allocate time to the tasks you plan to do off your "to do" list. Plan in enough flexibility to deal with the unexpected, and at least one review point at which you can check your direction and make adjustments.

• Integrate project tasks with your day-to-day tasks and diary. Do this by recording them on the same list and ensuring they are broken down to around the same size. If the average task size on your "to do" list is 15–30 minutes, for example, don't have project tasks of four hours in length – they won't get done.

• Motivate yourself to do longer-term tasks every day. Set yourself a goal of doing one longer-term task per day on each of your projects, or one task preparing for the next deliverable (i.e. not the current one) on every project.

CHECKLIST MANAGING YOUR TIME

	YES	NO
• Do you allocate "interruption-free" time in your diary, when you get away from your desk and turn off your email and phone, for tasks that require uninterrupted thought?	☐	☐
• Do you factor reactive time – spent responding to emails and phonecalls and attending ad-hoc meetings – into your day-to-day planning?	☐	☐
• Do you discourage reactive requests?	☐	☐
• Do you delegate work early and effectively?	☐	☐
• Do you ensure, where possible, that meetings begin on time and stick to the agenda?	☐	☐

Delegating effectively

Set time aside on a regular basis to plan which tasks and activities can be delegated to others. This may not be restricted to project tasks: in order to have the time for project management, you may find that you have to delegate other parts of your job, too.

Getting delegation right

Successful delegation is not always easy, especially if you are managing a small project within a multi-project environment. As the manager of a small project you can expect to find yourself delegating longer-term tasks to busy people who may only have partial understanding of what you are trying to achieve, and for whom your project is a relatively low priority. When deciding which tasks and activities to delegate, take time to consider the benefits you could expect from delegating a particular task, and the blocks that you would need to overcome. Once you have identified potential opportunities for delegation, clarify the specifics of how you could achieve them by asking yourself:

• What is the required outcome or deliverable from delegating this task?
• Why is this important?
• How will it be used and when is it required by?
• What constraints are there on how the result can be achieved?
• What could go wrong?
• Who should I delegate this task to?
• Why should they do it?
• What objections might I need to overcome?
• What help will they need?
• What level of authority can they handle?

BEAT INDECISION
Try to make quick decisions as to who to approach and what precisely has to be done, and don't procrastinate about approaching the sponsor if their involvement is required.

FIGHT GUILT
Nice people don't like delegating unpleasant tasks. However, effective leadership requires a hard head as well as a soft heart.

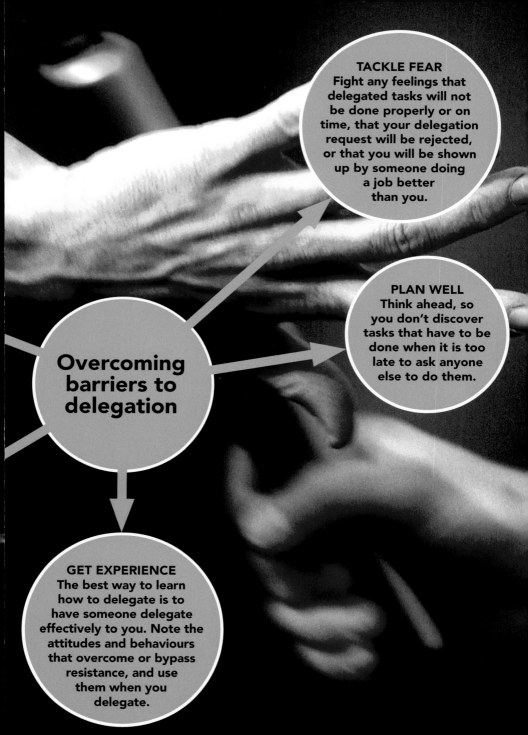

TACKLE FEAR
Fight any feelings that delegated tasks will not be done properly or on time, that your delegation request will be rejected, or that you will be shown up by someone doing a job better than you.

PLAN WELL
Think ahead, so you don't discover tasks that have to be done when it is too late to ask anyone else to do them.

Overcoming barriers to delegation

GET EXPERIENCE
The best way to learn how to delegate is to have someone delegate effectively to you. Note the attitudes and behaviours that overcome or bypass resistance, and use them when you delegate.

Preparing to delegate

Where possible, delegate straight from the plan: as soon as you have identified a task that needs to be done, select someone to do it. If they are present when the task is identified, use that moment to pass responsibility to them. Give delegatees as much warning as possible: it is preferable to have three weeks' warning of a deadline, rather than three days. Warn people of impending delegation, even before you are clear on what you want done. Brevity is of the essence and it's not a bad idea to use a standard format for this "heads-up message" (see right).

Setting the details

Arrange a formal meeting with the person you are delegating the task to. The success of the task depends on your ability to transmit the details and parameters of the task to the delegatee at this meeting. When delegating complex tasks, in particular, it is vital that you are confident that your colleague has fully understood and is committed to what they have been asked to do. Asking "Do you understand?" is simply not good enough: it is a closed question and as such will generally receive just a "yes" or "no" answer. Instead, try to ask

HOW TO... COMPOSE A HEADS-UP MESSAGE

DEFINE THE SCOPE OF THE TASK
Give a general description of the task to be delegated, e.g. "I've got some figures I need you to analyze."

↓

SET A TIMEFRAME
Describe when work is likely to start and when it will be needed, e.g. "I will brief you on Monday for a deadline on Friday. The task should take about four hours."

↓

ASK THE DELEGATEE TO PREPARE
Let the person know what they can be doing to prepare themselves for the work, e.g. "Can you set aside that amount of time next week?"

↓

SET A MEETING DATE
Give a time and a place for a delegation meeting, e.g. "We'll meet in the boardroom on Monday at 10am. Please bring your diary."

open questions, such as "How do you plan to do this?" This will give you more information about their level of understanding, but it can be quite challenging for the delegatee to answer without time to reflect. The following model for holding a split delegation meeting has proven successful in delegating project tasks to some very difficult characters.

Holding a split meeting

Organize your delegation meeting in two parts separated by a "gap" to give the delegatee time to reflect before being invited to explain how they will approach their task.

• **Part one** Describe what is required, by when, and at what cost; why it is required; and the context and parameters of what is required, including any restrictions on the methods to be adopted. By giving people whole jobs or the context of the whole job you will increase people's understanding and motivation leading to a more satisfactory outcome all round.

• **Gap** Give your colleague time for reflection on their own. Create the gap with a statement such as: "Let me get us a cup of coffee while you stay here and have a think about the task. When I come back you can tell me how you're going to go about doing it and what help you'll need from me."

• **Part two** Ask your colleague to brief you on any modifications they feel should be made to the goal (where appropriate); the way they plan to approach the task; what help they will need from you; and when they would like to review progress.

Once delegation is compete, give your colleague immediate feedback on their contribution, and pass a summary on to their manager where appropriate.

TIP

DON'T SKIP THE GAP

Creating thinking time within a formal meeting structure is important. Although people sometimes protest that they want "time to digest" or that they "haven't got time right now", giving them immediate time for reflection is always worthwhile.

 IN FOCUS... GIVING FEEDBACK

Longer-term delegation benefits greatly from formal (diarized) review and follow-up sessions. Follow the adage: "People don't do what you expect – they do what you inspect!" Ad-hoc checking is generally sloppy and inefficient – in fact, imprecise questions such as: "How are things going?" result in inexact answers, such as: "Oh, fine!", and almost invariably lead to problems at completion with missed deadlines or partial delivery. When reviewing a delegatee's work, accept what is good enough, don't criticize irrelevant details. Accept that a task may have been done differently to how you would have done it.

Maintaining momentum

Project work often requires effort over a prolonged period with little to show for it, so maintaining motivation can be a challenge. Procrastination is an ever-present danger, particularly on tasks that require high levels of concentration or challenging conversations with colleagues or clients.

DON'T PROCRASTINATE

Avoid putting off challenging tasks – every time you do so, you put a brake on your motivation for the project as a whole.

Motivating yourself

Before you can start to motivate your team, you first have to motivate yourself; if you are not enthusiastic there is little chance that others will be. Do this by a combination of revisiting the end result – reminding yourself of its value and what it will be like to achieve it – and monitoring progress. Be alive to the first signs of procrastination and act quickly to ensure internal resistance is never given the chance to build up.

Beating mental blocks

Sometimes you can reach a point of near paralysis on a task. If this happens, try using this technique for re-energizing yourself: take a blank piece of paper and write the task on it. Then write for three minutes continuously about the task. Keep the pen moving, and jot down anything that comes to mind: why the task needs to be done; why you haven't done it; who else is involved; other ways of doing it; and steps to dealing with it. Now go through what you have written and highlight any insights or action points. Decide what one thing you will do immediately to progress the task – and then do it. Most people report an immediate rise in energy which, coupled with an increased understanding of the task, enables them to get over what had built into an insurmountable hurdle in their mind.

Motivating others

Motivating members of your project team can be difficult for a number of reasons:
• Long-term deadlines are always in danger of being pushed into the background by the distractions and crises of the day-to-day workload.
• Non-routine tasks are prone to procrastination.

HOW TO... MOTIVATE YOUR TEAM

Break the project down into meaningful products that can be completed on a regular enough basis to maintain a sense of progress.

↓

Be open about the possibility of procrastination and discuss ways to overcome it.

↓

Always delegate in the context of the overall project.

↓

Find an engaging way to represent progress, rather than just marking ticks on a list (stars on a chart, perhaps, or sweets from a jar).

• Team members may not see a connection between their effort on tasks, the project achieving its objective, and any benefit to them.
• People with a hierarchical mindset may resent doing work for a project manager who is less senior than them. Approach such people positively, but be prepared to escalate a problem as soon as you recognize that it will be beyond your capability to deal with it.

Take positive steps to motivate your team (see above), but also use your risk assessment to identify points where momentum may be lost, recording potential counter-measures in the risk log.

Communicating successfully

As the project manager, you are the hub of all communication within the project team and between the project team and the outside world. At different stages of the project you will find yourself dealing with different stakeholders, but the three constant axes of communication you need to maintain are with the sponsor, the client, and the team.

TIP

PASS ON KEY INFORMATION

Operate a "no surprises" policy in your dealings with the sponsor – he or she should never have to say "You should have told me about this before."

Engaging your sponsor and client

Communication with the sponsor should be characterized by a high level of openness and trust from the start of the project. Spend time establishing how your communication will work. Discuss scheduled communication (such as diarized review meetings) and agree on when and how you expect ad-hoc communication to take place. Give warning of any decisions that need to be made and present facts to the sponsor in a written form for consideration. Record notes of all meetings, in particular any action points.

Communication with the client will tend to be more formal than with the sponsor. The challenge is often to be assertive, particularly when requesting decisions, access, or information. As with the sponsor, give the client notice of any decisions. The client relationship can occasionally contain an element of politics, particularly if the client is under pressure from members of his or her organization. As a general rule, aim to do everything you can to make your client look good. If it becomes apparent that this is not possible, use the sponsor to bypass the obstacle.

? ASK YOURSELF... AM I A GOOD LISTENER?

- Do I quieten my self-talk, so that I can focus on the speaker and understand his or her perspective?
- Do I clarify vague statements, to find out whether what the person is saying is factually and logically correct?
- Do I try to assess how people are feeling, and ask probing questions to understand what lies behind those emotions?

Talking to your team

Maintain an open and honest relationship with your team. In large teams, there is always a danger of some people being left out of the loop when decisions are made or new information becomes available. Make sure you have accurate distribution lists set up for email and documents. On larger and longer-running projects, you may find it helpful to post general information on an intranet site to which team members have access.

Choosing the method

Care is needed when selecting the medium by which you will communicate a particular message. Sending a sensitive message by email, for example, runs the risk of a potentially damaging misunderstanding with the recipient. Before pressing "send", take time to think about your purpose in communicating, what you want the outcome to be, and how "complex" the message is in emotional and intellectual terms.

Selecting a medium for your message

HIGH

Emotional complexity

Message: simple but emotionally charged, possibly requiring action from the recipient

Medium:
• Ad-hoc meeting
• Telephone conversation

Message: complex, with a high risk of misunderstanding or hurt feelings; need for the recipient to buy in to an idea and perhaps take action

Medium:
• Formal meeting
• Video conference

Message: simple, with a low risk of misunderstanding or hurt feelings; no need for high levels of emotional buy in

Medium:
• Voicemail message
• Email
• Note on the desk

Message: intellectually complex but emotionally non-contentious facts and figures

Medium:
• Fax
• Email
• Letter
• Memorandum

LOW   **Intellectual complexity**   **HIGH**

Reviewing progress

Getting the team together is costly in both time and resources, but well-run review meetings are an essential ingredient in any project, offering you the opportunity to check past progress and confirm future direction. They also renew people's identification with your project team.

Keeping track of progress

An effective review meeting should be one part of a continuous cycle of activity. Prior to every meeting, each team member should work towards completing their tasks, and if they fail to do this within the set timeframe, non-completion should be reported to you. Use this information to formulate and circulate an agenda for the review meeting, with minutes of the last meeting attached as preparatory reading. At the meeting, start by discussing progress since your last

RUNNING SUCCESSFUL REVIEWS

FAST TRACK	**OFF TRACK**
Sending the agenda for the meeting in advance	Holding ad-hoc review meetings with no preparation
Ensuring that agenda items run to time, without having to be rushed	Allowing the discussion to wander and side issues to dominate
Allocating action points to attendees with agreed deadlines	Assuming that everyone will know what they have to do
Finishing with a discussion about what has been learnt for next time	Accepting excuses without discussing how things can change

✔ CHECKLIST PREPARING TO CHAIR A REVIEW MEETING

	YES	NO
• Are you up to date with all aspects of your own project work? (If your project work is behind schedule, you won't have the authority to chase others for theirs.)	☐	☐
• Do you know who will be there and how they are doing with the tasks they have been set?	☐	☐
• Have you set aside extra time so that you can arrange the room and set up equipment before other people arrive?	☐	☐
• Are you feeling calm? (If you are stressed, this is likely to rub off on other people.)	☐	☐
• Are you prepared to challenge people who have not done what they are committed to, or who are behaving in a disruptive manner?	☐	☐

review, then make decisions about what tasks need to be completed before the next time you meet. Delegate specific actions to individuals. Record these actions in "Action minutes", which should be circulated as soon after the meeting as possible to give people the best chance of completing their tasks prior to the next meeting.

Scheduling review meetings

Review meetings can be scheduled as a regular event – at the same time of every day, for example, or on the same day of every week or month. Alternatively, the meetings can be fixed to the expected delivery date of certain products or to stages of the project. Both of these approaches have their strengths and weaknesses: regular meetings in the same place and at the same time are more prone to "game playing" and a lack of concentration amongst attendees, but meetings set by the delivery dates of your project are more difficult to schedule to ensure that everyone can attend.

TIP

KEEP IT BRIEF
During busy periods, hold short "stand-up" review meetings early in the day, or at a point when most people would expect to be taking a break. Insist on a prompt start, brief contributions, and no deviation from the main purpose of reviewing progress and coordinating activity through the next period.

Managing project information

"Filing" lacks the star quality of other aspects of project work and rarely rates in people's top three most enjoyable or rewarding job roles. Nevertheless, if you want to be in full control of your project, management of paper-based and electronic information is essential.

Assembling your project file

Set up a project folder or filing system to manage your project documentation as part of the initiation phase of your project. Compile a checklist – the document schedule – listing the records that it contains, and place this at the front of your project file. This will enable anyone looking for a document to see at a glance whether it is in the file. Use the

The contents of a project file

1 DOCUMENT SCHEDULE

Like the index in a book, the document schedule should tell you at a glance what paperwork the file contains. It can be a useful checklist: score through the documents that are not needed and put the date of entry for any document you put into the file

4 CHANGES TO SCOPE RECORDS

Keep these records close to the definition documents so that the material they contain is always accessed alongside the original scope to which they refer.

5 PROJECT PLAN AND BUDGET

Always keep the baseline plan and budget in the file, along with the most up-to-date versions. Archive intermediate versions elsewhere to avoid confusion.

TIP

TAG YOUR DOCUMENTS

Use different colours of paper for different types of document (minutes, sign-offs, etc.), and mark every project document with the date/time of creation and a version number from the outset.

document schedule to structure your conversation with the sponsor about the various records that will be required at different points in the project.

Even small projects can generate large amounts of paperwork, so it is important that you plan how you will organize the contents of your file. Version control can be helpful, because the drafting and signing-off processes can generate multiple versions of individual documents. Mark every document with a version number, and keep archive versions (back copies you are keeping pending a final review, for example) in a separate part of the project file from "reference" information – such as the current project plan – that is in regular use.

File active documents (those requiring a specific future action) in date order using a "Bring Forward" file, and use the reminder system in your electronic task list or calendar to flag important dates.

2 TEAM ORGANIZATION CHART

Keep a chart setting out who is doing what in your team. This allows anyone examining the file to see who they should approach on a particular matter. Include contact information and distribution lists.

3 DEFINITION DOCUMENTS

Keep a suite of documents that set out the definition of your project. This may include the mandate, brief, business case, PID, and any legal contracts or client agreements.

6 RISK LOG

You will refer to this document almost as often as you do to your plan and budget, so make sure you keep the risk log in your project file up to date with constant review.

7 THE MINUTES OF REVIEW MEETINGS

Keep records of minutes that include live action points or significant points of reference in the project file. Archive all others to ensure the file doesn't become cluttered or confused.

Monitoring costs

While it is important for you to monitor the schedule of the project and maintain focus on the outcome, it is equally vital that you keep track of the costs your project is incurring. Failure to do so can result in a project that, while seemingly successful is, in fact, uneconomic.

Managing project accounts

Effective cost monitoring throughout the lifecycle of a project is important for a number of reasons: it enables you to give the sponsor a true picture of progress whenever you are asked for it; it reduces risk by ensuring decisions to modify or cancel the project are taken early; it identifies areas of inefficiency; and it provides valuable information for planning future projects. Keeping track of your costs is also important because it could highlight theft or fraud. Like any other pot of money, project budgets occasionally attract criminal attention. If you are the person responsible for controlling expenditure, you may be liable unless you can demonstrate that you have used suitable procedures for monitoring costs.

CASE STUDY

Adjusting to change

The property department in a law firm won a contract to review 6,000 files for a local government agency. They priced the job at £900k, based on two hours per file after a start-up period. This proved accurate – experienced team members took just under two hours per file. However, the volume of work and tight schedule meant that morale dipped and staff turnover increased. The constant need to induct new staff pushed the average time per file for the first thousand files up to 2 hours 15 minutes. This would have caused the contract to overshoot by 12.5 per cent, costing the firm £112.5k in lost revenue. The head of the department negotiated secondments from other departments to spread the workload, and offered incentives to raise morale. Thanks to the early intervention, productivity returned to less than two hours per file, and the project hit its projected profit margin.

Keeping track of costs

If you are managing a small project, you may not have a budget for out-of-pocket costs – paid to external organizations for materials or services – but you would do well to keep track of the invisible cost of the work undertaken by your internal team. Particularly in a multi-project environment, timesheets provide a mechanism for charging costs back to the right client or cost centre.

Out-of-pocket costs generally attract heavy scrutiny. Nevertheless this budget can come under pressure either because of inaccurate estimates at the definition stage, additional features added to the scope without parallel increases in the budget, or poor risk management. If you are responsible for the budget, ensure you are clear on the reasons for any unforeseen expenditure before authorizing payment. Check the impact on other aspects of the budget: are you using money for desirable but non-essential features, leaving later essential features under-funded?

Dealing with cost overruns

Not every cost overrun is serious – sometimes costs run ahead of plan simply because work is progressing more quickly than anticipated. On other occasions, you may have underestimated the cost of a "one-off" item of expenditure, but feel this is likely to be offset by an overestimate elsewhere. The point at which even a minor overspend should be taken seriously is when it is early warning that you have underestimated a whole class of activity upon which the project depends. Tell the sponsor as soon as you perceive that unforeseen costs may require an increase in the overall project budget. If the budget is fixed (critical), identify any non-essential features you can remove from the scope to bring costs back in line.

HOW TO... MONITOR INVISIBLE COSTS

Use a timesheet system to keep track of time spent by your internal team.

↓

Allocate a financial value to the time recorded on the timesheets.

↓

Base calculations on the worker's salary broken down into an hourly rate.

↓

Add in the overhead cost of employing that person (heating, lighting, office space, etc.)

Chapter 4

Going live

At the end of every project, there comes a point at which whatever it has produced needs to be handed over to the end users. As the culmination of all your efforts, this should be an exciting time for the project manager, but there will also be challenges to face, and careful management is required to deliver a smooth handover and a successful outcome.

Implementing the project

Ensuring that the client, the team, and your organization have a positive experience as your project "goes live" is one of a project manager's most important responsibilities. The decisions you make during every phase of your project's lifecycle should be with implementation in mind.

Overcoming challenges

Implementation is primarily a client-focused phase of a project. However, you should also consider its significance for the end user, the project team, and your organization. As the project goes live, end users have to assimilate changes and come out of their comfort zone, while project team members have to let go of a project and move on to something new. Your organization simply wants swift and trouble-free implementation in order to realize the benefits of their investment. Your role as project manager is to help all three groups deal with these challenges.

KEY ACTIONS FOR SUCCESSFUL IMPLEMENTATION

PHASE OF PROJECT	ACTIONS
Initiation phase Describe the issue to be addressed or opportunity to be exploited.	• Conduct research among end users to establish how widespread the issue or opportunity is. • Document findings and, where confidentiality allows, circulate them to those who contributed.
Definition phase Design an end product that satisfies the need identified in initiation.	• Wherever possible, design the product in consultation with the client/end user – attribute good ideas to those who offered them. • Give an indicative date for implementation. • Use prototypes and mock-ups to bring the idea alive both for the client and the project team.
Planning phase Design a communications plan that delivers the information that different stakeholders need; and ensure the resources are available for successful implementation.	• Find out what aspects of progress the stakeholders are interested in and how frequently they want reports, then create a communications plan to deliver this. • Plan in time and budget for implementation activities such as rehearsals, marketing, training, and change management. • Book facilities, equipment, and personnel required for implementation as soon as you have a launch timetable.
Control phase Ensure all stakeholders are kept informed on progress and manage people's expectations.	• Deliver the communications plan, and take advantage of any unexpected opportunities to promote your project. • Find opportunities for listening to stakeholders' hopes and concerns. • Tell all stakeholders about any changes to the product or launch date, explaining why these have occurred. • Create the materials (documentation, guides, manuals, etc.) required to support implementation. • Train those who will support the product once it has gone live. • Recruit end users who will test the product as soon as it is ready for implementation. • Plan and rehearse implementation events.
Implementation phase Present the product in the most positive way possible, demonstrating an understanding of all stakeholders' needs.	• Get end users to test what you have produced (User Acceptance Testing). • Hold implementation events to roll out the end product. • Train or brief end users and distribute supporting documentation as necessary. • Get the sponsor to inspect the finished product and sign it off as complete. • Hold a celebratory event with the project team. • Reassign project personnel, providing feedback to them and their managers as appropriate.

Preparing for handover

Although the majority of work has been done, projects can sometimes stall at the implementation stage. You may run out of budget, or lose members of your team to other projects, or there may be last-minute changes from the client as they realize that implementation is imminent. Careful management at this stage ensures that your handover to the end users goes as smoothly as possible.

TIP

HOLD ON TO YOUR TEAM

Tell team members that they are finished on your project only when you are absolutely clear that this is the case.

Managing the final stages

As a project nears completion, team members can often feel jaded; the novelty that drew them to the project in the first place has become a distant memory. To reinvigorate your team, hold a pre-implementation meeting with all those involved, including clients and end users wherever possible. The core purpose of this meeting is to produce a detailed route map through to completion, but a well-run meeting can do wonders for your team's motivation and focus – especially if they see the client's enthusiasm for what you are about to deliver.

HOW TO...
HOLD A PRE-IMPLEMENTATION MEETING

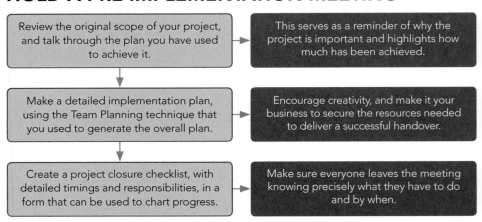

Review the original scope of your project, and talk through the plan you have used to achieve it.

This serves as a reminder of why the project is important and highlights how much has been achieved.

Make a detailed implementation plan, using the Team Planning technique that you used to generate the overall plan.

Encourage creativity, and make it your business to secure the resources needed to deliver a successful handover.

Create a project closure checklist, with detailed timings and responsibilities, in a form that can be used to chart progress.

Make sure everyone leaves the meeting knowing precisely what they have to do and by when.

Steering the end game

Your role in the lead up to implementation is primarily one of problem solving and coordination of the activity required for the project to "go live". Get round and see all stakeholders, particularly team members. Show an interest in what they are doing but resist the temptation to step in unless they really cannot do what has been asked of them without your help. Increase the frequency of review as you get close to your final date, but do not allow these meetings to get in the way of the work they should be doing. If everyone is in the same building, for example, a 10-minute "stand-up" meeting may work best, while conference calls are a sensible alternative for multi-site projects.

Running final tests

For some projects, User Acceptance Testing* is one of the last steps before implementation. Most frequently found in software development, UAT can be applied in a variety of situations. The testing is carried out by a representative panel of end users, who work through as many different scenarios as necessary to be sure that the product will perform as expected when it goes live. UAT must not be used to confirm that the product is what the end users want – that should have been defined in the project scope and any subsequent "changes to scope" documents.

*User Acceptance Testing (UAT) — the final technical test of a product, to make sure that it works as it is supposed to.

Handing the project over

The way in which a project "goes live" varies from project to project depending on the nature of its product. With time-critical projects there is rarely any doubt about the "go live" point, but where quality is the critical factor the opposite is often the case, and it takes a conscious effort to mark the point at which a project is complete.

TAKE ADVICE

Speak to your sponsor about your plans for marking "go live". Ultimately it is up to him or her to decide when the project is complete.

Signalling the end point

Projects are different to business as usual because they have an end point at which they can be declared complete and then have their success evaluated. Even if you are the only person working on a project, it is still helpful to mark the "go live" point, to signal that the project is finished before moving on.

For most projects, implementation should coincide with the transference of responsibility from the project team to an ongoing support function. Perversely, the better you and your team have been at managing the client while the project was underway, the more difficult you will find it to get them to transfer their allegiance to a new group. By marking the "go live" point, you make a definitive statement to your client that the time has come for this to happen.

✔ CHECKLIST MARKING "GO LIVE"

	YES	NO
• Have I made a clear declaration to all stakeholders that the project is complete?	☐	☐
• Have I clearly signalled to the client and end users that they are now responsible for the product?	☐	☐
• Have I marked the point at which project personnel are available for other assignments?	☐	☐
• Have I taken the opportunity to say thank you to those who have contributed to the project?	☐	☐

CASE STUDY

Oiling the wheels

A project manager charged with moving 40 people from an office in the heart of the West End of London to more spacious but cheaper premises in a less affluent part of London faced a challenge to ensure smooth implementation: the move was for financial reasons and no-one wanted to go. He decided to put together a welcome pack for each member of staff, and asked every shop, bar, café, restaurant, and gym in the area around the new offices whether they would make introductory offers to the newcomers on production of their company ID cards. On the day of the move, he placed the finished pack – worth approximately £100 of discounted goods and services – on each desk in the new offices. The offers it contained actively encouraged people to explore the area rather than simply sitting at their desks and complaining about their new surroundings. And when they did take up the offers, they found that they were welcomed as valuable additional custom.

Holding an event

Hold a "go live" event (perhaps couched as a final review meeting) in which you review the whole project. Evaluate the changes and benefits it has achieved. Consider how you can organize or stage manage the event so that there are things for people to see, do, and talk about. However, the watchword is appropriateness – if you over-play "go live" you lay yourself open to accusations of self-promotion. Involve the project sponsor in the event – get him or her to offer an assessment of the project and thank all those who have contributed.

Another pretext for an event might be to introduce the client or end users to the people who are about to take on responsibility for supporting them. Reiterate the post-implementation support that will be available and how snagging will take place. Snagging is the process of identifying and resolving minor defects that takes place during the implementation phase, prior to the project being declared complete. Make sure that everyone understands the part you need them to play in bedding the project in.

Providing support

In a quality-critical project, the quality of post-implementation support given to the end user is essential to its long-term success. Never declare a project complete until the end user has been trained to use the product and first-line support is available from outside the project team.

Evaluating success

Once the end product has been delivered, the project manager's final act should be to review the outcome of the project and evaluate its overall success. It can often be illuminating to make this post-implementation review against both the original scope and any subsequent modifications.

Analyzing the outcome

You should review the success of your project in a number of ways. Firstly, look at your immediate impression: did the project deliver what was expected? This level of review is best done at the same time as implementation – indeed it should be part of the sign-off procedure involving sponsor, client, and project manager. The review process should also look at whether the project has delivered a long-term benefit. In time-critical projects, this may already be at least partly evident at implementation or shortly afterwards, but in quality-critical projects the benefits may take longer to become clear. Finally, your evaluation should look at the benefits gained in business terms. Was the project worth it financially?

TIP

INVOLVE THE SPONSOR

Try to get the sponsor involved in the review process – experience suggests that without their involvement, the review rarely gets done as people are busy and move on to the next job.

EXPRESS YOUR THANKS
Hand write a personal letter to each team member expressing thanks for his or her personal contribution, making the effort to write something different in each one.

COMMEMORATE THE OCCASION
Have a team photograph taken or a group caricature drawn, create a collage of memorable moments, or frame an appropriate piece of the project plan and give it to each team member with a hand-written comment.

Ideas for celebrating success

GIVE A PROJECT GIFT
Give an inscribed desk ornament, to thank people for taking part. This does not have to be expensive but should be tasteful, fun, and/or useful. A distinctive pen or mug often stays around for a long time if the associations with the project were positive ones.

GIVE BONUSES
Team members will always appreciate a cash bonus, if funds are available.

GIVE A PERSONAL REWARD
Send an appropriate gift to members of the team at their homes with a personalized note: a bottle of Champagne, a bunch of flowers, vouchers for a spa, or tickets for an event can all deliver a far bigger message than the money that they cost.

ALLOCATE FUNDS
Put a small "celebration fund" into the project budget, which increases or decreases depending on whether the project is in front or behind time and budget. At the end of the project, hold a social event, involving everyone who contributed, at which you and the sponsor (and client if appropriate) can express your thanks.

Reviewing the process

A "lessons learnt" review allows you to learn from the process you have been through and helps you find ways to improve your project management. Because the project process should be repeatable, the main purpose of review is to establish what went well, what could have gone better, and what you can do to improve future projects.

Looking back at your project

The review process is your chance to learn from experience. It is not just about spotting errors or identifying parts of the process that did not run as smoothly as they could have – evaluation of what was successful is equally informative. If something worked particularly well (such as a technique or a supplier), it should be noted for future reference.

However, inevitably there will be some things that go wrong in your projects, and these also provide valuable lessons for the future. Although they may have been unforeseeable the first time they occurred, by taking the time to understand what has happened and why, you should be able to gain insights that would otherwise be missed, and take action to prevent their recurrence in future projects.

PLANNING PROJECTS FOR LEARNING

FAST TRACK

OFF TRACK

FAST TRACK	OFF TRACK
Establishing quality assurance procedures from the outset	Allowing an experienced project team to perform their roles out of habit
Giving personal learning objectives for the project to all team members	Being cynical about the organization's ability to do things differently
Including "lessons learnt" as a regular agenda item for meetings	Considering change a threat to what has been successful in the past
Having a team culture characterized by high levels of feedback	Allowing a blame culture, in which it is dangerous to admit mistakes
Establishing mechanisms for disseminating new ideas	Holding the project plan centrally and discouraging discussion of its details

Learning from the details

When reviewing the project, consider all aspects of the process in detail. Do not rely on opinions about what went well or make assumptions about what went wrong: talk to those involved and try to discover the facts. When these are in dispute, ask for evidence. Be curious about why things happened, and explore how this could inform future project decisions. When searching for the truth, be sensitive to the feelings of those involved: reviews should never become witch-hunts.

Once you have a good understanding of how everything worked, make sure that you act on your findings. Project learning is done for a purpose – to improve performance on future projects. Don't keep useful information and ideas to yourself – pass them on to where they can make a difference.

Holding a project review

A "lessons learnt" review meeting is your opportunity to get the team together and discuss how the project went. Hold the meeting as soon as implementation is complete – you can always call a second one, if necessary, once the project has bedded in. Far from duplicating effort, you will find that you actually save time using this approach, because memories are clearer and conclusions are reached more quickly.

Involve as many stakeholders as is practical in this meeting. A process review should take account of the views of everyone involved, within the constraints of cost, time, and availability. If possible, include the views of the client and end user, although in commercial projects, you may need to think carefully about how you are going to get these.

Be clear on what you want to achieve and have an agenda for the meeting. A review meeting can become unfocused and descend into generalizations unless there are specific items to discuss. If you have held interim learning reviews, use the notes from these as a structure. If not, then the PID, plan, and risk log can be a good basis for discussion.

TIP

PLAN AHEAD
Set a date for the review meeting when you are planning the implementation of the project – this should make it easier to get the time in people's diaries.

? ASK YOURSELF... WHAT CAN WE LEARN FROM THIS PROJECT?

- How good was our original scope?
- How accurate were the time and cost estimates?
- Did we have the right mix of people on our team?
- How effectively did the stakeholders work together?
- Where might we have anticipated risks better?
- How effectively did the technology we used perform?
- How well did our project methodology work?
- What project documents were most useful? Which, if any, were missing?

Documenting your review

Brevity is often the key to a successful project review document, so record the recommendations that you generate following the "lessons learnt" review meeting succinctly. Aim for three key learning points clearly described so that anyone encountering a similar problem in the future can implement your recommendations. If you have to write more because the project was large and complex, structure the document in a way that enables people to gain an overview quickly and then select only the detail that is relevant to them. It can be useful to generate a main document that you distribute to all stakeholders – containing a limited number of key recommendations for the conduct of future projects – and a number of annexes. These can either cover each recommendation in detail or provide more detailed feedback to specific individuals or departments.

Discuss your recommendations with the sponsor. Even if the sponsor does not want to be fully involved in the review process, at the very least you should discuss the findings with him or her before disseminating them to a wider audience.

TIP

THINK SMALL
Don't underestimate the value of small, easily implemented improvements to your approach. A "lessons learnt" review should identify several of these, and their combined effect can be significant.

Giving personal feedback

The review phase of your project should also look at the performance of individual members of your team. Although you should have been giving regular feedback throughout the project, people appreciate a final review once it is completed, especially when they've put a lot of effort into making a project successful. You will find that the best workers use feedback from project reviews as a way to build their CV or gather testimonials. Equally, people will be more likely to make a second effort if they know that failure will be investigated and recorded.

ACHIEVING HIGH PERFORMANCE

Contents

Introduction

There is no single technique for achieving excellence at work. High performance is attained through a combination of understanding yourself and your strengths and limitations; knowing what you want to achieve; and ensuring you are in an environment where you enjoy working and have some freedom to achieve what you want. *Achieving High Performance* gives you the tools you need to address these areas, and so become more successful at what you do.

Your route to improvement starts by getting to know yourself. The more fully you understand yourself, the more confident you will be. By understanding and playing to your strengths, you have a better chance of succeeding at your endeavours. Of course, you need to develop skills and knowledge in your chosen fields. There are some skills, such as managing your time and presenting, that will apply whatever you are doing and wherever you are doing it. These are like the tools in your work box, and the key to acquiring and honing them is to practise.

To become more effective at work, you need to be creative and confident, to communicate and listen well, and to make difficult decisions. If you can master these sometimes intangible skills, you can really differentiate yourself from other people. Finally, achieving high performance is about developing your skills further into management and leadership, broadening your horizons, and making use of what other people have to offer you.

Chapter 1

Knowing yourself

To prosper in both life and business you need to understand yourself. What are your strengths and limitations, what do you enjoy, and what do you really want to achieve? By reflecting upon and analyzing your own characteristics, and how you are perceived by others, you can begin to produce a plan for self-development and ultimate success.

Looking in from outside

Other people's perceptions of you may be significantly at odds with your own view of yourself. Finding out what others think of you is an important element of self-exploration, and helps you modify your behaviour so that you can take up opportunities that you might otherwise have missed.

MAKE AN IMPRESSION
Lasting judgements can be made, based on subconscious cues, within the first few seconds of meeting. Think about any visual cues you display and the tone of voice you use – these can often be more significant than what you actually say.

Seeking new perspectives

You may feel you lack confidence, or that you are too quiet, but others may see you primarily as someone who is trustworthy, honourable, and wise. Conversely, you may describe yourself as assertive and confident, while others see you as aggressive and avoid involving you in their projects. Other people's views are important because they shape the way they behave towards you. That's not to say you should always aim to please others, or change the person you are, but being aware of how others see you will enable you to change the signals you send out.

Getting answers

The only way to find out what others think of you is to ask. Many international companies use a process called 360-degree feedback, which is a formal means of eliciting comment from colleagues, staff, and bosses. It is often used to develop senior management teams, but you can carry out a similar process yourself on a smaller scale. Approach people who see you in different roles – perhaps your business partner, work colleagues at the same management level, your immediate boss, some of your suppliers and clients, and a couple of friends. Think of the best way to ask the questions: a questionnaire has the advantage of ensuring consistency, while structured face-to-face interviews give respondents the chance to elaborate, but may also inhibit honest responses. When drafting a questionnaire, keep it short and simple, and concentrate on specific questions that you really want answered, such as:

• How confident do I appear to you?
• Am I approachable?
• Do I communicate clearly?

Using feedback

The feedback process won't give you a definitive view of what you are like in the eyes of others, but it is certain to produce some valuable insights. It's too easy to focus on criticisms when you see them in black and white, so make sure that you value and reflect on the positive points that emerge, and use them in your planning for the future.

 IN FOCUS... PSYCHOMETRIC TESTING

Psychometric tests, such as the widely used Myers Briggs, offer a more scientific approach to self-understanding. These tests look at personality and attempt to give an indication of the type of environment in which an individual is likely to thrive. Myers Briggs positions people against four pairs of factors:
• Extroversion and introversion
• Sensing and intuition
• Thinking and feeling
• Judging and perceiving.

There is nothing wrong with any of these traits. However, if, for example, you are at the extreme end of the scale on "thinking", you may be ignoring people's feelings when you make decisions. If you are a "perceiving" rather than a "judging" person, you may need to set more goals and deadlines for yourself.

Setting goals

Work takes up a large chunk of your life, so job satisfaction is important. Achieving it doesn't necessarily mean changing job, it could just be a matter of broadening your existing role. Knowing what you enjoy and want to achieve will help ensure you're in the right job. If you're in the right job, you're more likely to succeed at what you do.

TIP

THINK BIG

Reach for the sky – it is important to dream before you do a reality check.

Examining your ambitions

Getting a clear view of your ambitions is not quite as easy as it seems. First, you may have arrived where you are more by chance than by design and it can be hard to avoid being influenced by your current situation. So, if you are working in sales, you may not look beyond a future in which you progress through the ranks to become sales manager and then sales director. Second, you will have family ties or other responsibilities that limit your freedom to follow your dreams. Third, your "ideal" job will change over time as you develop skills and experience.

Looking at the future

There are many ways to look systematically at your career and life goals. Some prefer to work with a coach – an objective, sympathetic, and experienced person who can help identify directions for progress. Others favour less formal consultation with their colleagues or peers, but it is equally valid to work through the options on your own. Indeed, the question is so central that it is worth applying more than one approach and repeating the analysis from time to time as your circumstances change.

Visualizing the way

Visualization is a technique that can help you clarify your goals. Set aside some time to sit undisturbed and relaxed. Picture yourself at various points in the future, say in three, five, and ten years' time. Think graphically and generate images of your ideal world, asking yourself questions such as:
• Where will I be living?
• What job will I have?
• What type of organization will I be working in?
• Will I own and be running my own business?
• What will I be doing on a day-to-day basis?

HOW TO...
DISCOVER WHAT IS IMPORTANT TO YOU

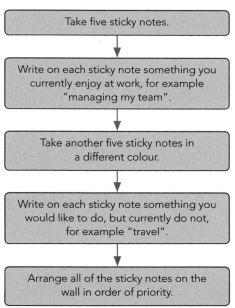

Take five sticky notes.

Write on each sticky note something you currently enjoy at work, for example "managing my team".

Take another five sticky notes in a different colour.

Write on each sticky note something you would like to do, but currently do not, for example "travel".

Arrange all of the sticky notes on the wall in order of priority.

• Will I have a team working for me or will I be a specialist?
• Will I be commuting or working from home, perhaps?
• What will my interests be?
Note down your thoughts and assess the picture that emerges against fixed constraints, such as your obligations to family.

Now reflect on the results. How can you work towards being where you would like to be? This process is not intended to make you dissatisfied with your present circumstances, but to open your eyes to new possibilities.

Analyzing your strengths and limitations

To achieve high performance in your workplace, you need to understand and play to your strengths. You also need to recognize what you are less good at doing, so that you can develop appropriate skills and acquire the necessary knowledge and experience.

REVIEW YOUR SKILLS
Even if you plan to stay in the same job, look closely at what's happening around you. Your work environment is in flux and you should constantly be learning and adapting, to cope with the new circumstances it presents you with.

Describing your capabilities

When you ask yourself what you are really good at, your answer should encompass three areas – your basic technical ability, your innate, or soft, skills, and the knowledge and experience that you have acquired.

Most people have a preference for what they like to do. Some are good at working with numbers, while others excel at languages. These skills are the building blocks of your job – sometimes called your basic technical ability.

Gaining skills and experience

"Soft" skills are less tangible than basic technical ability. You may be a good listener or a powerful communicator, or have the ability to influence people or negotiate well, or you may command respect, have great presence, and be highly motivated. You need to achieve a certain level of skill in these areas, but that level will depend on your precise role.

The third dimension of your personal strengths and limitations is your knowledge and experience, both of the sector and the role in which you work. For example, if you work in Human Resources, do you have sufficient knowledge of employment law? Reflect on your skills and knowledge: they may be good enough for your current role, but will they suffice in the future? Try to identify the role that best fits with your ambitions, and ask yourself what skills you'll need to fit that role. Published job descriptions and job advertisements provide a good guide to what employers are looking for. Set about gaining those skills through additional training, or by realigning your role with your current employer.

Carrying out a SWOT analysis

A simple way to assess yourself is to carry out a SWOT analysis. List your strengths and weaknesses, and the opportunities open and threats to you in your current role, as in the example below. This provides a picture of the development you need to excel in your present situation, and the skills, knowledge, and experience you'll need to acquire for your next role.

SWOT analysis for a Human Resources executive

POSITIVE	NEGATIVE
STRENGTHS • Experience in training • Presentation skills • Good communicator • Good knowledge of employment law	**WEAKNESSES** • Poor understanding of recruitment systems • No experience of disciplinary meetings • Don't like conflict
OPPORTUNITIES • Set up my own training business • Broaden my role to include recruitment	**THREATS** • Company may outsource training • Company may want all-round HR skills in the future

Developing your brand

We have looked at the importance of how other people see you and of understanding yourself, your strengths and limitations, and your ambitions. Developing your brand* is about how you bring these together, use them to differentiate yourself from other people, and develop your career.

Giving the right impression

*Brand — a unique and consistent set of values that underpins a product or service.

TIP

FOLLOW YOUR CUSTOMERS' LEAD

Match your personal style to that of your customers – it will help you create rapport with them.

Just as a company builds its brand, you need to know what you stand for and how you want to project yourself to others, and make sure the messages you give out are consistent with that. This doesn't mean you should try to be something you aren't. That may work for a short time but it's impossible to keep up over a long period. Your "brand" has to be something you are comfortable with. It should reflect your values and be uniquely yours.

There are some aspects of the way you look, sound, and behave that are essential to your brand, wherever you are working. Paying attention to your appearance, whatever your style, being polite, and fulfilling your promises, for example, are all "musts". Your brand needs to take into account your "target audience", such as the organization you work for and the customers you work with. If you work for an old-fashioned firm of lawyers, for example, wearing the latest fashion in shorts and large hooped earrings probably won't inspire your clients with confidence, but it may do if you work for a high-fashion retailer.

While appearance is important, how you behave becomes far more important as time progresses. If you look the part but fail to do what you have been asked or are bad-tempered and difficult, then no amount of image makeovers will help you succeed. The key to defining your brand is to pay attention to every element of the image you project.

What defines your brand?

LOOKING THE PART

- **The clothes, shoes, and jewellery you wear** – style and colours
- **The way you hold yourself** – no hunched shoulders
- **The way you style your hair** – always well groomed, but style is a matter of taste
- **The way you move** – with a purpose
- **The appearance of your hands and nails** – clean at all times and nail varnish appropriate to your situation

SOUNDING THE PART

- **The tone of your voice** – lower-pitched voices carry more weight
- **The pace of your speech** – slow enough to sound purposeful but not hesitant
- **The words you choose** – short, active, and positive, or longer and more descriptive?
- **The expression in your voice** – smiling makes you sound approachable and friendly

ACTING THE PART

- Shaking hands firmly, but not squeezing too hard
- Saying thank you
- Returning phone calls or emails within a reasonable time
- Respecting other people's views
- Giving other people the credit due to them
- Doing what you have promised to do
- Standing your ground when necessary

Planning the future

There is a saying that "all plans are useless, but planning is vital". Plans are useless as they become out of date very quickly. But without the process of planning, you won't prepare for the future. You need to plan, but don't stick to your plans so rigidly that you miss opportunities.

Knowing where you're going

Life is unpredictable, so why plan? First, all of the things you want to achieve in your life require effort and preparation. You need to ensure you acquire the qualifications and experience that will allow you to progress in your chosen career, and to do that, you need a plan. Having a plan gives you a framework against which to measure your progress. Have you achieved what you set out to do? If not, why not? What can you learn from your successes and failures? A plan also provides a reference against which you can judge new opportunities. How much will this opportunity contribute to achieving your goals? If it doesn't, why do you want to do it? Is it a distraction or have your goals and plan changed?

 IN FOCUS... WHAT'S ON YOUR CV?

One good way to plan the future is to create a version of your CV three, five, and ten years in the future. What qualifications would appear? What job titles would you have? Which companies would you have worked for? What experience would you have gained in each of the roles you have undertaken? If you don't know what to put on the CV, why not look in the papers or on the Internet for job advertisements. They will tell you what people are looking for when filling these roles today. Although this won't change dramatically, certain aspects, such as qualifications, computer literacy, and international experience, will be more in demand. So by looking at the job requirements today and thinking about the future, you should be able to construct an outline future CV to work towards.

HAVING AN EFFECTIVE FUTURE PLAN

FAST TRACK

OFF TRACK

FAST TRACK	OFF TRACK
Defining key measurable goals that logically lead to achieving your vision	Relying on chance rather than your own efforts
Setting goals that are believable and achievable	Choosing goals with unattainable qualifiers (e.g. needing to be born in a certain country if you weren't)
Always using your plan when making big real-life decisions	Reviewing and revising your plan infrequently

Creating a plan

A good plan needs to include four key elements:
• A vision statement that describes where you want to be
• A set of objectives that, if achieved, will lead you to the vision
• A "success map" showing how these objectives link together
• An indicator describing what success will look like at each stage.

Think first about your vision of the future: is it all about a single goal, such as becoming president of a multi-national company, or is it about a lifestyle, such as being a wealthy and respected partner in a law firm? Use some of the exercises described over the previous pages to help you to think about your vision. Next,

write your vision down in a vision statement. This should not be longer than a paragraph, but needs to contain all the attributes that are important to you. Spend time on this; it is the important first step in planning your future.

Developing a vision

Once you have a clear idea of your overall vision for the future, break it down into its main constituent parts. Do this by creating a set of top-level objectives you will need to achieve to reach your vision. Between two and five objectives should suffice, with each objective relating to a major theme in your vision. These objectives will form the top level of your success map.

Creating a success map for your future

A success map is a useful tool for thinking through the key actions you need to take to achieve your goals and for representing these in a single picture.

• To create your success map start from the top – your ultimate goal. Write this at the top of your map.

• Think about how you will achieve this goal. For example, imagine your vision is to become sales director for a major pharmaceutical company. To achieve this goal, you will need to have been a regional sales manager for three to five years, to have handled some major clients within your portfolio, and to have gained a professional sales qualification. These objectives become the second-level goals on your success map.

• Next, ask yourself how to achieve these objectives, and fill in the next level of your map.

• At all stages, use arrows to connect later objectives that are dependent on you having first achieved earlier objectives.

• To check that your success map is complete and follows a logical progression, work up from the bottom. For each objective, ask "Why am I doing this?" – the answer should be to obtain the objective above.

? ASK YOURSELF... AM I ON TRACK TO REACH MY GOAL?

Create an indicator of success for each of the objectives in your success map by asking yourself:
• Why is it important?
• Where does it link into my success map?
• What is to be achieved and by when?
• How will I measure this?
• How often should I reflect on progress?
• What should I do if the objective is not being met?

Handle large accounts and have major clients within my portfolio

Raise my profile within the company

Spend a secondment in brand marketing

Success map for an aspiring sales director

ACHIEVE PROMOTION TO THE LEVEL OF NATIONAL SALES DIRECTOR

Spend three to five years as regional sales manager

Obtain the relevant professional sales qualification

Attend the Sales Management programme

Spend five years as a sales executive

Develop an excellent sales record

Pass the Institute's exams

Chapter 2

Improving your skills

Think of your portfolio of skills as your toolkit. Just like a good set of tools, once you have acquired your skills, they will always stay with you – as long as you maintain them. From time to time you will need to add new tools to your kit as the requirements of your job change or evolve, and as new ways of doing things emerge.

Managing your time

While you can raise additional finance for your business, employ more people, and buy more machinery, there will only ever be 24 hours in a day. Time is one of the few commodities you cannot buy, but there are many techniques to help you use your time more effectively.

Tracking your time

Before you can start actively managing your time, you need to find out how you spend it. Rather than just guessing, measure and record your time expenditure over a period of at least a week in a time log. When you have completed the analysis, consider if the way you spend time reflects your key objectives. For example, you may find that you spend five per cent of your time visiting customers. Is this activity one that delivers key results (because it generates sales)? If it is, you need to consider whether you would be more effective by spending more time on this activity.

Making time

Planning encourages you to think not just about the day ahead, but also the more distant future. It's all too easy to put off big but necessary strategic projects, such as arranging training for your staff or creating a database of contacts, because you are immersed in day-to-day activity. Think about the longer-term projects you would like to implement in the next quarter. Break these tasks into manageable chunks, and estimate how much time it will take you to complete each chunk.

Planning your day

Write an action plan setting out your activities for the day ahead. The best time to do this is at the beginning of the day, when you feel fresh. Build time into your plan for day-to-day duties and the work you need to do towards your longer-term projects. Failing to stick to an over-optimistic plan can be demotivating, so be realistic in your timings, allowing for interruptions and breaks. When writing your plan, prioritize your tasks objectively – it often helps to use a matrix to categorize tasks according to importance and urgency. Give priority to those that are both urgent and important

(for example, producing up-to-date figures for the next day's sales meeting). Tasks that are important but not urgent (such as completing segments of your large projects) take second priority. Tasks that are not important but urgent (such as dealing with someone else's request for information) take third priority, and those that are neither important nor urgent should be delegated or not done at all.

HOW TO...
SET UP A TIME LOG

Categorize your tasks, e.g. answering emails, writing reports, planning, thinking, visiting clients, travelling.

↓

Assign a code or letter to each of these categories (e.g. emails = E, thinking = T).

↓

Keep a sheet of paper on your desk, divided into two columns.

↓

Split your day into 15-minute segments; enter these periods in the first column.

↓

As you work, record in the right-hand column the letter of the activity you have completed in the last 15 minutes.

↓

At the end of the week, analyze how you have spent your time and draw a pie chart to show where your time goes.

Structuring your day

To make the most of every work day, get to know the times of day when you are most effective and creative. If you are a "morning" person, plan to tackle your creative tasks – such as writing proposals or reports – and your challenging tasks, such as talking to a difficult client, in the morning. Take on routine tasks in the afternoon. If you are an "afternoon" person, do your routine tasks first, but make sure that you don't get hooked into doing them all day.

BE DISCIPLINED
Try to deal with paperwork only once. Mark a red dot on a document each time you pick it up; attempt to minimize the number of red dots on your paperwork – the discipline will slowly work its way into all your processes.

Working effectively

To help you work quickly and effectively, keep your desk tidy and ensure frequently used items are readily to hand. The same goes for information you use regularly. Set up favourites for websites; keep a list of who knows what, and of key phone numbers; and use an old-fashioned card index for storing nuggets of information you refer to often.

Build thinking time into your schedule: travel is often considered to be a time-waster, but it can also provide just the change of pace and scenery you need to do some creative thinking.

Dealing with interruptions

Make sure the working day is under your control by eliminating interruptions at key times. If you are working on a report that requires concentration, divert your phone or put it on voicemail; set aside 15 minutes every so often to collect messages and return calls. Let people know you will be unavailable between certain times. If someone drops in to talk to you, tell them you are working to a deadline and avoid making eye contact – they will get the message.

Streamlining your activities

Telephone calls

- Prepare everything you want to say before you call.
- Talking on the telephone helps to build relationships, but sometimes emailing instead avoids distraction.
- If someone calls you and you're short of time, tell them you will call them back at a specific time. Be sure always to follow up on your promise.

Emails

- Streamline your use of email by checking for new messages and responding to them only at certain times of the day.
- Use colour to highlight important or urgent emails.
- Target emails: avoid copying in people you don't need to, and ask others to do the same.
- Clear out your email inbox regularly.

Working quickly

- Make your decision and don't keep thinking about it afterwards.
- Balance time with quality control; a report may be excellent, but if it's too late it may be of no use.
- Concentrate on what you're doing at a particular time, and don't let your thoughts flit from one thing to another.

Participating in meetings

It's easy to forget the importance of meetings. This is where decisions are made that could affect your work and your future, where relationships are built, and where you have an opportunity to make an impression on others, make your views heard, and find out what others think.

TIP

MAKE YOURSELF HEARD

Have the first words of what you want to say in your mind; wait for a pause, then say those words clearly. Pause, then carry on with the rest.

Making your mark

Preparation is essential to ensure you make the most of your opportunity. Read any material in advance and note down issues you need to clarify and points you want to make. For important discussions, you may want to sound out other people's opinions to help you form your own view and get an idea of who will support your thinking.

When you arrive at a meeting try to sit near people who are likely to support your views, and ideally in the middle rather than at the end of the group. During the meeting, it is very important to find opportunities to speak. If you are nervous about making your own points, get used to hearing your voice by making short remarks in support of others. A clear, firm: "I agree with that point" will get you noticed. You can also ask questions for clarification, which will make you sound interested. Try drafting some points to make in advance, and introduce them early in the discussion, but make sure that you do so in the context of the discussion. Be careful, too, that you don't speak too much: it's better to be known as someone who makes good points than as someone who speaks all the time.

?

ASK YOURSELF... AM I PARTICIPATING WELL IN MEETINGS?

- Do I speak clearly and loudly enough to be heard?
- Do I look at everyone as I make my point?
- Do I contribute to the meeting early on?
- Do I support others?
- Do I listen to what is being said?
- Do I interrupt others only when it is necessary?

Taking minutes

Minutes should be produced for all meetings, even if they are just simple notes of who agreed to do what. For regular meetings, such as staff meetings or committee meetings, it can be useful if they take a formal style, because this helps to reinforce the importance of the meeting.

If you are the minute-taker, clarify what form the minutes should take with the chairperson. For some meetings it's important to know who said what. In that case you may need name plates for attendees. For most meetings, however, the key point is to record actions, who is taking them, and when they must be completed. If the chairperson doesn't summarize what has been agreed at the end of each agenda item, seek clarification. Produce the minutes as soon as possible after the meeting, when the discussion is fresh in your mind. Keep them as succinct as possible without detracting from the record of what was agreed.

✔ CHECKLIST GENERATING FORMAL MINUTES OF A MEETING

	YES	NO
• Have you stated the "title" of the meeting, where it took place, and when?	☐	☐
• Have you listed the people who were present at the meeting, and those who apologized for their absence?	☐	☐
• Have you agreed and noted that the minutes of the last meeting were an accurate record of what happened?	☐	☐
• Have you given a description of any additional discussion points that arose from the minutes of the last meeting?	☐	☐
• Have you detailed each agenda point, describing what was discussed and what decisions were made?	☐	☐
• Have you highlighted the action points, and stated who will be completing each task and by when?	☐	☐

Chairing a meeting

Chairing a meeting is an excellent way to gain visibility. You don't need to have expertise in the subject of the meeting, however you do have to develop a range of procedural skills. These range from the technical – how to produce an agenda – to the diplomatic, such as how to keep the discussion moving and stop participants from speaking for too long.

Calling a meeting

People often complain about how many meetings they have to attend. At a time when few of us have time to spare, going to a meeting that results in no action is just a waste of time. So before you call a meeting, ask yourself: is this meeting necessary or can it be done by another means, such as by email or a conference call perhaps? If you do decide that a meeting is necessary, next consider who should attend. This will obviously depend on the purpose of the meeting. If you are briefing employees about changes that are to be made to your department's structure, for example, then it's essential that everyone attends. If you want views on how the structure should change, on the other hand, you might want to invite just a few key people. Once you have decided who should attend, send out notices of the date and place in plenty of time. Give an indication of how long the meeting will take, to help your invitees plan their time.

Setting the agenda

An agenda is essential to ensure that your meeting has a focus and to enable participants to prepare beforehand. How you structure it will have a major impact on the success of the meeting. The best plan is to word the agenda so that the type of treatment necessary for each item is clear. "To discuss" means an open debate of the issues. "To note" means no real discussion unless there is a point someone is desperate to raise. The timings you allot to each item and where you place it on the agenda will give participants an idea of the importance of that subject. For regular meetings it's a good idea to ask participants if there is anything they want to add to the agenda or whether there is anything they want to raise under "any other business".

Running the meeting

The role of the chairperson is to ensure the meeting achieves its aims. There are a number of key techniques for doing this. One of the main characteristics of a successful chairperson is being able to make everyone feel they have been able to air their views, that their opinion has been valued, and that they have achieved something.

HOW TO...
RUN THE MEETING

Ensure there is someone to take the minutes and let them know the format you want the minutes to follow.

↓

Let each person speak, but move the conversation on to the next person when they have had their say.

↓

If someone is dominating the discussion, politely say "Thank you. That was useful and I think we've understood your point. I see Joe has something to add."

↓

Try to bring quieter people into the conversation. If you think someone may have something to contribute, ask them directly if they would like to add anything.

↓

Keep to time, but allow sufficient airing of the issues.

↓

At the end of the meeting, remind everyone what has to be achieved and summarize what has been agreed, to help the minute-taker.

Negotiating

Negotiating is all about bargaining to reach a mutually agreeable outcome. It is a skill that will give you an enduring advantage, not just at work, but in almost every aspect of your life. The keys to success in any negotiation are having clear objectives and being thoroughly prepared.

Knowing your ideal

A negotiation involves two (or more) parties, who have different needs, agreeing to compromise in order for something to happen. Preparation is vital: start by formulating a clear understanding of what you want to achieve, what you are prepared to concede, and how you will go about the process. Think about what you want the outcome of the negotiation to be, discussing and agreeing it with others where necessary. Break down your thoughts into three areas:
• The must-haves: these are the essential aspects of the deal – if they are not available, you will walk away.
• The ideal: this describes your perfect deal and defines all the elements that contribute to it.
• The give-aways: these are the aspects of the deal that you would be prepared to trade for must-haves or ideal components.

Q IN FOCUS... NEGOTIATING YOURSELF A BETTER SALARY

The best time to negotiate your salary is before you accept a job. Your prospective employer has invested money in recruitment advertising or consultants, and taken time selecting you. You are in a strong position until you accept, especially if you have received other job offers too. In these situations push for what you really think you're worth. Remember that every subsequent pay rise will be based on that initial agreement, so getting it right will influence your salary for many years to come.

Strategies for successful negotiation

1
TIME IT RIGHT
Start negotiating only when you are ready to do a deal. Don't begin the process on a fact-finding trip, for example.

2
TEST OUT YOUR TECHNIQUE
Practise your negotiating technique in situations where the outcome is not too significant.

3
LOOK FROM THE OTHER SIDE
Make a list of what you think the other side see as their must-haves, ideals, and give-aways.

4
OFFER TRADES
Propose trades with the other party: "If you could see your way to do this, we might be able to pay cash in advance."

5
SUMMARIZE AS YOU GO ALONG
At each stage, restate what has been discussed: "So, we have agreed that…"

6
DON'T MOVE TOO SOON
Make sure that everything is on the table before you decide to make an offer.

7
MAKE YOUR OFFER
When you have reached a position, make a clear offer and wait for a clear response.

8
DON'T BE FOOLED
If something looks too good to be true, it probably is – don't be taken in by slick sales patter.

NEGOTIATING SUCCESSFULLY

FAST TRACK

OFF TRACK

FAST TRACK	OFF TRACK
Stating your requirements clearly so the other party understands your position	Neglecting your preparation – if you don't plan you won't succeed
Being patient and accepting that negotiations take time	Giving way on a point you know you can't concede
Demonstrating empathy with the other party	Becoming confrontational, or showing aggression
Ending positively, even if you don't get exactly what you want	Continuing to negotiate after the deal is agreed

BE CLEAR
Make sure that you clarify all statements made by the other party. Ambiguity is the enemy of good negotiation.

Being prepared

Before you start any negotiation, it is crucial that you understand what else is on offer. Before you attempt to buy a car, for example, you need to have visited other showrooms to see what is available and for how much, and to have looked at the road-test report, price guides, and reviews. You also need to understand what you are buying. When you buy a mobile phone, the price may seem very reasonable, but you may be locked into a 12- or 18-month contract. So, unpack the product or service and understand all the aspects.

Such analysis helps in two ways. First, it helps you to identify your "must-haves", "ideals", and "give-aways". Second, it gives you negotiating power. If you can drop information about competitors into the negotiation, it forces the other party to respond in some way, giving you an advantage.

Doing the deal

Nearly every major negotiation requires a meeting. When you enter a negotiation meeting, you will have your objectives, but be prepared to modify your stance in the ebb and flow of the bargaining. As the discussion progresses, the other party will give you clues that indicate their position. For example, if the other person's tone becomes more reflective, they may be about to concede a point, so ease off to give them the time and space to make the step.

Look out for body language that reveals what the other person is thinking. If the other person leans away from you, for example, it may indicate that they are uninterested,

or are demonstrating their superior position: try to engage them more, without being confrontational.

If there is more than one negotiator present, keep a close eye on the person who is not speaking. Directing some of your questions to them may open up other avenues.

Once you have reached a position, offer it to the other side clearly and unambiguously. Wait in silence until they respond. They may ask for clarification or negotiate on a small issue, but if they raise a whole new issue, something is amiss: ask for an adjournment and reconsider the deal from scratch. When the deal is agreed, don't go back on it except under exceptional circumstances. People won't trust you again if you just change your mind.

CASE STUDY

Renegotiating terms
The managing director of a window manufacturer was introduced to a potential new customer, a small company wanting to buy window frames. A deal was negotiated based on payment with order, so there was no credit risk. The sales manager and MD had a good feeling about the new customer. They received the order for the end of the week and put it into manufacture early to make sure it was ready for a Friday collection. But on Thursday night, the sales manager received a call from the customer saying they had hit a problem

with their finance company, which had delayed the release of the money. Could they put back the order a week?

The windows had already been made, and could not be sold elsewhere. There was little to be lost and much to be gained by allowing the customer to have credit on this order. If they were dishonest, it would be better to find out sooner rather than later, but if things were as they said, the relationship would be strengthened. The customers were as good as their word and paid a week later. The trust created by this one act resulted in a flow of future orders.

Dealing with difficult people

A difficult person could be someone who is genuinely obstructive or just an individual who sees the world differently from you. In either case, to manage difficult behaviour, you first need to gain an understanding of the person, and then employ a set of tactics to manage the situation.

ACT EARLY

Tackle difficult behaviour as soon as it becomes evident – the longer you leave it, the harder it becomes to cope with, and it may affect other members of the team.

Planning for resolution

You can't change a difficult person by being difficult yourself. You have to set a target for the situation or relationship you wish to achieve, and then create a strategy to reach that goal. The approach you take will depend on the situation, the person, and the type of behaviour. Call a meeting with the difficult individual in a place where you won't be disturbed. Prepare what you want to say and how you will say it. Tell them how you see the problem, logically and without emotion. Ask them to tell you how they see it and don't interrupt, even if you disagree with their view. Ask them if they have solutions and, finally, add some ways in which you think the problems might be resolved.

CONDUCTING A MEETING

FAST TRACK	OFF TRACK
Letting the person speak	Interrupting
Putting your case calmly	Getting over-emotional
Standing your ground	Becoming argumentative
Breathing slowly and deeply	Taking it personally

STRATEGIES FOR DIFFICULT BEHAVIOURS

TYPE OF BEHAVIOUR	COPING STRATEGY
Negative Complains and disagrees with everything	• Keep positive – avoid being dragged down to their level • Point out earlier instances where your suggestion has worked • Put their "trouble-spotting" talents to good use on a project of their own
Unresponsive Uses silence as an offensive weapon	• Allow silences, rather than filling gaps in the conversation • Get them to talk by asking open questions to which they can't answer just "yes" or "no" • If you can't get them talking, call the meeting to a halt. Explain that nothing is being achieved and propose another meeting or course of action. Ask them to consider how the situation might be resolved
Overpowering Uses anger as an offensive weapon	• Let them express their anger • Try to empathize • When they have calmed down, find the real cause and possible solutions
Wants to "go it alone" Doesn't see themself as part of the team	• Tell them how they are seen by other team members • Explain what team membership requires • Point out how their strengths can help the team
Shows enthusiasm **but few results** Underachieves repeatedly	• Without dampening their enthusiasm, ask why something hasn't been completed • Help them understand how to get things done • Restrict their workload

Facing up to conflict

Truly difficult people are difficult with everyone. Few will fail to notice their behaviour, so it is important to face any conflict rather that allowing it to fester and affect the whole team. It is important to keep in mind that you need to act and not let the conflict affect you deeply. If the other person becomes threatening or abusive, walk away with dignity, saying you will consider the situation and get back to them. After a difficult meeting or telephone call, go somewhere quiet to stretch, move about, and get rid of your tension.

Presenting

It is wholly possible to become successful and achieve high performance without being good at speaking in public. However, presentations give you an unrivalled opportunity to shine and, most of all, be visible within your organization. There are two aspects to learning how to present well: the psychological side, overcoming your fear; and the process side, learning the techniques to do it well.

TIP

LEARN FROM THE GREATS

Take every opportunity to listen to the speeches of the great orators. Concentrate on their delivery. Notice how they grab your attention, how they use silence to give emphasis, and how they vary the tone and pace of their speech.

Being prepared

Successful speakers make delivering a presentation look effortless. In fact, the opposite is true: the key to speaking well is all about exhaustive preparation and practice. You need to get the content right, plan how to deliver it, and then practise your delivery until you are confident in what you are saying. Before you start to plan the content in detail, make sure that you know:
• Who your audience are and what they need from you – how much background information will they need to understand what you have to say?
• How much time you have for your talk – does this include question time?
• What audio-visual equipment is available – can you use a digital presentation?

 ASK YOURSELF...
ABOUT USING VISUALS

• Do your visuals – slides, photographs, or props – add value to your words?
• Are your slides clean, clutter free, and consistent in typeface?
• Do your slides include too much data?
• Do you have too many slides? As a general rule, aim for no more than one or two slides per minute.

Planning your presentation

1
SET OBJECTIVES
Decide what your objectives are – what do you want the audience to take away with them?

2
SET THE STRUCTURE
Structure your talk in three sections: scene setting, the main content, and a summary.

3
MAKE NOTES
Jot down notes for each section, keeping detail brief and only focusing on the key issues.

4
PLAN THE INTRODUCTION
Describe what you will be covering in the presentation, setting the scene and preparing your audience for what is to come.

5
MAP OUT THE MAIN CONTENT
Be selective about what you include. It is better to make three or four key points than try to rush through too much information.

6
WRITE THE SUMMARY
In the summary, briefly go over the main points that your talk has covered and emphasize any actions that need to be taken.

7
PLAN TRANSITIONS
Plan how you will "signpost" the start of each section – this helps your listeners concentrate and remember what you have said.

8
SUMMARIZE YOUR NOTES
Write out your presentation, using bullet points or short sentences, on small cards that are easy to handle.

9
USE COLOUR
Colour code your notes to help you quickly identify the transitions between different sections.

Practising your delivery

Research has shown that your voice – how you say something – is better remembered than the words you use, so practise how you deliver your speech. Begin by standing up, both feet firmly on the floor. Don't be too rigid and don't hunch, because you will smother your voice. Move your head gently from side to side to help you relax. When you speak, imagine your voice reaching the very back of the room like a wave rolling on to a beach. Voice control isn't just about projection: you need to add expression, depth, and resonance. Vary the pace of your speech to make it interesting. Cast your mind back to speakers you have heard who talk in a monotone – it's very difficult to concentrate on what they are saying without letting your mind wander. One of the best ways to practise putting expression and interest into your voice is to read children's stories aloud.

Techniques to help calm your nerves

- Banish negative "what will happen if..." thoughts. If you have prepared well, you needn't worry.
- Visit the venue ahead of time and familiarize yourself with the room you will present in.
- Stand at the podium and imagine the room full of people. Say a few words to get used to how your voice sounds.
- Visualize yourself delivering your presentation confidently and the audience applauding.
- Use relaxation techniques to keep you calm as the time of your talk approaches. For example, think about each part of your body, from your feet upwards, and imagine you're relaxing that part.
- Say to yourself: "I can do this!"

Creating rapport

Giving a presentation is a two-way process. You may be the person at the front doing the talking, but the audience will be giving non-verbal feedback all the time. Try to catch the eyes of people around the room throughout the presentation. Smile occasionally during your talk, but don't adopt a fixed grin.

Move around and use gestures if that feels natural for you. The more relaxed and natural you appear, the more rapport you will be able to create. Be careful not to move around too much, though, because it can make you seem nervous. If something does go wrong, such as your papers falling off the table or the bulb in the projector failing, take a deep breath. Unless they are very unusual people, your audience will empathize with you, because it's something nearly everyone dreads. If it's something you can remedy quickly, look at the audience, smile, and put the matter right. If it's a more difficult problem like the projector bulb, look to the organizers, ask for their help, and carry on as best you can. You will be remembered for coping well.

If you are interrupted, listen to the point being made and answer it briefly. Say you'll deal with it later or will speak to that person afterwards, then put it out of your mind.

- Picture a relaxing scene that you can call up if nerves threaten to get the better of you – practise this beforehand.
- When it is time for you to start, walk confidently to the podium and smile at the audience.
- Take a moment to put your papers down purposefully.
- Focus on what you are saying: it drowns out negative thoughts.

- Keep your feet firmly on the floor.
- Speak slowly and with purpose – it is easy to speak too fast when you are nervous.
- Keep breathing! Occasionally take a slow, deep breath.
- If you feel an attack of nerves, pick a friendly face in the audience and smile at them.
- Remember that no-one in the audience wants you to fail.

Chapter 3
Becoming more effective

There is a basic set of skills that can help you become more effective at everything you do. Like the oil in a machine, skills such as listening, decision-making, and communicating can help you work more smoothly and be more successful.

Reading and remembering

We are bombarded with information all day. The key to success is to be able to identify what is important and then remember it. Recalling an important fact can make the difference between success or failure in the heat of a negotiation or important meeting.

Reading rapidly

Reading a text book is not the same as reading for pleasure. There is a process for reading a text book. Start by reading the introduction. Then read the last chapter. At this point you should know what the book is about and how it's structured, and can decide whether it's worth reading the rest. If you think it is worth reading, turn the pages first, looking at the headings and diagrams; you will be surprised by how much you learn. Once you have done your initial review, leave a gap before you read the book as a whole – this greatly reinforces learning.

Scanning the details

The faster you read, the more you will remember. If you practise long enough, you will be able to scan a document and remember enough to hold a conversation about it. Start by reading whole sentences in one go. To do this, focus your eyes on the sentence rather than on each individual word. Move to looking at paragraphs. Eventually you should be able to look at the page towards the top, in the middle, and finally at the bottom before you turn over. When you are learning, try scanning the whole document first. Then read it at your normal pace. Just scanning first will improve your understanding and memory. If you are late and unprepared for a meeting, try scanning your documents. You will be surprised how much you pick up. Even if it doesn't work, you will be able to find the information you need much more quickly.

Using mind maps

A mind map is an effective way to record information in a succinct format that you can easily remember. To create a mind map that summarizes the content of a book you have read, for example, start by writing the subject of the book in the centre of a sheet of paper. Then draw branches radiating from the subject that sum up the major themes of the book. Next, fill in smaller branches containing the sub-themes, and finally add detail to these sub-themes in the outer "twigs" of your mind map. Use pictures and colour liberally, as they make your mind map more memorable and will increase your recall of the information. If you want to be sure that you will remember the content of your map, review it the day after you have drawn it, one week later, one month later, and finally one year later.

IN FOCUS... REMEMBERING NAMES

Most people worry about remembering the names of the people they meet. If you have difficulty, try the following: when you are introduced, always repeat the person's name. While you are doing this, look into the individual's face and identify a feature that reminds you of their names. Does Sr. Marrón have brown hair, or is his hair so startlingly different that you will remember his name? If there isn't a feature that is memorable, try imagining the person acting their names – Julia Stokes the steam train, for example, or Paul Parsons giving the sermon.

Being creative

Many problems have simple solutions, but those are the problems that everyone can solve. Being creative enables you to solve, or contribute to solving, difficult problems. This will get you noticed. Some people appear naturally creative, but creative problem-solving is a skill that you can learn and hone through practice.

Finding creative solutions

Creativity comes from abandoning linear thought and making leaps of the imagination. All your brain needs is the stimulus to make these leaps. Brainstorming is one technique for helping do this. Getting a group of people together to throw out possible solutions without the constraint of evaluating the suggestions creates energy and sparks new ideas. Another technique is asking people to consider the problem from a different perspective, such as: "How will our customers see this?" or "What if we turn the question on its head?"

Practise being creative in your private life, and it will develop your ability to be creative at work. Stimulate your brain by taking a different route to work, completing crossword puzzles, learning a new language, taking an activity holiday, or finding a new experience.

TIP

STIMULATE CREATIVITY

Very few good ideas have been created by sitting alone at a desk. Change your scene, have a coffee and relax, or interact with others.

Asking the right questions

When you are faced with a problem, it is often the boundaries or rules that constrain your thinking. "We can't do this because…" is a phrase that stifles creativity. Instead, asking the question: "What if this constraint wasn't there?" will allow you to consider all the new options and benefits open to you, and can create a new world in your mind. You will often find the opportunities open to you when you remove a constraint are so great that it is worth the time and effort it takes to remove it. Did James Dyson ask the question "What if we don't have a bag?" when he invented his revolutionary bagless vacuum cleaner? Did Trevor Baylis ask "What if there is no electricity?" when he invented his clockwork-powered radio?

Using benchmarking

Not every problem has to be solved again from scratch. Most problems have been solved before so all you have to do is find the solution. Benchmarking is a very useful tool for doing this.

Benchmarking is about comparing processes. It is about weighing up the way your organization does something against the way that another organization performs the same function. Start by making sure that you understand your own processes. Who does what, when, how, and why? Just doing this will create ideas for improvement, but it also forms the basis for benchmarking: comparing your processes with those of your chosen benchmark subject.

Who should you benchmark yourself against? Ideally, find an organization that is really good at the process you are trying to improve – for example, if you want to improve your despatch function, you might benchmark yourself against a company that is efficient at dealing with complex orders.

TIP

USE PRESSURE
A tight deadline can increase your creativity. You will often find that with a short deadline you'll come up with more alternatives and a better solution. However, it's also true that if you have a complex problem, "sleeping on it" can help you find the answer.

Being confident

Confidence is precious. It enables you to do what you want to do without constant fear of failure, or even despite fear on some occasions, and to maintain your sense of self-worth and not be dependent on what other people think. If you're confident, you can take centre stage when you want – you don't always have to linger in the background.

Thinking positive

The first step in building your confidence is to pay attention to what you're thinking. Concentrate on your positive thoughts. It's very easy to focus on the negative. You probably find that when you have been given feedback, at your appraisal perhaps, you concentrate solely on the one negative comment even though there were five positive comments. To help overcome this, build a bank of achievements and positive comments on which to draw. Sit down with a pen and paper, and answer the following simple questions:

- What have I achieved in the last year and in the last five years?
- What am I most proud of? What did it feel like when I did it?
- What am I good at? (create a list)
- What compliments have I received from others?

Concentrate solely on the positives of each situation, don't let negative "but" thoughts creep in. Commit the answers to your "achievement bank" and draw on them in moments of doubt.

CASE STUDY

Drawing on experience

A young executive was given the authority by his boss, the group managing director, to negotiate the purchase of a company. This in itself was a daunting task, but, arriving at the meeting with a partner from the company's lawyers as his only colleague, he was ushered into a room to find 11 people sitting opposite. The owners of the company he was buying were there, as were their accountants, tax advisors, and lawyers, and three merchant bankers. For an instant, he was totally overwhelmed. Then he remembered an industrial relations negotiating course he had attended a few years before. He recalled how he had handled that situation successfully, his confidence immediately returned, and he successfully negotiated the deal.

Managing thoughts

Most of us have a voice in our heads telling us to be careful and stopping us from doing things that would harm us. The same voice can also prevent us from doing new things and progressing: "If you do this, you'll make a fool of yourself. Let someone else do it." When you hear that voice, ask yourself: "What's the worst that can happen if I do this?", "How likely is that to happen?", and "What's the best that can happen?" In most cases you will find the good outweighs the bad, and you should go ahead. If not, at least you will have evaluated the risk logically and assessed whether it is one you are prepared to take.

Looking confident

It is also important to build confidence on the outside – how you appear to others. Even if you don't feel it, "acting" confident can have an effect on both you and those around you. If you have a confident demeanour you will be treated like a confident person by others. This will reinforce your self-belief and help you to feel confident in yourself.

All of us get into bad habits, whether it's slumping in our seat, forgetting to acknowledge people when we meet them, or not taking care over our appearance. Take a moment to think about the image you portray – is it one of a confident and professional person?

✔ CHECKLIST APPEARING CONFIDENT

YES   NO

- Do I maintain good posture? (An upright posture, keeping your shoulders down and your neck relaxed, makes you look and sound confident.) ☐ ☐
- Do I control my breathing when I'm nervous? (Fast, shallow breaths make you light-headed and raise the pitch of your voice, betraying your lack of confidence.) ☐ ☐
- Do I avoid closed body language, such as crossing my arms, and instead use open gestures and occupy the space around me as if I own it? ☐ ☐
- Do I sit comfortably rather than rigidly, avoiding jerky movements and fighting the urge to fidget? ☐ ☐
- Do I always dress neatly and appropriately and feel comfortable in what I wear? ☐ ☐

Making decisions

The place that you have reached in your career or your personal life is the result of the decisions you have made. Every decision closes off some opportunities and opens others. Life is full of difficult choices and that is why making good decisions is essential.

HOW TO...
MAKE A
DECISION

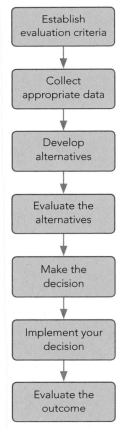

Establish evaluation criteria

↓

Collect appropriate data

↓

Develop alternatives

↓

Evaluate the alternatives

↓

Make the decision

↓

Implement your decision

↓

Evaluate the outcome

Defining the process

Making big decisions isn't simply about mulling over a few options. Big decisions require thought, information gathering, and the creation and evaluation of alternatives before the decision is finally taken. Timing is critical: you may sometimes be able to delay a major decision – although think carefully through the consequences if you do – but for many you will have to seize the moment.

When faced with a major decision, use the process described here to give structure to your decision-making. This will work for large personal decisions that you take yourself, but is even more important if you are working with others in making the decision.

Making group decisions

Group decision-making can be very powerful, as it creates ownership of the decision. Make sure that all involved understand the process you will use, and are aware of the input that is required at each stage. The decision will even be supported by those who disagree with the outcome, as long as the process by which you have made the decision is seen to be transparent and fair. However, you will have to abide by the outcome of the process. If you don't, the decision will be seen as arbitrary and the team will be reluctant to be involved again.

Establishing criteria

There are two reasons to establish early on the criteria by which you will evaluate your decision. First, these criteria determine what information you need to collect to make the decision. Second, they make the decision process transparent. Everyone involved knows what the alternatives will be judged against.

In joint decisions, create and agree the evaluation criteria in a group. Your organization will have its own criteria, so make sure these are included on the list. If the result is a long list, get the group to agree the most important criteria for making the decision.

In business, the evaluation criteria are often hard numbers – to do something for the least cost, for example, or to make the most profit. In your personal life, the criteria are usually more subjective – the relative size of the property you are buying, or the desirability of its location. Often you need both types, which is why you need to use judgement.

TIP

GO WITH THE FLOW

If your company culture is for decisions to be made by consensus, do that. If you act alone, you will not be supported and are likely to fail, regardless of whether the decision you made was correct or not.

Finding alternatives

Decisions are usually choices between alternatives; so successful decision-making depends on identifying the best possible set of alternatives to evaluate. Search widely, but remember you can't evaluate everything. You may need to be creative and on occasions "to think the unthinkable", but don't forget the obvious.

One alternative you should consider is doing nothing. This is not always easy, but may be a real alternative. At the very least it gives you a benchmark against which to compare the other possibilities. In some circumstances it may be possible to do two of the alternatives at the same time. This will require greater levels of evaluation than discussed here, but asking the question can sometimes overcome major dilemmas.

Using decision trees

Creating a decision-tree diagram can help you weigh up a number of alternatives. For example, imagine you are considering buying a house and have found two options, one of which is more expensive than the other. To buy house A you will need to borrow £300,000; to buy house B £500,000. You are concerned about how much each of the houses will cost you to buy over the lifetime of your mortgage. To compare the two options, first consider what the interest rates are likely to be. For example, you may evaluate three possibilities: interest rates

rising to 10 per cent, staying at 6 per cent, and falling to 4 per cent. Next estimate the percentage chance of each happening.

Now create your decision tree. To calculate the expected cost, multiply the annual cost by the percentage chance for each interest rate and then total the costs. The expected annual cost for house A is £18,600 and £31,000 for house B.

Use this information to evaluate your alternatives, but remember that this is the average expected cost. Averages very rarely happen, so you also need carefully to assess risk, for example, by asking yourself: "Can I afford the house if the interest rates are at 10 per cent for a long period?"

Decision-tree diagram for choosing between two houses

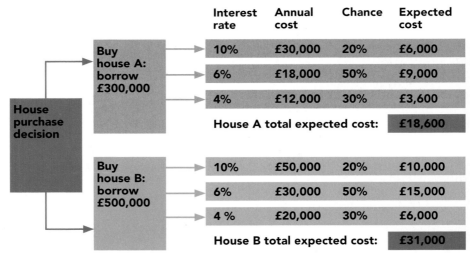

		Interest rate	Annual cost	Chance	Expected cost
House purchase decision	Buy house A: borrow £300,000	10%	£30,000	20%	£6,000
		6%	£18,000	50%	£9,000
		4%	£12,000	30%	£3,600
		House A total expected cost:			£18,600
	Buy house B: borrow £500,000	10%	£50,000	20%	£10,000
		6%	£30,000	50%	£15,000
		4 %	£20,000	30%	£6,000
		House B total expected cost:			£31,000

IN FOCUS... DEALING WITH RISK

All decisions contain risks. To assess the riskiness of your alternatives, ask:
• What is the best outcome I can contemplate?
• What is the most likely outcome?
• What is the worst outcome I can contemplate?
You can then estimate the probability of each outcome occurring and calculate the likely cost using a decision-tree diagram. However, regardless of the outcome of these calculations there are two further questions you need to ask:
• Can the project survive if the worst-case scenario happens?
• Am I prepared to risk that probability of failure?
Your choice may depend on your appetite for risk. Others may have a different view, so ensure everyone understands the risks involved.

Taking the decision

By the time you have created the evaluation criteria and evaluated the alternatives, the decision should be all but made for you. Remember, however, that after all of your calculations and analysis, you will have to make the decision based on your judgement of the situation. You will have to decide whether one factor is more important than another, and will choose to value some things above others. There is evidence to suggest that you can't make decisions without making emotional choices such as these. Decision-making isn't wholly rational, so be very careful about taking a decision that you are not comfortable with. Your emotions may be telling you something that the "rational" analysis has missed.

Acting on your choice

Once the decision is made, communicate it to those who have been involved in the process and to those it will affect. Draw up an implementation plan and delegate authority to individuals who will be held responsible for implementing the decision. Appoint a project manager and a project sponsor to oversee the whole project where appropriate.

Once the project or task has been completed, evaluate how it went. This isn't a witch-hunt, but an opportunity to learn. Some of the best-performing companies regularly re-evaluate their projects to gain insight and learning for the future. You can even improve your personal decision-making ability by reflecting on what went well and what didn't.

successful people know what they want and how they are going to get it, and say "no" when what they are being asked to do doesn't fit in with their plans. Being successful is as much about what you decide not to do as what you decide to do.

TIP

Maintaining a balance

We all have to keep a balance in our lives. You have to balance what your employer wants from you with what you get from your employer. The latter doesn't only mean money, but also the training you receive, the experience you get, and the opportunities that working for the company opens up for your career.

You also have to balance your working life and your family life. If you want to get ahead, the company you work for will expect some commitment and flexibility, but don't be a doormat. Decide how much time you will give to the company and how much you will keep for your family, and then stick to it consistently. There will be times when intensive effort is required and you may have to put in long hours, but if your employer doesn't reciprocate, you should consider your position.

ASK YOURSELF... WHAT'S IN IT FOR ME?

- Am I doing this because I have to, or because I want to?
- If I have to do it, what will I get in return?
- If I have to do it, can I make the task more enjoyable, or develop the task to align more with my goals?
- If I have to do it, what recognition will I receive?
- If I do this, is it helping me achieve my goals and ambitions?
- If I do this, is it giving me an experience that can go on my CV?
- If I do it, how can I maximize the benefit?
- If I say no, what are the consequences?

Getting it right

TIP

Use your judgement to assess when and how often it is appropriate to say no. It doesn't look good if you are seen as someone who always says no, or who only says no to the difficult jobs, so make sure that you get the balance right. When saying no is appropriate, do so quickly and politely.

You may sometimes find yourself in the situation where colleagues try to offload work on to you because they don't want to do it themselves, and they see you as being accommodating enough to do their work for them. If this happens, think very carefully before you accept. Assess the situation: if there really is a crisis and you can help, then of course you should do so. However, if there are no good reasons and you feel the other person may make a habit of offloading their work, you should say no. Do this politely but firmly. Don't make complicated excuses, just say something like: "I'm sorry, but I can't help out this time. I have a heavy workload myself."

THINK IT THROUGH

Think about the impact your decision to say no could have. For example, if your boss or a friend is in serious trouble, saying no to helping out could damage your relationship with them.

Communicating successfully

Communication is about sharing and receiving information through a variety of channels, from formal presentation to general conversation, emails, reports, and letters. How you communicate, and the channel you use, say something about you – so take care!

Knowing your audience

The first lesson in effective communication is to think about your audience: the person reading your email or report or listening on the other end of the telephone. Communication is a two-way process and your job is to make it easy for that person to understand and focus on what you are saying or writing. Think about their level of knowledge of the subject, whether they are likely to understand technical terms or jargon you may be using, and what is their particular interest in what you have to say.

COMPOSING AN EMAIL

FAST TRACK	OFF TRACK
Keeping it concise but clear	Using sloppy grammar
Keeping it short, but not abrupt	Using too many abbreviations
Putting key information in attachments, not in the main body of the email	Including so much detail that the email runs for several pages
Reading your email carefully before pressing "send"	Copying in others without thinking about the implications

CHOOSING THE RIGHT COMMUNICATION CHANNEL

CHANNEL	ADVANTAGES	DISADVANTAGES
Telephone Best used for delivering good news or testing out an idea quickly	• You get an immediate response to your message • You can test the reaction of the other person • More personal than written communication, so helps build a relationship	• No written record of your discussions • You may be calling at the wrong time, and may get an ill-considered response
Face-to-face meeting Best used for influencing people; delivering bad news; and discussing an important or sensitive matter or one that involves detail	• Personal contact helps to build relationships • You will be able to gauge the reaction to your message by reading the body language of the other person • You can present your case using more than just words, and so be sure to get your point across	• Setting up and attending meetings is time consuming • The person's response to a negative message may be difficult to handle
Letter Best used for lengthy and detailed information, especially legal documents and thank-you letters	• Provides a written record of your communication so may avoid dispute at a later date • As fewer letters are sent now, it makes your message stand out	• Your message will take time to arrive • You will not know whether your message has been read – or even delivered • You cannot see the reaction of the recipient
Email Best used for quick, short messages and urgent communication	• Instant delivery of your message • Quick to compose and to send • You can get a quick response	• You cannot see the reaction of the recipient • The "tone" of your message may be misinterpreted • Ease of sending may mean insufficient thought is given to the composition of the message
Report Best used for proposals and to make persuasive arguments where back-up evidence is required	• The formal structure helps in constructing arguments and presenting evidence for decision-making • You can detail your thought processes and rationale	• Much more time consuming to compile and write than other channels • If it is too long, it may not be read thoroughly

Getting your message right

HIT THE RIGHT LEVEL
Adjust your level of formality to match the individual, the organization, or the culture of the person you are communicating with.

KEEP IT SIMPLE
Use short words and uncomplicated sentence construction to aid comprehension – sending a clear message will give the reader a good impression of you.

BE CONCISE
Don't put in unnecessary words – they will dilute your message and may confuse the reader. Use "when...", for example, rather than "at a time when...".

HIGHLIGHT KEY POINTS
Use bullet points to help isolate important points for emphasis, but avoid using too many or they will lose their impact.

CHECK YOUR PUNCTUATION
Clear punctuation helps your reader understand what you have written, and is key to delivering a precise message.

BE DIRECT
Use the active rather than the passive voice to deliver your message. For example, say: "Mr. Skoog took the machine away" rather than "The machine was taken away by Mr. Skoog."

Shaping the content

Whether you are composing an email, writing a letter, or just speaking to someone on the telephone, you should prepare what you are going to say and how you say it. For something relatively simple, this may just mean organizing your thoughts and thinking about the best way to express them. For a more complicated or sensitive matter it's useful to jot down your ideas on a piece of paper and see how they link together, to help you to structure your message.

Always read what you have written in an email or letter, to check that it means what you want to say. For every message you write, ask yourself:

• Will the reader understand this?
• Have I captured their interest?
• Does this mean what I want it to mean, and have I got the tone right?
• Will this achieve the aim I want?
• Have I structured my thoughts in a logical way?
• Is it well laid out, concise, and jargon-free, and is the grammar correct?

Writing reports

A report is normally designed to present facts, figures, and recommendations for action. The structure, tone, and length will depend on the purpose. A report on a serious accident, for example, which may have legal ramifications, will have to be more thorough and detailed than, say, a recommendation to buy a particular model of printer.

All the essentials of good communication apply to the writing of a report. Keep it concise, without losing meaning, make it understandable and interesting to the reader, and make sure it reflects what you want to say. If you have to present facts and figures, remember that visuals are often much clearer than words.

Listening effectively

Many people can talk, but few listen well. If you are good at hearing what others miss, it gives you a distinct advantage. Good listeners are also better at building rapport with others, so listening effectively is a good skill to develop and practise.

Being a good listener

Listening is not the same as hearing. You can hear something but not take it in or respond to it. The words are just flowing over you. When you are truly listening, the person talking to you knows you are listening and will appreciate it. Listening requires concentration and you won't be able to concentrate if you are busy thinking about what you are going to say next. Be in the present. If you are really listening you will find your next words come intuitively.

Listen to what the speaker is saying, not just what you are hearing. Think about what the tone and inflection in the voice tells you about what's behind the words. Are they congruent? If not, what is not being said? Their body language is important too and you will probably pick this up subconsciously. Does the speaker's body language match their words?

As you listen, make sure that you understand what the speaker is saying. Summarize your understanding and, if necessary, ask the speaker to repeat what they have said, or ask for clarification if you are unsure. Never pretend to understand if you don't. Finally, make sure that you end the encounter on the right note.

✔ CHECKLIST LISTENING WELL

	YES	NO

Think about the last real conversation you had:
- Was I really listening to what was being said? ☐ ☐
- Were my responses appropriate while the speaker was talking? ☐ ☐
- Did my actions encourage or interrupt the flow? ☐ ☐
- Were my questions well crafted and appropriate? ☐ ☐
- Did I close the discussion appropriately? ☐ ☐
- Was I helpful? ☐ ☐

If you need to take further action as a result of your conversation, summarize what you have heard and then discuss the action you are going to take. Make a note of what is going to happen, ideally in your colleagues' presence. This will emphasize the importance of what has been discussed and decided. Always make a note of important points even if this has to be after the meeting.

Giving advice

There will be times when you get the impression that a conversation is actually a request for advice. Be wary of this. It's better to be asked for advice than to offer it unsolicited. If you really feel you have something important to contribute, ask the person if they want your advice, but be prepared for them to say no. Alternatively, give advice by telling a personal story of how you dealt with something similar. Do this carefully, however – no two circumstances are identical.

There are some times when there is nothing you can do. The person may be telling you something simply because they want someone to tell. Here, your role is simply to listen and empathize, letting them know you are always available when they need you. Above all, when someone tells you something in confidence, keep that confidence.

TIP

GIVE THE RIGHT SIGNS

Give signs of encouragement – nods, smiles, and winces in the right places – to the person you are listening to. If what they are telling you is distressing or embarrassing, it is better to vary your eye contact.

Chapter 4

Becoming successful

To achieve success in your professional life you need to bring together a coherent set of higher-level skills, from leadership and management to networking and personal development. Regularly monitoring and steering your progress, whether alone or with the help of an experienced mentor, is an integral part of the process.

Moving into leadership

A leader has the personal characteristics that make people want to follow them, the ability to create and communicate a purpose, and the personal touch to deal with people. To be a leader, you must want to become a leader and be committed to learning and practising leadership skills.

Making a great leader

To be a great leader, you don't necessarily have to be a good organizer, but you must ensure that work is capably organized and managed. You don't have to be a great strategist, but you must ensure that strategy is developed, delivered, and communicated. You don't have to be a brilliant decision-maker, but you must ensure that tough decisions are taken at the right time and implemented sympathetically. The first lesson of effective leadership, therefore, is that you must surround yourself with good people with the right skills, whom you can trust to deliver.

Defining leadership

While it is true to say that leaders are made, not born, they tend to share certain characteristics. They have integrity, displaying standards and values that make people trust them. They show enthusiasm, and can create it in others. They tend to have a warm personality and interact well with others and they are tough but fair, with high standards and expectations, but always dealing with people fairly and openly.

Aiming for the top

When you become a leader you will usually have three main aims, which often overlap and sometimes conflict with one another:
• To create a vision for the organization
• To ensure team cohesiveness to deliver the vision
• To satisfy the needs of the individuals within the team.
Juggling these balls is your task: if you drop any one, the organization or team is likely to stumble. Teams and individuals don't work well without a purpose or goal to achieve; individuals find it hard to achieve goals if they don't work as a team; and teams fail to achieve their goals without motivated individuals.

Characteristics of success

HIGH-PERFORMING ORGANIZATIONS
• **Are very clear on where they want to be and the measures of success**
• **Know where they have come from and respect their past**
• **Understand where they are now and where they stand against their competitors**

HIGH-PERFORMING TEAMS
• **Have clear and realistic objectives**
• **Share a sense of purpose**
• **Create an open atmosphere**
• **Regularly and objectively review progress**
• **Build on their experiences**
• **Work through difficult times together**

HIGH-PERFORMING PEOPLE
• **Feel valued and respected**
• **Know what is required of them at work**
• **Have the tools and resources to do their jobs well**
• **Know how what they do helps the organization to be successful**
• **Are nurtured and developed**

Succeeding as a manager

The role of the manager is to implement the organization's strategy through his or her stewardship of the available resources. Just like the leadership role, there are conflicts and tensions that have to be resolved, and all managers need to be leaders to some extent.

Defining the role

As a manager, your focus is on the delivery of tasks, on the efficient use and coordination of resources, and on developing capabilities of people within your team or organization. You must quickly realize that you cannot do everything yourself, and develop skills in setting objectives for yourself and for others, in delegating tasks, and in managing your team.

Delegating tasks

Delegation is about giving responsibility to others for part of a project, so freeing time for you to co-ordinate the work of all members of the team, like the conductor of an orchestra. It's also a good way of developing people – of growing their skills, experience, and confidence. You need to be clear in communicating the tasks to be delegated, the standards and goals to be achieved, and the boundaries of what can and can't be done. Not all tasks are suitable for delegation. Don't delegate unless the objectives of a task are:
• Clear, specific, and measureable
• Targeted and achievable in a set time
• Worthwhile and realistic, but challenging
• Written and recorded
• Consistent with the goals of the organization
• Set participatively.

8

Share the team's success and accept personal responsibility for failure.

7

Meet as a team regularly to review progress, track the performance measures, reallocate resources as necessary, and revise the plan when needed.

1

Communicate the big picture. What is the organization trying to achieve and how does your team fit in?

2

Explain the objectives you have to achieve and the measures on which you will be judged.

3

Discuss, as a team, how these will be achieved and develop an outline plan.

Managing team performance

6

Meet individual members on a one-to-one basis at regular intervals. Monitor progress, listen to their needs and concerns, and provide support.

5

Delegate tasks to team members. Avoid telling people in detail how the task is to be performed. Once the task is delegated, leave them to get on with it.

4

Decide how the tasks in the plan will be distributed between the team, the milestones to be achieved, and who will be responsible for what.

Working with a mentor

Finding and using a good mentor* can be highly beneficial both to your career and to your personal well-being. A good mentor is impartial, has more experience than you in key areas, and acts as a safe and effective sounding board for your ideas.

Defining the role

*Mentor — a person who guides you through a period of change towards an agreed objective.

A mentor can help you in a number of ways. First, they can enable you to work through your problems in a safe environment. They will not necessarily solve your problems for you (the idea is that you learn to do so), but they will ask questions to make you analyze your position and alert you to pitfalls or alternatives.

Second, they can give advice. This may be in the form of what to do, or who to approach within the organization to obtain help. They may point you towards training and development programmes, or suggest projects that you should get involved with.

Third, they may open up your career. They may have access to job opportunities before they become widely available and may suggest roles that you would never have considered. If they are external, they may have their own network of contacts, but don't expect this as part of the relationship.

Choosing a mentor

Your organization may run a mentoring service, but if they don't, you will have to set up a more informal mentoring relationship. The person you select as your mentor must, of course, possess the experience you want to access and should also be someone with whom you can build a good relationship. He or she may not be a technical expert in the field in which you are working. This can be a real advantage because they can work through issues with you from a fresh perspective. Mentors are typically separate from the line-management relationship, but your boss may be the ideal candidate, especially when the difference in age and seniority is large. Some companies establish roles where this is designed to happen – Assistant to the Managing Director, for example.

If you have a very senior manager or director as your mentor, it can open doors to people whom you wouldn't normally meet, give you insights into the organization's political process, identify career opportunities, and protect you when things go wrong.

Qualities of a good mentor

The attributes of a good mentor depend on your circumstances and on your specific role, but he or she should always be:
• Someone you respect and trust, and who won't always just agree with what you say
• Someone you consider as a role model
• Someone who listens, probing what you say in order to understand you
• Someone who is genuinely interested in you and what you want to do, and who is available when you need them.

TIP

THINK BEFORE YOU SPEAK

Remember that your boss is part of the organization, so if he or she is your mentor, be cautious about being completely open about every aspect of your ambitions or personal life.

❓ ASK YOURSELF... WHAT TYPE OF MENTOR DO I NEED?

• Do I need someone who is internal or external to my current organization?
• Is there a specific issue I really want help with?
• Is this a short-term need, or a long-term relationship?
• Is there an area of expertise my mentor should have (psychology, leadership, career guidance)?

Moving on

For some, the ideal career is a series of well-timed promotions within one organization, but gaining job satisfaction often necessitates finding a new role in a new company. Each move you make should give you the experience to progress in your career, so you should choose your opportunities carefully. But when is the right time to change and when is it better to stay put?

Achieving promotion

Getting promoted within your organization depends on being seen to be doing a good job and having the capability of doing a bigger job. You will probably need to improve your visibility within the company and cultivate key internal contacts, so become known more widely. Try putting yourself forward as a spokesperson for your team, or devise presentations on aspects of your work that you can deliver to a wider audience. Many large organizations run fast-track schemes, so make sure both your boss and the Human Resources department know you are interested.

Considering options

A job is not just its title – it is the experience you gain and what you can make of this experience in your later career. If you are in a clerical role, for example, why not volunteer to be involved in the continuous improvement programme. And if people don't see you as management material, volunteer for an external role, perhaps with a charity, and develop your leadership skills that way. Talk to your boss about opportunities that may be open to you. If you are a valued employee, your organization will be interested in your future.

You may need to leave your current organization to achieve your aims, but don't act without careful consideration. Ask yourself where you want to go to next, rather than focusing on escaping from the present. How will your move look on your CV three or five years from now? Future employers look favourably on an internal promotion on your CV. Above all, try very hard never to leave a job on a sour note – you will probably need a testimonial from your current employer to get your next job.

Seeking opportunity

Prospective employers are looking for evidence of five attributes:
• Appropriate qualifications
• A relevant range of experience
• Specific skills required for the post
• Previous positions held
• How successful you have been.
At the interview stage they will also assess your attitude and "fit" with the organization. Examine any job advert and try to decode it in the context of these attributes.

✔ CHECKLIST DECIDING IF IT IS TIME TO LEAVE A JOB

	YES	NO
• Have I already gained all the experience I can get from my current role?	☐	☐
• Have I exhausted all the development opportunities open to me?	☐	☐
• Do I have the appetite for a change?	☐	☐
• Am I in good health?	☐	☐
• Is the new job really a promotion?	☐	☐
• Will the new job provide the experience and opportunities I need for my future?	☐	☐

Getting that job

When seeking your next position, make sure that you consider and address each of the five qualities that recruiters are looking for:

1 Qualifications These give an indication of your potential and so are particularly important in more junior jobs. Even working towards a qualification signals commitment and ambition to your current, or future, employer. Examine job adverts in your area and analyze what qualifications employers are seeking; if you don't have them, enrol on a suitable course.

2 Experience There is no substitute for experience, but employers are not necessarily looking for candidates who have spent long periods in the same role – two or three years is often adequate. If you have spent less time in a role, and particularly if you have moved several times, you may be seen as someone who lacks commitment. If you have held one job for much longer, you may be perceived to be too set in your ways.

Experience is what you gain from each job and each project you undertake. If you make a mistake, learn from it. Reflect on what you have done and what you have learnt. Also, use

someone to help you through a project so you can learn in real time. A mentor, a good colleague, or even a family member can sometimes fulfil this role.

3 Skills Many of the basic skills you will need in any job, such as negotiating, presenting, managing your time, and chairing meetings, have been covered in this book. To hone your skills, identify your preferred learning style and choose development experiences that best suit you:
• Do you learn best from reading books, trade magazines, or online training material?
• Do you prefer learning in the classroom, at conferences, or from colleagues? Short courses give you the opportunity to develop specific skills away from your colleagues, in a safe environment.
• Do you learn best by doing the task? A great way to learn something is by teaching it to someone else.

4 Position Grand job titles will look good on your CV and may get you shortlisted for interview, but they are no substitute for experience. Discrepancies are sure to come to light when you are interviewed by your new employer, so be realistic.

When you apply for a new job, check that the content of the

advertised role matches the title. Is it really going to offer you the experience you want? For example, the title of Assistant General Manager may sound great, but in reality, will you be deputizing for the General Manager or will you be little more than a clerical assistant?

5 Success Most recruiters are looking for success and may not even shortlist you for interview if they don't see evidence of progression on your CV. More astute recruiters will want to examine how you have dealt with difficult and challenging situations. They want to see if you are someone who learns. To address this requirement, present yourself through a success story about your past. For example, compare the two statements below:

• "I was financial controller of a division in Cape Town for three years and every month the books were closed on time."

• "I led a project to replace the accounting system with new software: it was delivered on time and in budget."

The second statement clearly conveys success, where the first simply describes a role. Showing that you have taken up development opportunities and have been successful makes your CV stand out from the crowd.

TAKING YOUR CAREER FORWARD

FAST TRACK

OFF TRACK

FAST TRACK	OFF TRACK
Working towards qualifications you will need in the future	Focusing only on improving your technical skills
Demonstrating progression from junior roles to positions of responsibility	Expecting to be promoted purely on your impressive qualifications
Seeking out new experiences, and actively learning from them	Leaving responsibility for your development to your employer
Using a mentor to help with your personal development	Resenting your lack of promotion

Reviewing your plans

Planning your personal and professional development is essential to achieving high performance, but plans have a habit of being overtaken by events. New opportunities will arise and circumstances change, making it vital to review your progress.

Monitoring your progress

At least once a year, you should review your progress against your development plan. Ask yourself questions such as:

• Have I attained the goals I set myself in my plan? If not, why?

• Are my goals unattainable or are they just going to take a bit longer?

• What have I achieved that wasn't in my plan? What new opportunities does this give me?

Then review the plan itself to see if it still reflects what you want to do with your life. Think about whether your development has made your plan unfeasible, whether new opportunities have arisen, or whether your objectives have changed. Do you need to modify your plan or create a new one from scratch?

Development encompasses more than your position and progress at work. Successful people tend to be well rounded, with a variety of interests and experience, and they measure their success in terms other than how much money they have made and the status they have. Assess and review your own development by asking yourself questions about your current level of success – for example, how well you perform and are developing and learning, how you benefit from work, and how you look to your employer.

HOW DO I LOOK TO MY EMPLOYER?

Does my employer:
• think I am helpful?
• value my contribution?
• think I am promotable?
• trust and respect me?
• use me in projects beyond my role?

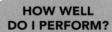

HOW DO I BENEFIT FROM WORK?

Am I satisfied with:
- my level of pay?
- the benefits I receive?
- my work–life balance?
- the opportunities this job gives me?
- my current role?

Scoring your success

HOW WELL DO I PERFORM?

Do I:
- work in a team that achieves work objectives and targets?
- consistently meet my own work objectives and targets?
- support my colleagues?
- have the experience and skills and the support and tools to do my job well?

HOW AM I DEVELOPING?

Have I:
- met the development targets I have set myself?
- kept my skills up to date?
- learnt something new at work this week?
- reviewed my development plan in the last six months?

EFFECTIVE
COMMUNICATION

Contents

Introduction

Communication is, without question, the most valuable skill any manager can possess. It is the link between ideas and action, the process that generates profit. Communication is the emotional glue that binds humans together in relationships, personal and professional. The ability to communicate is what connects people to others in an organization, an industry, or a society. To be skilled at it is to be at the heart of what makes enterprise, private or public, function successfully.

Effective Communication focuses on the processes involved in business communication and concentrates, in particular, on ways in which you can become more effective by becoming more knowledgeable and skilled as a communicator. All forms of communication, whether writing, listening, or speaking, are the end-products of a process that begins with critical thinking.

This book covers a wide range of topics designed to help you understand the communication process better, from planning a strategy to the analysis of your audience. It provides you with guidelines for preparing and delivering an effective speech, as well as ideas for expressing yourself on paper. There are tips for dealing with the specific challenges of team communication, including how to run a meeting, give feedback, and resolve conflict. Finally, it gives you ideas for communicating with clients and customers and thinking about your brand and identity. It's all here. The next step is up to you.

Chapter 1

Understanding communication skills

Communication is more than just a way to get ideas across or exchange points of view. It is the process by which we interact with others and seek out information essential to our daily lives, allowing us to control the circumstances in which we work.

Defining communication

Think of communication as a process, involving senders and receivers who encode and decode messages that are transmitted by various media and that may be impeded by noise*. The aim of this process is to elicit feedback in order to generate a desired effect or outcome.

*Noise — anything that interferes, at any stage, with the communication process.

Understanding each other

Humans aren't the only beings who communicate – virtually all forms of life are capable of sending and receiving messages. People, however, are the only living organisms known to communicate not just with signals and signs, but through the use of symbols with agreed-upon meanings. If we think about communication as the transfer of meaning, then for each of us, successful communication means that you will understand something just as I do: we are in agreement about what the sender intended and what the receiver ultimately understood.

Understanding the principles

Communication involves a number of basic principles, which apply across time and cultures. The communication process is always:

- **Dynamic** It is constantly undergoing change.
- **Continuous** Even when you hang up the telephone, you're communicating the message that you have nothing more to say.
- **Circular** Communication is rarely entirely one-way. We each take in information from the outside world, determine what it means, and respond.
- **Unrepeatable** Even if we say something again in precisely the same way, our listeners have heard it before, and so respond to it differently.
- **Irreversible** We cannot "unsay" words.
- **Complex** We all assign slightly different meanings to words. This variation is a product of our backgrounds, education, and experience, and means that there is always the potential for misunderstanding.

TIP

REDUCE NOISE
The ultimate success of the communication process depends to a large degree on overcoming noise, so make an effort to keep your messages clear, concise, and to the point.

DEFINING LEVELS OF COMMUNICATION

LEVEL	AUDIENCE
Intrapersonal	Communication within ourselves, sending messages to various parts of our bodies, thinking things over, or working silently on a problem.
Interpersonal	Communication between or among people, sending messages from one person to another – verbally and nonverbally – with the hope of transferring meaning from one person to another.
Organizational	Communication in the context of an organization, sending and receiving messages through various layers of authority and using various channels to discuss topics of interest to the group we belong to or the company we work for.
Mass or public	Sending messages from one person or source to many people simultaneously, through television, the internet, or print media.

Overcoming barriers

Why do attempts at communication often fail? Broadly speaking, there are two barriers that keep us from communicating successfully: the operations of our bodies and our minds, and our assumptions that other people understand and react to the world in the same way that we do.

Unblocking your communications

The information we receive about the world comes from our senses. It is possible, however, for our senses to be impaired or for the source of the message to provide inadequate information to be reliably decoded. In sending messages to others, we must be sensitive to the fact that they may not see, hear, touch, taste, or smell in the same way we do.

Ensuring understanding

Communication is more than sending and receiving messages; if the message has been delivered but not understood, no communication has taken place. Everything, from the culture in which we live to the norms or standards of the groups to which we belong, can influence how we perceive the messages, events, and experiences of everyday life. Even individual mindsets, such as holding stereotypes, can set up barriers, affecting what we understand and how we react to outside stimuli.

CONSIDER CULTURE
Be aware that different backgrounds, education, and experience give people different expectations. Your way of seeing the world is not the only one.

Learn to recognize the barriers likely to block your communications, and focus on what you can do to overcome them. When speaking to someone, for example, constantly monitor their reactions to confirm that you are being fully understood.

Overcoming barriers to communication

BANISH PREJUDICE
Never make a judgement before knowing the facts about a situation. Acknowledge that you are usually working with incomplete data.

FIGHT STEREOTYPES
Don't assume that all members of a group share the same characteristics. Put aside any stereotypical views you may have; treat each person as an individual.

CONTROL YOUR FEELINGS
Try to present your arguments rationally rather than emotionally, and accept that other people may have strong feelings about a subject.

WATCH YOUR LANGUAGE
Recognize that language has different levels of meaning. People will respond differently to the same words, especially if the words are vague or general.

Communicating at work

Communication is a fundamental skill, central to the human experience. We each know how to do it; we've done it since birth and receive additional practice each day. So why is it so difficult to communicate on the job? As a manager, it is important to understand how the workplace changes the nature of communication for both sender and receiver.

TIP

LOOK ABOVE AND BELOW

Notice how communication differs throughout your organization and always tailor your message style and content. Is one style of format, content, or message preferred by management, and another by those at more junior levels?

Tailoring your approach

Several factors in business life alter the way in which we look at communication. We all have a personal communication style, but within an organization you often have to adapt your approach to accommodate the needs of those you work with and work for. If you put the preferences of your audience – particularly your boss and your clients – above your own, you will often get what you want faster. The way you communicate also depends on your position within the organization. The higher your level of responsibility, the more you have to take into account when communicating. And as you become more accountable, you need to keep better records – a form of communication to yourself that may later be read by others.

✓ CHECKLIST ADAPTING YOUR STYLE

	YES	NO
• Do you understand how the culture of the organization you work for affects the way in which you need to communicate?	☐	☐
• Have you adapted your writing and speaking style to the expectations of the culture in which you are working?	☐	☐
• Have you changed your style to accommodate any changes in the structure of the company or the conditions of your industry?	☐	☐
• Have you noted the communication preferences of your supervisor and adapted your writing, speaking, and listening styles accordingly?	☐	☐

Adapting to your environment

Organizations, like the people who work in them, are in constant flux. Businesses change by necessity with the conditions of the marketplace and the lives of the managers who run them. Your communications must adapt to the conditions in which you find yourself. However, this never constitutes a reason for signing your name to a document that is false, or passing along information that you know isn't true.

Matching the culture

All communication must work within an organization's culture. The accepted approach can vary considerably between different organizations: some companies, for example, require every issue to be written in memo form and circulated before it can be raised in a team meeting. Other organizations are much more "oral" in nature, offering employees the opportunity to talk things through before writing anything down.

Many companies rely on a particular culture to move day-to-day information through the organization. To succeed in such a business, you must adapt to the existing culture rather than try to change it or ask it to adapt to you.

Planning your approach

Getting people to listen to what you say, read what you write, or look at what you show them isn't easy. How do you persuade them that paying attention to your message is in their best interest? The key to ensuring that your communication hits the mark is detailed planning.

TIP

QUESTION YOUR OWN ROLE

Ask yourself whether you are the right person to send the message. Will your signature compel people to action, or might the message be more effective coming from your manager, or someone closer to the intended audience?

Choosing your approach

The choices you make, from the content of the message you send to the medium you select, all have a direct impact on the outcome of your communication. Whatever the situation, ask yourself about the following:

• **Message** What should your message contain? How should your message impart the information? Should your message be broad or detailed?

• **Medium** What's the best way to send this message? Is one medium quicker or cheaper than another? Will one offer a better opportunity for feedback or carry more detail?

• **Code** Will your audience understand the words you've used? Will the words and images mean the same thing to the audience as they mean to you? Do these words and images have multiple meanings for various audiences?

• **Feedback** How will you know if you've communicated successfully? Will the audience response be delayed? Will it be filtered through another source?

• **Noise** How many other senders and messages are out there? Whose message traffic are you competing with? Will others try to deflect, distort, or disable your communication attempts?

• **Effect** What are the goals or communication outcomes you're hoping for? How will you know whether you've achieved them? How will the audience know that the information and ideas you've communicated are useful and worth acting on?

Targeting your communication

Planning targeted communication involves ensuring that you:

WORK WITHIN OBJECTIVES
All of your communication should be consistent with and directly supportive of the strategic objectives of your organization – its vision, values, and beliefs.

ADAPT TO YOUR AUDIENCE
Appeal to the basic needs (shelter, sustenance, safety, companionship, or social approval) of your intended audience or their senses (use motion, colour, and sound). What can you do to hold their attention?

EXPLAIN YOUR POSITION
Use words that your audience will understand and concepts they can relate to. This means, of course, that you must know who your audience are, as well as what they know and how they feel about the subject.

MOTIVATE YOUR AUDIENCE
Encourage your audience to accept and act on your message by appealing to authorities that they respect, the social conformity displayed by others they know or admire, the rationality of your argument, or their desire to behave in consistent ways.

KEEP THEM ON SIDE
Make your audience resistant to counter-persuasion by asking for a tangible, preferably public, commitment from them, or reminding them of the benefits to be derived from doing as you ask.

MANAGE EXPECTATIONS
Always let your audience know what to expect, and deliver what you promise, never less. People are disappointed only if their expectations exceed what they actually receive.

Understanding your audience

Who are these people you're communicating with? What do you know about them? What do they know about you or your subject? How do they feel about it? When preparing to communicate, ask a few simple questions about the people in your audience. Once you know more about them, you can find ways to motivate them to listen.

TIP

GET TO KNOW YOUR AUDIENCE
It's all too easy to stereotype an audience, especially when you are working against the clock. Make sure you have collected all the information available about your audience, and refer to the key characteristics as you prepare your speech or document.

Pinpointing backgrounds

When you're assessing your audience, look for any similarities in personal backgrounds. For example, what is the average age of audience members? Consider whether they will be familiar with the concepts you plan to speak about, and the sort of life experiences they may have had. Next, think about the education level of your audience. This will have a significant influence on the content of your talk or document, including its central themes and the vocabulary you employ. The personal beliefs of your audience are an important factor to take into account when planning what you will say. Are they liberal or conservative? What is their political affiliation? Are they committed to a particular religious or social point of view?

Considering ethnicity

The ethnic origin of members of your audience may be worth knowing, but don't overestimate its value. The utility of this information may lie in knowing which issues and positions are of greatest concern to members of a particular ethnic group. The limitation lies in knowing that you cannot reasonably stereotype the views of all members of such a group. Sensitivity to ethnic issues and language styles should be sufficient as you prepare a speech.

Positioning status

For certain forms of communication, knowing the economic status and lifestyle of your audience is especially important. Gain as much information as you can about the following:

• **Occupation** Knowing how people earn their living will tell you something about their educational background and their daily routines, as well as their motivations and interests.

• **Income** Knowing how much money an audience makes can give you some idea of what their concerns are. The less they make, the more they will be driven by basic needs, such as food and housing. American psychologist Abraham Maslow documented the Hierarchy of Human Needs, showing that higher level needs – such as self-actualization – are only relevant to people once their more basic needs have been met.

• **Socioeconomic status** This term describes where your audience is located in the social/economic spectrum. It is, of course, a direct function of other factors, such as income, education, occupation, neighbourhood, friends, family, and more. Think of this as a single descriptor that explains just how much prestige your audience has in the eyes of others in their own society, and use it to target your words to address their problems, hopes, and needs.

IN FOCUS... GENDER TRAITS

Gender refers to the social and psychological expectations, roles, and views of men and women.

Considerable evidence now indicates that this may be among the least useful pieces of information to know about your audience. Why? Because study after study has shown no statistically significant difference in the responses of professional men and women to a wide range of stimuli. Clearly, knowing that your audience might be composed exclusively of one sex or another might alter your approach somewhat, but you would be unwise to assume that you should communicate in one way for men and another for women.

Matching the message

Once you know something about the individuals who make up your audience, begin to think about how to approach them. You'll need a strategy to help devise the right message and to choose the most effective method of communication for your audience.

Hitting the right knowledge level

A thorough knowledge of what your audience already knows about your speaking subject is useful in a number of ways. First, it tells you where to begin. Don't speak down to the audience by explaining fundamentals they already understand. Second, don't start above their heads. Begin at a point they are comfortable with and move on from there.

GETTING YOUR MESSAGE ACROSS

FAST TRACK	OFF TRACK
Knowing as much as you can about who will read or hear your words	Assuming the audience knows all or nothing about your subject
Tailoring your message to the needs and interests of your audience	Acting as if the audience already shares your ideas and interests
Understanding who the key decision-makers are, and their criteria for making decisions	Failing to check who exactly is in your audience, and what they need to know in order to act
Knowing who is respected by your audience and seeking their approval for what you recommend	Assuming your ideas are good enough to stand up on their own, and discussing them with no-one

Managing emotions

Even more important than what the audience knows about your subject is how they feel about it. What they know about taxation is far less relevant than how they feel about it when they listen to a talk about tax reform. You need to tailor your words carefully to what the emotional response of your audience is likely to be. The greater the degree of ego involvement (or emotional response) to a given topic, the narrower the range of acceptable positions open to you. In other words, people are much more open-minded on topics they are indifferent about than they are on topics they care about passionately. If you misjudge an emotional response, your communication will fail.

Establishing the audience's role

Your message may need to reach only the audience before you, or you may be relying on those people to pass on the message to others. Think about everyone who might see or hear your message, including:
• **Primary audience** These are the people who will receive your written or spoken message directly. Make sure that you understand and address their needs, interests, and concerns.
• **Secondary audience** Others might read or hear of your message indirectly. Could the communication be given to a reporter, union organizer, or competitor?
• **Gatekeepers** These are the individuals who you have to route your message through, and who might filter or block it. Does someone in particular stand between you and the audience you hope to reach?
• **Opinion leaders** These are individuals who have significant influence over members of the audience. Who do they admire or listen to on this subject?
• **Key decision-makers** These are people with the power to influence the outcome of the communication.

HOW TO... MOTIVATE YOUR AUDIENCE

Begin by expressing shared values before moving on to more contentious areas.

↓

Grant a favour to win a concession from an audience.

↓

Finally, use the promise of reward or the possibility of punishment, if appropriate.

Choosing your medium

Most managers make decisions about whether to write or speak to someone based on two criteria: convenience and their own personal preferences. But an effective choice of communication medium or channel depends on much more than what suits you at the time.

TURN OFF THE AUTOMATIC PILOT
Most of us reach immediately for our preferred form of communication. Learn to stop, consider your options, and purposefully choose the right channel and medium for the message.

Learning to ignore instinct

Many managers choose a form of communication instinctively, and not always for the right reasons. For example, if you need to pass bad news to a colleague but don't want to provoke a confrontation, you might choose to send an email, even though your colleague would prefer to hear from you in person. On another occasion, you might choose to make a phone call rather than write a letter, because it seems quicker or easier. You might make this choice even when the message is complex and would benefit from extensive explanation, detailed description, or visual aids.

In fact, just two factors should govern your choice of medium for any message. You should think first about the preferences of the person or audience receiving your message, and second about the characteristics and benefits of speaking versus those of writing.

IN FOCUS... THE PLATINUM RULE

We're all familiar with the old rule: "Do unto others as you would have them do unto you." It's a good rule, but it contains a small flaw. What if others don't want to receive the same treatment as you? What if their preferences are, in fact, significantly different? The Platinum Rule, devised by communication expert Tony Alessandra, is a variation of that age-old maxim: "Do unto others as they want to be done unto." This means treat others as they want to be treated, not how you think they should be treated. Communicate with others in the manner that they prefer and you'll get what you want: their time, attention, and cooperation.

Knowing when to write

Writing produces a permanent record, can be used to convey great detail, is often much more precise, and can be used for careful wording. If it's important that you say something in a specific or exact way, you may want to write it down. And, of course, if your audience has a preference for source material or large amounts of detail, such as tables or large lists, you can provide that information as an appendix or attachment to a memo, report, or proposal.

Keep in mind that you may have to share your message with many people and it may be impractical or impossible to speak to each of them. Writing in a precise, persuasive way may be the best approach to influence your audience.

Identifying when to speak

Speaking provides a richer context – it includes the use of nonverbal cues and allows for more emotion. This communication form is less rigid, as it leaves no permanent record. It may also be much quicker.

Speaking to others also invites their participation. It may be the best way to elicit ideas, size up other people's feelings, and even discover any possible objections to your message before decisions have been made and formalized in writing. Once something is written down, people tend to feel committed to that course of action, even if the documents can easily be revised. A conversation or discussion, on the other hand, has a more transitory feel to it: it is flowing and flexible, and less permanent and formal than written forms of communication.

Chapter 2

Speaking and writing

Two of the most important skills for a manager, and often also the most daunting, are to stand up in front of an audience and deliver a presentation, and to communicate effectively in writing, whether in formal business letters, email correspondence, or detailed reports. For both, clear thinking, preparation, and practice are the keys to success.

Planning your speech

Preparing for a business presentation is the most important stage of the process. While it may seem daunting at first, planning your speech becomes much easier once you break the task down into manageable steps, ensuring that you address all the relevant issues at the right time.

Defining substance and style

When it comes to giving a speech, content is king. Substance matters and there is absolutely no substitute for knowing what you're talking about. This means that, whenever possible, you should select a topic that you know and understand, so that you can talk about it with confidence. However, this also depends on your audience; never forget that they are the reason you are in the room. Using your knowledge of your audience to tailor the content to meet their expectations is not a guarantee of success, but it is certainly a step in the right direction.

Determining your purpose

TIP

Before you start to plan the details of your speech, make sure that you know why you are speaking. If you can't come up with a reason for speaking, then don't speak. Identifying your role as a speaker and your importance to the listeners is especially important. It may be that this audience wants your views on the subject at hand and is keenly interested in your opinions. Alternatively, your purpose may be purely to inform them about a topic, and the demand for your opinions may not be as high as you imagine.

Find out, too, all you can about the context in which the presentation will take place. You need to know the answers to questions such as: is your audience still in the fact-gathering stage, or are they ready to make a decision? What is their reason for listening to you? How urgent is the subject you'll be speaking about? Have recent events, either locally or globally, affected their view of the topic in any way? Are your listeners involved in a process that will require them to take action after hearing what you have to say?

MAKE TIME FOR RESEARCH

You're being paid for your time preparing and delivering the speech, but the 80:20 rule applies – spend around 80 per cent of your time on research and preparation, and only around 20 per cent on practice and delivery.

CASE STUDY

Preparing to succeed

Elizabeth Allen, chief communication officer of the international office supplies firm Staples, Inc., was given the task of drafting a press-conference speech for her CEO, Tom Stemberg, to announce Staples's sponsorship of a new sports arena in Los Angeles. Ms Allen knew that this financial arrangement would be covered by the sports press, not the business press. She also knew that sports figures, civic officials, investors, and reporters would be in the room: "Many people thought the name would be a local, California company.... This was a Boston company putting its name on a Los Angeles landmark. There were cultural factors at work here, as well as political and business factors." As she considered how to prepare the speech, she decided three things: she would reduce her thinking to one or two main points; she would include a few examples and anecdotes that the local audience would relate to; and most importantly, she would cite at least one powerful reason why the relationship between her company and the City of Los Angeles would be productive and long-term.

Preparing your speech

Once you have a clear picture in your mind of why you are giving the presentation, who your audience is, and what they want to hear from you, start to make a detailed plan of your speech. This planning stage is vital, so make sure that you don't leave it to the last minute. You need to be completely familiar with the structure and content of your speech by the time you deliver it. There are eight key steps to preparing a successful presentation.

1 COMPOSE A THESIS STATEMENT
Write a one-sentence declaration of what you want the audience to know, understand, believe, or do. Make it brief, simple, comprehensive, and as complete as possible.

2 DEVELOP THE MAIN POINTS
Restrict yourself to just two or three main points, so that you will have time to explain and support them all. Make sure that all of your evidence relates to and is supportive of your principal reason for speaking.

5 PREPARE YOUR OUTLINE
Write a one-page outline of your speech. Think about the issues you plan to raise, the sequence in which you will address each of them, and the evidence you'll offer your audience in support of those ideas.

6 CONSIDER VISUALS
Think about what visuals will best enhance your speech, by helping to explain, reinforce, and clarify your main points. Sometimes it is easier to show the audience something than to say it.

Steps to preparing a speech

3 GATHER SUPPORTING MATERIALS
Now gather evidence to support your main points. Use your knowledge of the audience to select the kinds of proof that they will find most convincing. Make your evidence compelling, recent, and fully transparent to your listeners.

4 THINK ABOUT STRUCTURE
Consider the order in which you will deliver the information, and think about what you will say in your introduction, in the body of the speech, and in your conclusion.

7 WRITE THE SPEECH
Now prepare the content of your speech in detail. Some people choose to write in short bullet points, others write their script out more fully. Choose the way that best suits you, but remember that your audience want to hear you speak to them, not read to them.

8 PREPARE YOUR NOTES
Finally, transfer your speech into the notes you will use to deliver it. These may be bullet points on a PowerPoint presentation, written notes on notecards, or the full manuscript.

Developing visual support

Behavioural scientists have known for many years that visual images can have a powerful effect on the process of learning. In some cases, pictures may reach people who simply don't listen well to the spoken word, or who may not understand what the words mean.

TIP

CHOOSE THE RIGHT CHART

Charts and graphs are a useful way to display data. Be sure to select the type of chart (such as a pie chart, bar chart, or line graph) that most clearly illustrates any comparisons you want to make, and use colour carefully to emphasize your point.

How does visual support help?

Behavioural scientists have found that visual support is important in communication for three main reasons:
• It can help explain, reinforce, and clarify the spoken word during a presentation. If you can't say something easily, you may be able to show it to your audience.
• Some people pay more attention to what they see than what they hear, and can more quickly and easily recall information and concepts with a visual component than those that are just spoken aloud.
• People tend to recognize ideas most easily when they are presented as a combination of both words and pictures, rather than when presented as either words or pictures alone.

Choosing when to use it

Displaying information in a visual manner will enhance most presentations, but tends to work best:
• When you have new data for your audience
• When the information you hope to convey is complex or technical in nature
• If your message is coming to the audience in a new context
• For certain types of information – such as numbers, quick facts, quotes, and lists
• For explaining relationships or comparisons
• For revealing geographical or spatial patterns.

Using visuals effectively

Good visuals have a number of characteristics in common. The most important is simplicity. The more complex a visual display becomes, the more difficult it is for an audience to understand. Keep your visuals clear, ordered, and simple when trying to explain an important idea or relationship.

Good visuals use colour to explain and attract. Very few people tend to have exactly the same taste in colours, but almost everyone appreciates occasions when colours are used meaningfully and consistently. Certain traditions, such as using red numbers or bars to indicate a loss and black ones to indicate profit, allow audiences to quickly grasp information. Try using a simple legend to explain colour use on your charts and graphs; it helps the audience and will ensure consistency and simplicity in your visual aids.

USING VISUALS WELL

FAST TRACK	OFF TRACK
Thinking carefully about the needs and interests of your audience as you plan your visual aids	Including large amounts of text in your visuals so the audience has to read much of your message
Choosing visuals that capture the essence of your main points	Using stock visuals that are only indirectly related to your main points
Using colour in a consistent, careful manner so that related items are colour-coded and grouped together	Failing to explain any coding in your visuals, including your use of colour, symbols, and graphic depictions
Making sure your visual support is simple, crisp, clean, and uncluttered	Not worrying about the overall look and hoping it will work adequately

Improving your confidence

It's one thing to know your material. It's another matter entirely to believe that you can get up on stage and speak with confidence to a group of strangers. Understanding your message and having a well-organized speech are important to your success, but so is self-confidence.

TIP

KEEP NOTES SIMPLE

Losing your place in lengthy notes can give your confidence a serious knock, so make sure your notes are quick and easy to use, giving you the information you need at a glance.

Improving your delivery

Rehearsal will help improve your speech and raise your level of self-confidence. Simply knowing that you've been through the contents of your speech more than once builds familiarity and is reassuring. It will also ensure you talk for the correct amount of time. A run-through or two will show whether you have too much, too little, or just enough to say. Rehearsal will also help you to improve your transitions. By practising your speech, you'll be able to identify the rough spots and work on smoothing the transition from one main point to another and from one part of the speech to another.

Using notes

The best speakers seem to confidently deliver their speeches extemporaneously, or "from the heart", without notes. Such speeches aren't really memorized word-for-word, but rather are thoroughly researched, well rehearsed, and professionally supported. Many extemporaneous speakers will use their visual support – acetate transparencies, 35-mm slides, or electronic slides – to prompt their memories. Others prefer to work from bullet points on notecards, or use the full manuscript. Whichever you choose, make sure that your notes are simple, easy to follow, and allow you to maintain eye contact with the audience.

Gaining confidence

The better prepared you are, the more confident you will feel at the podium. Make sure you have thought about all aspects of your presentation, from the layout of the room to the type of microphone you will use. The knowledge that you have personally arranged every detail, and have meticulously planned and rehearsed your talk, will help build your confidence. If you get cold feet, remember that you've been asked to speak because the audience is interested in your expertise and viewpoint. Just approach this speech as you would any other managerial task, knowing that you have the ability, the intelligence, and the confidence to get it done.

"The audience wants to hear what I have to say."

"I'm the expert. I know this subject better than anyone."

"I know my speech, and I'm confident that it reads and flows easily and well."

✓ CHECKLIST BEING PREPARED

	YES	NO
• Have you double-checked the time and location for your speech?	☐	☐
• Are you sure about the length of time allotted to the speech?	☐	☐
• Have you decided how to arrange the room?	☐	☐
• Have you found out whether you are using a lectern or are free to walk around the room during the speech?	☐	☐
• Have you tested the microphone and sound system?	☐	☐
• Are you familiar with the arrangements and systems for visuals?	☐	☐
• Do you know what lighting is available, and have you planned whether it needs to change for screen visuals or handouts during your talk?	☐	☐
• If you are using a computer during the presentation, are the relevant files backed-up on a second computer to use if necessary?	☐	☐

Delivering your speech

You've researched the topic thoroughly, written and organized your thoughts, and rehearsed your remarks. Use the confidence that you've developed in planning and rehearsal to take the next step: get up and speak. You are the medium, or bearer, of the message, and your delivery is critical to the successful communication of your ideas.

Improving your delivery

As you approach the challenge of becoming an accomplished public speaker, keep in mind that no-one is born with great public-speaking ability. Language is the habit of a lifetime, and your ability to speak with conviction and sincerity is a function of your willingness to work at it. Your skills will improve with every speech that you make, and as you master the art of presentation, chances are that others in a position of influence will and reward you for your effort.

CASE STUDY

Capturing audiences

How does Apple Computer CEO Steve Jobs garner so much attention when he speaks at industry events and product launches? Much of his ability to mesmerize a crowd comes from his methodical preparation and passion for the subject. "Jobs over-prepares and knows his material cold, so his mind is free to do audience calibration," says Bill Cole, CEO of Procoach Systems in San Jose, California, US. "He reads the audience instead of being in his head, remembering what to do or say next. He knows his material and mechanics so well

that he can go with the flow." In 2005, Jobs gave the commencement speech at Stanford University. He centred his talk on stories about his life, such as being given up as a newborn for adoption, dropping out of college, founding the Apple Computer company, and then getting fired from his very own company. "His personal stories are brief and powerful," says Ginny Pulos, a communication consultant from New York. "You can see the emotion on his face and hear it in his words." The lesson for executives, says Pulos, is to "learn to tell stories about the passions in your life."

Ways to keep your audience interested

MAKE A CONNECTION

- Step up to the lectern, breathe deeply, smile, think positively, and speak
- Humanize and personalize your speech – share your experiences, values, goals, and fears
- Do your best to be one of them (unless it's clear you are not)
- Use humour where appropriate (unless you are not funny)
- Actively involve the audience as much as you can
- Focus on current local events and issues known to the audience

HELP THEM UNDERSTAND

- Blueprint the speech: tell the audience where your talk is going
- Begin with the familiar, then move to the unfamiliar
- Talk process first, then add in the detail
- Visualize and demonstrate your ideas where you can
- Use interim summaries and transitions to guide your audience through what you have to say
- Give examples to illustrate your concepts and ideas
- Tell stories, and dramatize your central theme

Becoming a better writer

Very few people think writing is easy. Good writing – that is, writing with power, grace, dignity, and impact – takes time, careful thought, and revision. Such writing is often the product of many years of training and practice. Even though writing may sometimes seem like hard work, with a little effort you can learn to do it well.

ALWAYS EDIT
Revising and editing are critical to good writing. Putting some time between writing and editing will help you be more objective. Revise your writing with the intent to simplify, clarify, and trim excess words.

Organizing your writing

Good business writing is simple, clear, and concise. By not calling attention to itself, good writing is "transparent", helping the reader focus on the idea you are trying to communicate rather than on the words that you are using to describe it.

The key to good business writing is organization. You need to know where you are going before you start, so do your research and identify the key issues you need to cover. Compose a list of the most important points, and use them to create an outline. If your document will include an overview section containing your purpose for writing, write this first. Next, tackle the most important paragraphs, before filling out the details and any supplementary material.

ASK YOURSELF... HAVE I EXPLAINED ADEQUATELY?

- Does my writing flow in a logical way, and have I given complex explanations in a step-by-step form?
- Have I "translated" any technical terms?
- Have I said enough to answer questions and allay fears without giving too much detail?
- Have I used visuals to help explain complex facts?
- Have I cautioned the reader, where necessary, against common mistakes and misreading of the information?

Meeting your reader's needs

Before you write, find out what the reader expects, wants, and needs. If you later discover that you must deviate from these guidelines, let the reader know why. When composing your document, don't include material that you don't need: you may be accused of missing the point. Make sure, too, that you always separate facts from opinions in your writing. The reader should never be in doubt as to what you know to be true, and what you think may be the case. Always apply a consistent approach to avoid misunderstandings.

Writing for clarity

When composing a memo, letter, or report, keep in mind that your reader often doesn't have much time: senior managers, in particular, generally have tight schedules and too much to read. They need your written communication to quickly and clearly give them the details they need to know.

Ensure that your writing style is both precise and concise. Use simple, down-to-earth words, and avoid needless ones and wordy expressions. Simple words and expressions are more quickly understood and can add power to your ideas. Be direct, and avoid vague terms such as "very" and "slightly"; this will show that you have confidence in what you are saying and will add power to your ideas. Make sure, too, that everything you write is grammatically correct – you don't want your busy reader to have to re-read your sentences to try to decipher their meaning.

Keep your paragraphs short; they are more inviting and more likely to get read. If your document must include numbers, use them with restraint – a paragraph filled with numbers can be difficult to read and follow. Use a few numbers selectively to make your point, then put the rest in tables and graphics.

TIP

MAKE IT PERFECT
Eliminate factual errors, typos, misspellings, bad grammar, and incorrect punctuation in your writing. Remember that if one detail in a memo you have written is recognized to be incorrect, your entire line of thinking may be considered suspect.

Making your writing come alive

To escape from outdated, excessively formal writing styles, try to make your writing more like your speaking, and then "tidy it up". Imagine your reader is in front of you and aim all the time for writing that is clear, fresh, and easy to read. You may need to write a first draft for structural purposes, and then go back over your document. Make sure that your writing is:

• **Vigorous and direct** Use active sentences and avoid the passive voice. Be more definite by limiting the use of the word "not".

• **Free of clichés and jargon** Tired, hackneyed words and expressions make your writing appear superficial.

• **Made up of short sentences** This won't guarantee clarity, but short sentences will prevent many of the confusions that can easily occur in longer ones. Try the ear test: read your writing aloud and break apart any sentence you can't finish in one breath.

• **Connecting with the reader** Reach out to your reader by occasionally using questions. A request gains emphasis when it ends with a question mark. Rather than writing, "Please advise as to whether the meeting is still scheduled for February 21st", simply ask: "Is the meeting still scheduled for February 21st?"

> **WRITE WITH PERSONAL PRONOUNS**
> Use "we", "us", and "our" when speaking for the company. Use "I", "me", and "my" when speaking for yourself. Either way, be generous with the use of the word "you".

IN FOCUS... THE RIGHT ORDER

A poorly organized letter reads like a mystery story. Clue by clue, it unfolds details that make sense only towards the end – if the reader makes it that far. Your job is to make it easier for the reader, by explaining each point with an overview, followed by details. To avoid any confusion, always give directions before reasons, requests before justifications, answers before explanations, conclusions before details, and solutions before problems. Try the approach used in newspaper articles. They start with the most important information and taper off to the least important.

Capturing and keeping your readers' attention

USE CONTRACTIONS
Make your writing softer and more accessible by occasionally using the contractions that we naturally speak with, such as "I'm", "we're", "you'd", "they've", "can't", "don't", and "let's".

ALLOW SENTENCES TO END WITH A PREPOSITION
Don't reword a sentence just to move a preposition (e.g. "after", "at", "by", "from", "of", "to", or "up") from the end. You are likely to lengthen, tangle, and stiffen the sentence.

USE SHORT TRANSITIONS
Use "but" more than "however", and "more than" rather than "in addition to". Use more formal transitions only for variety. Don't be afraid to start a sentence with words like "but", "so", "yet", "and", or "or".

USE THE PRESENT TENSE WHENEVER POSSIBLE
This adds immediacy to your writing. Be careful, however, not to slip from the present to the past tense and back again, as this will make your writing confusing. Select one tense and stick to it.

Writing a business letter

Business letters are primarily external documents, although managers will occasionally use letters to correspond with subordinates and executives within their organization. Good letters are crisp, concise, and organized so that readers can follow and understand the content with little effort.

TIP

BE PROMPT

When you receive a business letter, always send an answer within three business days. If you can't reply within this time – because you need to speak with someone else or gather information – drop the writer a note to let them know that you are working on their problem.

Writing successful letters

Your success as a business writer depends, in large measure, on your ability to convince others that what you have written is worth their attention. This is more likely if your letter meets three criteria: it should be compact, it should be informal, and it absolutely must be organized. Be careful, however. Brevity is desirable, but you can overdo it. Make sure that your letters are not too brief or curt. It is extremely important to make sure that your reader has enough information to understand the subject. Include each issue relevant to the subject, and explain the process, the outcome, or the decision to the satisfaction of the reader. If you were receiving the letter, would the information be sufficient? Would you be satisfied that the writer had taken you seriously?

Showing interest

When writing in response to a letter you have received, aim to show that you are genuinely interested. The person writing to you thought the issue was important enough to write about; you should think so, too. Show by your words and actions that you care about them and the issue they've written about.

Give everyone the benefit of the doubt. Don't automatically assume that the person corresponding with you is doing so for the purpose of cheating you or your company.

Q IN FOCUS...
FORM LETTERS

It may be tempting to compile a "one-size-fits-all" approach to writing when there are many recipients, but it is usually a recipe for disaster. A letter must answer all of the questions its audience is likely to have, responding to their fears, doubts, and concerns. In situations in which it is absolutely necessary to use this approach, you can test market form letters, by showing them to several people who are (or have been) members of the audience in question and asking for suggestions for improvement.

Hitting the right tone

If a correspondent makes (or attempts) a joke, play along. Show that you have a sense of humour. Racist, sexist, or profane humour is never appropriate, but ordinary self-deprecating or directionless humour can often lighten or improve a difficult situation.

If you have to deliver bad news by letter, say you are sorry. Use phrases such as, "I am sorry to say that…" or "I regret to say that we'll be unable to [do something] because…". You can soften the blow by saying that you're sorry it happened, or that you regret the outcome. If it's bad news and your reader thinks you don't care, you

may spark an unwanted reaction. If you're bearing good news, say that you are glad: "I am delighted to tell you that…". Alternatively use a phrase such as: "You will be pleased to learn that…".

Never write and quickly send off an angry letter. Venting your spleen in an angry, hostile reply to someone may make you feel good, but it's almost never a good idea to post such a letter. Take your time and cool down before you compose an angry letter. Then, if you have written something you aren't sure about, wait until the following day so that you can re-read what you have written before sending it. Chances are, you'll think twice about posting.

Using email effectively

Email is now a global means of staying in touch, passing data and graphics, and managing the flow of information needed to run a business. It's also a gateway for unwanted spam and viruses. Properly managed, though, email can become a productivity booster, a link to distant markets, and an essential communication tool.

TIP

ESTABLISH A RESPONSE TIME

If you usually respond to email messages immediately, people grow to expect an immediate response, and become annoyed if you differ from this. The rule of thumb in business is to respond to emails by the end of the same day. If it's really urgent, use the telephone instead.

Reducing your emailing time

Email is a tool; don't let it become your master. Limit the time you spend on email by following these tips:
• **Send less, get less** Think carefully about whether you really need to draft new messages or respond to those you've already received.
• **Escape the endless reply loop** Silence in response to an email message may feel rude, but is acceptable. If you wish to reassure someone that no reply is necessary, finish a message with "no reply needed," or a request with "Thanks in advance." Avoid asking any questions for which you don't really want or need answers.
• **Think twice about the "cc" box** If you copy in a large number of people to your emails and they all respond with a reply that needs an answer, your message backlog may become unmanageable.

✔ CHECKLIST KNOWING WHEN EMAIL IS INAPPROPRIATE

	YES	NO
• Do I need to convey or discern emotion?	☐	☐
• Do I need to cut through the communication clutter?	☐	☐
• Do I need to move quickly?	☐	☐
• Do I want a remote communication to be private?	☐	☐
• Am I trying to reach someone who doesn't have (or check) email?	☐	☐
• Do I want to engage people and get an immediate response?	☐	☐

Improving your habits

Don't check your email constantly. Check it at regular intervals, such as first thing in the morning, once after lunch, and again before going home. Be disciplined about your email management. Aim to handle each message just once. If it's unimportant or irrelevant, hit the delete key. If you spend more than three hours a week sorting through junk mail, you have a problem and need to reorganize your system.

If a message is something you'll need to respond to, decide whether to do it now or later, when you will have the time and information you need. Once you have responded, move the message out of your inbox and into an archive folder.

Avoiding the pitfalls

It's all too easy to send an email quickly, only to regret it later. Before sending any email, always check the "To" field before you click "Send". Make sure you're sending this message to the address you intend. Double-check to make absolutely certain you haven't clicked "Reply All".

Make sure your computer – and your company's email server – are set to the correct time and date. Messages with an incorrect time or date can be misfiled or overlooked.

HOW TO...
SEND A BETTER EMAIL

Pick the subject line of the email carefully: make it informative and brief so the recipient can easily find and act on it.

↓

Now write the main body of the email, using correct grammar, punctuation, and capitalization.

↓

Avoid abbreviations and cyberjargon: most business professionals dislike them. WIDLTO (when in doubt, leave them out).

↓

Be careful with criticism: be sure to provide enough context and background to avoid a misunderstanding.

↓

Keep it short. If you need more than three paragraphs, phone instead or send the material as an attachment.

↓

Use a signature to conclude your email, but keep it simple: don't be tempted to add humourous or "inspiring" quotes.

↓

Before you send the email, check your attachments. Send only those that your recipient needs or wants to see.

Writing reports

Reports are longer and more comprehensive than most documents, and are written for the purpose of documenting actions, describing projects and events, and capturing information on complex issues. They are often written by more than one person for audiences with multiple needs and interests.

TIP

INCLUDE A COVER LETTER

As a courtesy to your reader, always include a cover letter to accompany the report, explaining what the report covers and why. Where appropriate, include the report's most important recommendations or findings.

Planning your report

There are four main questions to consider when compiling a report:
• **Who is in your audience?** Think about their level of interest in the content, and their familiarity with the issues, ideas, and vocabulary you plan to use.
• **What is the ideal format?** Consider how your readers will use the document – will they start from the beginning and read through page by page, or will they skip to sections that interest them most?
• **Have you collected the right information?** Make sure your information is relevant, correct, and sufficient, and that you know how to explain it most usefully.
• **Is the document properly organized?** Consider using a bold typeface for headings and sub-headings to help organize the information and make it retrievable.

Writing the report

Reports are divided into three sections: front matter (including title page, abstract, table of contents, and list of figures and tables), the main body of the report, and end matter (bibliography, appendices, glossary, and index). Begin the main body with an executive summary, detailing the report's key points and recommendations. Busy executives may only read this section, so it must tell them all they need to know in order for them to agree with your recommendations.

DIVIDING YOUR REPORT INTO SECTIONS

SECTION	CONTENT
Title page	A single page, containing the full title of the report, the names of the authors, the date on which the report was issued, the name of the organization, and often the people or organization to whom the report is submitted.
Abstract	A paragraph that briefly summarizes and highlights the major points. Its primary function is to enable a reader to decide whether to read the entire work.
Table of contents	A list of all of the headings within the report in the order of their appearance, along with a page number for each.
List of figures and tables	When a report contains more than five figures or tables, it should include a page listing each by title, with page numbers.
Foreword (optional)	An introductory statement usually written by an authority figure who will be well recognized by prospective readers. It provides background information and places the report in the context of other works in the field.
Preface (optional)	This describes the purpose, background, or scope of the report. It is sometimes used to acknowledge assistance provided in research or preparation, and sources used.
Executive summary	This provides more information than the abstract, and enables readers to quickly scan the report's primary points. Executive summaries are usually restricted to a few pages.
Main text	This forms the main body of the report, and explains your work and its findings.
Conclusion	This contains not only concluding remarks but also any recommended actions for the readers.
Bibliography	An alphabetical listing of all the sources you consulted to prepare the report; this suggests additional resources the reader may wish to consult.
Appendices	Information that supplements the main report as evidence, such as lists, tables of figures, and charts and graphs.
Glossary	An alphabetical list of definitions of unusual terms used.
Index	An alphabetical list of topics with page numbers.

Chapter 3

Communicating with your team

A team is only as good as its communication; misunderstandings can cause a huge amount of extra work and lost time. When managing a team, focus on giving constructive feedback, briefing thoroughly, and dealing effectively with conflict.

Listening effectively

Studies show that adults now spend more than half of their daily communication time listening to someone else speak. As a manager, being able to listen effectively and understand others is at the heart of creating a team that performs to the best of its ability.

Learning when to listen

Listening is a skill you acquire naturally, but can improve upon if you're motivated to do so. The first step towards becoming a better listener is, surprisingly, to stop. You need to stop talking, stop trying to carry on more than one conversation, and stop interrupting. Let the other person speak. As others are talking, allow yourself to respond cognitively and emotionally, taking in the factual information and the tone of their remarks, without responding. Then ask carefully thought-out questions that will clarify what they have said and reassure you of its basis in fact.

Getting the message

Start by trying to see things from the speaker's point of view, and let your actions demonstrate this. Show interest with your body language: look the speaker in the eyes and maintain an open and non-threatening posture. Give the speaker physical signs of your undivided attention: close the door, hold your calls, and put aside whatever you're working on.

Listen carefully to how something is said: look out for hints of sarcasm, cynicism, or irony in what you hear. Try to tune in to the speaker's mood and intention. Remember that communication is a shared responsibility, so it is up to you to ensure that you understand the message.

Once you have listened to what a person has to say and clarified anything you're not sure of, evaluate the facts and evidence. Ask yourself whether the evidence is recent, reliable, accurate, and relevant.

TIP

BEWARE WISHFUL THINKING

Just because you want to hear something doesn't mean it is what the speaker is actually saying. It is all too easy to fall into the trap of selective hearing, so make sure that you listen to everything that the speaker is telling you.

LISTENING ACTIVELY

FAST TRACK

OFF TRACK

FAST TRACK	OFF TRACK
Listening regularly to difficult material to hone your listening ability	Assuming that everything interesting should be provided in written form
Giving your full and undivided attention to the speaker	Pretending to listen while actually doing something else
Listening to the argument in the speaker's terms, and in the order he or she wishes to follow	Criticizing the speaker's delivery and interrupting the flow of what they are saying to ask questions
Focusing on the reasons for the speaker's approach and discussion	Assuming you already know what the issue is and how to resolve it

Giving feedback

When he was mayor of New York City, Ed Koch frequently walked the streets of his hometown asking his constituents, "How am I doing?" The question wasn't simply rhetorical. He asked the question of friend and foe alike, and he cared about the responses, because his performance as mayor depended on feedback – direct, honest, current, unfiltered feedback.

Knowing when to give feedback

Good feedback doesn't just happen. It is the product of careful, deliberate communication strategies, coupled with good interpersonal communication skills. You can significantly increase the probability that the feedback you give helps others to improve by understanding the role of feedback in both personal and professional settings.

Feedback is vital to any organization committed to improving itself, because it is the only way for managers and executives to know what needs to be improved. Giving and receiving feedback should be more than just a part of an employee's behaviour; it should be a part of the whole organization's culture.

 IN FOCUS... LANGUAGE

Not everyone has the same understanding of language, and certain words, phrases, or terms that mean one thing to a manager may mean something very different to a person receiving feedback. It is important, therefore, that the language used for feedback is acceptable to the person being spoken to and appropriate for the circumstances. The words used must be clearly understood and agreed upon by both parties. Acronyms or company jargon are only acceptable if it is clear that both parties know what they mean. Successful managers make sure they know whether the person they are giving feedback to shares the same frame of reference they do, avoid language that will cause confusion, and choose words that are universally understood.

Knowing how to give feedback

Providing constructive, useful feedback involves more than simply responding to people as they speak to you. Consider the context in which the communication takes place, people's intentions as they speak (or choose not to speak), and your objectives as a manager.

• **Get the timing right** Before deciding to offer feedback, decide whether the moment is right for both people involved. Constructive feedback can happen only within a context of listening to and caring about the other person. If the time isn't right, if the moment isn't appropriate, you can always delay briefly before offering your thoughts.

• **Understand the context** This is the most important characteristic of feedback: find out where an event happened, why it happened, and what led up to it. Always review the actions and decisions that led up to the moment; never simply give feedback and leave.

• **Give both positive and negative feedback** People are more likely to pay attention to your complaints if they have also received your compliments. It is important to remember to tell people when they have done something well.

TIP

FOCUS ON BEHAVIOUR

If you are giving negative feedback, defuse any hostility and minimize the fear felt by the other person by depersonalizing the conversation: focusing your comments on the behaviour involved, not the people.

Hitting the right tone

"Why can't you fill out trip reports properly?"

"These trip reports need more detail."

"You've messed up again. Fix it."

"There are errors in this report. Can we talk about it?"

Understanding nonverbal communication

Most of the meaning transferred from one person to another in a personal conversation comes not from the words that are spoken, but from nonverbal signals. Learning to read, understand, and use these wordless messages isn't easy, but is essential for effective communication.

Reading nonverbal signals

The movement, positioning, and use of the human body in various communication settings serves a number of functions:

- To highlight or emphasize some part of a verbal message
- To regulate the flow, pace, and back-and-forth nature of verbal messages
- To reinforce the general tone or attitude of a message
- To repeat what the verbal messages convey (holding up three fingers to indicate the number three, for example)
- To substitute for, or take the place of, verbal messages (such as giving a "thumbs up" gesture).

USE VOCAL DYNAMICS
Tone, volume, rate, pitch, forcefulness, and enunciation all convey meaning about a subject, and how you feel about the people in the room.

Nonverbal cues are often difficult to read, especially because there are few body movements or gestures that have universally agreed-upon meanings. A colleague who looks tired or overworked to one person may appear disinterested or indifferent to another. While looking for meaning in a particular movement, position, or gesture, be careful not to miss more important signals that reveal the true feelings of a speaker. Body language can sometimes contradict the verbal messages being sent. Tears in a person's eyes, for example, might involuntarily contradict a message telling you that they are fine.

Using nonverbal signals

WATCH YOUR APPEARANCE
Make sure that your clothing and grooming are appropriate to your audience, your reasons for communicating, and the occasion.

RESTRAIN YOUR MOVEMENTS
Small gestures, close to your body, will convey an image of confidence and authority. Keep your voice low but audible and your posture relaxed.

WATCH YOUR EYE CONTACT
Eye contact usually reinforces trust; however, in some Asian cultures, looking a superior in the eye as you speak can be considered disrespectful.

TAKE CARE WITH TOUCH
The rules on touching others in a business context vary from culture to culture. Make sure you know and respect local customs.

Running briefings and meetings

Briefings and meetings are an inescapable part of business life. They are a means of sharing information, initiating strategies, perpetuating a culture, and building consensus around business goals. Done well, they're good for business and good for morale.

TIP

ANTICIPATE QUESTIONS

Do your best to address audience concerns, questions, doubts, and fears in advance. Plan the content of your briefing around the needs of those in the audience.

Organizing a meeting

Be clear about the purpose of any meeting before you start planning. Invite only those people who are directly related to your goals, and make sure you include all the key decision-makers. Once you've arranged a time, place, and date that is convenient to everyone, send them all an agenda, making clear the meeting's theme and goals. In putting together the agenda, consider the following questions: What do we need to do in this meeting? What conversations will be important to those who attend? What information will we need to begin?

Prioritize the most important items so they will be discussed early on in the meeting, and assign a certain amount of time for each agenda item.

❓ ASK YOURSELF... DO I NEED TO CALL A MEETING?

- Do I need to motivate people, giving them a "jumpstart" to get going?
- Do I need to share general company or market information with people to help them do their jobs?
- Do I need to initiate a new programme or project?
- Do I wish to introduce people to one another, so they can benefit from each other's experiences?

Giving a briefing

Briefing is a process by which you provide information to those who need it. As with any form of communication, think about your audience, your purpose, and the occasion. Find out all you can about the audience, and what they hope to take away from the session. State your purpose clearly and simply at the beginning of the meeting: "The purpose of this briefing is to look at budget projections for the next 90 days." Let them know why you're calling the meeting now.

Delivering a brief

When giving a briefing meeting, choose the form of delivery that best suits your speaking style and the needs of the audience. There are three forms to choose from:
• **Memorized presentations** These are delivered verbatim, just as you wrote them. This gives you total control over the material, but unless you're a trained actor, there's a risk that you'll sound wooden and the material contrived. Worse yet, you may forget where you are and have to start again or refer to notes.
• **Scripted briefings** These are more common, but they can also sound stilted. The problem with reading is that you risk losing eye contact, lowering your chin, and

CASE STUDY

A competitive advantage
As CEO of the international retail giant Wal-Mart, David Glass knew the company would have to be quick off the mark with merchandising strategies, particularly in response to moves made by competitors. Each Saturday morning, when sales results for the week were transmitted to the corporate headquarters, Glass would gather key subordinates to share information from people in the field. They would tell the sales team what their competitors were doing; the senior team would then focus on corrective actions they wanted to take.

By noon, regional managers would telephone district managers, and each would exchange ideas on the direction they wanted to take that week, along with changes they would implement. "By noon on Saturday," Glass said, "we had all our corrections in place. Our competitors, for the most part, got their sales results on Monday for the week prior. They were already 10 days behind."

compressing your vocal pitch. If you do use a script, rehearse carefully and look up frequently, making regular eye contact with your audience.
• **Extemporaneous briefings** These are delivered either without notes or with visual aids to prompt your memory. They are the most effective choice, looking more spontaneous, while actually being thoroughly researched, tightly organized, and well rehearsed.

Communicating to persuade

Most successful attempts at persuasion involve four separate, yet related, steps. Following these steps won't guarantee success with any particular audience, but they will set the stage for the attitudes you're trying to shape in your team and the behaviour you hope will follow.

TELL THEM ABOUT THE BENEFITS

Make sure you cover the WIIFM question: "What's in it for me?". Don't just tell your team what you want them to do – make sure they understand the many ways in which they themselves will benefit from it.

Getting their attention

If you want to motivate people to do something, you first have to catch their attention. Research shows that we selectively choose what to pay attention to, both as a defence mechanism against sensory overload, and because we seek out messages with particular value for us. We ignore virtually everything else. There are two ways to capture attention:
• Use physical stimuli, such as bright lights, sound, motion, or colour
• Present stimuli that relate directly to the needs or goals of those you want to persuade.

Providing a motivation

Next, you need to provide a reason for people to act. A persuasive writer or speaker is one who can lead others to believe in what he or she is advocating, and then encourage some form of behaviour in line with that belief. This amounts to giving good reasons for what you believe. These are not reasons you think are good, but reasons your team thinks are good.

Identify the needs and interests of your team and connect them to your message. Which of their needs are you fulfilling? Appeal to their sense of rationality – show why it makes sense to act on your message. Or call on their sense of conformity, by showing how well others will view them if they act on your message.

Moving others to act

Once you have captured the attention of those you want to persuade and have given them good cause to believe the message, you must provide them with a clear channel for action. First, however, take time to reassure them: show them that there is a high probability that you can deliver on the promised reward. Your team needs to know that what you've promised will actually come true.

Next, recommend a specific proposal for action. Tell your team exactly what you want them to do, describe how you would like them to go about it, and set out a realistic timescale. Make sure that everyone on your team knows how and when progress will be measured and identify the end point and the rewards for achievement that lie ahead.

Keeping them on side

The arguments that you use to persuade others can be one-sided, presenting your case alone, or two-sided, presenting your case as well as dealing with real and potential counter-arguments. Choose your approach based on the knowledge and preconceptions of your audience. If you decide to use a two-sided argument, you should:
• Warn your team that others may try to influence them to change their minds.
• State some opposing arguments and then refute them. If you are aware of an opposing message, consider previewing at least part of it to the audience and then explaining why it is flawed.
• Encourage commitment in some tangible or visible way. It's more difficult for someone to back away from a position for which they've publicly proclaimed their support.

WHEN TO USE ONE- OR TWO-SIDED ARGUMENTS

ONE-SIDED ARGUMENT	TWO-SIDED ARGUMENT
The audience initially agrees with you and your aim is simply to intensify support.	You suspect or know that the audience initially disagrees with your position.
The audience will not be exposed to any form of counter-persuasion.	You know the audience will be exposed to subsequent counter-persuasion.
The audience is not well-educated or may become easily confused by an opponent's argument or evidence.	You hope to produce a more enduring result with a knowledgeable audience.

Managing conflict

Conflict* can arise from a variety of sources, but many experts see it as a function of such workplace issues as personality, personal and professional relationships, cultural differences, working environments, demands of the marketplace, and of course, competition. As organizations increasingly use teamwork, differences among team members can lead to conflict.

*****Conflict** — *a state of opposition or hostilities between two or more people that may arise as a result of clashing principles or incompatible wishes.*

Identifying the sources of conflict

Not all conflict within an organization is unhealthy, but conflict between and among people within an organization can quickly become counter-productive, divisive, and destructive if not properly managed.

Conflict may develop over any number of issues or factors, but these five appear regularly:

• **Limited resources** Everything from office space to budgets may put people in competition with one another. Allocate scarce resources fairly to avoid this.

• **Values, goals, and priorities** Confrontation can occur when people in an organization don't agree on strategic direction or basic priorities. Agreement on goals, large and small, can help to avoid this.

• **Poorly defined responsibilities** Conflict may result from differences between formal position descriptions and daily expectations of the job. Review and agree who is responsible for what (and to whom).

• **Change** Many changes, including those to annual budgets, organizational priorities, lines of authority, or limits of responsibility, as well as restructuring, mergers, divestitures, and lay-offs, can create anxiety, uncertainty, and conflict in an organization.

• **Human drive for success** Conflicts can arise as a result of the natural sense of goal orientation that every human experiences. Many organizations actively foster a sense of competition among their members, creating many competitors and few rewards.

Ways to manage conflict within your team

1 LISTEN CAREFULLY
Find out what's on people's minds, and ask them what they're thinking and how they feel.

2 SEPARATE PEOPLE FROM PROBLEMS
Rather than saying "I can't support you", say "I'm not in favour of that solution."

3 FOCUS ON INTERESTS
Don't focus on a person's demands, but on their interests – the reasons behind their demands.

4 RECOGNIZE FEELINGS
Accept feelings in others, and work to communicate empathy. Keep your own emotions in check, to ensure that you act professionally.

5 FIND THE SOURCE
Track the conflict to its source. Don't accept the first answers you find; employees may have underlying concerns.

6 KEEP COMMUNICATING
Keep the lines of communication open and speak as frankly and honestly as possible.

7 START SMALL
Get people to agree on the small stuff first. Once they start to agree on a few things, the big issues won't be as difficult.

8 DEVISE OPTIONS
Find alternatives for mutual gain. By working together on the options, you can shift the dynamic from competition to cooperation.

9 SUMMARIZE THE AGREEMENT
Review all the details with everyone involved. Make sure all are in agreement.

10 CUT YOUR LOSSES
Sometimes the conflict has simply gone too far, and you must decide to make personnel changes.

Communicating externally

In today's global economy, you may find yourself communicating across companies, countries, and cultures, through a variety of media, including the internet. Focus on your company's core goals and identity to ensure consistent messaging.

Negotiating successfully

Negotiation is a process in which people attempt to persuade others to cooperate or assist in attaining goals or goods that they value. The process often involves bargaining – giving up something in order to get something else – as well as collaboration, cooperation, and compromise.

Exploring interests

A key distinction to make in negotiating is recognizing the difference between interests and positions. A position is a hard line in the sand: a statement of a single acceptable outcome. Interests, on the other hand, are the reasons behind that position. Spend time seeing the negotiation from the other party's point of view; this may help you anticipate what is really important to them. This is important because there may be more than one way of meeting those interests. Can you find an alternative, workable position that will still satisfy the other party's interests?

Recognizing significant points

Before negotiating, you need to decide upon three main points about your position:
• **Your target or aspiration point** What you hope to achieve. Set this at a high but reasonable level.
• **Your reservation or walk-away point** The least desirable outcome that you will accept. At anything less than your reservation, you would be better off walking away without a deal.
• **Your Best Alternative to a Negotiated Agreement (BATNA)** This is your back-up plan in case you are unable to reach agreement with the other party.

TIP

CONSIDER COMPENSATION
Sometimes parties can be enticed into an agreement through the offer of something unrelated to the issues in negotiation. Think about what might be valuable to the other party, but inexpensive for you to offer.

Making the opening offer

If you have done your homework and have a good idea of the bargaining range, then you should make the opening offer. That offer anchors the bargaining process. Your opening offer should reflect your aspirations, but not be ridiculous. If it is way out of range, you risk insulting the other party and damaging trust. If the other party makes the opening offer, and it is outrageous, don't discuss it. Simply dismiss it, indicate that it is not a possibility, and start again.

Your opening offer should leave you room to make concessions, but bear in mind that any you do make will provide the other party with information. If they make concessions, you should reciprocate, or they may view you with distrust and become more competitive. Don't make too large a concession right away, however, or the other side may think there is considerable "give" in your bargaining range.

? ASK YOURSELF...
AM I PREPARED TO NEGOTIATE?

• What do I really want?
• What does the other party involved really want?
• Should I compete, or should I cooperate with them?
• How honest should I be? Should I reveal all that I know?
• How much should I trust the people I'm negotiating with?

Selling is both a form of persuasion and a process of relationship building. Most people don't want to feel as if they're being sold something; they would prefer to believe that they're buying it. This involves a balance of thoughtful questions, active listening, and a well-prepared presentation.

Prospecting and presenting

Selling involves actively looking for prospects who have the money, the authority, and a desire to buy. Before you contact a prospect, make sure that they fulfil these criteria, and that you know both what you want to achieve, and how. Develop a presentation that you can deliver confidently. This may be entirely memorized, formulaic (allowing some buyer–seller interaction), or entirely flexible and interactive.
If you're offering a solution to a specific problem, base your proposal around a detailed analysis of the buyer's situation. Before you contact a prospect, always:
● Determine your call objectives. Are they specific, measurable, achievable, realistic, and well-timed?
● Develop a customer profile. What do you know about the person who is making the buying decision?
● Familiarize yourself with all the customer benefits.
● Develop a sales presentation.

Closing the sale

First ask the prospect's opinion about the benefits you're offering, using a question such as: "How does this sound to you?" If this throws up any objections, handle them as they arise. Don't repeat negative statements or concerns; focus on positive outcomes. There are various ways to close a sale, so choose the one that is most appropriate to your situation.

TIP

MAKE A POSITIVE FIRST IMPRESSION

Be positive: smile, be enthusiastic, and open conversation with a thoughtful compliment or a prediction related to your product.

USE THE MINOR POINTS CLOSE
Ask the prospect to make low-risk decisions on minor, low-cost elements. Then ask for the order.

Ways to close a sale

GIVE AN ALTERNATIVE CHOICE
Give two options, and then ask: "Which of these do you prefer?"

USE THE ASSUMPTIVE CLOSE
When the prospect is close to a decision, say: "I'll call your order in tonight."

SUMMARIZE THE BENEFITS
Present the main features, advantages, and benefits, then ask for the order.

USE THE SCARCITY CLOSE
If true, tell the prospect that these items are so popular, there may not be many of them left.

USE THE CONTINUOUS "YES" CLOSE
Develop a set of questions the prospect will answer "yes" to, then ask for the order.

Communicating across countries and cultures

The industrialized nations of the world are experiencing unprecedented change. In much of Europe, for example, it is possible for EU citizens to travel from country to country without a passport, conducting transactions in a common currency. Barriers to trade have tumbled or vanished in recent years, but through it all, each of us has retained something essential to our identity as humans: our culture.

Defining culture

Culture is everything that people have, think, and do as members of their society. Culture affects and is a central part of our economy and the organizations that employ us. It is composed of material objects, ideas, values, and attitudes, as well as expected patterns of behaviour. Whatever your business, you're likely to encounter people of different ethnicity, citizenship, and cultural origin. Dealing with people of different cultures, conducting business over international borders, travelling safely, and communicating effectively are not always easy, but are essential for success in today's business world.

 IN FOCUS... ETHNOCENTRISM

All cultures, to one degree or another, display ethnocentrism: the tendency to evaluate a foreigner's behaviour by the standards of one's own culture, and to believe that one's culture is superior to all others. We tend to take our own culture for granted. We're born into it, and we live with its rules and assumptions day in and day out. We quickly come to believe that the way we live is simply "the way things should be". As a result, we often see our behaviour as correct. However, culture is not value-neutral. We have good reasons for believing and behaving as we do, but that doesn't necessarily mean that others are "wrong".

TIP

INVESTIGATE THE SUBCULTURES
Virtually all large, complex cultures contain subcultures. These are small groups of people with separate and specialized interests – essentially, they are niche markets.

Understanding culture

When you're communicating with a culture other than your own, you need to be sensitive about the particular beliefs and values of that culture, and how they differ from your own. Bear in mind that:

• **Culture is ingrained** Few of us would give a moment's thought to learning how to be a part of the culture we have grown up in. Our first culture is so closely defined for each of us that we're barely aware that we have one. Learning a second culture, though, takes a purposeful effort.

• **Culture is universal** All societies have an interest in passing along values and norms to their children, thereby creating and defining a culture. No matter where you travel, you'll find people with cultures that differ from the one in which you grew up; noticing these differences will strengthen your communications.

• **Cultures allocate values** Some cultures engage in behaviours that others might consider reprehensible. Be careful never to cause offence when communicating by inadvertently breaking taboos or talking about matters that are considered "off limits".

Recognizing change

The culture of any country is constantly undergoing change. The clothing people wear, the transportation they use, the books they read, the topics they talk about, and so on, all change over time. This is due to the internal forces of discovery, invention, and innovation; and external forces, including the diffusion of ideas from other cultures. Some cultures change fast, while others evolve more slowly, either by preference or because they are more physically isolated. Changes in culture are often reflected in changes in the way people speak and write; make sure that your own communications reflect these changes.

Communicating internationally

On a personal level, communicating across international borders means becoming more aware of the ways in which your thinking or actions are culturally biased. Start by recognizing that your own education, background, and beliefs may be considered fine, or even laudable in your own culture, but they may not count for so much to someone from a different country. Take a non-judgemental position towards those from other cultures, and you are likely to find that they will extend the same hospitable tolerance towards you. If you find yourself making personal judgements, keep them to yourself.

When you're writing or speaking to people from another culture, try to understand life from their perspective. Learn to communicate respect for other people's ways, their country, and their values.

Adopting the right attitude

You don't have to adopt the local culture and begin doing things the way they do. Just be aware and respect that they do things differently. "Your way" of communicating might work brilliantly in your own culture, but less well in another. Try to adopt an open-minded approach, focusing on:

• **Developing a tolerance for ambiguity** Accept the fact that you'll never understand everything about another culture. You can still appreciate and function within that culture satisfactorily.

• **Becoming more flexible** Things won't always go the way you want. A small measure of flexibility will prove enormously helpful.

• **Practising a little humility** Acknowledge what you do not know or understand. Because you weren't raised in another's culture (or may not even speak the language well), you'll never fully understand all aspects of it. Displaying humility and acceptance will win friends, influence people, and make life easier. Communication consists of the transfer of meaning, so do everything you can to make sure that your messages are not misunderstood.

TIP

LEARN TO RECOGNIZE "NO"
Some cultures consider it rude to say "no". If you are met with vague answers to requests, such as "I'll try", or "yes, but it may be difficult" in these cultures, it may be safer to assume that your request has been refused.

? ASK YOURSELF... DO I UNDERSTAND THE CULTURE?

• Do I understand the basic business etiquette of introductions and meetings in this new culture?
• Do I know how to recognize the key decision-makers within a group?
• Am I familiar with the culture's business dress code?
• Do I know how many languages are spoken, and which is the official language?
• Have I learned the preferred forms of negotiation?
• Do I know which forms of media are popular among which demographic groups?

Writing for the web

The way that people read a website is very different to the way in which they read other written information. You must take this into account when developing content for a website. It is not sufficient to simply repurpose content written for print; you need to write specifically for the internet, thinking carefully about your audience and what they need.

Engaging your readers

Why is writing for the internet different? First, people rarely read websites word-for-word. Instead, they scan the page, picking out individual words and sentences. Rather than starting at the beginning of a page and reading from start to finish, internet readers will scan a site looking for relevant items and then, if they find something useful, print it for later reference. Guide your reader by highlighting the most important or useful points in your document using headings, lists, and eye-catching typography.

AVOID FRAGMENTATION
Be careful not to subdivide your information into too many pieces. Your readers may be overwhelmed or frustrated if they have too many choices. Ensure that each segment is sensibly organized, coherent, and easy to scan.

Web readers generally do not read pages in sequence. Instead, they jump around on a website looking for content that interests them, navigating back and forth across images, ideas, and words. Providing information in precise segments or "chunks" will allow readers to quickly find what they're looking for. A well-constructed chunk provides readers with a comprehensive account, as well as links to related or supporting pages. When your content lends itself to such treatment, use lists rather than paragraphs. Readers can pick out information more easily from a list than from a fully developed paragraph.

Preparing content for the web

THINK ABOUT LENGTH
Limit the length of each paragraph and each page to about half of what you might consider for a printed page. Don't arbitrarily divide a page that is likely to be printed.

USE SUMMARIES
Include brief but comprehensive summaries of longer documents, so that readers can easily tell whether they need to read more or can move on to other content.

ENSURE EASY ACCESS
Your principal goal should be to provide access to the information people are most likely to want. Provide easy-to-follow clues that will lead people to chunks of information that will be useful to them.

PREPARE FOR PRINT
Make it easy for your readers to find, print, and save information. If some aspects of your content are more detailed or lengthy, consider linking to a PDF file that is both downloadable and printable.

Running a teleconference

Recent improvements in both the cost and quality of teleconferencing equipment have made the prospect of connecting people with audio and video technology over vast distances seem increasingly attractive. It is vital to plan carefully, however, to avoid technical hitches and make the experience rewarding and successful for those involved.

Preparing for a teleconference

Running a successful and productive teleconference depends largely on the time you spend planning and preparing for it. If possible, find out as much as you can about the facility you have chosen before the day of the teleconference. If you're in charge, it is up to you to make sure that the setting has everything you need. Try to meet the support technician, and learn what your physical responsibilities will involve.

CHAIRING A TELECONFERENCE

FAST TRACK	OFF TRACK
Asking people to give their names, titles, and locations	Introducing some of the participants, but ignoring others
Keeping to the agenda and staying on time	Introducing new items not agreed to in advance
Taking control and providing people with opportunities to speak	Allowing people to talk with one another in side conversations
Making notes of what is being said and by whom	Failing to capture what's been said and agreed to

Appearing well

On the day, dress conservatively: avoid busy patterns, thin stripes, and small prints that draw attention. Act always as if people are watching you, and refrain from quirky mannerisms – these may go unnoticed in a meeting but are magnified in a teleconference. Sit up straight, pay attention, and project a professional image. Do your best to look at the camera lens when you are speaking. You'll enhance your credibility dramatically if you focus squarely on the camera; others will think you're speaking directly to them.

Sounding good

Once you're in the room, avoid idle talk or unguarded comments – assume that someone may be watching and listening. Speak a bit more slowly than usual, to ensure that everyone understands you. Don't read a speech or a prepared statement, but keep summarizing key issues as you move along. Refer to the agenda and remind people of elapsed time as you move from point to point.

At the end of the teleconference, summarize the issues discussed and agreed to. After the event, prepare and distribute minutes within a few days.

HOW TO... PLAN A TELECONFERENCE

Identify the purpose of the teleconference: explain to people what they will be doing and why.

↓

Visit the facility in advance and try to identify any aspects of the location or equipment that affect how you need to plan the teleconference.

↓

Identify a chairperson who will be responsible for starting, stopping, and running the teleconference.

↓

Plan the agenda; don't just try to "wing it" as you go along. Place easily accomplished items first on the list.

↓

Distribute the agenda so other people know what will be discussed and will have time to gather necessary information.

↓

Schedule the teleconference for a time and date that suits everyone.

↓

Confirm the teleconference with all participants and send a reminder just before it is due to take place.

↓

Share important resources in advance; send through any materials that are important for everyone to see.

Communicating in a crisis

There is a huge difference between business problems and crises. Problems are commonplace in business. A crisis, on the other hand, is a major, unpredictable event. Without careful communication, crises have the potential to damage an organization's reputation and financial standing, together with those of its employees, shareholders, products, and services.

Identifying the crisis

Some business crises can be prepared for (to a certain extent), while others require an immediate and creative response. There are two main types:
• **Internal crises** These arise within the company, such as accounting scandals, or labour strikes.
• **External crises** These are caused by an external factor, such as a natural disaster, a technological disaster, or external threats by special-interest groups.

It is important to recognize the type of crisis you are facing, as this will help you pinpoint the groups of people you will need to communicate with, and give you an idea of how fast and how far the effects of the crisis could potentially spread.

CASE STUDY

Merck & Company

In September 2004, pharmaceutical firm Merck & Company made the decision to remove its painkilling drug Vioxx from the market because of cardiovascular risks. More than 100 million prescriptions had been written for the drug. Within 60 hours of the initial announcement, Merck's communications team launched a website and established a toll-free telephone number to address concerns.

Traffic on the company's Vioxx website grew from 4,000 hits daily to 234,000 in just 24 hours. The toll-free number received more than 120,000 calls in the first six days following the announcement. Without its sophisticated web presence and competently staffed call centre, Merck would not have been able to address the enormous wave of public concern that arose overnight about Vioxx, and its reputation would have been badly damaged.

Dealing with a crisis

Communicating in a crisis is different from managing a business problem. You are likely to be unprepared, and have insufficient information. This is accompanied by intense time pressure and an escalating flow of events. Crisis communication often offers few precedents to work from and intense scrutiny from outside the organization. This can lead to a loss of control and a sense of panic, so it is important to keep your head, and address the crisis systematically.

ADDRESSING A CRISIS

WHAT TO DO	HOW TO DO IT
Get information	• Deal from an informed position and separate fact from rumour. Document what you know and don't know for sure. Become the source of reliable information, and keep the information flowing. • Determine the real problem in the short term and the long term. Check whether this is really your problem.
Put people in place	• Put someone in charge. Give them responsibility, authority, and the resources to get the job done. Tell people who it is. • Assemble an effective but nimble team. Staff it with the expertise needed, and provide resources. Isolate team members from other day-to-day concerns.
Draw up a plan	• Develop a strategy, which should include ways to resolve the problem, deal with affected parties, and communicate both today and in the long term. • Establish goals. Define your objectives for the short term, mid-term, and long term. Measure relentlessly and don't be discouraged by critics, negative press, or short-term failures.
Start communicating	• Centralize communications. Incoming communication provides intelligence, while outgoing communication gives a measure of control over what is being said about the situation. • Rely on a strictly limited number of spokespersons who are knowledgeable, authoritative, responsive, patient, and good humoured. • Consider all markets – local, regional, national, and international. Don't overlook allies in other markets who may be able to provide assistance or credibility.

Dealing with the media

Being the subject of a news media interview is never easy, and can be stressful and risky. You might say the wrong thing or forget to say what's most important about the subject of the interview, or your comments might be taken out context when they're aired. However, by following a few basic rules, you can limit risk and use the interview to your advantage.

TIP

REVIEW THE DAY'S NEWS

Make sure you're up to date on events surrounding the topic of the interview. If you're caught by surprise, don't comment on events or quotes on which you are uncertain.

Capitalizing on opportunity

Learn to see media interviews as an opportunity to reach a large audience. They represent a chance to tell your story and to inform the public of your business or expertise. They also offer an opportunity to address public concerns and set the record straight, if you're the subject of misinformation in the press. They can be a forum in which to apologize if you've done something wrong, and a chance to reinforce the credibility of your organization and its leadership. Don't feel bullied into giving an interview if you're not ready: you can say "no" or delegate to another staff member who is more accustomed to dealing with the media.

✓ CHECKLIST SUCCEEDING IN MEDIA INTERVIEWS

	YES	NO
• Are you clear about what you hope to achieve from the interview?	☐	☐
• Do you know which items of information you can share, and which are confidential?	☐	☐
• Have you decided on a method for avoiding arguments if the reporter goads you?	☐	☐
• Do you know how to respond to false allegations, without repeating the phrases the reporter uses?	☐	☐
• Are you focused on remaining professional and likeable, no matter what happens in the interview?	☐	☐

Preparing for an interview

The best way to ensure a good interview is thorough preparation. Gather your information, and also:
• Research the reporter; deal only with established, professional journalists.
• Ask your Public Affairs or Corporate Communication office for help and guidance.
• Find out the subject and background of the story and ask who else is participating.
• Double-check the time, date, and location.
• Refine and practise your message: rehearse aloud the words you actually plan to use.

TIP

GET YOUR POINT IN EARLY
A reporter may not ask the one question you're most hoping to talk about. Raise the issue yourself, get your points in, and repeat them frequently. Use the free air time or print space to your benefit.

Conducting the interview

Arrive at the appointed interview site early and introduce yourself to all those involved. Dress smartly and accept the offer of make-up if appropriate: knowing that you look good will add to your confidence and sense of professionalism.

During the interview, it's perfectly acceptable to refer to facts and figures on a pocket card. Be yourself, and use words that everyone will understand; explain any technical or complex concepts in simple ways, as though you're talking to a friend. Make sure that you stay focused on the central theme of your message and always speak in terms of the public's interest, not your own.

Building brands

Communicating the essence of a brand is more than simply using words and visuals to convey an image. This is because a brand is both a process and a product. It's a living, breathing organism that must be nurtured and protected if it is to survive and thrive.

HOW TO... BUILD A BRAND

First, deliver something of value.

Then, meet expectations every day.

Be clear and certain about who you are.

Represent the same thing to every customer.

Winning hearts and minds

A brand is, first of all, a promise of an experience. It is what a product, service, or company stands for in the minds of customers and prospects. At its very core, a brand is a perception or a feeling. It's the feeling evoked when we think about a product or the company that delivers it. And, of course, a brand is the basis for differentiation in the marketplace – a way to separate yourself from all other competitors in the hearts and minds of your customers.

Defining the brand

The most crucial characteristics of a brand are content and consistency. To succeed, a brand must make a clear and unambiguous promise to its stakeholders (customers, employees, investors, suppliers, creditors, and others) and then deliver on that promise.

The Starbucks brand, for example, is clearly aligned with the customer experience. When regulars in Starbucks' coffee shops began to complain about the smell of hot breakfast sandwiches, the company's CEO Howard Schultz decided to focus on the core experience (and aromas) of freshly ground coffee, and the relaxing experience of visiting a Starbucks. Retail giant Wal-Mart's brand promise is "Everyday low prices". It makes no promises about customer service, brand-name products, or the shopping experience.

Communicating brand image

TIP

LOOK TO YOUR CUSTOMERS

If you feel your brand needs updating, turn to your customer research. What is it they seek in your brand? What do they value the most? And what changes will they accept?

There are five key points to consider when defining and maintaining a successful brand:
• **Vision** Be certain that one consistent, strategic vision drives your goals for the brand. Prioritize your plan to deliver on the promise (what is most important and why?). Align all stakeholders behind the vision.
• **Culture** Empower your entire organization to get behind the brand. Give them the authority, responsibility, resources, and training to satisfy customer expectations.
• **Innovation** You cannot stand still; you must continually innovate to stay ahead of the demands of the marketplace and the shifts in everything from demographics to target-group tastes and preferences. Demonstrate that you are both innovative and protective of the brand experience.
• **Action** Specify and communicate those actions that are essential to brand success to those within the organization who must deliver on the promise.
• **Value** Consistently and continually measure results. Show your investors, associates, and business partners what you've accomplished and what improvements you have yet to make.

 IN FOCUS... BRAND VALUE

Brands that have a clear sense of themselves and have worked diligently to deliver on their promises are often quite durable, withstanding economic down-turns, changes in customer preferences, and game-changing innovations in their product category. The value of developing brands is highlighted in two quotes. John Stuart, former CEO of Quaker Oats Company, said: "If this company were split up, I would gladly give you the property, plant, and equipment, and I would take the brands and trademarks... and I would fare better than you." Carlton Curtis, VP of Corporate Communication at Coca-Cola, stated: "If all of Coca-Cola's assets were destroyed overnight, whoever owned the Coca-Cola name could walk into a bank the next morning and get a loan to rebuild everything."

INTERVIEWING
PEOPLE

Contents

Introduction

The key to success for any organization is its people. Getting the right people depends on how an organization recruits, and a fundamental element of the recruitment process is interviewing.

As the business environment becomes more dynamic, organizations' needs change, and so do the skills they require of their employees. Moreover, simply having the right skills does not guarantee that a candidate will benefit your organization. Today's most creative and progressive recruiters recognize that understanding the aptitudes, attitudes, and motivations of their employees is essential to ensuring that the people they hire represent the best possible fit for current vacancies. As a result, those who conduct job interviews on behalf of their organizations not only hold the present, but the future of their employer squarely in their hands. That is a lot of responsibility.

The aim of *Interviewing People* is to guide you through the minefield of interviewing candidates: organizing the interviews and other supplementary activities, helping you to ask the right questions, deciding which information sources you should consider in finding out who the person really is, and preparing the groundwork for successful partnerships between the new employees and your organization. The end result should be to make interviews rewarding for candidates and recruiters.

Chapter 1

Planning the interview

Interviewing a potential recruit is a long and complex process, but the reward is seeing the person you interviewed contributing to your organization's success and happy in their job. Achieving that success takes careful planning.

Developing a checklist

Your checklist is your step-by-step guide to ensuring that you and your organization make the most of the candidate interviews. Create it at the very beginning of your recruitment process so that you can always visualize where you are at a given moment and what you need to do next.

PLAN TILL THE END

Include time in your plan to check references and make an offer once you have chosen a candidate.

Planning to plan

Preparing for and conducting an interview involves a number of steps. However, the actual interview is only one part of the process. Your checklist should cover the steps required before the interview, during the interview, and afterwards. Your plan should also incorporate points along the way at which you assess progress to date and make any necessary amendments. Leave room to add extra stages if necessary. Remember it won't always be possible to execute each step perfectly. Concentrate on fulfiling each point and keep a record of what you do and the results.

Breaking it down into steps

First, analyze and understand the job itself and its significance in your organization. Next map out the steps of your strategy for filling it: where you will publicize the vacancy, what support you will need to screen and rank incoming curriculum vitaes (CVs), how to define your shortlist, the kinds of questions to be asked of candidates at interview, and selecting any other measures that would be required to supplement the interviews. Then there will be logistics issues to be worked out, such as where the interviews will be held.

TIP

SOLICIT EMPLOYEE REFERRALS

Reward employees for recommending friends and relatives for jobs in your organization. The new employee gets recognition, and the organization gets a well-recommended new employee.

Budgeting for your strategy

Know what your budget is from the start; finances play a role in identifying top, secondary, and optional priorities on your checklist. One key spend is likely to be on recruitment advertising. Hiring a venue for interviews and getting expert help to assess candidates' skills may also mean spending some money. Get estimates on every expenditure before you spend anything.

CHECKLIST PRE-INTERVIEW PLANNING

	YES	NO
• Do I understand the job and where it fits in my organization?	☐	☐
• Have I planned a recruitment/interview/assessment budget?	☐	☐
• Have I decided whether supplementary meetings such as assessment centres are necessary?	☐	☐
• Have I placed the recruitment advertisements in appropriate media?	☐	☐
• Have I considered meeting places and venues for interviews?	☐	☐
• Have I designed the questions?	☐	☐
• Have I decided on the interview format (panel or pair, for example)?	☐	☐
• Have I fitted in reassessment times to look back at what I have accomplished to date and consider what needs to be done next?	☐	☐

Creating the job description

The job profile starts by acting as a sort of recipe for the person you are looking for, but comes to define expectations of the job holder as well as aspects of your organization's purpose. The profile reveals one individual piece of how your organization sees its future.

TIP

LOOK AHEAD
Make sure the job description gives the role context in terms of the organization and the types of challenges and growth opportunities provided.

Setting the "rules of the game"

A well thought out job description can help to attract candidates who are right for the job. It also serves as a foundation for appraisals and employee development plans, and it outlines for both job holder and manager the "rules of the game" in day-to-day activities and over the long term. The person specification, which is often part of the job description, defines the kinds of education, experience, skills, and personal characteristics that are likely to be necessary to succeed in the job.

ASK YOURSELF... WHAT ARE THE JOB REQUIREMENTS

- Why does this job exist?
- What must this job holder achieve for the organization?
- Which responsibilities could be re-allocated to allow the addition of new ones?
- What changes are planned for the organization that could affect this job?
- What skills should the job holder have to make the organizational transition easier?

Analyzing your needs

You may be filling an existing job that has just been vacated. A vacancy provides an opportunity to consider the continuing need for the job. If a need remains, then examine whether the role demands the inclusion of new responsibilities, competencies, and knowledge. Keep in mind that as organizations evolve, their needs and strategy change, and so must the dimensions of the work and the jobs created to carry out that work. Think about how your organization is changing and its impact on the role.

Defining the job's purpose

The starting point for both creating and refreshing a job description or profile is defining the job's purpose. What is the main reason for the job's existence and what is the job holder expected to achieve? From there, go on to construct the description's skeleton, which must include the following: job title, main duties and responsibilities, who the job holder reports to, who reports to the job holder, where the job is based, and whether it is full-time, part-time, or flexi-time. Use the profile to build a compelling case for the job's desirability, such as responsibility for certain projects.

Sharing the full picture

As one of the job description's purposes is to attract applicants, it can be tempting to exaggerate the most interesting aspects of the role and downplay the least interesting. Misrepresenting the job role does no one any favours. Highlight the job's best points, but balance the description so that applicants understand the full picture of what the role entails. Be truthful, skip the jargon, and write as clear and concise a description as possible.

Creating the person specification

Developing a precise person specification requires an in-depth understanding of the competencies, knowledge, skills, experience, education, aptitudes, and attitudes that the best possible selected hire for this role could have. Break requirements down into "essential" and "desirable" categories which can help to differentiate between candidates when the time comes to build your shortlist. Focus on qualitative aspects of experience instead of an arbitrary number of years or qualifications. Perhaps the most challenging part of creating the person specification is effectively building in personal characteristics that are desirable or necessary in the job holder. Recognize that you will need to link interview questions to the person specification, as well as the job description, so consider also how a candidate can best demonstrate to you that they have, for instance, "integrity" or "initiative". Avoid terms that could appear to be discriminatory such as "mature", "bright young graduate", "Christian values", and so on.

7 EXPLAIN SPECIAL CONDITIONS
Detail conditions such as working unusual shifts or on public holidays, regular travel, or wearing a particular uniform.

6 DESCRIBE THE SCOPE OF THE JOB
Explain the boundaries of the job holder's responsibilities and the potential for developing them further.

Developing a job profile to fit your requirements

1 DEFINE THE JOB PURPOSE
Ask yourself what is the person filling this role supposed to accomplish. This step influences the rest of the process.

2 IDENTIFY THE JOB TITLE
The job's purpose sets out what the role should be called. Keep the job title jargon free, brief, and as clear as possible.

3 DESCRIBE THE CONTEXT
Refer to the work conditions and nature of the business in which the job duties will be carried out.

4 OUTLINE THE JOB'S OBJECTIVES
Specify the key aims: for example, provide efficient customer service that ensures problems are dealt with effectively.

5 SET OUT THE BASICS OF THE JOB
Outline the day-to-day responsibilities and tasks, the skills needed to fulfil the job duties, and hours required weekly.

Using digital aids

Interviewing is a person-to-person interaction. However, technology can be a valuable ally in today's recruitment process. You can put technology to work for you early on to advertise your job via your corporate website or on job boards. Then well-chosen recruitment software can help to screen and organize the field of candidates who apply.

Maximizing your brand

Your organization's website is often the first port of call for two sets of job seekers. The first group knows of your organization and is interested in finding out what it would be like to work there and if there are currently any vacancies. The second is taking a look after seeing an advertisement for the job on offer. If your organization has the resources, its site should offer a careers section that features full job/person descriptions and on-line tools that allow candidates to upload CVs. Some organizations upload videos of current employees explaining what it is like to work there on their site. Other organizations showcase written testimonials and photographs. If you can't afford "bells and whistles", ensure as a minimum that it is easy to find up-to-date job listings on the site.

TIP

TAP INTO SOCIAL MEDIA
Build your own profile on a professional social media networking site to help attract potential candidates.

Using social media

Going on-line takes your recruitment effort into a whole new cyber realm. Savvy managers and recruiters turn to professional social networking sites like LinkedIn, Naymz, and Plaxo to reach "passive" job seekers (those who are not looking for jobs at the moment) and to spread the word that a job is available. To get the most out of such sites, join sub-groups that can broaden your outreach – by location, industry, or profession.

Using job boards

The use of on-line job boards* as a recruitment tool for all kinds of jobs is increasing rapidly. The generalist job board may be the right vehicle to get the word out about entry-level and less specialised types of roles, but career professionals tend to seek out the niche job boards. Although job boards specializing in vacancies for senior executives are growing in popularity, they do not attract as much interest from qualified applicants as on-line services that are aimed at more junior professionals. You may want to post your vacancy on more than one job board to increase its visibility.

*Job board — an on-line service on which employers can post details of vacancies for a fee.

Tracking candidates

TIP

Depending on your organization's size and the number of people hired each year, software that helps to manage the recruitment process from beginning to end may be a worthwhile investment. Widely known as applicant tracking systems (ATS), recruitment software can deliver services from posting job notices and importing candidates' on-line job applications to screening CVs, scheduling interviews, managing your communications with individual candidates, and more.

KNOW YOUR OPTIONS

Investigate a variety of recruitment software. Systems have been created specifically for large or small organizations.

CASE STUDY

Streamlining applications

British airline bmi increased the number of job applications it handled over a six-month period by 25 per cent by putting into place recruitment and talent management software. The airline often received hundreds of applications a week, but had only a few employees working in its recruitment department.

Paperwork constituted a major part of the team's workload because applicants would first send in a CV, and would then be sent an application form. The company saved thousands of pounds in printing and postage costs by taking its application process on-line. The on-line system also allowed more efficient screening of candidates.

Creating a matrix

Interviewing can become a very subjective process because it involves people, and their impressions and interpretations of information and how it is delivered. You can remove some of the subjectivity by building a framework that gives context to the relative importance of candidates' education, experience, skills, and key personal qualities.

Constructing a filtering matrix

Devising a matrix to filter the flow of candidates in the early stage of selection will save processing time. It consists of a list of candidates running down one side, and a list of minimum and preferred educational, professional experience and skills requirements running along the top. The requirements listed on the matrix should match those in the job posting. A simple "yes/no" or tick box system is best for indicating whether or not the requirements have been met. Ultimately, the filtering matrix is the document supporting the decision to interview, or not interview, a particular candidate.

Charting a qualitative matrix

TIP

DEVELOP A POINT SYSTEM
Decide before the actual interviews what different scores will mean in your interviewing matrix. For instance, if the top score for a given area is five, what must a candidate demonstrate to be scored at five?

An interview will require you to score candidates on information that is less factual and more qualitative in nature, so a matrix for this stage will reflect the quality of a response rather than a simple yes or no. The areas you measure will be personal qualities such as communication skills, business awareness, and knowledge. Each will receive points with, say, a top score of five. You may want to "weight" particular areas, by either raising the top score or by multiplying the given score by a number to reflect that area's importance to the hiring decision. You can use the same basic visual framework design as the filtering matrix.

Adding it all up

Organize your matrices so that information is easily accessible and your scoring system for each is easily understandable. Then create a single score sheet that outlines the accumulated score from each activity of the interviewing process for each candidate. Once you have completed interviewing and assessing your candidates, add up the scores to see which candidate has come out on top. If a question arises over selection later on, a transparent system will support and clarify your decision and the process used to make your choice.

Sample of a qualitative matrix

SCORING SYSTEM:
1 – **No evidence of competency**
2 – **Limited competency (one example)**
3 – **Acceptable (meets the minimum standard for the job)**
4 – **Significant (examples demonstrate confidence)**
5 – **Extensive (many excellent examples that reflect well-rounded professional knowledge and expertise)**

TIP

EXAMINE ALL AREAS

Keep in mind that if you incorporate complex activities in your interview process, an additional matrix will be necessary to reflect candidates' performance there as well.

CANDIDATES	COMMUNICATION SKILLS	INDUSTRY KNOWLEDGE	TECHNICAL KNOWLEDGE	REGIONAL KNOWLEDGE	TOTAL SCORE
Candidate 1	3	3	3	3	12
Candidate 2	5	4	4	5	18
Candidate 3	2	3	3	4	12
Candidate 4	4	5	5	3	17

Deciding the agenda

To make the most of your interview, you need a plan that sets out not only the informational ground you want to cover, but also outlines the time you want to devote to each segment of the interview. Your agenda should also include any "extras" that the interview process must incorporate.

Bringing the elements together

The question-and-answer segment of getting to know your candidates is referred to as "the interview", but to get the most out of your exposure to them, think instead of the interview as a multi-part event that may require several different settings and techniques. The core points to decide are whether you will have a single interview or first and second interviews, and if supplementary activities should be included. For example, when candidates come in for interviews, a tour of your facility may be appropriate to give them an idea of what the work environment is like and to show them employee facilities. It will also give you a chance to see their spontaneous reactions to the environment.

BUILD IN IN-BETWEEN TIME

Pleasantries take time, so be sure to plan in enough time to welcome each candidate as they come in, and tell a departing candidate goodbye and when they might expect to hear from you next.

Organizing your time

How long each interview should last will depend on the amount of information you must obtain from each candidate. This will be based on the complexity of the role or the seniority of the position. However, you should allow at least 45–60 minutes for the question-and-answer portion of an in-person interview. Reviewing the job description and person specifications is a good starting point for developing the questions. Use it also to plan the pace of your interview by deciding how much time should be devoted to each segment, based on its importance to your selection criteria.

Planning for contingencies

The best-laid plans can go awry when the unexpected occurs. Your interviews could be thrown off kilter by late arrivals, office emergencies, or any number of everyday events. Work out a "Plan B" to help you and your candidates navigate smoothly through any problems that could occur on the day of the interview. One common contingency is running behind schedule, which can threaten the goodwill of your remaining candidates throughout the day as well as raise the possibility that you won't get all the information you want during the interview. Perhaps the room you've arranged as the interview location has been double booked. A candidate, or you, could be faced with a personal emergency. Develop a list of "what ifs" in order to plan effective solutions for a range of contingencies.

Building the shortlist

The list of candidates who will be invited to the interview will form your shortlist. Following the interview, you may trim this list even further to choose some to participate in further selection activities in your search for the best possible candidate.

Selecting the best

Build your interview shortlist with the help of the filtering matrix, which will make it clear which applicants met most of your requirements and which did not. Your next steps depend on two factors: how many applicants met most or all of the minimum and preferred requirements, and how many people you want to interview for the job. If your list does not include the desired number of candidates to interview, look at the applicants who met the highest percentage of the minimum requirements. Examine their CVs for individual differentiators, such as evidence of promotions, recent training, or unpaid work experience.

Achieving a manageable shortlist

Work with at least one other person to develop your shortlist to eliminate the possibility of bias. For a manageable list, keep in mind how much time you will have to devote to interviews. A shortlist for a senior or complex role should be small because there will be few people with the right blend of skills, experience, and personal qualities who meet highly specific requirements. Too many applicants for a high-level role means that the job posting may have been written too broadly.

If you are hiring in volume, consider initial telephone screening to help you narrow your shortlist to interview. Telephone screening can also be useful for confirming the candidates' credentials, probing gaps in employment history, exploring their willingness to relocate, or determining whether their salary expectations are in line with what your organization is prepared to offer. Telephone screening can save money and time by eliminating unqualified or inappropriate applicants from the shortlist to interview.

Considering the overqualified

As a recruiting manager you may face the difficult task of deciding whether a job will sufficiently challenge and stimulate a potential employee. Some organizations disfavour overqualified candidates because of concerns that they might get bored or that they will cost too much. Other employers look at hiring such candidates as an opportunity to develop a role and, possibly, a team or the entire organization in new ways. If you have seemingly overqualified applicants on your shortlist, ask yourself what their impact would be in a particular job role.

Inviting the candidates

Extend the invitation to a job interview with the same enthusiasm with which you hope your candidates receive it. Be clear in the information you provide, and prepare to adapt your plans if some candidates require special assistance.

TIP

ADDRESS WITH CARE

Address candidates by first names instead of Mr or Ms initially, to avoid embarrassment over gender-neutral names.

Personalizing the invitation

An invitation to attend an interview is the first personalized communication you will send a candidate, and it must accomplish several things: provide information, get across a sense of your organization's style and culture, and communicate pleasure that the candidate has chosen to apply for this role. Using phrases like "I am pleased to invite you", "We look forward to meeting you", or "Your experience interested us greatly" will personalize the tone of your communication, whether delivered by phone, letter, or e-mail. Telephone the candidate to discuss and agree a time, and then send your letter or e-mail to confirm the arrangement.

 IN FOCUS...

PRE-INTERVIEW QUESTIONNAIRES

One of the world's most influential experts on recruitment, Dr John Sullivan, recommends that managers give candidates a series of questions to answer before an interview to save valuable time and to help interviewers find out more about them beforehand. Candidates might be asked about job preferences, career goals, and motivators, for instance, in questionnaires that are sent to them with the interview invitation and returned before the interview. Such questionnaires could be given only to those candidates who are selected for interview, but Sullivan suggests that they could also be used to screen out a few applicants from that pool.

Providing the right information

The invitation sent to candidates must detail the date, time, and place the interview will be held. Send a map or a weblink to a map of the area so that they can find the venue easily. Also say who will conduct the interview. Let them know if they need to bring passports, work portfolios, or other documents or materials. Provide advice on how to reschedule their interviews if the given time and date are not convenient. Also give names and contact details such as mobile numbers so that they can let you know if they have been delayed on the interview day.

Considering special needs

When inviting candidates to interviews, ask if they have any particular requirements. These could include:
• making the venue easily accessible if a candidate has mobility problems.
• allowing for or providing an interpreter for hearing- or speech-impaired candidates.
• allowing a friend or relative to accompany a candidate to support or help them.
• providing equipment to help sight-impaired candidates read any necessary material.
• offering a break mid-interview.

ISSUING INVITATION LETTERS

FAST TRACK

OFF TRACK

FAST TRACK	OFF TRACK
Addressing the communication to the candidate by name	Sending an interview invitation to "Dear Applicant"
Providing contact names and phone numbers for the interview date in case the candidate has an emergency	Offering no way to contact you on the day of the interview if a candidate has a problem
Taking a proactive approach to adapting interview conditions for candidates with special needs	Telling special needs candidates that they will have to experience the same interview conditions as everyone else

Chapter 2

Conducting the interview

The interview is the first opportunity for you to get to know the person behind the CV, so every element is extremely important. Keep in mind that the interview will also shape the candidate's impression of your organization.

Setting the tone

When you go to a live performance of a play, from the moment the curtain goes up, the scenery, the backdrop, and the background music give you clues as to what you are about to experience. The same is true for your candidates as soon as they arrive for the interview.

REMOVE DISTRACTIONS

Leave behind communications tools – office telephones, mobile phones, and PDAs such as BlackBerrys – or keep them turned off.

Selecting a venue

If you have chosen a neutral location such as a hotel as an interview venue, it is best to host your interviews in a comparatively formal setting, such as a suite or conference room instead of a lobby or restaurant where too many distractions await. Similarly, if you hold the interviews at your own premises, book a private room or office so that your meetings with candidates will be free from distractions such as phone calls and other interruptions. Check in advance that the setting is tidy, and does not have personal items such as inappropriate calendars or posters in view.

Getting to the right place

Make sure that your candidates know where they should go on arrival and who they will see for the interview – these basic details will help them begin the process with confidence. A further boost to the candidates' confidence will come when their first contact welcomes them at the meeting point. Then a comfortable, pleasant place to wait for their interview will suggest that your organization is well organized and committed to seeing candidates begin interviews in the most relaxed state possible.

TIP

MAKE THE VENUE ACCESSIBLE

Avoid sending candidates on their own on complicated routes around floors of offices that will look all the same to them – appoint an escort to guide them.

Meeting the candidate

Bring with you the candidate's CV and any other relevant material: the questions you are going to ask, the job and person specifications, organizational background, and a notepad and pen. When you meet them, offer a warm, professional greeting using their name and provide a glass of water. Some small talk about the weather or their journey to the premises is appropriate.

TIP

BE ON TIME

Be punctual – keeping the candidate waiting without a genuine emergency reflects poorly on your organization.

✔ CHECKLIST PREPARING FOR A CANDIDATE

	YES	NO
• Is your meeting place free from distractions and interruptions?	☐	☐
• Is the candidate aware of where they need to go?	☐	☐
• Do the relevant people such as a receptionist or security personnel know that the candidate is coming and where they are to be taken?	☐	☐
• Did you bring the candidate's CV and other relevant materials such as a list of the questions to be asked?	☐	☐
• Are drinking water and cups accessible nearby?	☐	☐
• Do you know how to pronounce the candidate's names?	☐	☐

Choosing the format

The format of the interview provides a framework for its content. Issues to consider include whether the interview should be conducted one-on-one or two-on-one, or if a panel is required. Circumstances may even dictate that the interview takes place on the telephone or by video conferencing.

Interviewing with a panel

To select a candidate for a very senior, highly technical, or otherwise multifaceted position, interviewing by panel may be the most effective option. A clear structure, so that the interview flows and each panel member knows what they are responsible for, is essential to a successful panel interview. So is having a lead or primary interviewer to guide the interview's direction. The secondary panellists can offer clarifying questions and provide additional thoughts later. But remember to limit the numbers – more than four panellists may overwhelm and confuse your candidates.

Teaming up

Most first-stage interviews involve one or two interviewers. Asking questions, listening to and recording answers, observing, and then deciding to either hire the candidate or move on to the next stage of selection is a lot for one person. During the interview, two interviewers can alternate between asking questions and taking notes. Later, two sets of observations and insights are likely to be more helpful towards building a complete picture of a candidate's suitability for a role.

Interviewing at a distance

TIP

Distance may make a face-to-face interview impractical. If telephone manner and customer service are significant parts of the job, it would make sense to have a first interview by phone. If you can use a video link-up, the interview will be much the same to conduct as if it was in person. If interviewing by telephone, speak distinctly and keep in mind that it will be even more important to convey warmth and professionalism in your voice. Try smiling naturally as you speak, so that it can be heard in your voice and choose a quiet place away from distractions and interruptions.

TEST THE TECHNOLOGY

Leave time to check that the video-conferencing equipment is working before you begin an interview. If it fails, you will waste time tracking down a technician to make it work.

❓ ASK YOURSELF... HOW SHOULD I CHOOSE AN INTERVIEW FORMAT?

- How complex is the job role?
- At what stage do we need to see the candidate in person?
- What resources are available to conduct an effective distance interview?
- Who else from my organization should be involved in the interviews?
- What will I look to a fellow interviewer to deliver?
- How would we structure a panel interview?

Competency-based questions

The goal of the interviewing process is to find the right candidate who will bring the right skills to the job. Asking candidates to explain how and when they have used the precise competencies in past experiences and situations will give you insight as to their suitability for the job.

Understanding competency

The idea behind competency-based questions is to link past behaviour and experiences with the skills needed for the job and future performance. These questions are also known as behavioural questions. Instead of asking what a person would do in a given situation, the interviewer asks candidates to describe how they have handled such a situation previously. This kind of questioning is seen by many professionals as the most reliable because past performance is the best predictor of how a person will perform in the future.

Using the STAR method

The STAR method can guide you through the dual responsibilities of preparing competency questions, and then listening effectively to candidates' responses. STAR is an acronym that stands for Situation, Task, Action, Response. First, outline the type of situation you want the candidates to refer back to in your questions. When a candidate responds, you are listening for a description of a situation that matches the requirements you outlined in the question, a logical approach to solving the problem, specific actions taken to address the challenge, as well as clear results.

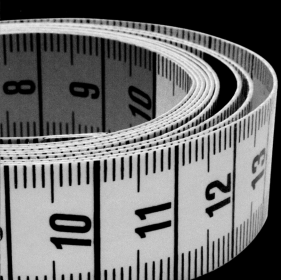

"Describe a situation in which you worked with another department."

"Give an example of a time when you had to work with a difficult customer."

"Tell me how you handled a situation in which you had to make a quick decision without having all of the facts."

"Tell me about a time when you had to motivate your team under difficult circumstances."

Assessing competency

"Give an example of how you managed a particularly demanding project."

"This job requires 10 days of travel each month. Please describe the travel requirements of a previous job, and how you dealt with the challenges."

"Please give an example of how you dealt with interpersonal conflict in your team."

"Describe a situation in which you handled conflicting requests from senior managers."

Asking further questions

A clear picture of each candidate's experience and background should emerge from interviews. While competency-based questions should deliver most of the "meat" from your interviews, you will want to obtain information from candidates that may require other types of questions.

VALUE TIME

While asking verification questions, be careful not to waste valuable interview time by asking candidates to recite their CVs to you word-for-word.

Verifying credentials

Exploring the credentials and past experience that candidates have cited on their CVs is an important part of interviewing. Basic verification questions would cover factual aspects of their education and experience, such as "How long did you attend that school?", and "Which courses did you take?" To obtain more value-based information about their education or experience, ask questions such as: "What motivated you to seek higher education?", and "How did you juggle school work with working at a part-time job?" Verification questions allow you to check for gaps that could tip you off to an untruth or exaggeration in their list of credentials.

ENCOURAGE STORYTELLING

To ensure fairness, you will be asking each of the candidates the same questions, but prepare to ask follow-up questions to clarify candidates' responses or prompt greater detail.

Diversifying your approach

Open questions, such as "Tell me about yourself", give your candidates a chance to list their skills and experiences to the requirements of the job. If you are seeking factual information, a closed question will be appropriate, for example, "How many staff did you manage?" Probing questions could also be described as follow-on questions because they are likely to follow a response and are intended to encourage the candidate to explain their answer in detail. Unorthodox or unusual questions may prompt intriguing answers, but be certain you know what you want to achieve by asking such a question that, on the surface, has little to do with the job at hand. Questions such as "What is your favourite film and why?" can inject a light moment into an interview, or they can offer some insight into a candidate's passions and creativity. Stress questions, on the other hand, are designed to reveal how a candidate reacts to pressurised questions. However, introducing added stress into an already stressful interview may be counterproductive!

USING DIFFERENT TYPES OF QUESTIONS

QUESTION TYPE	EXAMPLE	IMPACT
Open	"Tell us about yourself."	Allows candidates to match skills or experiences to the job
Closed	"How many new offices have you opened?"	Secures a brief, specific answer
Hypothetical/ situational	"What would you do if…"	Assesses how candidates think on their feet and gives insight into their priorities and judgment
Probing	"Could you elaborate on how you achieved that result under those circumstances?"	Follow-on questions that are intended to draw out more information
Verification	"Can you confirm when and where you completed your health and safety certification?"	Similar to a closed question; seeking brief answers to verify and confirm factual information
Leading	"Part of the job is publishing a monthly newsletter. Have you done this before?"	Intended to secure a "yes" or "no" answer with further elaboration by the candidate
Stress	"If you were on a plane that was going to crash, who would you save – yourself, your boss, or your mother?"	An aggressive form of questioning that puts the candidate under stress to see how they will react
Unusual/quirky	"If you were a vegetable, what would you want to be and why?"	Aimed at eliciting information about a candidate's creativity and how they think

Respecting diversity

Having a diverse workforce begins with recruiting men and women of different races, religions, nationalities, ages, and sexual orientation into the organization – and the interview is the first step to achieving this.

Attracting diversity

To attract the widest variety of employees possible, reflect the presence of diversity in your organization in all of your on-line and print recruitment materials. Improving interviewing skills is important to finding the right person – but it is also important to remember that the successful candidate can either be a man or a woman and come from varied backgrounds, ages, lifestyles, and life situations.

EMPLOYEE ASSOCIATIONS
Be aware of employee associations that your organization sponsors for members of different ethnic groups or religions, or if it supports special interest groups.

Recognizing differences

If your candidate pool is diverse, cultural awareness will be essential during your interviews – both to understand how candidates present themselves and how you respond. A smile and a pleasant manner go a long way towards bridging cultural gaps anywhere around the world. Ensure that your interview protocol reflects a positive attitude towards diversity – from your welcome, to the questions you ask and your body language.

CORPORATE DRESSING
Check if your organization's policy on corporate dress or grooming allows adaptation for different religious requirements for both men and women.

Addressing candidates' cultural concerns

GESTURES AND EYE CONTACT
Understand that a handshake may not be appropriate between men and women, and extended eye contact can signify anger in some cultures.

RELIGIOUS FACILITIES
Find out if there are facilities on-site for prayer or rituals during the day, and check the organization's policy on time off during religious observances.

EATING HABITS
See if the canteen offers vegetarian, kosher, and halal dishes, and if office refrigerators have separate shelves for vegetarian and meat dishes.

Avoiding illegal questions

You may want to ask certain questions to ensure that a candidate is the right choice for your organization. As you see it, you are probing the candidate's suitability for the job. But recognize that many questions may be not only inappropriate, but illegal.

TIP

CONCENTRATE ON JOB-RELATED QUESTIONS
Focus on potential recruits' past achievements, future ambitions, motivations, and what they can bring to your workplace.

Understanding the playing field

Laws vary from country to country regarding which questions are illegal to ask job applicants, and who can or can't work in a country. To avoid legal difficulties, consult your organization's employment law advisor. You might find it difficult to assess what is appropriate to ask candidates, but one rule of thumb is that if the question you want to ask refers to a candidate's personal life and not specifically to a job requirement, it is probably inappropriate to ask.

Asking the right question

Think about what you really want to know about when you consider asking personal questions such as "Which country are you from", "Are you planning to have children," "What religion are you", or "How old are you?" If you believe a candidate's national origin is important, what you probably need to know is, "Do you have a legal right to work in this country?" Your interest in a candidate's family plans may reflect your need to know if they are willing to travel, as the job requires. Instead of asking about a candidate's religion, the relevant issue may be whether they are willing to work particular hours and days of the week. Rather than asking about a candidate's age, pinpoint the issue at the root of the question: is the person physically capable of carrying a certain amount of weight necessary for the job?

Avoiding a wrong move

Using the interview to develop a personal relationship with a candidate is out of bounds. In show business, the phrase "the casting couch" refers to the practice of turning auditions, or interviews, into opportunities to leverage relationships with performers or with authority figures. Business has also suffered from the occasional scandal when a gatekeeper*, such as an interviewer, initiates or accepts inappropriate overtures. During the interview, you and the candidate may discover a common interest that both of you wish to pursue outside the business environment. However, pursuing a relationship – no matter how innocent – as a result of the interview could lead your organization's management to question your judgment on candidate selection. It could also lead to legal and reputation difficulties for you and your organization. Avoid at all costs.

*Gatekeeper — a person who controls access of people, commodities, or information to an organization or to the public.

NAVIGATING LEGAL ISSUES

FAST TRACK

OFF TRACK

FAST TRACK	OFF TRACK
Asking which languages they know	Asking where they were born
Asking if they are willing to relocate	Asking if they are married
Asking if they would be able to carry out all the job responsibilities	Asking if their religion allows them to do a certain type of work
Asking if they belong to any professional associations that are relevant to the job	Asking which kinds of social, religious, or political groups they belong to
Offering a glass of water before and during the interview	Inviting them out for a coffee on a personal basis

Effective observation

The point of the interview is to gather as much information as possible about the candidates who have applied for a particular job. To obtain this information, you must ask questions, and then listen carefully to the answers. Visual observation of the candidates is also important.

BE PATIENT
Fight the urge to interrupt or finish interviewees' sentences; be comfortable with a certain amount of silence before moving on to the next point.

Listening actively

Focus on what the candidate is saying, by both listening to the words and observing changing vocal tone, volume, and pace. If you are taking notes, listen for key ideas from the candidate's answer – don't try to write down every word they say. When the candidate has finished responding, ensure that you have understood by summarizing one or two of the key points back to them. Then gather more information by asking the candidate to clarify or elaborate their response.

Communicating non-verbally

Your non-verbal cues can either reinforce or contradict the interview's stated purpose. For example, encouraging a candidate verbally to "Tell me about yourself" while fiddling with a paperclip sends conflicting messages. Sitting back in your chair with arms folded can be taken to mean that you are sceptical of what they are saying, and suggest a closed mind, even if that is not how you actually feel. Checking your watch can be interpreted as a desire for the meeting to be over. On the other hand, leaning forward as the candidate speaks, maintaining eye contact, smiling, and occasionally nodding to acknowledge that you are taking on board what they say, lets interviewees know that you are engaged.

Non-verbal clues

When you observe the candidate during the interview, you too are looking for signs of engagement. The ability to listen and an interest in the job at hand are among the first requirements. Also look for non-verbal clues to character, ability to interact with others, confidence, and other traits that would affect a candidate's future success in the job. Physical gestures such as head nods and hand movements can suggest interest in a conversation or a particular topic. Other body movements, such as finger or foot tapping or leg swinging can reflect discomfort, perhaps boredom, or tension. Inappropriate laughter can be a sign of nerves. Be sure to write down what you observe.

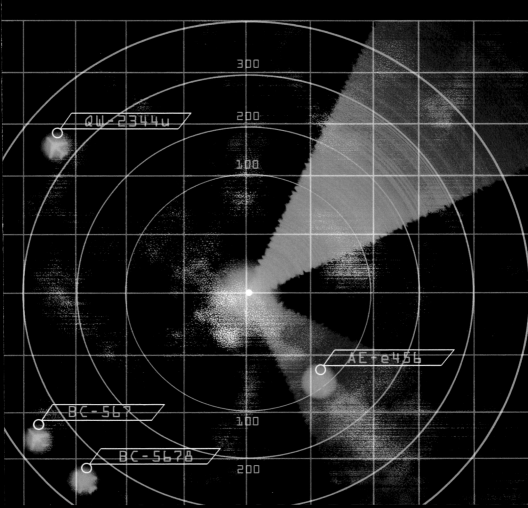

Concluding the interview

You have explored your candidate's CV, explained the job and person specification, and gained insight into the skills and knowledge that they would bring to the job. Now it is time to end the meeting. Bringing the interview to a successful close will help both candidate and interviewer move seamlessly into the next stage of the recruitment process.

TIP

GAUGE INTEREST
Post-interview, gauge a candidate's interest in the role by their enthusiasm and the eagerness they show in any follow-up.

Questioning the interviewer

When you have finished asking the questions, ask the candidate to offer any additional information they have not covered which is relevant to the job. Also invite them to ask any questions they have. Be prepared to answer questions about the impact of current events on your organization. If your organization has been in the news recently, candidates may want to ask you about the issues involved. The candidate who has researched your organization before the interview should know what your organization does, but you should be ready to answer any questions that they may have about the organization's plans for growth, diversification, or consolidation, and how the job on offer fits into a long-term strategy. This stage may well be too early to discuss salary and benefits, but come prepared to respond to such a question, even if it is only to say, "We will discuss those points at a later date." After they have asked their questions, ask the candidates if the job still interests them and whether they would like to proceed to the next stage.

IN FOCUS...
KEEPING THE END MOVING

Be alert to signs that the candidate suspects that the interview has not gone well, and that they are going to try to make up for any miscommunication in the last few minutes of the interview. If a candidate wants to return to a particular response to one of your questions or clarify a point, you could gain additional insight that will be helpful to your decision. However, letting them overexplain with no real point is helpful to no one. Know when it's time to cut the chat short.

Moving forward

The candidate will also want to know what will happen next. Be as open and clear as possible about the process ahead. If you plan to hire someone based on the first round of interviews, say so. If you will be conducting second interviews, skills tests, or an assessment centre, tell them. If you are basing your choice purely on the interviews, let them know the date by which you expect to have made a decision. Likewise, if you plan second-stage meetings, provide the candidate with as much information as possible about when they will be notified if their application is being taken forward and when the next round of selection will begin. You should also be as open as possible about when they will know if their application has not been successful.

Tidying loose ends

Closing out a job interview should leave both parties feeling that the meeting fulfilled their aims; the candidates should feel they have successfully communicated to you their suitability for the role, or alternatively that the role is not right for them. As the interviewer, you should feel that you have obtained all the information needed at the current stage of the recruitment process. You should also feel that you have a good idea of whether the candidate matches the job and person specifications closely enough to progress further to the next selection round. Housekeeping details that require attending to at the end include ensuring that the address, e-mail, and phone number you have on file for the candidate will remain current through the next stage of the selection process. Thank them for coming, and offer a smile and a handshake – if appropriate – to end the meeting.

**HOW TO...
END THE
INTERVIEW**

Complete your interview questions.

Invite the candidate to cover ground you missed.

Encourage the candidate to ask questions related to the job.

Confirm the candidate's contact details.

Enquire about the candidate's notice period.

Explain what happens next.

Thank the candidate for coming.

Chapter 3

Supplementing the interview

An interview may not be enough to fully gauge your shortlisted candidates' capabilities, on-the-job potential, and suitability for a particular role. Even after an in-depth interview, you will need the help of additional tools to find out more about the candidate.

Gathering further information

No matter how well planned, the basic interview does not guarantee that a complete picture will emerge of how well a candidate fits all the requirements of a given role. Background information is required, and you may have to take help from professionals to make the right decision.

KNOW THE LEGAL REQUIREMENTS
Some jobs may have mandatory minimum qualifications prescribed by law. Make sure you are aware of any requirements for the job under offer.

Uncovering skills

CVs and interviews are vehicles for candidates to "tell" what they can do and what they have done. However, they don't allow them to actually "show" their aptitude for certain competencies required. Nor do they let candidates demonstrate how they would perform in a typical work scenario. In jobs requiring high levels of skill, for example, it may be necessary to verify that candidates actually have the required specialist skills. Depending on the job's complexity, various kinds of tests and activities can be carried out to uncover a candidate's professional skills, ability, and aptitude.

Establishing background

In some cases, the sensitive nature of some job roles – such as working with children or hazardous chemicals – may need examination of the candidates' background to confirm that they are suitable for that role. As new technology offers opportunities to investigate the ways in which people put themselves forward to friends, family, and colleagues, you can now take other steps to make sure candidates are a good organizational fit.

Using professional assessment

Expert assistance will probably be required to help you conduct most of the in-depth assessments to ensure that you select the best person for the job. Ask your HR director to recommend assessment professionals. You can even consult psychologists and test publishers. But regardless of your consultant's knowledge, it is your responsibility to understand what information you need to know about each candidate – this will arm your experts with the knowledge to create the most effective tools in obtaining this information.

PLAN YOUR STRATEGY

Work with your expert consultants to decide the supplemental assessments needed before you advertise the role. Then you can advise candidates about the breadth of the selection process.

ASK YOURSELF... WHAT MORE DO I NEED TO KNOW?

- Are there specific personal characteristics which are needed in the job?
- Which hard competencies are required – for example, typing, standard office software, numeracy, proficiency in a foreign language, or data checking?
- How well would the candidate interact with clients or deliver a presentation?
- Will I want to verify past employment, qualifications or, in some cases, immigration status and right to work in my country?
- Does the job require working with vulnerable people such as children?
- How do the candidates represent themselves to professional and personal peers?

Holding an assessment centre

To test for job-specific skills, capabilities, and personal traits, you may want to hold an assessment centre. The term "assessment centre" doesn't refer to a specific place; it is a series of exercises designed to reveal candidates' personal characteristics, capabilities, skills, and potential to succeed in the job you are filling.

INCLUDE A SOCIAL EVENT

Hosting a reception or lunch for your candidates will allow you to see how they respond to others away from the assessment environment.

Matching tests and roles

The assessment centre is your opportunity to scrutinize candidates against the selection criteria you outlined in the job description and person specification. In addition to measuring job skills, an assessment centre also requires candidates to adapt to a variety of different challenges under the watchful eyes of qualified assessors who observe their behaviour while they perform tasks and participate in activities. The nature of the exercises and activities included will depend on the type of job to be filled and should require candidates to demonstrate the skills and abilities that they would actually need on the job.

GIVE FEEDBACK

Be sure that feedback on performance is offered to all participants – they need to know which traits or skills the assessments flagged up as meeting or not meeting the job requirements.

Planning exercises

At a typical assessment centre, exercises might include: on-line or paper-and-pencil tests to assess personality, aptitude, and skills; in-tray exercises based on day-to-day work situations; interviews; role-play and simulation scenarios; presentations; and group activities. For more senior and complex roles, the exercises may take several days. The event could be held at your organization's head office or a neutral location, such as a hotel, leased office space, or convention centre. Consider how many candidates must attend when deciding how much space will be needed.

Standardizing tests

Creating an assessment centre requires the involvement of experts to design the exercises and to assess candidates. Expert advice and analysis are especially needed when you want to use psychological testing in your selection process. The International Task Force on Assessment Center Guidelines underscores that training assessors is crucial to an effective assessment centre. It recommends that when you are choosing assessors, take into account their knowledge and experience with similar assessment techniques, plus their familiarity with the organization and the job to be filled. You may want to train people from within your own organization as assessors, but you could also consider using professional psychologists.

HOW TO...
PLAN AND RUN AN ASSESSMENT CENTRE

Conduct an analysis to pinpoint the behaviours, competencies, and characteristics necessary for the job.

↓

Deploy a variety of appropriate assessment techniques.

↓

Appoint a number of assessors to observe and evaluate each candidate.

↓

Train assessors thoroughly.

↓

Put in place a system to accurately record candidates' performance.

↓

Pool relevant information afterwards.

IN FOCUS... HISTORY OF MILITARY ASSESSMENT CENTRES

The purpose of assessment centres is to give an idea of how a candidate operates in a work situation. They were first used by the military to aid in the selection of officers. The German military used job simulations, along with other capability measurements, to select officers after World War I. From 1942, the British War Office adopted an officer selection system loosely based on observations of the German method. The US Office of Strategic Services ran a three-day programme of tests to improve its spy selection during World War II. In each case, the intention was to discover how candidates responded to the pressures of real-life situations.

Using psychometric tests

Organizations increasingly use psychometric tests to help identify in individuals the specific characteristics, abilities, and aptitudes that are likely to predict a person's success in a particular job.

Understanding psychometrics

Psychometric tests measure psychological variables such as intelligence, aptitude, and personality traits, and they are available from credible psychometrics providers. They often involve answering multiple-choice questions, and many can be administered both off-line and on-line. Sometimes these assessments are used to develop psychological profiles of candidates, covering personality and intellectual ability. They can also be used to measure emotional intelligence, preferred work style, candidates' ability to learn, and their potential to achieve in the future. An example of a psychometric instrument is the Myers-Briggs Type Indicator. With this tool, users' responses to a series of multiple-choice questions determine which of 16 personality types they most closely match.

CONFIDENTIALITY
Only people with a legitimate "need to know" as part of the selection process should have access to results.

Choosing what to measure

A thorough study of the manual which comes with each test will help you understand the research which has been conducted to assure the particular assessment's effectiveness. Statistical information outlining its reliability, predictability, and other factors can help you decide if a particular test is right for helping you find out what you want to know.

STANDARDIZATION
The tests must be given under controlled conditions and scored using standard criteria.

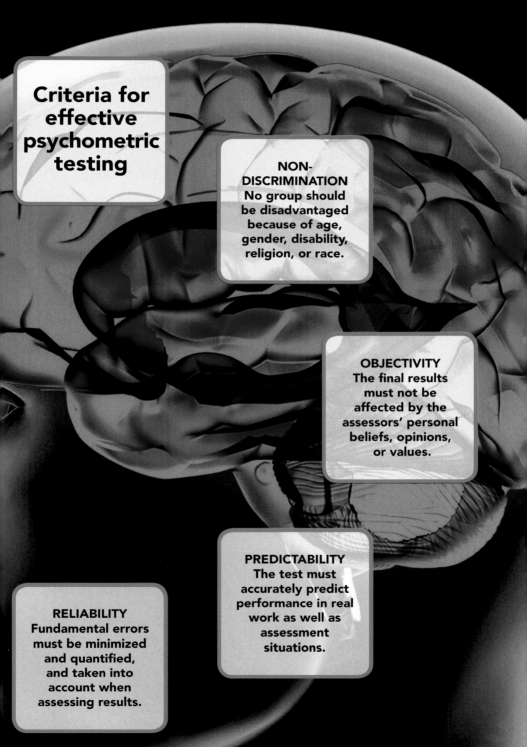

Criteria for effective psychometric testing

NON-DISCRIMINATION
No group should be disadvantaged because of age, gender, disability, religion, or race.

OBJECTIVITY
The final results must not be affected by the assessors' personal beliefs, opinions, or values.

PREDICTABILITY
The test must accurately predict performance in real work as well as assessment situations.

RELIABILITY
Fundamental errors must be minimized and quantified, and taken into account when assessing results.

Testing skills and ability

Depending on the kind of job you're filling, tests that measure certain types of learned knowledge and skills may be very useful to the selection process. Tests are available to assess your candidates' abilities and aptitudes in many areas, from IT skills to spatial reasoning*.

*Spatial reasoning *— the ability to visualize images, mentally move them around, and understand how their positions change with movement in one direction or another.*

Testing professional skills

How do you know if candidates can do what they say they can do? With certain types of professional skills, it is easy and cost effective to find out by testing for them. Today, it is possible to measure many skills using web-based tests, and it is possible to give candidates a choice as to where they take the tests – at a specified location, such as during an on-site assessment centre, at their home, or wherever there is access to the Internet.

A skill testing service will be able to provide you with myriads of tests that gauge proficiency in specific IT disciplines, foreign languages, administrative operations such as credit management, payroll and office software, industrial specialities, and virtually every kind of job in business that involves processes, technical knowledge, or data usage. Expect test scores to be accompanied by a report that analyzes the results, so that those making the hiring selection can understand candidates' individual strengths and weaknesses in depth.

🔍 IN FOCUS...
ABILITY VS APTITUDE

The terms "ability" and "aptitude" are often used interchangeably, but various tests may differentiate between the two. Ability might be defined as an enabling proficiency, which means someone can do a particular thing, often thanks to a learned skill or qualification. Aptitude reflects more a candidate's capacity or talent to do something. Some view "ability" as the basis of aptitude, and aptitude as more job-related than ability. Another way of looking at it is to think of ability as a person's capability to do something, and aptitude as the potential to become capable of doing it.

Measuring aptitude and ability

Aptitude is more about a person's propensity for a particular type of thinking or reasoning, which is necessary to succeed in the role, than it is about a well-developed skill. For example, an individual who understands the relationship between shapes, dimensions, and space could be said to have an aptitude for spatial reasoning, the focus of some specialist aptitude tests. Abstract reasoning, or the ability to analyze information and solve problems, is another common theme of aptitude testing. Aptitude for a given discipline can be very important, particularly when filling jobs in which you expect the successful candidates to undergo future training to become qualified or proficient at the job.

In some cases, instead of measuring aptitude, you may need to get an idea of candidates' abilities to communicate and use basic arithmetic. A verbal ability test would typically cover word usage, spelling, different parts of speech, reading, and following instructions. Multiplication, division, and reading charts and graphs might be included in a numeric ability test.

TIP

CREATE YOUR OWN TESTS

Explore the possibility of building your own tests – some test suppliers offer this option depending on the job and the skills you want to test.

CHOOSING APPROPRIATE TESTS

FAST TRACK

OFF TRACK

FAST TRACK	OFF TRACK
Defining which abilities and skills are needed for the job	Being unaware or doubtful about which abilities and skills are needed
Seeking out tests which will measure those skills and abilities	Believing all candidates when they say they can meet all requirements
Scrutinizing the analytical reports that should accompany the test	Considering only the overall scores on the tests

Carrying out group activities

Role play and group activities offer great benefits when they are used as part of the recruitment process. Unlike psychometric and aptitude tests, these exercises give candidates a chance to put their interpersonal skills centre stage and put theory into practice.

PRACTISE DISCRETION

Do take notes during group activities but take a discreet approach so not to make participants feel that you are waiting for them to make a mistake.

Watching candidates in action

You've been getting some insight into your candidates' aptitude and personality traits – now you will see them put their skills, experience, social abilities, and work habits to use in simulated workplace events. This is where you and your assessors will have to work your hardest to observe and record actions and responses. This blend of verbal communications and body language should fill in many of the remaining blanks about your candidates – for example, their ability to work in a team, how well they think in stressful conditions, and whether they are effective listeners. Although cultural differences may affect a person's non-verbal behaviour, you can often glean hints about someone's attitudes by observing basic facial expressions and body language.

Planning activities

Keep the rules simple and clear: specific time allowances must be met, the target goal of a team project must be defined, the guidelines for giving a presentation must be outlined, and the characters and scenarios to be portrayed in role-play events must be understood by the participants. The exercises must be well planned and pose genuine challenges to the participants. However, their structures must not be so complicated that participants are confused instead of stimulated.

Reading basic body language

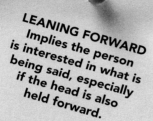

LEANING FORWARD
Implies the person
is interested in what is
being said, especially
if the head is also
held forward.

FIDGETING
Might reflect nervousness.
Examples include
constantly adjusting one's
clothes, or toying with
nearby objects.

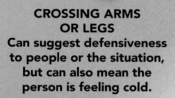

**CROSSING ARMS
OR LEGS**
Can suggest defensiveness
to people or the situation,
but can also mean the
person is feeling cold.

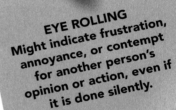

EYE ROLLING
Might indicate frustration,
annoyance, or contempt
for another person's
opinion or action, even if
it is done silently.

**DRUMMING OR
TAPPING FINGERS**
Could signify a person's
agitation, boredom,
or impatience in a
given situation.

**MAINTAINING
EYE CONTACT**
Can mean interest in what
is being said, while a fixed
stare can mean the person
is feigning interest.

TIP

WATCH YOUR COSTS

Use your budget on critical expenses such as the right staffing and essential exercise materials. Organizationally branded items such as paper, pens, and pencils are nice-to-haves, but won't help identify the best candidate.

Structuring the exercises

Do you want your role-play exercises to involve only your job candidates? Or do you want at least one of the roles taken on by a non-involved player? Remember: the more candidates you involve in the exercise, the more qualified observers you will need on hand to ensure that each job applicant is carefully and equally assessed. Sometimes assessment centre organisers bring in actors who are skilled in dramatic improvisation to portray other characters in role play exercises so that observers can focus their attention on the candidates. Bringing in additional experts will boost the cost of your assessment centre, which may already be expensive. However, the importance of getting the right person for the particular role or roles you are filling could justify the extra cost. An actor could also facilitate a chaired discussion, unless you would like to put a candidate in the role of chair. Putting one candidate in the role of chair can be an effective tool to assess that person's ability to facilitate a group discussion or project. However, that could lead to the participants getting an impression that the person portraying the chair is the favoured candidate to get the job. Rotating candidates in and out of the chair's role may draw better performance from the group as a whole.

✔ CHECKLIST PREPARING FOR GROUP ACTIVITIES

	YES	NO
• Have you ordered the right activity materials?	☐	☐
• Will the space accommodate the activities you have planned?	☐	☐
• Will you have enough assessors to effectively observe candidates?	☐	☐
• Have you structured the activities clearly with goals and allotted completion times?	☐	☐
• Do the assessors know what you are looking for from each exercise?	☐	☐

CHOOSING ROLE PLAY AND GROUP ACTIVITIES

ACTIVITY	HOW IT WORKS	WHAT IT REVEALS
Leaderless discussion	Candidates are given a problem to discuss for a specific amount of time, during which they must develop solutions.	Leadership, negotiation, influencing, and verbal communication skills, creativity, and non-verbal communication style
Practical task	This is a creative problem-solving exercise that may involve constructing an object with unusual materials or by moving them around in an unusual way.	Interpersonal, teamwork, project management, and problem-solving skills
In-tray or e-tray exercise	Designed to simulate a typical workload for the person who gets the job, the exercise may include memos, budget forecasts, trend information, reports, messages, and emergencies that must be dealt with within a given amount of time.	Managerial capabilities such as organization, task prioritization, delegation, time management, and attention to detail while also being able to take a holistic view to problem solving, decision making, and planning
Oral presentation	Candidates must prepare a talk on a given topic with minimal preparation time.	Creativity, confidence preparation, ability to think on feet, and to structure and effectively communicate a message
Role play	A scenario involving two or more people is created in which a candidate plays a specified role and deals with a specific on-the-job situation.	Communication, listening and negotiation skills, empathy, problem solving, responses to certain situations
Case study	Candidates are briefed on a typical business problem and must make recommendations.	Ability to analyze information and make decisions
Business game	Candidates working in groups compete to come up with the best solution to a business problem, such as a bankruptcy or hostile take-over bid.	Skills in teamwork, creative decision making, situational analysis

Background screening

Knowing exactly who a candidate is before you bring that person on board will be crucial to your organization's wellbeing. Issues such as identity, false career information, criminal pasts, and illegal immigration are important and need to be checked early on to avoid problems later.

HOW TO... CHECK OUT NEW RECRUITS

Verify their identity.

↓

Verify academic records.

↓

Verify professional credentials.

↓

Check right-to-work documents.

↓

Commission public and criminal records check.

↓

Consider other checks as needed.

Protecting your organization

It is obvious that an organization needs to be certain that new recruits will bring to the new job all of the education, qualifications, skills, and experience they claim to have, in order for the organization to benefit. You want to believe everything candidates have told you on their CVs and in interviews, and trust that they have told you everything. But strong competition for particular jobs and tightened employment standards in certain industries mean there is a greater likelihood of candidates falsifying, or omitting necessary information from their applications. Failing to take steps to confirm candidates' identity and background can leave your organization vulnerable to a number of serious risks such as employee fraud, legal liability and litigation, theft of sensitive organization and customer information, damage to the organization's reputation, and costs stemming from negligent hiring procedures.

Deciding what you need to know

Senior-level roles, certain specialist jobs, and positions giving access to sensitive information or vulnerable people may require more extensive and complex checks of candidates. You may want to out-source complicated screening to a specialist agency. But consider first which checks would be most relevant to the job, organization, and industry involved.

Confirming identity

The most basic vetting procedure is to check references for past schooling, membership in professional organizations, and employment details that candidates have given you. However, previous employers may be reluctant to confirm details other than dates of employment because of possible legal action if the candidate does not get the job. Get candidates to help you with simple methods of confirming identity and address by having them bring in identity documents with a photograph (such as a passport or driver's licence), a recent bank statement (within the last three months), and a utility bill addressed to them at their current home. Foreign candidates must provide documentation that they are currently eligible to work in your country.

TIP

AVOID DISCRIMINATION
Ask all candidates to show you their passports so that you are not singling out non-natives for travel document checks.

Using social networking sites

The Internet is used by many people to share details of their personal lives. Some employers use social networking sites on the Internet as yet another bank of information to check out potential new recruits, while others believe such checks invade candidates' privacy.

TIP

BE AWARE OF REPUTATION

Type your organization's name into a search engine to check on-line mentions to know what employees are saying about your own organization.

Knowing what to look for

Research by job site CareerBuilder.com revealed that in the US, one-third of the hiring managers who screened candidates via social networking profiles reported they dismissed some from consideration after finding inappropriate content. Material regarded as deal-breakers included information about using drugs, badmouthing employers or colleagues, lying about qualifications, criminal behaviour, and making discriminatory remarks related to race, gender, or religion. However, 24 per cent reported finding content that helped solidify their decision to hire a particular candidate, if for example, their profile reflected achievement or creativity. To use such sites effectively, you must know what information you are looking for.

CASE STUDY

Enterprise Rent-A-Car
There's no doubt that social networking sites are a major phenomenon, but not all of the world's top employers are inclined to use them – even when an employer is well known as a top employer of graduates, who are generally among the dominant users of such sites. To the accompaniment of considerable news coverage, the European human resources director

of international car hire organization Enterprise Rent-A-Car revealed that her recruiters would not research job candidates via social networking sites. According to her, scrutinizing personal web pages invades the candidates' privacy. By using personal web pages for business purposes, employers would be blurring the lines between what is personal and what is business, she told interviewers.

Exploring profiles on-line

To find out more about a candidate's professional affiliations, contacts, and background on-line, first type that person's name into your search engine to see if any web mentions come up. If a listing appears, click on the link related to a business-focused social networking site. However, it may be ultimately best to simply avoid social networking sites such as Facebook and MySpace, which focus more on personal life.

Your decision to research candidates on social networking sites must be based on your organization's values. If your organization has a conservative culture, exploring such sites may result in your finding material that turns a previously appealing candidate into a less interesting one. But if your organization has a creative culture, your view of some candidates could be enhanced if their web pages feature an innovative design or information about a meaningful project.

TIP

CHECK YOUR LIABILITY

If you out-source any recruitment to third parties, make sure they follow your policy on using, or not using, social networking sites to check out candidates. Using the sites inappropriately could mean joint liability.

CHECKING SOCIAL NETWORKING SITES

FAST TRACK

OFF TRACK

FAST TRACK	OFF TRACK
Visiting professionally-focused sites	Visiting sites that are used primarily for socializing with friends and family
Considering professional references on candidates' profiles	Looking for embarrassing photos or video clips
Looking at the on-line networking groups that they belong to	Seeking out personal details, such as a current pregnancy, which does not affect hiring decisions
Studying their public profiles for work-related information	Making inappropriate contact with candidates

Chapter 4

Making the final decision

The information required to make the hiring decision is in your hands, but the difficult task of analyzing and prioritizing the strengths and potential of each candidate still lies ahead – as does the decision of choosing the best person for the role.

Aligning goals

Hiring a new person into your organization is more than simply filling a slot. It is not enough for the new hire to meet today's needs; in this fast-moving world, new recruits must be capable of growing and developing along with the organization.

PREDICT THE BEST DEVELOPERS
Remember that past performance is a strong indicator of future performance. Candidates with a track record of embracing development elsewhere are likely to embrace it at a new job.

Developing tomorrow's team

To position themselves for future success, organizations must understand where they are at the moment and what they must do to reach where they want to go. New skills and new kinds of jobs will be essential to the forward-moving organization. The people who are recruited into their midst now must be sufficiently flexible to be effective contributors to the organization of tomorrow. Think about the candidates you are interviewing and choosing between: who wants to be comfortable and do the same task in the same way, and who seeks a challenge and wants to develop?

Matching values

TIP

SUPPORT DURING CHANGE

Sometimes a change in values is necessary for an organization. If this is true in yours, you must openly endorse and back the new recruit's moves to make changes happen in spite of organizational inertia.

In some cases, you may be recruiting a person specifically to lead the way towards development and growth. Consider your organization's other goals and values: how do you want to move ahead, and are there right and wrong ways to accomplish this? While it is important to allow and encourage creative differences when examining different options offered by candidates, bear in mind that bringing in a person with fundamentally different values could result in a costly mistake that sets your organization back.

Defining the right matches

Draw up a document that outlines your organization's strategic goals and defines the behaviours, skills, and abilities that would support them. Take the exercise further by outlining the strategic goals of the team for which you are hiring, and define the attributes, experience, and abilities that would help them achieve these goals. This approach will require you to understand the direction of both the organization and the team; hopefully, the two are complementary. It will usually be easier to define strategic goals for the organization; individual teams may not always outline theirs. Work with them to do so – however, be warned that this requires care and considerable thought. Then when matching up the abilities, attitudes, behaviours, and skills of each of your candidates to the items on the two lists, you will begin to see where alignment and compatibility exist and where they don't.

**ASK YOURSELF...
WHAT DO WE NEED
TOMORROW?**

- What does your organization want its unique selling proposition to be in five years' time?
- What new skills will you need to accomplish that?
- How must our organization develop to fulfil its long-term goal?
- What are the requirements needed by today's manager to lead the organization to achieve that aim?
- How do the above needs relate to the position you are filling now?

Assessing strengths

It is rare that a candidate offers all the required attitudes, characteristics, skills, and experience to succeed in the role at hand. Taking a methodical approach to weighing up and comparing candidates' strengths is the key to deciding which blend of strengths is best for the job.

Using the framework

At the beginning of the recruitment process, you drew up job and person descriptions to set out the demands of the role and the experience, character, and qualifications required. You may also have created a decision matrix to give these requirements some sort of priority. When you reach the stage of making a final decision, return to these documents and use them as a framework against which to review the information gathered from interviews, tests, assessment centre activities, and CVs.

Weighting responses

Ask yourself what percentage of your hiring decision will be based on information gained in the interview itself – 100 per cent, 50 per cent, or less? If the decision will depend primarily, or entirely, upon the interviews, then devise a weighting system for the responses to each question. Let's say that you decide each answer would be worth a maximum of five points. At the same time, each question would have a different value depending upon its importance to the hiring decision. For example, a candidate might earn four points for the quality of her response to a question, which has a weighted value of three points. The total earned value of her response to that question would be 12 points (4 x 3).

Scoring strengths

If you held an assessment centre, bring into the hiring equation the information obtained through the psychometric tests, exercises, and other activities. Create a score sheet or assessment sheet for each candidate. List each element or activity that you "tested" or "scored" them on, and note the appropriate score, points, or place on the behavioural spectrum*. Or you could keep it simple, and put ticks by the elements where they performed to an acceptable level and double ticks for outstanding performance. What kind of picture is emerging of each of the candidates? Is there one candidate who clearly stands out from the rest? Or are there several with a similar collection of strengths? Eliminate the most obviously weak performers among your candidates. Discuss with your colleagues and any external experts the strengths demonstrated by the candidates who remain contenders, and check if they are the most critical strengths needed by the organization.

*Behavioural spectrum — *the full range of behaviours a person may exhibit or actions they might take during an assessment centre activity.*

CONSIDER ANY ORGANIZATIONAL CHANGES

Take into account any changes that have occurred in your organization since recruitment began. It may be necessary to reconsider candidates' strengths in light of new priorities.

Linking goals

Next, consider the organization and team goals you identified, along with the list of abilities, behaviours, and skills that are required to support them. Compare these with the strengths of each individual candidate as outlined on the score sheet. Ideally, the candidate whose skills, experience, and other characteristics most closely meet the job criteria will also be shown to be a good fit with the organization and team goals. Remember throughout the selection process that you are measuring candidates against the required criteria, and not comparing them to fellow candidates. Being human, it is inevitable that some discussion will result in candidate comparison, but keep in mind that you are looking for the best match to the job and to the organization.

HOW TO...
MAKE YOUR DECISION

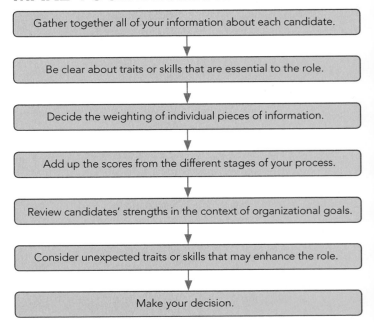

Gather together all of your information about each candidate.

Be clear about traits or skills that are essential to the role.

Decide the weighting of individual pieces of information.

Add up the scores from the different stages of your process.

Review candidates' strengths in the context of organizational goals.

Consider unexpected traits or skills that may enhance the role.

Make your decision.

Experiencing a surprise

As you approach your decision, remember that a methodical approach to hiring is the best way to ensure that the job criteria, person specification, and organization goals are given due consideration when choosing candidates. However, keep your mind open to the unexpected if a candidate has demonstrated an unanticipated skill, personality trait, or other quality that adds a new dimension to their application for the job. Perhaps the candidate lacks a qualification, trait, or experience that you initially considered essential for the role but offers something else that you had not thought about, in spite of your in-depth examination of the job requirements. If you are seriously considering this candidate, weigh up whether you can make that trade-off without it having a negative effect somewhere along the line. But also be clear about which characteristics, skills, or experience you cannot afford to do without. Traits such as integrity and a constructive, positive management style should be non-negotiable, and a specific qualification may be less important to your organization than a candidate's unexpected expertise in a new and exciting technology.

TIP

MAKE THE MOST OF UNEXPECTED SKILLS

When a candidate has an unanticipated skill that could be valuable to the organization, consider whether it is needed now or if a new role should be created to incorporate it.

ASK YOURSELF... WHAT ARE THE CRITICAL UNKNOWNS?

- How well will the candidate work in a team?
- How do they respond to stress?
- What is their management style?
- What motivates them to perform?
- How well will their personality mesh with their potential manager?
- How flexible and adaptable are they to new conditions?
- How well do they think on their feet?
- Are they problem solvers?
- Do they have an unexpected skill or ability that may enhance the role?

Making the offer

The process does not end once you have chosen a recruit. The next stage involves creating a job offer for them and inviting them to build a future in your organization.

Building the package

The salary is one of the offer elements that can make or break the deal. Most employers benchmark salary data to ensure that they pay their employees competitive wages for their marketplace, and offer an attractive selection of benefits. At the least, studying recent salary surveys for jobs in your industry sector will help you to adjust the basic salary that you will offer your new recruits, to reflect the appropriate levels of education and experience, as well as the geographic region.

Informing the selectees

Once you have put together an offer, telephone your chosen candidate to share the good news verbally before you send out the letter. Mention a few of the offer highlights, such as pay and start date. They may ask for a few days to consider the opportunity after studying the written offer, which is perfectly acceptable. However, an attempt to significantly renegotiate the offered salary should be viewed with caution, particularly if a range was originally advertised.

OTHER DETAILS
Confirm a deadline for accepting the offer, a start date, name of the line manager, and the job location.

WORK HOURS
Outline the typical work hours and days, any flexible working hours, and any probation period.

REFEREES
Make it clear to the recruits that the offer is contingent upon suitable references.

Making the offer

SALARY AND BONUSES
Be aware of average salary and bonus or commission levels for this role.

BENEFITS
Spell out in detail the benefits – for example, insurance, discounts, and holiday time.

COMPANY ASSETS
Advise which assets come with this role, such as mobile phone, car, or PDA.

Obtaining references

Confirming the hire of your top candidate will depend on obtaining suitable references. You may have explored their professional background and right to work in your country, but taking the additional step of gleaning specific, job-relevant information about your candidate from people who know him or her is crucial to sealing the deal.

TIP

EXPAND THE REFEREE BASE

Consider accepting a reference from a community group or volunteer project, who can discuss the person's skills and attributes relevant to the job.

Lining up references

Advise your candidates early in the recruitment process that if you should decide to hire them, you will need the names and contact details of two or three professional references who would be willing to speak to you about their current or previous jobs. Emphasize to candidates that employment will be contingent on your being able to obtain suitable references.

Requesting information

It is not uncommon for hiring managers today to send out forms requesting information on their new recruits, to make it easier for the referees to provide information. However, it is best if you can actually speak to a referee. If you are able to speak with a referee directly, ask the basics, but also inquire about the quality of the recruit's work, strengths and weaknesses, ability to work with others, and any anecdotes that offer insight into how your potential recruit made a difference in the workplace. Other questions may come to mind, too, but be sure that you ask only work-related questions. Avoid asking anything you wouldn't be willing to ask the candidate directly, such as anything to do with race, religion, ethnicity, marital status, or age.

Raising questions

Hopefully you will receive information that confirms your best impressions about the person you have selected for the job. However, do make contingency plans in case you get a negative report about your potential recruit. If you receive one less-than-favourable report but others that are positive, ask your candidate for another reference you may contact; there may have been a personality conflict between manager and employee, the manager may have been jealous of the employee, or perhaps that particular job was not a good fit for your potential hire. On the other hand, if none of the referees seem willing to confirm or verify information the candidate has given you, you may want to reconsider your decision to hire this person. However, sometimes former managers are simply not sufficiently interested to pass on any information, positive or negative, about former employees. This should not be held against the candidate; you will have to consider this a "neutral" reference, and ask the candidate for another. Another scenario that has been known to unfold is the use of family or friends as professional references, so be certain to verify the circumstances in which the referee knew the candidate.

TIP

GET IN TOUCH WITH THE REFEREES

Follow up reference forms and letters with a more direct approach – a phone call – to ensure you get the necessary answers regarding your candidates.

✔ CHECKLIST CREATING A REFERENCE FORM

	YES	NO
• Have you confirmed dates of employment and job title(s) during employment?	☐	☐
• Have you confirmed the candidate's final salary?	☐	☐
• Have you asked about any promotions or honours?	☐	☐
• Have you asked about their responsibilities?	☐	☐
• Can they list the training and development undertaken?	☐	☐
• Can they confirm the candidate's reason for leaving?	☐	☐

Sending rejection letters

Probably the most painful part of recruitment is telling non-selectees they did not get the job. Those candidates will no doubt share their experiences – good or bad – with their friends or family, so organizations can only gain by treating unsuccessful candidates well.

TIP

TREAT EACH CANDIDATE EQUALLY

Choose your language carefully so that no one could build a case for being discriminated against.

Handling with care

Failing to get a job you want is one of life's great disappointments. The bottom line is that you as an individual did not offer everything the employer wanted. Being able to empathize with that blow to self-esteem will go far towards guiding your treatment of the candidates you did not select. Treating them with dignity can create a good impression of your organization as an employer in the marketplace. Even though your attention may be focused on bringing on board your new employee, ensuring that your non-selectees walk away with a positive impression is time well spent.

"We received a number of very strong applications."

"I regret to say your application has not been successful."

"If you have any comments on your experience of our recruitment process, we would be delighted to hear them."

Contacting non-selectees

Send all non-selected candidates a formal letter confirming that they did not get the job. The tone must be businesslike, but inject some warmth with a comment referring back to an interesting bit of information the candidate revealed in the interview, if possible. Depending on the number of candidates you interviewed, you may have time to telephone non-selectees. If so, tell them that they have not been selected, but thank them for applying and wish them well in their job search.

Being positive in your approach

The rejecting letter's main purpose is to tell non-selectees they were not successful this time, but it also gives you a vehicle to encourage promising candidates to apply to your organization again. You could also invite them to apply for specific roles in your organization for which they may be better suited. However, letters to the candidates who would not be a good fit for the organization should be just as professional and courteous as those to the people whom you would like to see apply again in the future.

"Thank you for taking the time to come in."

"My colleagues and I greatly enjoyed meeting you."

"We would be happy to consider your application for the more junior position of..."

Reviewing your process

Once you have nearly completed your recruitment process, go back over the steps to examine the results and see where the process could be improved. Your own notes and the opinions of colleagues and experts involved in the process can help with this.

Looking for "red flags"

Analyze your collated data to look for indicators that your process is inadequate. Warning signs might include too few applications from candidates with the right skill sets, or information gaps about candidates' capabilities. Exchange feedback with the colleagues involved in the process about interviewing style, the relevance of questions asked, and what could be improved.

LOCATION
Make sure you place future advertisements in the places where the most appropriate candidates for the role are most likely to see them.

Measuring return on investment

Keep records of the number of days it has taken to hire for the role, from the beginning of the process to the candidate's formal acceptance. Closely monitor the total cost-to-hire – this will include costs incurred for advertising, recruitment consultants, assessment centre tests, background checking carried out by external consultants, venue hire, and staff hours. Effectively managing the time it takes to hire means balancing the quick and efficient filling of the position with not rushing to put the first available candidate in place. Keeping cost-to-hire at a fiscally responsible level is challenging, which means that you must keep tabs on the return-on-investment of each expense.

JOB DESCRIPTION
Ensure that future advertisements explain and "sell" the job, and effectively communicate your organization's brand and identity.

Planning your recruitment advertising

MEDIA
Consider which medium – print or on-line – produced the most candidates, and which specific title or site delivered the best-qualified applicants.

QUALIFICATIONS
Determine whether there was an overabundance or a noticeable lack of certain desired skills/ experience offered by candidates.

DIVERSITY
Check whether candidates had similar backgrounds, or they represented the diversity of your customers, clients, and geographic location.

Onboarding new employees

The candidate has been chosen and has accepted your offer. Now it is time to make sure that the transition from candidate to employee is seamless. Lay the groundwork for a successful future in the organization by providing the right information and equipment – and a warm welcome.

TIP

PERSONALIZE THE EXPERIENCE

Select a colleague to initiate contact with the newcomer and be a "buddy" during onboarding and induction, to answer questions, and keep the newcomer up-to-date with office projects and activities before they arrive.

Creating a link

If your organization does not already have a programme in place for preparing recruits for their new workplace, it is time to build one. One way to start making new employees feel as though they are already part of the team is to send them employee information, such as a staff handbook, before their first day. Or you could send them a link and log-in for the organization website's intranet so that they can get a feel for its day-to-day goings on as well as benefits, social events, dress code, and the organizational structure. If your organization has branded materials, such as pens, t-shirts, or caps, give these items as a gift to communicate the message "You are one of us." If the person is relocating from a distance, send information about the local area, such as accommodation, schools, and leisure facilities.

✔ CHECKLIST BRINGING THE NEWCOMER ON BOARD

	YES	NO
• Have I sent relevant employee information to the newcomer?	☐	☐
• Have I ensured that the line manager or a colleague is prepared for the newcomer's arrival?	☐	☐
• Have I organized a session to explain the team's current projects and how the new recruit is expected to contribute to them?	☐	☐

Planning Day One

Advise your new employees where they need to report on their first day, with directions on how to get there. If there is an organization-wide first-day orientation, plan for a colleague from their team to meet them afterwards. Then let them spend the first day getting to know the workplace, their work equipment, and their colleagues. A nice touch is for the line manager to take the newcomer out for lunch on the first day to spend some time over a meal discussing the job, plans for the first week at work, and the team's current projects. This can get the relationship off on a good footing by demonstrating the line manager's accessibility to team members.

TIP

MAKE THE MOST OF ONBOARDING

Remember that the best onboarding operations involve both technology and the human touch. Technology efficiently takes care of the bureaucracy, such as ordering equipment and passes, and generating necessary paperwork. Humans add a warm welcome.

Mapping the future

Most importantly, your new hire needs to understand your organization's mission, values, and strategy moving forward. They need to know where they fit in, and how they are expected to contribute to the organization's day-to-day operations as well as the future. Having their job description at hand to review will reinforce their duties and responsibilities. Mapping out a clear idea of the team's targets over the next few months will provide a view of how all the pieces fit together. A well-thought out and welcoming beginning will help newcomers to start this phase of their careers with confidence. And that is one of the best ways to retain the best and brightest talent.

IN FOCUS...
ONBOARDING

Top employers now take seriously the need to make joining an organization as smooth and enjoyable a process as possible for its new employees. There is certainly a business case for it, whether applied to an organization's most junior employee or its most senior. Evidence shows that when done well, onboarding promotes productivity, encourages employee retention, and leads to quicker assimilation of recruits. Well-planned onboarding ensures that all the necessary paperwork is completed early on, that they have the necessary work equipment from the first day, and that they get off to a running start with the new job.

PRESENTING

Contents

Introduction

The increasing pace and competitiveness of business makes the need for communication all the more urgent. It is not surprising that presentations have become an essential tool for business communication in workplaces around the world. After all, ideas need to be shared in a clear and convincing way if they are to influence others.

Every presentation is a pitch in which you must sell your ideas to colleagues or outside audiences. This holds true whether your intention is to inform or to persuade, whether you are delivering a formal speech from behind a podium, a presentation using visual aids, an informal address to your staff, or a briefing distributed through the media.

Successful presenters understand what they must communicate, who they are communicating with, and for what reason. With preparation and practice – and working through each of these elements – anyone can learn to plan, assemble, and deliver a successful presentation every time.

The elements of great presentations are described in this guide in practical detail, making it ideal for new managers and experienced communicators alike.

Chapter 1

Planning to present

A presentation is a way of informing, inspiring, and motivating other people. Whether your audience is a group of receptive colleagues, demanding clients, or strict regulators, your job is to influence the way they think and feel about your message. No matter how charismatic you may be, success depends on careful planning of your content and delivery.

Putting the audience first

Presenting successfully means stepping back from your own knowledge of your subject. Examine what you want to say and how you convey that information from the perspective of the audience. Their priorities will almost always be different to yours.

MIND YOUR LANGUAGE

Check the language abilities of your audience – if you do not share a first language, you will need to make allowances.

Identifying the need

A presentation serves a very different purpose to a written report – it is far more than just another vehicle for information. A presentation allows an audience to gain knowledge by watching, listening, and being inspired by you. Audiences come not to learn everything you know about a subject, but to gain your perspective – they are likely to remember only the big themes even a short time afterwards. Good presenters understand that audiences are looking for information in context, not in full detail, so ask yourself what *you* can add through *your* presentation of the subject.

Researching the audience

Get to know your audience, even before you plan your presentation. Talk to the organizer of the event about their expectations, and if possible, engage with those attending ahead of time; ask them about their existing level of knowledge, and what they hope to hear about. Work out if they need persuading, informing, educating, motivating, or a mixture of all these. The more you understand your audience's expectations, the better you'll be able to meet them.

TIP

MATCH THINKING STYLES

Is your audience made up of creative thinkers or analysts? You'll need to tailor your content and delivery to match their thinking style.

Focusing your message

Identify the essential information you want your audience to understand and remember. You should have no more than three such core messages. Build your presentation around these points and add supporting details where necessary – but remember that less is more when it comes to oral presentation. Make your key points emphatically and repeatedly and don't try to be too subtle or clever. Always look for the overlap between what you want to say and what your audience wants to hear.

ASK YOURSELF...
WHO IS MY AUDIENCE?

- Who will be listening?
- What do they already know? Is there a common understanding to build on?
- What are their expectations? Will they hold any preconceived notions about the subject?
- What do I want them to learn? What do I expect them to do with that knowledge?
- What will I say to accomplish my goals?

Presenting and selling

Presentations serve a great variety of purposes. They can be used to inspire and motivate people or they can be designed to simply convey information formally (as in a lecture) or informally (as in a team briefing). But most often, they are used to promote a product, service, or idea, or to persuade stakeholders about a particular course of action. In other terms – whether overtly or covertly – most presentations aim to sell.

TIP

GET TO THE POINT

Engage your audience by addressing what they want to know quickly. Avoid opening your presentation with background about you or your company – when it was founded, where it's located, and so on.

Pitching your ideas

The better you can meet the needs of your audience, the more successful your presentation will be. So when selling anything, from an idea to a product, your presentation should focus on how it will help your audience, how it will solve their problems. Whenever you talk about your idea, product, or service, don't just list its features – express them as benefits.

Throughout your presentation, your audience will be constantly assessing both your trustworthiness and the strength of your "sell". You need to be able to "read" their reactions so that you can address their concerns. Successful presenters do this by inviting many questions from the audience and encouraging them to interrupt; the questions and comments from the audience provide vital feedback.

IN FOCUS... THE TWO-MINUTE PRESENTATION

We often encounter people casually – between meetings or in quick conversations at conferences. It pays to develop a two-minute pitch that introduces you, your business, and the unique value you can offer. The pitch should be very easy to understand, describe the solutions you offer, and reflect your passion about what you do. A good two-minute pitch will get you a surprising number of follow-up meetings.

Selling successfully in your presentation

EXPECT TO CLOSE

If the presentation is effective, the decision to buy, or buy in, is a natural next step. Be prepared to ask for some kind of commitment and agree to take immediate action, even if it is only setting up a further meeting.

SHOW, DON'T TELL

Visual representations and physical demonstrations bring sales presentations to life. People remember what they see and do for themselves, so be creative.

KNOW YOUR STUFF

To establish your credibility, you need to know a great deal about your product or service. As well as handling general, predictable queries, be prepared to demonstrate your knowledge in every respect – commercial, technical, and practical.

BELIEVE WHAT YOU ARE SAYING

An animated, enthusiastic presentation is a must. Buyers do not want to buy from someone who doesn't appear fully committed to the product, even if it is relevant to their needs.

SELL BENEFITS, NOT FEATURES

The presentation must centre on what matters most to the buyer – general discussion won't do. Talk about specific benefits. How does the product or service help to solve a problem or improve a situation?

Presenting formally

In many presentations, you are in control of what you say and how you say it. But be aware that some types of presentation are much more formal, following rules, requirements, timescales, or formats dictated by the audience or by a third party. They include presentations to boards, regulatory bodies, and examination and assessment panels, all of which require high levels of planning and rigorous attention to detail.

TIP

EXPECT TOUGH QUESTIONS

Formal presentations to boards and panels may be met with adversarial questions – boards may view harsh questioning as perfectly acceptable, so come prepared with robust answers.

Keeping focused

When you are asked to make a formal presentation, always request guidance about what is expected from you – what is the desired length, content, and context of your material. Play safe – don't attempt to be too innovative with the structure, but stick with a tried and tested formula:

HOW TO...
STRUCTURE A FORMAL PRESENTATION

> Introduce the topic, the argument you are about to make, and the conclusion that you will reach.

> Develop your arguments clearly and persuasively, justifying what you say.

> Make a conclusion: summarize your main arguments and explain the relevance of the conclusion made; explain why you are confident of your conclusion.

> Facilitate discussion of your presentation; check that everyone has understood exactly how you have arrived at your conclusion.

Keep your presentation concise and limit the detail that you include. If presenting to a board of directors, for example, bear in mind that they don't get involved in day-to-day management and have many demands on their time. Focus on what they really need to know, but ensure you don't withhold anything important – choose your words very carefully to ensure that you cannot be interpreted as being misleading.

Preparing to succeed

Before a formal presentation, seek out people who know the members of the board. Find out everything you can about their backgrounds, concerns, and predispositions. Use what you have learned to prepare your arguments; if appropriate, try to gain advance support for your position with members of the board.

Confidence is another key success factor. You will be expected to take a strong stand and support it with compelling evidence. Handle challenges with calm assurance and keep in mind that it is your position, rather than your personality, that is under attack. Finally, if you are presenting with colleagues, make sure you "get your story straight" – that your materials are consistent.

Being a panellist

Panel presentations are often a feature of conferences. If you are asked to be a panellist, make sure you understand the specific areas or questions you have been invited to address. Find out who is talking before and after you, and what they are focusing on to avoid repeating their content.

Build flexibility into your presentation, since time slots often shift to accommodate delays. Make sure you have time to present your key points. If you feel the topic is too complex for the time frame, suggest an alternative.

Following protocol

Some expert panels are very formally structured, with individual members asked to stand and present on a topic in turn before fielding questions from other panellists or the audience. Others are much looser, with any panellist permitted to interject, add remarks, or pose questions at any time. If the format of your panel is unstructured, always be attentive while others are speaking, don't interrupt others too often, and don't speak for too long. No matter how informal the structure, always take the time to develop your key messages in advance.

Planning the structure

There are many ways to organize your ideas to create an effective and convincing presentation. Sometimes, the content you need to convey will fall more naturally into one type of structure rather than another. There may also be an element of personal preference – you may simply feel more comfortable with one type of structure than another. But however you choose to organize, the end result must achieve your communication aim. In other words, content always dictates form, not vice versa.

Setting out the basics

All presentation structures share three high-level elements: the introduction or opening, the body or main content, and the conclusion or close. Most of your time will be spent delivering the body, but don't underestimate the importance of opening with an introduction that captures the audience's attention, and tying everything together at the close.

QUICK AND EASY STORYBOARDING

Sticky notes are a useful tool when storyboarding your presentation. Use a different coloured note for each type of element: here, blue for a key message, pink for each proof point that backs up a message, and orange for a visual aid. Reposition the notes to experiment with running order, the balance between "showing" and "telling", and to identify weak sections. Storyboarding is a method of sequencing your ideas that can help you decide how to represent them in a logical and compelling order when planning your presentation. It adds a physical dimension that is especially useful for organizing and understanding the impact of a presentation using visual aids.

- **The introduction:** Think of your opening as a promise to the audience. It should tell them what they are going to hear, and why it is important. This section needs to get their attention and give them a reason to keep listening.
- **The body:** This is where you deliver on the promise you made in your introduction. Here you deliver the facts, analysis, explanation, and comment to fill out your message. Sustain interest by keeping the opening promise in mind, and making sure every element advances that goal.
- **The conclusion:** Your close is the "so what?" of your presentation. Remind the audience of your key points and clearly articulate where they lead, or conclusions that can be drawn. An effective close demonstrates your conviction about the action you are suggesting or the position you hold. While you should spend no more than 15 per cent of your presentation time on the close, remember that it will probably be the section that your audience remembers most clearly. Whatever you want them to remember, say it now.

TIP

KEEP IT BALANCED

Your structured content should fall roughly into these proportions: 10 per cent introduction, 75 per cent body, and 15 per cent conclusion. Let each section fulfil its function: don't overload the introduction or bring in new ideas in the conclusion.

Selecting a framework

To structure your presentation for maximum impact, choose a framework sympathetic to its content. For example, if your material is data-driven, use a numbered list; if you are selling a concept, employ case studies. Described here is a selection of useful structural alternatives.

NUMBERED LIST

Use this model to present modular information such as the top competitors in your market. Quantitative information helps your audience to understand the relationship between a list of items.

PROBLEMS AND SOLUTIONS

Outline a problem, then reveal how to fix it. This structure is excellent when discussing change. It can help to position you as someone who can read a situation clearly, explain it, and offer a way forward.

FEATURES AND BENEFITS

Work through the elements of a product or proposal and explain the positive outcomes each one can generate. This method works well for more persuasive sales presentations.

DEDUCTIVE OR INDUCTIVE?

Deductive reasoning moves from general principles to specifics ("our market is growing, we should do well"); inductive reasoning moves from specifics to principles ("we've done well, our market is growing").

MESSAGING

Tell them you are going to tell them, tell them, and then tell them you have told them. This simple structure works well provided the messages are clear and backed up with proof.

STORIES AND CASE STUDIES

Present your argument through narrative. People love hearing stories, making this a compelling and forceful presentation method. Keep your story simple and explain the "moral".

COMPARE AND CONTRAST

Put your material in context by comparing it with something else. Ensure your content is coherent and well chosen so that similarities and differences are clear to your audience.

OPTIONS AND OUTCOMES

List some choices and the pros and cons of each. Make sure the options are different, not refinements of one idea. If you are going to suggest the best way forward, be prepared to back it up with data.

TIMELINE

A chronological structure is useful for showing progressive developments. Its linear structure is intuitive and easy to understand. To avoid seeming one-dimensional, ensure your material has both purpose and pace.

Opening and closing

Two simple observations of human interaction will help you plan a powerful presentation. First, you only have one chance to make a first impression; and second, people remember longest what they hear last. These observations suggest that the opening and closing parts of your presentation have particular importance. It pays to practise getting these moments right – making them clear, powerful, and engaging.

TIP

MAKE FRIENDS
Establish a good rapport with the audience early. Greet them warmly; ask them how they are enjoying the day.

Opening powerfully

The opening to your presentation serves many functions: it grabs the attention of your audience, establishes your credibility, and sets the stage for what is to come. Don't begin with an extended introduction, lengthy thanks to your hosts, or a recitation of the agenda – you may not be able to engage your audience after such a slow start. Instead, explain to your audience how listening to you will be of benefit to them, and through your confidence, let them see your competence.

IN FOCUS...
ESTABLISHING YOUR CREDIBILITY

Credibility is everything. Your audience needs to buy into you in order to buy into your message. Introducing yourself (or being introduced) with your academic or professional credentials in specific fields may help, especially at formal or academic conferences, but credibility isn't just a function of title – it is a product of confidence, preparation, and experience. Explain to your audience what experience you bring to the issue and why you are qualified to speak; then show that you understand the information and can apply it independently. In order to keep your credibility throughout, you will need to show that you want to communicate, and are prepared to work to do so. You don't have to be word-perfect, but you do need to be focused and organized with what you do know. Your preparation and readiness will speak volumes.

Capturing attention

Be yourself at your most engaging. Rehearse your opening many times – out loud and in front of a mirror – and don't be tempted to improvise. Pump it up, but don't force jokes or stories into the opening if it's not in your character. Most of all, be audience-centred; find common ground with the audience early on. Try using:
• Interesting or entertaining quotes
• Unusual or startling statistics
• Interesting survey results
• Short anecdotes
• Personal stories of experiences or lessons learned
• Outlines of problems and how you would solve them.

Elevating endings

You will probably feel relieved as the end of your presentation approaches, but don't be in a rush to finish: your final words are likely to be those that persist longest in your audience's memory. End with a summary of your key points, or deliver a call to action resting on those points, which will make sure they are remembered – in other words, make sure your ending addresses the objectives you had when starting out.

However you choose to end your presentation, make it meaningful and memorable. Don't end by introducing new ideas that you don't have time to support.

TIP

BACK IT UP
Always provide follow-up materials so that you continue your dialogue with the audience. Keep these printed materials concise and relevant to the presentation – too wide a reach can be off-putting.

CLOSING A PRESENTATION

FAST TRACK	**OFF TRACK**
Ending on a positive note, even if you've delivered negative information	Ending abruptly without a summary or call to action, or by calling for questions prematurely
Restating, rather than re-examining, key points in your material	Introducing new information towards the end of your presentation
Being concise	Running out of steam or rushing for the finish line

Winning with words

When you make a presentation, your job is to make the audience understand, recall, and respond to your message. Your success as a speaker depends on your delivery of the message, and this cannot be separated from your choice of words, forms of expression, and the mental images that you conjure up as you bring your words to life.

TIP

STAND UP
Whenever possible, present standing rather than seated. You will command attention, and gain better breath and voice control.

Convincing and persuading

Persuasive speech, or rhetoric, asks that an audience goes beyond passive listening. Its purpose is to elicit agreement – for example, that a crisis is looming and action is necessary – "to avoid crisis, we must...". The tools of rhetoric were developed in classical times by great thinkers such as Plato and Aristotle, for whom verbal artistry was not just a means to an end, but a way to arrive at truths about politics and justice. Aristotle, for example, relied most heavily on logic to support his arguments, but also recognized the importance of ethos and pathos.

CLASSICAL RHETORIC

TYPE OF RHETORIC	CHARACTERISTICS	EXAMPLE
Ethos	An appeal based on the integrity and reputation of the speaker. You may not understand the reasoning, but you trust the speaker.	"As a leading orthopedic surgeon, I recommend this child safety seat."
Pathos	An appeal to the emotions of the listener, such as love, compassion, fear, or greed. Often personalizes the argument.	"Give your children the protection they deserve with our safety seats."
Logos	An appeal to the listener based on logic. This would include evidence and reason.	"Fatalities drop 37 per cent with our safety seats: the conclusion is clear."

USING ACTIVE PHRASING

FAST TRACK

OFF TRACK

FAST TRACK	OFF TRACK
"Sales are rising. That's better than we expected."	"Surpassing our expectations, sales are rising."
"We're making real progress."	"Progress is being made."
"Training is necessary and it fits our timeline."	"Training, with respect to our current timeline, has been found necessary."
"We can understand complex ideas if they are presented well."	"Complex ideas, provided they're presented well, can be understood."

MIX YOUR MESSAGE

A rounded presentation combines several different types of arguments – try mixing ethos and pathos in your summing up for a powerful closing.

Creating moments

Beyond the use of clear structure and good narratives, there are many verbal techniques to help your audience remember what you say. Use these sparingly to emphasize key points – sprinkling these devices too liberally throughout your presentation will dilute and therefore spoil their effect:

• Alliteration: "the sweet smell of success"
• Grouping words in threes: "friends, Romans, countrymen"
• Acronyms: "Audience, Intent, Message – AIM"
• Allegory: "I have a dream"
• Repetition: "Location, location, location"
• Mnemonic: "Thirty days has September..."
• Personification: "This product will be your faithful companion"
• Rhetorical questions: "Can one product really deliver all these benefits?"
• Using a motif: returning to a symbol or visual image throughout your presentation to add continuity.

Eliminating interlopers

Many speakers insert a word or syllable to fill what they perceive as an awkward gap. These filler words – er, um, ah, and so on – bubble up because we are all used to two-way conversation. When you pause, the other person speaks, and so on. When you are presenting, there is no feedback and the silence can be unnerving. Practice and awareness of your own habits will help you become comfortable with natural pauses while you consider the right phrasing, but knowing your material is the best defence against needing to use unnecessary words to fill a space.

Certain phrases detract from your authority as a speaker. There is a temptation to inject words like "possibly" and "perhaps" to soften what you are saying, so that you seem less severe. Don't bother. Eliminating such words and phrases will instantly power up your presentation.

"So..."

"Kind of" "Um" "You know?"

"Literally" "Ah"

"Hopefully" "Ok?"

"In my opinion"

"Might be" "Right"

"A little bit"

CASE STUDY

The personal touch

Steve Jobs, the co-founder of Apple Computers, is widely renowned for his memorable presentation skills. Jobs often fuels his public appearances and speeches with some personal anecdotes that allow those who are outside his industry to understand and be inspired.

"Because I had dropped out and didn't have to take the normal classes, I decided to take a calligraphy class... None of this had even a hope of any practical application in my life, but ten years later, when we were designing the first Macintosh computer, it all came back to me... It was the first computer with beautiful typography. If I had never dropped in on that single course in college, the Mac would have never had multiple typefaces or proportionally spaced fonts. And... it's likely that no personal computer would have."

Steve Jobs, Commencement Address, Stanford, California, 2005

Using narrative

Six of the most powerful words in the English language are "Let me tell you a story". Narratives bring facts and figures into context and lift presentations out of the realm of dry tutorials. They provide a showcase for the presenter to demonstrate real passion and grasp of the issues, particularly if the narrative resonates on a personal level. Crucially, like no other device, they will captivate the listener.

Learn to use stories effectively, by reading and listening to accomplished storytellers. Draw on your own experiences and practise honing them into stories by telling them in informal situations.

Stories can take diverse forms, but to be useful in a presentation they should have two basic elements – the "what happened", or sequence of events, followed by the "lesson learned" or moral, based on those events.

To further increase the likelihood that your audience will retain your message, distribute a printed handout to supplement your oral presentation. It may be a simple reprise of your presentation; it may contain additional information, elaborating on points you have made; or it may be a list of additional reading. A handout is a useful tool (essential in academic environments), as long as it is thoughtfully structured – it should not just be a place to dump your additional research. Always explain the purpose of your handout to your audience, and never assume that it will be read – it is no substitute for your oral presentation.

Introducing visual aids

It is said that a picture is worth a thousand words, and using visual aids in your presentation undoubtedly heightens impact and improves audience retention. In business, the term "visual aid" often reads as shorthand for PowerPoint™ or other presentation software, but you don't need computer technology to add visual flair. A simple prop can make an unforgettable point, and flip charts are foolproof, cheap, and portable.

TIP

BUILD SUSPENSE
Keep a prop covered on the table in front of you before you use it; this will help create intrigue and anticipation.

Preparing to impress

Visuals are of little value unless they clarify and illustrate your message. When planning your presentation, first establish its basic outline; then refer closely to the content to identify the points that would benefit from visual treatment. Consider what kind of visuals will help you communicate your information and where you can use them in your presentation to greatest effect. Will maps help your audience get to grips with locations? Will graphs or pie charts really help them to understand figures?

Then consider how much time you will need to invest in finding or generating the visual aids – would your effort be better spent refining and practising your delivery?

Some visual aids require little or no preparation. Props are objects that help reinforce a point or grab attention and they are particularly useful if you want to evoke an emotional response. Props can also be passed round the audience to engage their senses of smell, touch, and even taste. Use props sparingly, and integrate them well into your presentation so they are not perceived as gimmicks.

IN FOCUS...
RETAINING VISUAL INFORMATION

A study at the University of Pennsylvania's Wharton School of Business found retention rates of verbal-only presentations ran at about 10 per cent. Combining verbal with visual messages increased retention rates by nearly 400 per cent to 50 per cent.

Making images work

The most common presentation tools today are the slide or digital projector, which can carry text and graphics, and the video player. Each needs to be used thoughtfully and sparingly; if you bombard your audience with slide after slide, chances are they will retain very little, and a long video presentation is the perfect time to grab a nap.

Remember that the audience needs to be inspired and gain your perspective on the subject. You can only provide these yourself.

When using an image to make a point, cut down on narration and allow the audience to discover the message for themselves. Don't talk over a photograph – introduce it. Even a simple photograph of a building will generate more impact than a verbal description alone.

Think very carefully before using video. Most people are used to high production values and as such anything less could play against you. Customer testimonials work very well as video clips, but if you are planning on using a video element you do need to be selective since the average time allocated for a speech is five to seven minutes. Anything over a couple of minutes of clips and it will appear that your speech is just a distraction for the main event – the video clip!

Using presentation software

Multimedia projection software has become a standard tool for business presentations. Used with care, the software can greatly enhance the impact of your communication, but beware its seductive nature, which invites you to fill your slides with ever more content and embellishment.

Getting to the point

Creating slides in a dedicated presentation package, such as PowerPoint™ or Keynote™, is easy. But using these tools to communicate effectively is a bigger challenge. First ask yourself if your presentation will actually benefit from slide formatting; it may be just as effective – or more so – to use props, videos, handouts, or just your own voice and authority. For example, slides are not the best way to present lots of data (handouts are much better), but they are effective for showing the relationships between sets of data.

Slides are not a magic bullet: they won't organize a disorganized presentation; they won't give a point to a presentation that doesn't really have one; and they'll never make a convincing presentation on their own. What your slides can do is reinforce your points, drawing attention to them as you present.

KEEP IT SIMPLE
If you find yourself apologizing for the complexity of a slide, take it out.

Choosing the cues

When you elect to use multimedia projection tools, use them for what they are good at – showing rather than telling information. Findings from cognitive scientists suggest that because visual and verbal information is processed separately, audiences have a difficult time absorbing both at the same time. This means that you should let images do their own talking, and keep text minimal.

Streamlining your content

AVOID "EXTRAS"
Don't leave your audience wondering why you didn't address something you put on a slide.

Less is more. Use your slides to emphasize key points in your presentation rather than as a comfort blanket – they have far more impact when used sparingly. Don't include complex charts or graphs, or assume people will look at your handouts later to decode them – if a graphic can't be understood during the presentation, take it out or simplify it. Try breaking it into several separate slides; it can be very effective to use a series in which information is "built" with each slide.

Simplify the information on each slide – use no more than five lines of text per slide, and no more than six words per line. Some presenters tend to load their slides with bulleted lists, then deliver their presentation by expanding upon the points. This approach fails to engage the audience; rather than recapping bullet points, try replacing them with intriguing keywords that invite your explanation.

WRITING EFFECTIVE SLIDE TEXT

FAST TRACK

OFF TRACK

FAST TRACK	OFF TRACK
Using punchy key word bullets, such as: • Revolutionary • Adaptable	Using long bullets or paragraphs of text, such as: • Powered by rotary not conventional engine • Able to work in temperatures of −10 to 50°C
Capitalizing only the first word of each sentence	Using all capitals, excessive underlining, or type effects
Proofreading your text by reading it backwards	Using abbreviations or industry jargon

Making great visuals

You don't need to be a graphic designer to produce effective slides. The key – as with text – is to keep things simple, and stick to one, consistent graphic language. Limit yourself to two fonts and two type sizes for the presentation, and use the same conventions throughout – for example, bold text to denote a heading, and italics for quotes. Keep font styles and colours consistent from slide to slide so your audience doesn't have to stop and consider whether any differences are significant to their meaning. Use sans serif* fonts for their clarity and clean lines, and consider using white text on dark backgrounds to reduce glare.

Resist the temptation to present every graphic you have access to: use no more than two images on one slide, and no more than three separate curves on one graph. Be imaginative with your images. They don't need to be literal or combined with text – projecting a single, powerful image will help to vary the pace of your presentation and open up discussion.

? ASK YOURSELF WILL MY VISUALS WORK?

- Will the type you've used be legible when projected? Colours and sizes may be fine on your computer screen, but not when enlarged by a projector.
- Are image file sizes manageable? Over-large files tend to load slowly and may stall your presentation.
- Is the room dark enough for your slides to be seen? Balance the illumination in the auditorium so that you can still see your audience, and vice-versa.
- Is the type large enough? A good guide is to add 5cm (2in) of character height for every 6m (20ft) of distance between your slide and the audience.

*Sans serif — a typeface that is without serifs – decorations added to the ends of the strokes that make up letters.

TIP

LOOK AT THE AUDIENCE

Don't use your slides as prompts for yourself. It will encourage you to make slides that are for you rather than your audience. What's more, it will make you look at the screen, rather than at the audience.

Using conventions

Your audience won't have long to interpret complex graphics, so always simplify to the essentials, and take advantage of familiar visual conventions: for example, use the colour red to suggest negative numbers, stop, or danger; use pie charts for relative proportions; and use ascending lines to indicate growth. There is no need to reinvent the wheel. Beware of gimmicks, such as animated transitions between slides. Movement is very distracting when processing information, and such effects should be used sparingly.

HOW TO...
WORK WITH SLIDES

Begin your presentation with a title slide that introduces the topic.

Show slides only when you are talking about them. Don't leave them up.

Spend no more than two minutes addressing a slide.

Direct your audience to a slide using a hand gesture.

Walk your audience through each slide following natural reading patterns (left to right, top to bottom in Western cultures).

When presenting a complex slide, allow the audience some time to absorb the information before you talk.

Presenting virtually

Fast and near-ubiquitous broadband connections have made the delivery of remote, virtual presentations cheap and reliable – a far cry from the days when video conferencing involved expensive, complex equipment for both the sender and receiver. Getting the best from virtual delivery methods involves combining conventional presenting skills with a new range of techniques.

CHECK IT WILL WORK
Always check the compatibility of technologies used for conferencing. Some are dedicated applications that must be installed on the users' computers; some are web-based. The presenter may talk over a telephone line, pointing out information being presented on screen, or audio may be incorporated into the software package.

Benefiting from technology

Delivering your presentation online means your audience can watch, listen, and take part from anywhere in the world. It saves time, travel, and expense, and it appeals increasingly to generations of business people for whom the computer has always taken centre stage.

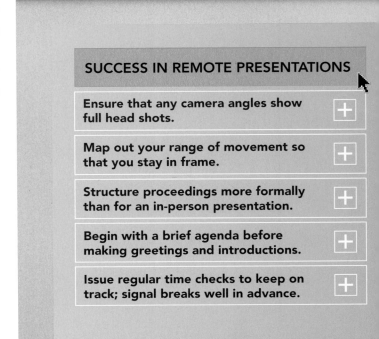

SUCCESS IN REMOTE PRESENTATIONS

Ensure that any camera angles show full head shots.

Map out your range of movement so that you stay in frame.

Structure proceedings more formally than for an in-person presentation.

Begin with a brief agenda before making greetings and introductions.

Issue regular time checks to keep on track; signal breaks well in advance.

Choosing your format

Web conferencing is the direct descendent of video conferencing, allowing live meetings or presentations to take place over the Internet or company intranet. The meeting may be referred to as a webcast, where there is little or no audience participation, or a webinar, where participation is encouraged – via the web, phone, or email. Podcasts can deliver messages that can be viewed on handheld devices or mobile phones. All these technologies are increasingly being used to reach staff, investors, and the media, but should always be considered as additions to face-to-face presentation, rather than a replacement. The biggest challenge is keeping your audience engaged when you are not physically present.

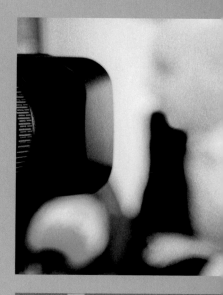

Don't over-answer questions. Attention spans in this media tend to be short.	
To retain interest, make sure you build in regular feedback breaks.	
Try to keep things simple and remind other participants to do so too.	
Use illustrations, graphs, and videos wherever possible.	
In audio formats, use repetition to drive home points.	
Acknowledge participants, and give everyone an opportunity to be heard.	

Chapter 2

Preparing and practising

Every presentation is a performance. The stage needs to be set, the props and costume put in place, lines learned, and delivery rehearsed. Practice is vital to improve confidence and fluency, and to fine-tune your material for oral delivery.

Getting word perfect

Don't try to be anyone but yourself. Identify your strengths – story-telling or humour – and put them to good use in your presentation. Practise as much as possible; your audience deserves a presenter who can make the material fresh, understandable, and relevant.

REHEARSE YOUR ATTITUDE

The energy you put into a presentation, and your enthusiasm for the subject, will drive home your message. These apparently natural characteristics need practice too.

Practising aloud

Your presentation will be delivered orally, and to reach your confident best, you should practise this way too. You need to literally deliver your presentation out loud and, if possible, to a test audience that can offer constructive feedback. Run through the presentation in the same (or similar) room or auditorium where you will deliver the real thing, rather than in the car or in your bedroom. Ideally you should run through your presentation out loud five to ten times; this sounds like a lot, but the applause you will eventually receive from your audience will make all the effort worthwhile.

Honing your delivery

Your goal is to refine your content to make it as powerful as possible and you comfortable enough with your material to set the script aside. Here are a few practice tips:

- Practise your presentation with an outline, not a full script.
- If possible, practise in front of someone who has knowledge of the material.
- After several rehearsals to help you remember the contents, practise delivering it without stopping in order to judge its flow.
- Time your presentation with each round; make sure to stay on track.

- Absorb your material well enough to give your presentation the look of spontaneity.
- After you are satisfied with the content, try recording a practice round on video. It will give you a new perspective on how you look and sound to others.

With experience, presenters naturally develop their own style of delivery. Some have a talent for keeping an audience engaged with questions or exercises; others excel at helping an audience understand issues through narrative. No single structure serves all presenters in all circumstances, so it pays to try out many different approaches.

 IN FOCUS...
THINKING LIKE A PRESENTER

Growing your presentation skills means thinking like a presenter 24/7. There are many real-life situations where you can develop your skills.

- Practise narrative techniques in casual conversations.
- Identify and follow your natural characteristics when communicating.
- In everyday conversation, watch how your listener responds to different approaches. What works to keep their attention?
- Attend presentations by others. Which styles of presenting keep your attention and which do not?
- Be a collector: gather anecdotes, stories, and quotes for later use.

- Work on building one skill at a time. Before your next presentation, select one area – narrative skills, or presenting statistics, for example. Concentrate on improving your delivery in that area.
- Get as much feedback from your peers as possible. It is very difficult to evaluate yourself objectively as a communicator.
- Get targeted feedback. Ask someone you know to listen to your presentation with a specific purpose in mind. Tell them in advance, for example, that you'd like feedback on how strong your eye contact is or how many "filler" words you use.

Pacing yourself

Effective presenters know that good timekeeping can be as important as good content. A presentation that starts and ends on time gives a strong impression of competence. Achieving this goal is the result of excellent preparation, making time for rehearsal and flexibility on the day.

RECRUIT A TIMEKEEPER

Placing a friendly "timekeeper" in the audience who can unobtrusively signal the time remaining to you is a good way of staying on track.

Preparing notes

A formal presentation or speech is the wrong place for an original thought. Effective communicators plan, prepare, and practise their material. Most presenters use notes. Even if you don't need to consult them, they can be reassuring. Treat them as prompts rather than a script. Write them in the form of bullet points or keywords, not complete sentences, and rehearse "joining up" the points. Don't worry if your words aren't the same every time.

Notes are most useful when they are accessible at any point during the presentation. Use numbered sheets or cards, ensuring that your numbers match up with handouts or slides. Your notes can also serve as a backup if you can't use your visual aids.

If you do need to refer to notes, don't try to hide it. Take a moment, review your material, and continue. Your audience will take the pause in their stride.

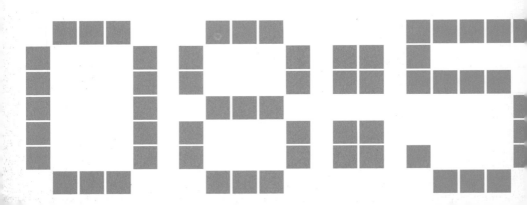

Timekeeping tips

- Never, ever go over your allotted time. Your audience will thank you.

- Watch your breathing. If you are running out of breath, slow down your delivery.

- If you tend to speak too quickly, try delivering each point to one person, maintaining eye contact with them before allowing yourself to move on.

- It takes about two minutes to deliver a page of double-spaced text.

- When rehearsing, remember that the pace of the actual presentation will probably be slower due to summarizing, natural pauses, and nerves. Compensate by erring on the side of less material, rather than more.

- Don't use automatic scrolling features for projected slides. The presenter, not the technology, should set the pace.

- Practise using a stopwatch – don't rely on guesswork or estimates.

- If a colleague is going to "drive" the slides for you, practise your timing together so you don't have to say, "next slide, please".

- Interactivity is an advanced skill, because it complicates pacing. If you use it, consider imposing a limit on the number of questions, or group them together by saying, "I see there are a lot of questions here. If you would, hold your questions and I will address them after this section."

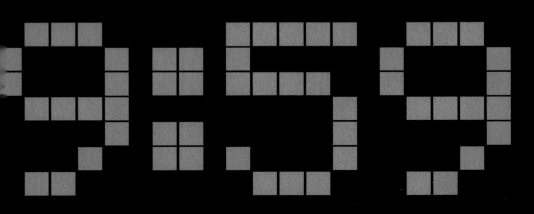

Being spontaneous

Planning for spontaneity appears, at first, to be a contradiction. But building in opportunities to digress from the main path of your presentation allows you to shine in front of your audience, making you appear the master of your material, and so helping to retain attention.

Making room for digression

Memorizing your presentation word-for-word is not a good idea. Unless you are a skilled actor, your delivery is likely to be flat and uninteresting. The same goes for reading from a script; listeners may misjudge your authorship, or question your commitment to your words. Instead, practise your material so that you know it so well you can deviate from it with confidence. By all means use short notes as prompts, but plan moments into your presentation where you can elaborate on a point of interest, or talk with great passion about an area very close to your heart. Digressions are very useful tools as they can provide "oases" – places where you can take a short respite from the focused intensity of your presentation to talk about topics you know inside-out. These moments will give you a breather and allow you to relax and regain your poise before continuing.

PRESENTING WITH HUMOUR

FAST TRACK

OFF TRACK

FAST TRACK	OFF TRACK
Rehearsing your jokes	Forcing humour if it does not come naturally to you
Turning humour on yourself and being self-deprecating	Being sarcastic or making jokes that may embarrass others
Employing humour sparingly to lighten a mood or diffuse tension	Relying on jokes so much that your message becomes diluted
Using humour that flows naturally from your own experiences	Using humour that depends on context or detailed explanation

TIP

KEEP ON TRACK

Treat any digression as a chance to connect with the audience. Move from behind the desk or lectern, and make eye contact with the audience as you speak. Your audience will perceive your delivery as a one-off – a presentation tailored to them.

Using levity

Humour can be a powerful icebreaker, and used carefully, will demonstrate that you are attending to your audience because you are sensitive to what they find amusing. If you choose to use humour, be careful how you do so. The wrong joke or story that may have seemed funny at the time can easily backfire and cause irreparable harm to how you are perceived by your audience. The benefits and drawbacks of humour are magnified tenfold when presenting to culturally different audiences: a timely joke will light up the audience and show that you have made an effort to understand their perspective; conversely, an inappropriate joke can be disastrous.

Remember that using humour is not essential, and if you don't feel comfortable being funny, don't try. Similarly, if you have any doubts about the suitability of a joke or type of humour, just leave it out rather than risking offence.

Planning the practicalities

The physical environment has a significant impact on the way you communicate and connect with your audience. The success of your presentation depends crucially on whether people can hear and see it clearly. So make sure you consider the physical space in which you will present and the equipment you will need.

CHECK LINES OF SIGHT

If you are using visual aids, consider whether everyone will have a clear view of them, bearing in mind where you will be standing as you describe them.

Assessing the location

The practical side of your presentation demands as much foresight as the content itself. Don't leave the details to others, on the assumption that everyone knows what is required to make your presentation a success. Instead, plan ahead and give yourself enough time on the day to ensure everything is well prepared and make final adjustments. If possible, view the venue and layout (*see opposite*) well in advance, and arrange a meeting with the facility's manager to request any necessary changes.

✔ CHECKLIST SCOPING OUT THE VENUE

	YES	NO
• Will everyone be able to see and hear the presentation from all vantage points in the room?	☐	☐
• Can you be heard at the back of the room? Take someone with you to help check.	☐	☐
• Can you control the lighting in the room, if necessary?	☐	☐
• Can windows be shaded to eliminate glare?	☐	☐
• Are power points conveniently located? Do you need extension leads?	☐	☐
• Is there a table for handouts, business cards, or follow-up information?	☐	☐
• Will additional seating be available if needed?	☐	☐
• Will a sound system be necessary for audience questions?	☐	☐
• Is all audio-visual equipment tested and in good working order, and are you happy that you know how to use it?	☐	☐

Layout pros and cons

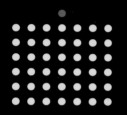

CLASSROOM
The classroom-style layout features rows of seating, perhaps with desks or tables.
Pros: Ideal for larger audiences; desks make it easy to take notes.
Cons: Less conducive to interactivity; people finding or leaving their seats can be disruptive.

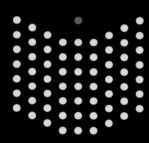

CHEVRON OR WING LAYOUT
This is similar to the classroom style, but the seating is split into blocks angled towards the presenter.
Pros: Audience is brought closer to the presenter; better potential for interactivity.
Cons: Takes more space for fewer seats compared with classroom style.

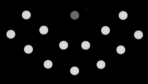

HORSESHOE
Audience members are arranged in curved rows around the presenter.
Pros: Ideal for smaller groups; good for interaction; good lines of sight; provides work space for audience.
Cons: This layout can only accommodate a limited number of seats.

BOARDROOM
Audience members are seated around a long table, with the presenter at the head.
Pros: Generates a sense of formality.
Cons: Some seats have poor lines of sight, making prolonged viewing and listening uncomfortable; showing visuals can be awkward for the same reason.

Making yourself heard

ASK FOR QUIET

Before you start, ask for all phones and electronic devices to be turned off, and make sure noise from nearby rooms or hallways is abated.

If you know you will be speaking with a microphone and public-address system, make sure you arrive early to allow time for a sound check. Your aim is to make sure you will be heard clearly around the room, over the level of normal background noise.

Practise projecting your voice to fill the room's farthest corners without shouting, and without getting too close to the microphone.

Remember, microphones only amplify your voice; they don't improve your delivery. The rhythm, pitch, and expression of your voice need to be as carefully controlled as in any other situation.

Microphone technique

- Don't tap the microphone to test it – speak into it

- Don't get so close that you "pop your P's" or amplify your breath

- Keep jewellery, hair, and buttons away from the microphone

- Don't pound or tap the lectern or rustle papers near the microphone

- Keep your voice natural and varied

- Do check with your audience, even after the initial sound check, to make sure everyone can hear

Selecting a microphone

Choose the type of microphone suited to the mode of your presentation. Hand-held models allow presenters to move while speaking, but limit gestures to your free hand. Clip mounted, or Lavaliere, microphones solve that problem: their small size allows them to be secured to a shirt or lapel, and wireless models allow for even greater freedom of movement. However, they must be placed correctly to avoid volume drop-off as you turn your head. Stationary microphones work well if you are using a podium, but limit movement. Whatever your choice, make sure you practise positioning and projection beforehand. On the day, ensure you know when your microphone is on, and how to turn it off.

Using lasers and remotes

Any tool or device that helps audience understanding is worth considering. Laser pointers and wireless remotes have become widely used, and each has their place.

TIP

CHOOSE SIDES
If you are right-handed, stand to the left of your screen or flipchart so you don't have to reach across your own body when pointing. If you are left-handed, stand to the right.

Laser pointers direct a thin beam of light at a screen or other medium. They can be useful for highlighting a particular area of a slide or other visual aid without obscuring the image with a physical pointer.

However, bear in mind that if your visual material is too busy or complicated to be understood without you using a pointer to explain it, there may be a case for simplifying it, or perhaps assigning the various points to more than one slide. If you use a laser pointer, make sure you keep it directed away from the audience to avoid a distracting light show.

Wireless remote controls allow presenters to advance to the next slide without having to stand right next to the equipment. Since this gives you the physical freedom to move around, it can help you achieve the right level of interaction and deliver a professional, free-flowing presentation.

Respecting other cultures

All cultures have their own unique customs and rules, particularly when it comes to speaking and interacting in formal and work settings. While those from outside the culture are generally given some latitude, it is wise to consider any relevant cultural issues before you present.

TIP

GET UP TO SPEED QUICKLY

If you can, get some basic cultural information from your hosts, then supplement your learning with additional resources such as guidebooks and websites.

Knowing the norms

Presenting in a foreign country can be a daunting experience. On top of all the usual issues of preparation, you must deliver your material in an unfamiliar place and setting. However, you can still build rapport with your audience by doing some prior research into basic rules of conduct, or "norms", and how they differ from those of your native culture.

For example, emphasizing points through a strong voice and definitive hand gestures is a sign of confidence in the United States. In the UK, however, this style may come across as abrasive – and in China, it could seem vulgar. Passing a microphone over someone's head or pointing to a member of the audience may be perfectly acceptable in Western cultures, but it's the height of rudeness in Thailand.

While direct eye contact is generally valued as a sign of trustworthiness in many Western societies, it is generally considered rude in India and South Asia. Western-style "casual Fridays", when dress codes are relaxed, may be regarded as unprofessional in other parts of the world. Bare legs for women may be considered normal and practical in some cultures, but unprofessional or offensive in others.

In the United States, Canada, and Australia, the use of first names in business settings is quite common. However, in Hong Kong, Portugal, and Germany, using first names without being invited to do so is considered over-familiar.

? ASK YOURSELF... AM I APPROPRIATE?

- What are the proper forms of address?
- What are the appropriate standards of dress?
- Am I aware of any idioms or slang I use? Can I avoid using them while presenting?
- Do I know which hand gestures or body language are appropriate and inappropriate to use?
- Are my visuals clear and simple enough to express my message even if my audience doesn't understand everything I say 100 per cent?
- Have I run my presentation past a person familiar with local culture before the big day?

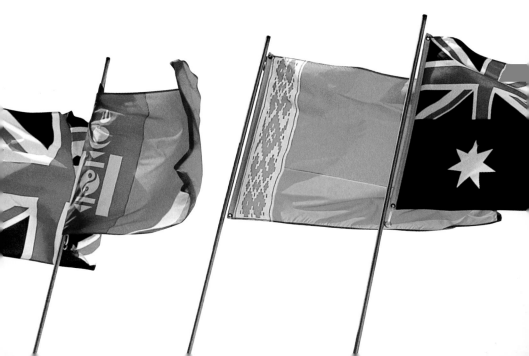

Solving problems

Planning for problems isn't negative thinking. It is simply common sense. Consider the industries that devote enormous resources to preparing for unfortunate events that they hope will never occur. From airlines to utilities, it is a wise policy to expect the unexpected and arm yourself to handle problems with ease.

REST UP

Get a good night's sleep before your presentation. This will help you project relaxed confidence.

Preparing a "Plan B"

Even the most carefully crafted presentations will come up against unexpected technical or human problems. Glitches in equipment, logistical delays, or lack of preparation on the part of others may conspire to upset your plans. It pays to plan for problems, and develop a "Plan B" for every eventuality.

When a problem occurs, you need to act fast. Don't waste time apologizing or fretting out loud about the disruption, just carry on as if nothing has happened, by putting your "Plan B" into action.

Always make sure you are one step ahead and have thought of everything. If your computer presentation fails, for example, fall back on the note cards you prepared containing your key messages. Better still, carry an extra laptop as well as a spare projector bulb.

When you rehearse your presentation, identify topics that you can leave out if you have been allocated less time than you had expected; similarly, plan an audience discussion or question and answer session that you can quickly and easily deploy if you run short. Your audience will tend to take their cues from you. If you take any mishap or change of plans in your stride, so will they. Displaying a cool head and calm disposition in front of your audience will pay dividends. If there is a mishap, show that you are fully in control and you will get right back on track through body language and your words and actions.

Handling interruption

There is usually no need to stop your presentation for latecomers – continue speaking while they take their seats. However, there are exceptions. If a key decision-maker arrives late, pause and provide a quick summary to bring that person up to speed. Make sure it is brief enough so the latecomer does not feel embarrassed. Be ready to handle interruptions of all sorts: the most common of these is the ringing mobile phone. If you notice audience members using phones or other electronic devices, others will almost certainly notice too; such distractions can quickly disrupt and undermine your presentation.

HOW TO...
STOP A PHONE PEST

Request that all phones are switched off before you start.

↓

If a phone then rings, don't try to speak over it. Pause, let the owner switch it off, and stay calm.

↓

If the owner picks up the call, pause and wait quietly until he/she has dealt with it.

↓

If it happens again, call a break and speak privately to the offender.

If you can hear chatter or side conversations, pause. This will draw attention to the culprits who will hopefully realize they are at fault and stop. If they persist, don't single out individuals, but ask firmly if there are any questions that the audience wishes to raise. Add that everyone will want to devote their full attention to the next part of the presentation because it contains some very important information.

Recovering poise

There are times when you will find yourself – briefly – lost for words. It can happen to anyone; even actors forget their lines from time to time. Don't panic – you know your material, so skip ahead or summarize what you have covered already: it will appear to the audience to be part of a well-planned delivery. There are tried and tested techniques that will buy you a few moments to get back on track. Try one of the following for a quick recovery. Stay calm, and you won't lose momentum:
• Repeat the last thing you said
• Return to a key message
• Pause and review your notes
• Ask the audience if they have any questions
• Use your visuals as a prompt
• Call for a break.

Getting ready for the off

The number one strategy for boosting presentation skill is to devote as much time as you can to preparation and practice. Don't take shortcuts. By doing the work in advance, you can make your presentation work for you and communicate successfully every time.

PRACTISE THE TRANSITIONS
If rehearsal time is short, spend it practising your transitions from one point to another, rather than delivering details. Getting these moments right will make your presentation appear much smoother.

Making final checks

Run through your presentation perhaps once or twice, either alone or with a "friendly" audience. You are looking to reaffirm your material, not pick holes in it. You may feel the temptation to rework everything from top to bottom. Resist this urge and stick with the ideas you have developed over time – there is no time to assess the implications of any big changes.

Check your visual aids one last time, making sure you are up to speed with all the practicalities of your presentation. Again, don't be tempted to make any major changes at the last minute.

Speaking at short notice

There may be times when you have to prepare or alter a presentation at very short notice. In this situation, the overriding concern is to use whatever time you do have to best effect.

Focus on your key messages rather than supporting details, and write them into a streamlined one-page outline. Prepare for likely questions, but forget about creating elaborate visuals – you will more often than not get bogged down in layout rather than content. Use existing materials, or do without. When you give the presentation, explain the situation to the audience and offer to answer their questions as best you can, and provide additional material should it be needed.

Am I ready?

Could I deliver this presentation without any materials or notes if I had to?

Am I confident that I am making my "best case"?

Do I believe everything I am saying?

Is there any part of my presentation I couldn't fully explain if I had more time?

Have I anticipated any questions I might get?

Have I vetted the information I am presenting with others?

Do I fully understand my audience's expectations?

Am I ready with follow-up or additional information?

Do I know what next steps are called for?

Am I looking forward to this presentation or dreading it?

Chapter 3

Taking centre stage

As your presentation approaches, all the preparation you have put into your material and delivery may be overshadowed by the prospect of having to perform. Don't worry. There are plenty of techniques that will give you a real advantage on the day of your presentation, boost your confidence, and help you deal with nerves or mishaps.

Creating a first impression

The first thing your audience will notice is how you look, and this first impression is hard to shift. Give plenty of thought to the message you want to send through your attire, grooming, and posture. Study yourself in a mirror, and ask colleagues for their opinion on your appearance.

LOOK SHARP

Change into a fresh, pressed outfit just before your presentation; check beforehand that changing facilities are available.

Connecting with the audience

Appearance alone won't win over your audience, but it plays an important role in setting out your intent and credibility. When choosing what to wear, consider which outfit will have the greatest influence on the people you would like to impress the most.

For example, if the audience consists mostly of your casually dressed peers, but also includes two suited directors, dress up not down. And if you are the manager of a factory addressing the shop floor, think how differently your message will be perceived if you are wearing a suit or clean corporate overalls.

KEEP IT REAL

While you shouldn't forsake style for comfort, avoid wearing clothes so formal that they make you feel self-conscious and false.

Dressing to impress

There are no fixed rules about dress and appearance, but if unsure, veer towards smart, professional, and conservative rather than trying to reassure your audience by "blending in" with their style. You are dressing to create an air of authority and confidence rather than to please yourself, so steer clear of casual clothes like jeans and trainers, leather, shiny fabrics, and anything with prominent emblems or designer labels. Avoid distracting blocks of bright colour, though colour can be used to provide an accent. Make sure your shoes are clean, polished, but comfortable – if it is painful to stand in them for the length of the presentation, change them.

Minimize jewellery – you don't want your accessories to be the most memorable part of your presentation – and always pay attention to details, even if you won't get that close to the audience. You can bet that they'll notice if your clothes are wrinkled or your cuffs are frayed. Remove bulging keys, change, and other loose items from your pockets, and check that your lapels are free from name tags.

Whatever your dress, always take the time to groom yourself – your audience will not forgive an unkempt appearance or poor personal hygiene.

? ASK YOURSELF...
AM I WELL GROOMED?

- Is my hair clean, neatly styled, and away from my face?
- Are my fingernails clean and trimmed?
- Have I trimmed my beard and moustache?
- Are any tattoos visible?
- Is my perfume/cologne overpowering? Many people find scent unappealing, so it should be avoided.
- Have I applied antiperspirant?

Looking confident

The audience is on your side – they want you to succeed; they want to learn and be inspired by you. But to win their attention and trust, and to exert your influence, you need to impose your presence and demonstrate confidence in yourself and in your presentation material.

ACCENTUATE THE POSITIVE

Avoid crossing your arms or leaning backwards, away from the audience; these actions send out very strong negative signals.

Growing self-belief

Inner confidence comes from a combination of self-belief and real enthusiasm for your message. When you are confident, you behave naturally, and in the full expectation of a positive outcome; your self-assurance is genuine and your audience buys into your message.

You can build your confidence over time through exercises in which you visualize success and, of course, through experience. Looking confident and feeling confident may seem two very different things to you, but to your audience, they are one and the same. Employing techniques that make you appear more confident will bring positive feedback from your audience, which will boost inner confidence.

Establishing your presence

USE PROPS

If nerves deter you from moving your body, hold a prop – such as a pen or wireless remote – in one hand until you find your comfort level and confidence.

You can win the attention and respect of an audience before you begin simply through your posture, and by the way you occupy the space around you. Even if you cannot rearrange the seating in the room, you should become familiar with the room, your position, and the lines of sight – "owning" the space will make you feel more comfortable and confident. Give yourself room to move, and make sure the audience can see your hands; don't trap yourself behind a desk or use the lectern as a shield – the audience may interpret your position as defensive.

Using body language

If your content is irrelevant or your delivery dull, you shouldn't be surprised if your audience switches off. But they will also disengage if the non-verbal messages that you send out are inconsistent with your words. Your stance, gestures, and eye contact must support what you say; in the event of any conflicting information, the audience will tend to believe what your body language appears to be saying.

Start your presentation with a neutral but authoritative posture. Maintain a balanced stance, with your feet slightly apart and your weight spread evenly between them. Keep upright, facing the front, with shoulders straight, not hunched, and your arms loosely and comfortably at your sides. Don't lean on a chair or perch on furniture for support. For the first 30 seconds of your presentation, try not to move your feet. This "anchoring" will help establish your authority with your audience. As you build rapport, you can relax your posture – this will help win you trust and make the audience feel much more comfortable – leaning forward sends a positive, friendly message.

ASK YOURSELF... DO I APPEAR CONFIDENT?

- Is my eye contact strong?
- Am I projecting my voice?
- Am I maintaining good posture?
- Are my hand gestures natural?
- Is my language conversational?
- Are my movements purposeful?
- Do I appear calm and in control?

**SPRING-CLEAN
YOUR BAD HABITS**
Rid your performance
of any visible signs of
discomfort you may
be feeling. Avoid
nervous mannerisms
such as putting your
hands stiffly behind
your back, looking
down at the floor,
playing with jewellery
or hair, or fiddling
with your sleeves
or buttons.

Moving for effect

Human attention is drawn to movement – it is
programmed into our genes – so one of the most
powerful ways to hold on to your audience, and to
make viewers focus on you, is to move.

Always use movement purposefully and intentionally
– merely walking back and forth will be interpreted as
nervous pacing and will distract the audience.
However, using movement in tandem with your words
will boost impact. Here are a few examples where
actions will reinforce the message:

• When you want to refer your audience to a
projected slide, take a step back towards it, and
sweep your arm to guide the viewer's eyes up
towards the slide: be careful not to turn your back
on your audience as you move.

• Move to a different spot on the stage area when
moving from point to point – this can help the
audience to separate out your key messages.

• Coordinate your movements to emphasize an
important point – for example, walk across the
room, and turn quickly to coincide with the
conclusion of a point.

Your movements need not be too theatrical – your
aim is to hold the attention of the audience rather
than to entertain them.

IN FOCUS...
THE 7-38-55 RULE

According to a study by Dr Albert Mehrabian of the
University of California, how much we like someone
when we first meet them depends only 7 per cent on
what they say. Tone of voice accounts for 38 per cent.
The remaining 55 per cent is down to body language
and facial expression. This is known as the 7-38-55 rule.

SHAKING HANDS CONFIDENTLY

ON TRACK

OFF TRACK

ON TRACK	OFF TRACK
Bending your elbow and extending your right arm	Offering just the fingers of your hand
Pumping your hand two or three times before releasing	Holding on to the other person's hand too long or too lightly
Making and keeping eye contact with the person you are greeting	Looking around the room while shaking someone's hand

Using gestures

Use gestures to reinforce points, just as you would in casual conversation; you may need to "amplify" small movements to take into account the scale of a room: for example, a hand gesture may need to become a movement of the whole forearm if it is to be seen from the back. You may need to practise to make such gestures appear "natural". Avoid at all costs any intimidating gestures, such as pointing fingers at your audience or banging your hand or fist on the table or lectern.

Many presenters deliberately avoid making eye contact with the audience. But if you can keep your nerve, engaging with the audience in this way creates trust and intimacy, and is one of the most effective means of keeping attention, especially throughout a longer presentation.

Unless you are presenting to a very large group, attempt to make eye contact with every member of the audience at least once. Maintain contact for no more than three seconds – longer contact may be seen as hostile. If you find this unnerving, start by making eye contact with someone who looks friendly and approachable before moving round the room.

Remember also to target people at the back and sides, or those who appear less enthusiastic. If you remain too nervous, look between two heads or scan the room – never avert your eyes from the audience. Not only will you lose their trust, your voice may become muffled and indistinct too.

Holding the audience

Novelty and expectation will keep your audience focused through the early parts of your presentation. But keeping their attention once they are accustomed to the sound of your voice and your presentation style can be more of a challenge. Look out for signs of disengagement, and be prepared to act quickly to bring the audience back on track.

Keeping interest

You have prepared an interesting presentation. You are delivering it with conviction using a good range of visual materials and rhetorical devices. Yet when you look out, you don't get the reassurance of attentive expressions on the faces of the audience; you may even detect signs of distraction.

Reading signs from the audience

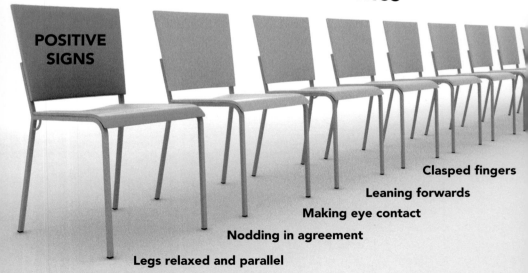

POSITIVE SIGNS

Clasped fingers

Leaning forwards

Making eye contact

Nodding in agreement

Legs relaxed and parallel

Chin resting on hand

Perhaps your audience is tired, or your presentation is the last in a gruelling day, or maybe you are delivering some difficult material. In any case, you need to take action fast:

• **Ask the audience** if they can hear and understand your words and if they are comfortable (it is hard to concentrate in a hot auditorium). Take remedial steps if necessary.

• **Consciously change** your delivery; slow your pace, or introduce pauses after key points. Change your pitch or volume.

• **Get interactive** and pose questions to the audience and invite answers. Field questions. Leave your position behind the podium and walk out into the audience, making extensive eye contact.

• **Don't get frustrated** with the audience. Compliment them so that they feel valued.

• **Tell your audience** what's coming up, and when – "we'll work through a few examples before moving. on to a question and answer session in five minutes". This will help them feel more involved in proceedings.

TIP

MONITOR THE MAJORITY

Regularly assess your audience for signs of discontent or agitation, but remember that isolated displays of body language may be misleading, and they can vary between cultures.

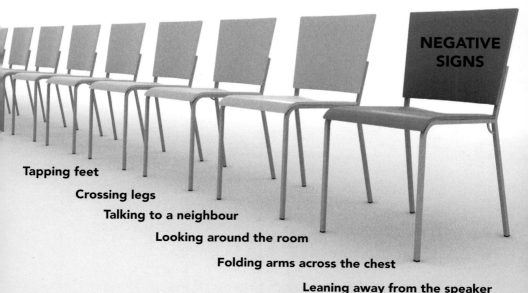

NEGATIVE SIGNS

Tapping feet

Crossing legs

Talking to a neighbour

Looking around the room

Folding arms across the chest

Leaning away from the speaker

Taming nerves

Public speaking ranks at the top of many people's list of worst fears. Be assured that this fear is understandable and normal – and even highly experienced presenters sometimes feel some anxiety. Rather than fighting your fear, try to harness it so it works for you; as ever, this requires preparation, practice, and persistence.

TIP

CONTROL THE SYMPTOMS

There are many symptoms of nerves: feeling "butterflies" in your stomach is common, as is dryness of the mouth; twitching eyes; fidgeting or playing with your hair or a pen; and rocking from side to side. Work on controlling the external signs so they are not visible to your audience.

Channelling your energy

Before your presentation, you will be brimming with nervous energy. Start by giving that energy a release: vent any concerns to a trusted colleague, then go for a walk, or do some gentle stretching and warm-up exercises. Your body's physical response to stress tends to work against your mental preparations. Take the following preventative action before you begin:

• Take several deep breaths, holding each for a count of four, then slowly release through your mouth. This will help moderate a quickening pulse and heartbeat.
• Don't take your position too early. Keep your body moving in the moments just before your presentation.
• Shrug your shoulders to help ease tension.
• Give your voice a warm-up by humming; stretch and release your facial muscles.

IN FOCUS...
RITUALS AND CONFIDENCE

Repeating the same sequence of actions and thoughts before each presentation is a helpful tool in preventing nerves. Rituals are used by people to combat much stronger fears – such as agoraphobia and fear of flying – because they set up a safe zone of familiarity. Your ritual can be anything from cleaning your spectacles to arranging your papers geometrically on the desk – just make sure that it is a sequence of simple, undemanding tasks that won't cause stress themselves.

Letting yourself shine

Once you begin the presentation, control the release of energy. Don't dissipate it too early by pacing around or rushing your delivery. Maintain eye contact with individuals in the audience; this will help your nerves because it gives you a mental focus, and you will probably get positive feedback from your audience (smiles and nodding heads) that will boost your confidence. Behavioural research has found visualizing a stressful event is enough to trigger a real physical reaction. Conversely, we can all achieve a calmer state through positive images. So before your next presentation, try visualizing your own success.

HOW TO...
VISUALIZE SUCCESS

Imagine yourself taking the stage confidently and speaking well. See yourself enjoying the moment.

↓

Remember how you feel at your most confident. Tell yourself you can and will succeed.

↓

Picture yourself as relaxed and prepared – you look more confident than you feel.

↓

Tell yourself you don't need to be perfect; the audience is on your side.

↓

Tell yourself you are well prepared. You CAN do it!

Speaking powerfully

How do you sound? In control? Authoritative? Dynamic? Voice is a powerful tool in the presentation arsenal. Don't worry – you needn't have the booming resonance of a stage actor to convince your audience that you are fully involved in what you are saying.

TIP

PROTECT YOUR VOICE

Don't drink milk or milk products before speaking – they will coat your mouth. Rest your voicebox (larynx) for at least a day before your presentation, and take regular sips of water while speaking.

Using confident vocals

As you speak, your audience "reads" your voice – its nuances of pitch, volume, pace, and so on. This process happens imperceptibly, below the radar of consciousness, yet it shapes your audience's perceptions of your message. Sound hesitant and your audience will question your content. Sound confident and your audience will side with you. Try using the various facets of your voice (see right) when you practise your presentation and use them to effect.

PACE
Vary the pace of your delivery. This helps keep your audience alert. Speak slowly when delivering key messages: new ideas need time to be processed.

Remaining calm

Slow and deep breathing enhances your performance. It boosts the supply of oxygen to your brain, making you more alert; it helps you stay calm; and it increases the flow of air over your vocal cords, enhancing the clarity of your voice. To avoid stumbling during your presentation, declutter your speech by removing unnecessary words and any trite expressions.

Finally, learn to be comfortable with silence in front of an audience: it feels odd at first, but "dramatic pauses" after key points add memorable emphasis.

Master your voice

VOLUME
Be comfortable projecting your voice so that it can be heard everywhere in the room. Vary your projection to grab and keep attention. Your aim is not only to be heard, but also to alert listeners to the importance of what you are saying.

INTONATION
Using an upward inflection (upspeak) at the end of sentences may signal you are uncertain. Using declarative sentences with the voice ending in a downbeat will give even neutral phrases an authoritative touch.

TONE
Whether presenting good or bad information, do so with a tone that matches the content of what you are saying.

DICTION
Enunciate words clearly, adjusting the pace of your delivery where needed. Be careful with acronyms or unusual words your audience might misunderstand. Repeat important numbers for emphasis and to be certain they are heard.

PITCH
Slow your delivery and breathe deeply. Only then will you be able to use the full range of highs and lows of your voice. A confident speaker varies pitch more than a rushed one whose pitch is flat and unengaging.

Succeeding with formal speeches

Formal speeches such as keynote addresses, appearances at award ceremonies, and addresses to trade conferences and plenary sessions follow structured formats and are often delivered in large group settings. Look on them less as a chance to inform – more to entertain your audience while enhancing your own reputation.

TIP

KEEP DOWN THE DETAIL

There is a limit to the level of detail people can absorb while listening as opposed to reading. Test your speech on someone who hasn't heard it and check that they understand.

Crafting your content

Delivering a formal speech at an official or ceremonial occasion requires a particular method of preparation. Formal speeches may be read verbatim from a script, delivered from detailed cards, or delivered extemporaneously based on careful preparation. However, they lack important features of other presentations: visual aids are rarely used, and the speaker is physically separated from the audience, limiting the degree of interaction.

As with other presentations, consider the audience and what they need, as well as the messages you want them to receive. Match your delivery to the nature of the occasion; evening receptions, for example, are not the time for complex content – the audience is more inclined to be entertained.

Without visual aids, handouts, or interactivity, your words must carry the full weight of your message. Keep your sentences short and confine yourself to one point or idea per sentence.

As far as possible, emulate the natural rhythms of speech in your script, keeping your sentences flowing naturally. Although the occasion may be formal, don't fall into the trap of using "sophisticated" vocabulary solely to impress your audience. Instead, use everyday language in a concise and accurate way.

Adapting your delivery style

Even though you will probably be reading your speech, look for different ways in which you can show personality and commitment to your message. Use hand gestures as you would naturally when you speak, to emphasize your points. A simple device such as this will help to keep things interesting for your audience.

Don't feel you have to read each word or phrase exactly as written. You should feel free to depart from your speech as required; this will give your delivery a much more spontaneous feel. Aim for a style of delivery that does not call attention to itself, but that conveys your ideas without distracting the audience.

• Break up your sentences more than usual so you can deliver them more easily.
• Write delivery reminders to yourself on your script – for example, highlight words you want to emphasize or write in "pause" to remind yourself of pacing.
• Err on the side of brevity.
• Practise your speech until it becomes second nature to you.
• Practise reading ahead so you can speak with your eyes on the audience for as long as possible.
• If someone else has drafted your speech, rewrite or adapt it so that it reflects your own "voice". Add a few personal references to make it seem less formal.
• Visualize yourself as a professional TV presenter – try to inhabit the role.
• Ask for and learn from feedback.

TIP

Working the room

MAKE IT READABLE

Print out your speech in a large, clear font on single-sided pages. Mark your script for points of emphasis, but make sure you can easily read any handwritten edits or notes.

Speaker podiums give the presenter a place to stand, room to place a hard copy of the speech, and, sometimes, a stationary microphone. However, podiums can also pose problems. While they do provide some comfort, they also create a physical barrier between speaker and audience that is a challenge to overcome. Even transparent podiums, designed to mitigate this problem, still force the speaker into a small, tightly constrained space, making it difficult for the audience to gauge their commitment and belief in what is being said.

USING A PODIUM

FAST TRACK

OFF TRACK

FAST TRACK	OFF TRACK
Placing papers high up on the podium to reduce "head bobbing" as you read	Maintaining a "death grip" on the sides of the podium
Sliding rather than turning pages to reduce noise and distraction	Leaning on the podium
Allowing the audience to respond; pausing to acknowledge applause or laughter if interrupted	Tapping fingers on the podium or near the microphone
Varying voice, tone, and pacing throughout the speech	Allowing your voice to trail off at the ends of sentences
Testing and adjusting podium height before beginning	Turning your head away from a stationary microphone
Standing squarely balanced on both feet at all times	Fiddling with pens, paper clips, or anything else on the podium

To counteract the constraints of a podium, exaggerate your gestures so you can be seen clearly. Use a hand-held or lapel microphone to avoid obstructing the audience's view of your face. Plan moments where you can move towards the audience, however briefly, to address a point – question and answer sessions following the speech can offer this opportunity. Freedom of movement will signal your willingness to engage with your audience.

If you are stuck behind the podium, keep in mind that you must still find ways to connect with the audience. Make eye contact at points around the entire audience, and find a natural delivery that lets people know that the words and thoughts you are speaking are indeed your own.

Using teleprompters

TIP

ACT NATURAL
To make your delivery more human and natural, imagine a member of the audience (or a friend) on the other side of the teleprompter.

Text-display devices such as hidden screens and teleprompters can avoid the need for a podium. They allow you to appear more fully engaged with your audience by looking in their general direction as you read and delivering your text more naturally.

However, it takes practice to use these devices well. You need to be sufficiently at ease with them, so they aren't a distraction, either to you or your audience.

Follow these simple steps in order to ensure a smooth performance:
• Teleprompters do vary. Rehearse with the actual device you will be using.
• As with every visual aid, make sure you are in control. Be sure to set your own pace of delivery.
• If your script is hard to read in this format, rewrite it. Adjustments now will pay off later.
• Build in and script pauses to sound natural.
• Read ahead in phrases to look more natural.
• Deliberately increase your blink rate in order to prevent "teleprompter stare".

Running the Q&A

The question and answer part of your presentation is a great opportunity to drive home your key points and cement the bonds you have established with your audience. Q&A sessions keep an audience engaged and provide you with an invaluable insight into how they have received and understood your communication.

TIP

MAINTAIN OPENNESS

Stay away from defensive language – phrases such as "You misunderstand my point" – and seek to be empathetic: "I can certainly understand your objections."

Making time for questions

Always allow time in every presentation for questions and answers or some other form of audience feedback. If your format doesn't allow for a session following your presentation, consider addressing questions as they come up.

Audiences often look forward to the question and answer session more than to the presentation itself. It is at this time that their needs move to centre stage – they can engage with you directly and test the strength with which you hold your ideas. You should welcome the Q&A because the questions will indicate if you have been effective, and if you have addressed what the audience really wants to know. Consider the Q&A as feedback – a way of strengthening your presentation content and delivery.

Staying in control

Clearly signal the start of the Q&A session not only with your words but through body language; an open posture indicates you are ready for questions. Stay in control of the session at all times by directing the format and focus of the questions. Although this part of the presentation is unscripted, there are techniques to help keep the session focused:

• Keep questioners on track: if they begin to wander off the point, you could say, for example, "We're running short of time and I want to make sure we return to the immediate issue at hand."
• Don't allow audience members to engage in their own separate debates, or to interrupt one another. Step in and direct the process with a quick assertion of control: "Susan, I'd like to hear your question, then we'll turn to the issue Brian is raising."
• Seek to find common themes, or larger points that will get the discussion back to a message: "These are good points that deal with different ways to reach the goal we've been talking about."
• Don't dismiss questions even if it is clear that someone missed a key element of your presentation. Graciously repeat a quick summary for the questioner without making them feel awkward.

TIP

USE TOUCHSTONES

Keep returning to key words and phrases – or touchstones – in your answers. This will emphasize crucial points and help audience retention.

TIP

GOOD QUESTION!

Don't overuse the response: "That's a good question!" or it will lose its meaning with your audience.

 IN FOCUS... WRAPPING UP

Signal in advance your intention to close off questions, with a statement such as, "We have time for two more questions and then I'll wrap this up." Don't just end abruptly after the last question is answered. Instead, take a moment to summarize your key points and offer your audience next steps or actions they can take. Be succinct in this final closing, and restate without repeating what has come before. Remember to leave on an upbeat and positive note, and thank people for their time and their attention.

Answering tough questions

Even the best-prepared presenter will come up against hard questions, or difficult questioners. How you deal with these challenges can win or lose you the presentation, as the audience waits to see just how confidently and competently you can defend your position. In many cases, just staying calm and remaining in control under pressure is more important than having all the answers.

TIP

REPEAT THE QUESTION

In larger rooms, when wearing a microphone, repeat or summarize each question for the benefit of others in the audience before offering an answer.

Anticipating situations

It is always easier to appear confident when you have done your homework, and it pays to be well prepared for your Q&A session. Although it is unscripted, you should – with a little knowledge of your audience – be able to anticipate those questions you are most likely to be asked, and those you hope not to be asked. Be ready with suitable answers to both types, but also prepare to be surprised by unconventional questions. No-one expects you to have all of the answers all of the time, so don't be afraid to say, "I don't know".

The key to handling difficult questions is keeping your poise. Maintain a calm demeanour, even if the questioner does not. Avoid signalling any discomfort through body language – stepping back from the audience or breaking eye contact, for example.

If you have been standing up for the duration of the presentation, remain standing for the Q&A session. Keep a level tone, even if your answer is a candid "I don't know". If caught off guard by a question, buy some time; ask for the question to be repeated, or say that you will need some time to consider and that you will return to the question later. Even if your audience perceives the question as hostile or unfair, they will still want to see how you handle the response.

Try not to take statements or questions personally, and address the answer to the entire audience while responding. Avoid being provoked and remember, you are in charge of your presentation.

RESPONDING TO QUESTIONS

PROBLEM	SOLUTION	EXAMPLE
Long-winded or unfocused questions	Pose the question differently	"So what you're saying is there's been a lack of progress – is that right?"
	Ask for clarification	"I want to be sure I understand the question. Are you asking why we haven't made progress?"
Sceptical or hostile feedback	Validate the concern	"You're right about this approach carrying some risk, but we can mitigate that risk by the way we handle this."
	Empathize with the concern	"I understand your frustration. This has indeed been a long process. We'd all like to move forward now and get on with implementation."
	Stand firm	"I hear your concern, but let me respectfully disagree with your statement. Here's why."
Questions that stump	Keep your cool	"That's a good question. I don't have the answer for it. Here's what I can tell you though…"
	Return the question	"Let me ask you how you would answer that?" or "Can you clarify why you're asking that question?"
	Delay	"We can certainly discuss it after the session."

Dealing with the media

Media attention carries more credibility with audiences than advertising because it is perceived as being less partial and not paid for. It can help your organization to advance ideas or products, and build awareness and credibility with a targeted audience. However, not understanding media priorities can have negative consequences, even for smart businesses.

Understanding your role

Dealing effectively with independent media means recognizing the nature of the relationship that you are about to enter into. When you are interviewed, your role is not just to passively answer questions, it is to shape the agenda so that you can present your key messages succinctly and effectively. While you can't control the questions asked or the context, you do have control over access and over what you say. Maintaining a balance of control in interviews is a matter of delivering your messages well, through preparation and practice.

Investing in training

Having expertise on a subject doesn't mean you are media-ready. In fact, being close to a topic often makes it difficult to speak in the broad and brief terms media interviews demand. Given that every media interview can impact on your organization's image and reputation, it is worth thinking about investing in training for all managers who are likely to come into contact with the media. Media training provides managers with the means to prepare for interviews, to shape a story through responses to the reporter's questions, and to meet the organization's needs and those of reporters at the same time.

" GROUND RULES FOR MEDIA INTERACTION "

BE CONCISE AND CONSISTENT
Understand your own message, and its context. Be firm when communicating it to the reporter.

EVERYTHING IS ON THE RECORD
Reporters will assume that you know this. Anything you say can and will be quoted or broadcast.

AN INTERVIEW IS A BUSINESS TRANSACTION
Set yourself a goal for each interview, then accomplish it as briefly and as memorably as you possibly can. Know when to stop talking.

AN INTERVIEW IS NOT A CHAT WITH A FRIEND
Reporters are focused on getting a story. They do not work for you and will report a story whether it serves your interests or not.

Talking to reporters

Anyone in business is a potential interview subject for a reporter searching for an expert opinion. Whether it is TV, radio, or print media, that opportunity, provided you get it right, can win you a wider platform to gain attention for a product or service, or to raise your own profile.

MAKE INDEPENDENT STATEMENTS

Make sure everything you say to a reporter can "stand alone"; that is, make sure your statements are not dependent on a specific context to be understood correctly.

Preparing for the interview

Reporters are always under pressure to produce their stories. You will need to respect their deadlines while allowing yourself time to prepare thoroughly for an interview. Before the interview takes place, ask the reporter for the following information:

• What was it that captured their interest?
• What do they think that you can add to the story?
• What approach is being used – do they want a personal story, or a balancing opinion?
• What other sources will they be using – what can you uniquely add?
• Who is their primary audience?

Speaking to reporters under such circumstances – especially about controversial or news-based subjects – makes many people worry that they will be taken out of context. You can reduce the likelihood of this happening by planning ahead:

• Work your messages into a short, memorable form – sound bites for broadcast and quotes for print media. These are what you want the reporter to take away with them.
• Formulate "bridges" – ways of moving between an answer to an anticipated question and a sound bite that you have prepared.
• Seize the initiative by telling the reporter what you have to say about the subject, even before the questions begin. This is your opportunity to influence the direction of the interview.

Getting your message across

FORM CONNECTIONS

Let the reporter know if there are others you are aware of who can provide information or points of view that can aid in understanding. Help the reporter get in touch with those resources.

A standard line of questioning for reporters concerns the "worst case scenario". Reporters who are seeking interesting comments are prone to press subjects to speculate on what might happen in a given case that the public might need to know. However, speculation – no matter how carefully phrased – is likely to create problems if you are quoted out of context. Replace speculation with an interesting comment about what you do know. You will be in a good position to do that if you understand what the reporter wants and develop your own well-crafted messages to provide it.

BEING INTERVIEWED

FAST TRACK	OFF TRACK
Setting a clear goal for every interview	Assuming the reporter will explain your points for you
Taking the initiative in getting your points across	Hoping the reporter asks the right questions
Keeping answers short and memorable	Giving detailed responses and letting the reporter select the relevant parts
Staying focused on your messages and speaking about what you know	Guessing at a correct response or the views of others
Keeping your voice natural and lively	Speaking in a monotone
Anticipating the obvious questions as well as the toughest	Winging your way through and hoping for an easy ride
Correcting any inaccurate assumptions posed within questions	Letting inaccuracies stand

NEGOTIATING

Contents

Introduction

Negotiation is challenging, complex, and exciting, and requires a mixture of knowledge, skills, experience, and intuition. Each negotiation is unique and there is no single technique for improving your success. Thus, to be a successful negotiator, you should use a mixture of moves and countermoves, driven by the nature of the specific negotiating situation. This book describes various practices and techniques that can help to make you a more successful negotiator in every situation you face.

Negotiating distills negotiation theory and practice to give you practical advice on how to become a successful negotiator. It addresses questions such as: "Should I make the first offer?", "How should I present and respond to offers?", "How can I obtain concessions from my counterpart?", and "How can I make concessions effectively?" It helps you understand and put into practice ways to analyze your and your counterpart's power, and to increase your negotiating power by building winning coalitions.

However, negotiating successfully goes beyond mastering tactics and strategies. It is also about having the right attitude and mindset, such as being diligent in your preparation and planning; being resilient in the face of multiple challenges; being creative by inventing mutually beneficial options; and being ready to walk away from poor deals. By mastering these negotiating tactics and strategies, and by developing the right attitude and mindset, you will achieve superior results.

Chapter 1

Preparing to negotiate

Negotiation is a skill that you can learn and develop through practice and experience. By framing the process correctly and by searching in advance for creative options, you will be able to find solutions that satisfy the interests of all parties.

Becoming a negotiator

Many people shy away from negotiation because they think it implies conflict. In fact, negotiation is what you make it. When undertaken with confidence and understanding, negotiation is a creative interpersonal process in which two parties collaborate to achieve superior results.

Seeing the benefits

When you become skilled in negotiation, you can create real value for your organization. Negotiation allows you, for example, to secure cost-effective and reliable flows of supplies, enhance the financial value of mergers and acquisitions, settle potentially damaging disputes with union leaders or government officials, or resolve internal conflict constructively. Negotiation is increasingly recognized as a core competency. Many companies develop their own methodologies and offer training and mentoring programmes for negotiators.

Understanding the basics

Good negotiators are made rather than born. Although some may be naturally gifted and intuitive (possessing, for example, the ability to empathize with others), most have developed their principles and tactics over time and recognize that negotiating is a largely rational process.

To be a successful negotiator, you have to feel psychologically comfortable in the negotiation situation. This means being able to tolerate uncertainty, deal with unexpected behaviour, take measured risks, and make decisions based on incomplete information. You need to think about solving problems and creating opportunities rather than winning or losing: if you are confrontational, you are likely to have a fight on your hands. And if you "win" there will necessarily be a loser, with whom you may have to work in the months to come.

TIP

LEARN YOUR ART
Developing the skills needed to be a successful negotiator can take time, so be patient. Try to learn from every negotiation you undertake, both for your organization, and in your life outside work.

BUILDING A FOUNDATION

FAST TRACK

OFF TRACK

FAST TRACK	OFF TRACK
Keeping an open mind to learning new techniques	Believing that negotiating is an innate ability
Treating negotiation skills as a mixture of rationality and intuition	Negotiating from a fixed viewpoint
Developing trust slowly	Appearing too eager
Expressing empathy while negotiating assertively	Behaving assertively without expressing empathy
Having a strategy and sticking to it	Chasing haphazard opportunities

Understanding negotiation dilemmas

The negotiating task is very complex because it embodies a number of fundamental dilemmas. To be successful in your negotiations, you need to understand the difference between the true dilemmas that you need to address, and the many myths that surround negotiating.

Identifying true dilemmas

Over time, a number of myths have evolved about the nature of negotiations. Many negotiators continue to hold to them, failing to recognize the difference between these myths and the real dilemmas they face. For example, it is a popular misconception that a negotiator must either be consistently "tough" or consistently "soft" if they are to be successful. In reality, effective negotiators do not need to choose between these approaches, but are flexible and use a repertoire of styles.

THE STRATEGY OR OPPORTUNITY DILEMMA
Unexpected opportunities sometimes arise in negotiation. It can be tempting to divert from your well-planned strategy, but be aware that this may distract you from achieving your objectives.

Many also believe that negotiation is largely an intuitive act, rather than a rational process. It is true that an effective negotiator will use their intuition to a certain extent (to know the right moment to make a concession or present an offer, for example). However, most of the negotiating task requires systematic processes such as masterful due diligence, identifying interests, and setting clear objectives.

Skilled negotiators are able to recognize the myths and focus their energy on the true negotiation dilemmas, balancing their approach and making the difficult decisions needed to achieve the most successful outcomes in their negotiations.

The five negotiation dilemmas

THE HONESTY DILEMMA
How much should you tell the other party? If you tell them everything, they may exploit the information and take advantage of you, so you need to strike a balance between honesty and transparency.

THE TRUST DILEMMA
Trust is needed for a negotiation to move forwards, but if you trust the other party completely, you put yourself at risk of being taken advantage of. Invest in building trust, albeit with measured caution.

THE EMPATHY DILEMMA
If you develop empathy with the other party, it may stop you from acting assertively and negotiating for your interests. Try to do both well – maintain good relationships, but protect your interests too.

THE COMPETE OR COOPERATE DILEMMA
You must compete for the benefits on the table, but also cooperate to create them with the other party. You therefore need to be skilled at both, to be able to create and then claim value.

Understanding your counterpart

It is important to understand the issues and interests of the other party before you start the negotiations. Negotiators come to the table because they each need something from one another, so you must identify your counterpart's key issues and interests. How important is each one? Which are the deal breakers and which may they be willing to concede?

Try to assess whether it is you or your counterpart who holds the power. What are your counterpart's strengths and weaknesses? What is their level of information and expertise? How badly do they want to make a deal with you? Do they have other attractive options? Can they walk away from the table and exercise a BATNA*? Are they pressed for time? If you know that the other side has a tight deadline that you are able to meet, you may be able to negotiate a better price. Similarly, if you know that your counterpart has recently expanded production capacity, you may be able to gain better terms for larger volumes of orders.

*BATNA — acronym of Best Alternative To a Negotiated Agreement. This term is used by negotiators to describe the course of action that you (or your counterpart) will take if negotiations break down.

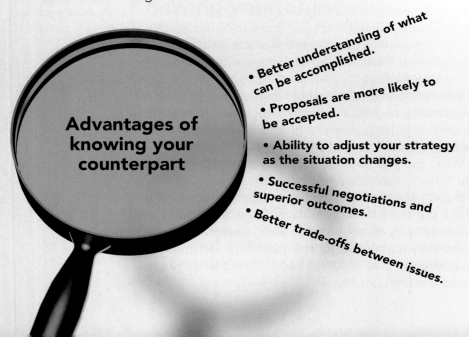

Advantages of knowing your counterpart

- Better understanding of what can be accomplished.
- Proposals are more likely to be accepted.
- Ability to adjust your strategy as the situation changes.
- Successful negotiations and superior outcomes.
- Better trade-offs between issues.

Thinking strategically

Much of what occurs in the negotiating room is, in fact, determined by what happens outside the negotiating room. This requires you to think strategically about your situation in relation to the situation of your negotiating counterpart. For example, in some negotiations, you and the other party may be representing others. Make sure you are very clear about the identity of your constituency, and that of your counterpart. What are their expectations and can you influence them?

If there are several negotiating parties, analyze all of them and begin to think in terms of coalitions. With whom and how can you build a winning coalition and how can you block a threatening coalition?

CONSIDER THE TIMESCALE
Shape your negotiating strategy with respect to the timescale. You can be more blunt in a short, one-off negotiation than in a long negotiation that is part of an ongoing relationship.

Tailoring your strategy

Make sure that your negotiating strategy and behaviour reflects the other party's situation and approach. For example, in many negotiations, the other party is free to leave or join the negotiating table as they wish. In some cases, however, the parties are bonded together over the long term and cannot simply walk away, and your strategy should reflect this.

Some negotiators prefer to negotiate away from the public eye, while others insist on keeping all stakeholders and the public informed. Consider which mode is more advantageous to you, taking into account the sensitivity of the issues, the history between the parties, and the legal and governance systems of each party.

Some negotiation counterparts observe formal protocols in negotiations, while others are freer in what can and cannot be said. Take particular care to do your research when negotiating internationally to learn the formalities expected of you.

Designing the structure

Before producing a blueprint for a building, an architect first studies the functionality of the structure – the purpose it will serve. When you are planning a negotiation, you need to think like an architect and devise a structure and a process that will best fit the purpose of the negotiation.

TIP

CREATING THE RIGHT TEAM

In team negotiations, carefully consider the size and composition of your team so that you include all necessary skills and represent all key constituents.

Structuring your approach

Every successful negotiation starts with a clear structure: defined roles, agreed rules, a set agenda, and a schedule for action. A framework for the negotiation will most likely be suggested by each of the participants. It is then subject to negotiation and joint re-creation so that all parties are satisfied that it reflects their concerns. Consult with your opposite number before you negotiate to agree all procedures that you will use. If you cannot agree on the procedures, it may be better to postpone or abandon the negotiations altogether.

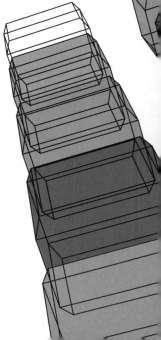

Making a framework

Your agreed framework needs to be sufficiently flexible to accommodate changes in circumstance, but should at very least cover the following:

• **Basic ground rules** These need to be agreed with your counterpart. For example, is it acceptable to change negotiators mid-stream? Are observers allowed? Is the meeting open or closed? How should people be addressed and how should priority of speech be given? What will be the course of action if you cannot reach agreement? All parties should agree to listen respectfully to one another, attempt to understand the positions of others, and refrain from legal proceedings for the duration of the negotiation.

• **A clear agenda** This should include all the substantive issues and interests that you and your opposite number wish to negotiate. Clarify the level of importance of each issue and decide the order in which issues should be discussed. Some negotiators prefer to start with easy issues, others tackle everything together.

• **An agreed venue** Chinese philosopher Sun Tzu's *Art of War* states that one should "lure the tiger from the mountain" – that is make your counterpart leave their comfortable environment. Ask yourself how the choice of venue will affect you and your team. At the very least, ensure that you will have access to the necessary support (computers, secure phone lines, and advisors).

Managing processes

Once you have an agreed framework in place, you also need to structure the processes that will steer the negotiation through its various phases. There are three distinct processes – the negotiation process, the temporal process, and the psychosocial process – that come together in any negotiation. Each requires a different set of skills.

The negotiation process involves managing information and communications during the discussions, planning and re-planning, coordinating efforts between negotiators, making moves and countermoves (all in real time), and making important decisions under conditions of uncertainty and time pressure.

Keeping time

The temporal process involves managing time and the way in which the negotiation moves from one stage to the next by appropriately pacing the speed of each stage and synchronizing the actions of the negotiators. Many negotiations (and sales presentations) stall because the negotiators labour points for too long and are unable or unwilling to move the process towards its closure phase.

Thinking straight

The psychosocial process requires a sound knowledge of human behaviour and an understanding that people will take on "roles" during negotiations. You need to be able to overcome barriers to rational negotiation and avoid psychological traps, such as the illusion of optimism, a sense of superiority, and overconfidence. Other hazards include a reluctance to reverse a decision that produces poor results or intense conflict, and competition between negotiators in the same team.

Playing by the rules

The purpose of processes and structures is not to constrain the progress of the negotiation, but to give you tools to resolve challenges or impasses. Having clear rules will allow you to:
• Move from multiparty negotiations to one-on-one negotiations.
• Change the level of negotiation, upwards or downwards.
• Replace negotiators who are self-serving or too rigid.
• Expedite the process by issuing a deadline.
• Change the venue or schedule.
• Conduct some of the negotiations behind the scenes by introducing a back channel.

Avoiding common mistakes

Never underestimate the risks associated with poor preparation: when you fail to plan, you plan to fail. The most common errors in forward planning include:

RELYING ON SECONDARY INFORMATION
Always seek out reliable sources of primary information. By all means read industry report analyses, reports of management projections, and corporate annual reports, but consider that these reports may sometimes be inaccurate or biased.

AVAILABILITY BIAS
It is easy to find information that is widely available. Make an effort to uncover information that is not so easy to obtain.

CONFIRMATORY BIAS
Do not filter out important information because it does not fit with your existing points of view and beliefs.

INFORMATION ASYMMETRY
Do you really know as much as you think? To be safe, you should assume by default that you know less than the other party.

OVERCONFIDENCE
If you underestimate your counterpart you will neglect to plan well. If you already think you know how a negotiation will end, you may exclude new sources of information and creative solutions.

UNDERESTIMATING RESOURCES
In any negotiation you must be able to present supporting facts, anticipate how the other side will respond to your arguments, and prepare counterarguments. Do not underestimate how long it can take to assemble such information, especially if you require input from experts and colleagues.

Chapter 2

Setting your style

There are many approaches to negotiation. Some negotiators advocate a hard-line, uncompromising style. Skilled negotiators know that you are more likely to achieve a satisfactory outcome by taking the interests of the other party into account and trying to create win–win deals, develop mutual trust, and build relationships for the future.

Defining negotiation styles

Negotiators come to the negotiation table because they have needs that they believe may be fulfilled through negotiations. In order to fulfil these needs, negotiators use different styles and engage in a variety of behaviours that they trust will help them get what they want.

*Value-claiming behaviour
— *competitive actions undertaken by a negotiator in an attempt to ensure a win–lose outcome in their favour. Such actions include making excessive demands or threats, concealing interests, and withholding information.*

Spotting different approaches

There are three styles of negotiation: distributive, integrative, and mixed motive. Negotiators that use the distributive style view negotiations as a competitive sport, a zero-sum game with a winner and a loser. Such negotiators compete fiercely for the distribution of the outcomes (the size of the pie) and engage in value-claiming behaviour*. They dismiss the value of building relationships and trust as naive, tend to use threats to obtain concessions, and exaggerate the value of the small concessions that they make. They also conceal their needs, do not share information, do not look for possible creative ideas, and even use deceptive tactics. In contrast to value-claiming negotiators, integrative negotiators believe that the size of the pie is not fixed and can be expanded, and that the negotiation process is able to produce a win–win solution. The integrative style of negotiation is designed to integrate the needs of all the negotiators. Negotiators engage in value creation behaviours. They invest in building relationships and nurturing trust, share information openly, and are cooperative, flexible, and creative.

TIP

TAILOR YOUR APPROACH

Utilize all of the negotiation styles – distributive, integrative, and mixed – where appropriate, depending on with whom you are negotiating and what their negotiating style is.

Using mixed-motive tactics

The true nature of effective negotiations is often mixed, requiring both cooperative and competitive tactics. The rationale for this is that, through cooperation, negotiators create value; they put money on the table. Following this, once value has been created and the money is on the table, the parties have to split it amongst themselves. In order to secure the most profitable split, a negotiator has to switch from the cooperative mode to the competitive mode.

 IN FOCUS... RESPONSES TO DISTRIBUTIVE TACTICS

If the other party is using a distributive win–lose approach, a negotiator who favours the win–win style must protect their own interests. Some respond with the same hard tactics, meeting toughness with toughness. However, since the win–lose negotiation style is most likely to produce sub-optimal outcomes, it is advisable to first try to influence the other party to move towards a more integrative style.

Value claimants often think the other party is oblivious to their tactics, and so some negotiators inform the other party tactfully but firmly that they know what they are doing and that it doesn't contribute to productive negotiations. If all approaches to dealing with value-claiming tactics fail, however, and if they do not require the deal, many negotiators will simply leave the table.

Defining interest-based negotiation

Negotiators often make the mistake of turning the negotiation process into a contest of positions. Some are hard bargainers, thinking of the other party as an adversary; others take a soft approach, considering the other person to be a friend and making concessions easily. Instead of utilizing hard or soft bargaining tools, effective negotiators tend to focus on the interests of both parties.

Focusing on interests

In interest-based negotiation, the negotiators come to the table with a clear understanding of what they want and why they want it, but also with an understanding that the other party has its own set of needs to fulfil. Knowing that both parties' needs can be satisfied in multiple ways allows for the negotiation process to be more about constructive problem solving – that is, collaborating to find out what they can do together in order to achieve their respective interests.

Focusing on interests involves concentrating on the "why" instead of the "what". People always have a reason for wanting something. For example, imagine that you and your friend are arguing over who should have the last orange in the fruit bowl. Your friend may want the orange because she wants to make juice, while you may want it because you need the peel to make cake. If, rather than arguing, you talk about why you need the orange and uncover the underlying interests behind your respective positions, you will discover that one orange can satisfy both of you.

AIM FOR JOINT GAINS
Instead of limiting the thinking to only one or two options, work jointly with the other party to creatively explore many potential solutions.

SEE BOTH SIDES
Assess the situation from the other party's perspective. This improves communication and helps the other party understand how they stand to benefit from the deal.

SEPARATE THE ISSUES
Keep people issues, such as emotions, separate from substantive issues (such as price or delivery dates).

FOCUS ON INTERESTS
Make sure that you have a clear understanding both of your own interests and those of the other party.

EXCHANGE INFORMATION
Before making any decisions, exchange information with the other party in order to jointly explore possible solutions.

Conducting interest-based negotiations

KNOW YOUR BATNA
Make sure that you have a clear understanding of your BATNA (Best Alternative To a Negotiated Agreement) – the best option available to you if the negotiation process falls apart.

USE STANDARDS
Base your negotiation on precedents, laws, and principles, rather than arbitrary judgements. This makes the agreement fair and makes it easier to explain the rationale to others.

Negotiating from the whole brain

We all think differently, and naturally bring our own "style" to the negotiating table. Understanding the strengths and weaknesses of your thinking style, and tailoring your approach to take into account the style of your counterpart, can greatly improve your success in negotiation.

Understanding your own style

Ned Herrmann, author of *The Creative Brain*, proposed that there are four thinking styles: the rational self, the safekeeping self, the feeling self, and the experimental self, which relate to dominance in different quadrants of the brain. Negotiating is a whole-brain task, requiring the ability to be diligent and rational (quadrant A activities), to plan and organize well (quadrant B activities), to interact well with others (a quadrant C trait), and to be bold and take risks (a quadrant D characteristic). However, only four per cent of the population is dominant in all four quadrants. Most negotiators, therefore, have strengths and

✔ CHECKLIST UTILIZING THINKING STYLE DIFFERENCES IN NEGOTIATION

	YES	NO
• Have you determined what your own thinking style is?	☐	☐
• Have you identified your weaknesses in negotiation and are you working to improve in those areas?	☐	☐
• If putting together a team of negotiators, have you taken each person's thinking style into account? Do they complement one another?	☐	☐
• Are you able to quickly assess the thinking style of others?	☐	☐
• Do you take your counterpart's thinking style into account when negotiating with them?	☐	☐

weaknesses in performing the negotiating task, and should work to improve in their weakest areas. A negotiator who has limited abilities in the feeling self (quadrant C), for example, can improve by developing his or her emotional intelligence. A negotiator who has limited abilities in the experimental self (quadrant D) can improve by developing his or her creative abilities by taking creativity workshops.

Influencing others

The whole brain model can sometimes help you to influence your counterpart negotiators. For example, if you believe that your counterpart's strength is in the feeling self (quadrant C) and their weakness is in the rational self (quadrant A), you will be more successful if you connect to him or her emotionally by building the relationship, and not by trying to connect cognitively through long speeches or rational arguments.

The four types of thinking styles

A
THE RATIONAL SELF
Individuals with brain dominance in quadrant A tend to be logical, analytical, fact-oriented, and good with numbers.

B
THE SAFEKEEPING SELF
Individuals with brain dominance in quadrant B tend to be cautious, organized, systematic, neat, timely, well-planned, obedient, and risk-averse.

C
THE FEELING SELF
Individuals with brain dominance in quadrant C tend to be friendly, enjoy human interactions, engage in open communication, express their emotions, enjoy teaching, and be supportive of others.

D
THE EXPERIMENTAL SELF
Individuals with brain dominance in quadrant D tend to think holistically and see the big picture. They are also often creative, comfortable with uncertainty, future-oriented, and willing to take risks.

Creating win–win deals

Some negotiators talk about wanting to create win–win deals, but when they hit major roadblocks leave the negotiating table prematurely, thus missing out on an opportunity to make a good deal. Effective negotiators utilize techniques to ensure they can create win–win deals.

SHOW THE WAY

If you are dealing with a win–lose negotiator who thinks that the idea of win–win deals is naive and unrealistic, show them how to create value and reach superior agreements by focusing on interests and bundling issues together.

Getting the conditions right

Effective negotiations, unlike competitive sports, can produce more than one winner. However, it takes motivation by both parties to find creative alternatives that fulfil their interests to create a win–win outcome. To promote win–win deals, effective negotiators focus on both the substantive issues of the deal (price, terms of payment, quality, and delivery schedule) and on formulating a social contract between the negotiators – the spirit of the deal. This involves setting appropriate expectations of how the deal will be negotiated, implemented, and re-visited, in case future disputes arise. If, by contrast, negotiators believe that negotiations are a zero-sum game that must inevitably be won at the expense of the other party, a win–win deal is not possible.

Bundling the issues

Effective negotiators do not negotiate a single issue at a time because this implies that there is a fixed pie and only leads to a win–lose scenario. Instead, they bundle several issues together. Trade-offs can then be made between negotiators because negotiators do not place equal importance on every issue. The principle of bundling issues involves placing an issue that is of high value to you (for example, price) with another that you consider to be of low value (for example, warranty). When you trade-off on issues, you can then keep your high-value issue (price) and give your low-value issue (warranty) away to the other party. The other party, in return, will allow you to have your high-value issue, because your low-value issue is, in fact, of a high value to them. If your low-value issue is also considered to be a low-value issue by the other party, then they will reject the trade-off. Therefore, it is important for you to know what the other party considers to be their high-value issues.

Capitalizing on risk

You can also capitalize on differences in risk tolerance. Some negotiators are more comfortable with high-risk situations than others. As a win–win and risk-taking negotiator, it is possible for you to design a deal where you assume more risk and receive more benefits while your counterpart, who is also a win–win negotiator but risk-averse (avoider), assumes a lower level of risk but receives fewer benefits from the deal.

WIN–WIN NEGOTIATING

FAST TRACK	OFF TRACK
Negotiating on multiple issues simultaneously	Negotiating on only one issue at a time
Understanding what is important to the other party	Focusing exclusively on your own interests
Identifying and leveraging differences in the interests of and the risks to the other party	Ignoring differences in your counterpart's interests and risks

Building relationships

Contract negotiators are typically task-oriented and pragmatic, tend to focus on negotiating specific issues, and do not invest in building relationships. Relationship negotiators, in contrast, invest first in building good relationships before negotiating on specific issues. Effective negotiators need to be skilled at both approaches.

Making a personal connection

Today, more and more Western negotiators value what the Asian, Arabian, and Latin societies recognized thousands of years ago – the value of good relationships. Experienced negotiators invest in building relationships because good relationships "oil" the negotiation process and make it more efficient. For example, Former US Secretary of State James Baker has stated that he has seen this occur time and again – that once negotiators have a good relationship, even the most difficult and conflict-inducing issues have been resolved, simply because the negotiators were more transparent and flexible with each other.

Making contact

Effective negotiators know that, in the long run, good relationships are best built through face-to-face interaction rather than by talking on the telephone or corresponding via email. Where possible, try to create opportunities to socialize with the other party before the negotiations begin. This is not to talk about the negotiations and "discover secrets", but rather to get to know the other person better and connect with them on a human level. The atmosphere of the negotiation process may be very different if you are not meeting your counterpart for the first time at the negotiation table.

CASE STUDY

Being prepared
When US businessman Robert Johnson was looking for investment to enable him to create a new cable channel, Black Entertainment Television, he did his homework. Before pitching the idea to John C. Malone – one of the industry's biggest players – he learned about Malone's business philosophy of believing in the entrepreneurial spirit and of individuals helping themselves rather than relying on others. When they met, Johnson was able to connect with Malone by highlighting their shared business values. This similarity provided a positive start for their successful business negotiations.

Interacting informally

In your interactions with the other party, take advantage of any opportunities to genuinely express your appreciation and congratulate them for their achievements. Use small talk and humour where appropriate – taking opportunities to interact informally will help you build a relationship. Be cautious, however, and use "safe humour" in order not to risk offending the other party. Where possible, focus on the common ground between you. You may find that similarities are personal (the same hobby, for example) or ideological, such as a similar business philosophy. Such findings offer a solid start for building a long-lasting, friendly, and constructive relationship.

Thinking long-term

You should also protect the "face", or dignity, of others and treat them with respect when you are taking more from a deal than they are. This is especially helpful when you are trying to build long-term relationships. In team negotiations, it can work well to include socially skilled negotiators in your team who can take greater responsibility for building lasting relationships, while others (contract negotiators) focus more on the specific issues.

Developing mutual trust

Trust is an essential component of success in all types of negotiation, whether business, diplomatic, or legal. Ambassador Dennis Ross, former US Coordinator of the Middle East, has stated that the ability of negotiators to develop mutual trust is the most important ingredient of successful negotiation, and that without it, negotiations fail.

TREAD CAREFULLY
Although there are many benefits to a trusting relationship, it is not always possible to build trust. Some individuals and groups are simply untrustworthy, so be cautious in your efforts to develop trust.

Understanding the benefits

Trust involves a willingness to take risks. It has to do with how vulnerable one is willing to make oneself to a counterpart. There are many benefits to having trust between negotiators: it promotes openness and transparency, and makes the negotiators more flexible. Negotiators who trust each other take each other's words at face value and do not have to verify their statements. This reduces emotional stress and other transaction costs, and makes the negotiation process more efficient. The likelihood of achieving good and lasting agreements is also higher.

Keeping your commitments

Building trust is difficult but losing it is easy, especially if you break your commitments. The French diplomat Francois de Callier, who wrote the first negotiation book in 1716, stated that a relationship that begins with commitments that cannot be maintained is doomed. Shimon Peres, the President of Israel, has said that promises have to be delivered, otherwise one's reputation is at stake. Although people do sometimes make genuine mistakes and promises in good faith that they ultimately cannot keep, if you want to build trust, you need to make every effort to keep your commitments.

Building your reputation

One of the most important currencies negotiators have is their reputation. It may sometimes be tempting to maximize short-term gains by overlooking the long-term consequences, but experienced negotiators know that people prefer to do business with those that they trust, and guard their reputation fiercely.

Developing trust

Reciprocation is important for building trust. When negotiators offer information or concessions, they expect the other party to reciprocate. Without reciprocation, no further gestures of goodwill will be offered. With reciprocation, the negotiating parties will be able to find ways to collaborate and create value for both.

It is also important to be seen to be fair. As fairness is a subjective matter, however, make sure that you understand the standard of fairness that your counterpart adheres to. Past behaviour is often used as a predictor for future behaviour, so try to behave consistently.

Examples of actions used by negotiators to build trust

When Henry Hollis sold the Palmer House in Chicago to Conrad Hilton, he shook hands on Hilton's first offer of $19,385,000. Within a week Hollis received several offers more than a million dollars higher. However, he never wavered on his first commitment.

In 1873, US financial markets were in poor shape and "king of steel" Andrew Carnegie needed to cash in a $50,000 investment with J.P. Morgan. Expecting a $10,000 profit, he asked Morgan to send him $60,000. Morgan sent $70,000 – the investment had made $20,000 profit.

Negotiating fairly

Fairness is an important characteristic in negotiations. Negotiators need to believe that the negotiation process and its outcomes are fair, otherwise they may choose to end the negotiations without coming to an agreement, or fail to put the agreement into action.

Ensuring fairness

There are several categories of fairness that contribute to successful negotiations. Distributive fairness relates to the distribution of outcomes (the splitting of the pie). Negotiators use three different principles of distributive fairness:
• Equality: this states that fairness is achieved by splitting the pie equally.
• Equity: this states that the outcome should relate to the contribution made by each party.
• Needs: this states that, regardless of their contribution, each party should get what they need.

In addition, a negotiator's level of satisfaction and willingness to follow through with an agreement are determined by their perception of the fairness of the procedure (procedural fairness), and also the way they feel they have been treated by the other party (interactional fairness).

Fairness is a subjective issue. When negotiating, if you first define what you consider to be fair, you can then use this "fairness frame" as a bargaining strategy in your discussions with the other party. Alternatively, if you state the importance of fairness at the beginning of the negotiation process, it may encourage the other party to be fair.

CLARITY
Be certain that the final decision is clear, without any potential misinterpretations.

JUSTIFIABILITY
Make sure that all parties are able to explain why you are slicing the pie this way to somebody else.

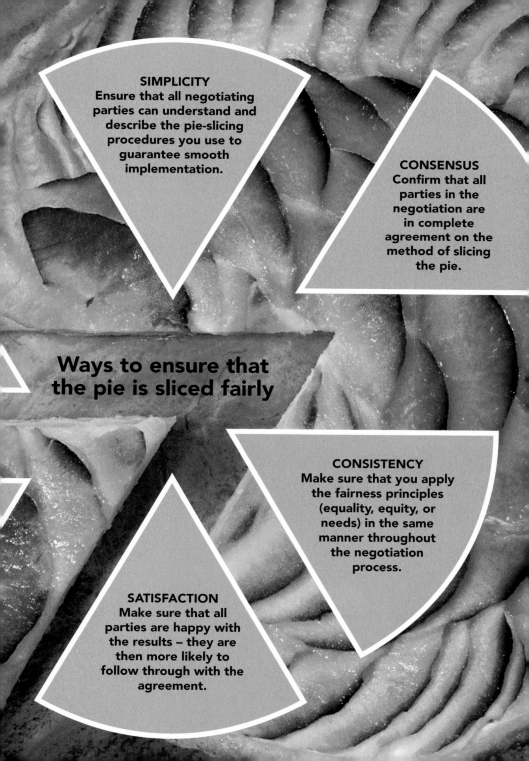

SIMPLICITY
Ensure that all negotiating parties can understand and describe the pie-slicing procedures you use to guarantee smooth implementation.

CONSENSUS
Confirm that all parties in the negotiation are in complete agreement on the method of slicing the pie.

Ways to ensure that the pie is sliced fairly

CONSISTENCY
Make sure that you apply the fairness principles (equality, equity, or needs) in the same manner throughout the negotiation process.

SATISFACTION
Make sure that all parties are happy with the results – they are then more likely to follow through with the agreement.

Chapter 3

Conducting negotiations

The negotiation process is a strategic interplay between the parties on either side of the table. To be successful, you need to know how to build a strong position, influence your counterpart, deal with difficult situations, and close your deals.

Negotiating with power

Power is a central factor in determining the outcomes of the negotiation process. Effective negotiators understand that power is not static and thus engage in continuously assessing and enhancing it. However, it is equally vital to know how to negotiate when you do not have power.

Understanding power sources

Power can come from a number of different sources:
- **Information** Being well informed enables you to support your arguments and challenge the other party's arguments.
- **BATNA** Having an attractive alternative to a negotiated agreement gives you the power to say "no" to a bad deal and walk away from it.
- **Resources** The party that has more resources – financial, technological, or human – has more power.
- **Needing the deal** The less badly you need the deal, the more power you have not to settle for it.

• **Time** The fewer deadlines you are pressed with, the more power you have to wait and explore opportunities for better deals.

• **Sunk costs** The more willing you are to let go of your sunk costs (such as financial and emotional expenses), the more power you have.

• **Skills** The more skilled you are in the art of negotiation, the more power you have to produce better joint outcomes.

Negotiating from a weak position

If your position is weak, never share this information with the other party. New information or opportunities may arise at any point, which may strengthen your BATNA and your negotiating position. Even if your position is weak overall, try to identify any areas of strength you have and use them as leverage. Even the most powerful party will have some weaknesses, so try to discover these and target them.

Never make "all or nothing" deals from a weak position – you may miss out on opportunities that would have arisen as the value of what you are bringing to the table increases during the negotiation process. Instead, make deals sequentially and in small chunks, to ensure that the other party will be more likely to recognize the added value that you bring to the table.

TIP

RECOGNIZE YOUR TRUE POWER

Weak parties often underestimate their own power and overestimate that of powerful parties, so try to make an objective assessment of the amount of power you have.

TIP

USE LIKEABILITY AND INTEGRITY

When in a weak position, do not underestimate the power of personal likeability. People do business with people they like and whom they can trust to keep their promises and deliver good value.

CASE STUDY

Creating power

When Thomas Stemberg, the founder of office products retailer Staples, needed a new round of capital to expand his business, he went back to the venture capitalists who had already financed the company. This time, however, they closed ranks and demanded a higher equity share than Stemberg was willing to provide. Determined to break the venture capitalists' cartel, Stemberg sought alternative sources of funding – the pension funds, the insurance companies, and high net worth individuals – with which he could negotiate from a more powerful position.

Making offers and counteroffers

Before you go into a negotiation, it is vital to plan your opening move. Do you open negotiations and make the first offer or do you wait and allow the other party to go first? Make sure that you have an opening offer in mind, and plan how you will respond to your counterpart's offers.

Knowing when to go first

Some experts suggest that you should not make the first offer and should always allow your counterpart to go first. Skilled negotiators, however, question the conventional "never open" rule. They choose to tailor their approach to each negotiation. How should you decide whether to go first or second? You should present your offer first when you are confident in the thoroughness of your due diligence and also when you suspect that your counterpart is ill-informed. By going first, you will "anchor", or set a benchmark, that will be used as a reference point for the counteroffer.

If you are not fully informed, do not go first. Consider the other party's first offer, do not respond to it, and do your due diligence. In some cases, two negotiators are equally skilled and well informed and neither wishes to go first. Such cases often require the involvement of a trusted third party to act as a neutral go-between and get the negotiations started.

Setting your offer

Whether you present your offer first or second, how high should your offer be? Former US Secretary of State Dr Henry Kissinger believes that a negotiator is better off starting with a high offer. Most negotiators, however, tend to negotiate first with themselves and thus restrain themselves from making bold offers. They tend to justify their modest offers by thinking that their counterparts would not go for a higher offer. Experts today suggest that a seller who puts forward a high offer may risk his or her credibility and offend the buyer, who may very well walk away without even providing a counteroffer. Instead of coming up with offers that are either too high or too modest, it is often better to make offers that are bold and daring. Bold and daring offers are reasonably high, tend not to be acceptable, but are still negotiable.

TIP

CONSIDER THE LONGER TERM

If you are hoping to form a long-term relationship with the other party, do not take advantage if they make you a very low first offer. You will generate goodwill and nurture the relationship if you instead respond with a counteroffer that is higher, but still reasonable to you.

IN FOCUS... POSSIBLE RESPONSES TO TOUGH OPENING OFFERS

It is easy to be thrown if the other party's opening offer is extremely low. Effective negotiators make sure that they are not startled by a tough first offer, and avoid making a quick, emotional reaction. It is vital that a low opening offer does not become a benchmark for the negotiation. Possible responses to low offers include rejecting the offer as unreasonable; asking the other party to revise the offer; or asking questions and probing the other party for justifications for the toughness of the offer.

Making concessions

Experienced negotiators know that successful negotiations involve a certain amount of give and take, and are well versed in the process of making concessions. They tend to develop offers that leave room for concessions, as these are the oil that lubricates the making of a deal.

Conceding in small steps

Each negotiation event is unique, so there are no absolute rules for how to make concessions that apply to all situations. However, it is generally true that people like to receive good news or benefits in installments, rather than all at once. Skilled negotiators, therefore, tend to make multiple small concessions in order to increase the level of satisfaction of their counterparts.

Knowing what to concede

TIP

WATCH YOUR TIMING

Think carefully about the timing of your first sizeable concession. If you make it too soon after your initial offer, it will give the other party the impression that the initial offer was not a credible one.

Inexperienced negotiators often make a first sizeable concession as an expression of goodwill. However, this can set the expectation that there are many concessions to be provided. Experienced negotiators, by contrast, tend to untangle the relationships from the concessions. Sometimes, in order to set the tone of reciprocating concessions, they concede first by making a concession on a minor issue.

Wait before you make the first sizeable concession. During this time, advocate for your initial offer and convey the idea that it is not that easy to make concessions. The second concession should be smaller in size than the first and be a longer time in coming. Making concessions in progressively declining installments will then lend more credibility to when you finally say: "There is no more to give."

Making and interpreting concessions

ENABLING RECIPROCITY
Label the concessions you make as ones that are costly to you and then reduce your value. This sets up the expectation that you will receive a concession in return, implying value for value.

USING CONTINGENCY
If you suspect that your concession will not be reciprocated, offer a concession that is contingent upon the other party providing a concession in return. For example: "I will be willing to extend the terms of payment to 45 days if you will increase your order by 500 items."

SETTING BOUNDARIES
Some negotiators put the deal at risk by asking for too much. Set boundaries for the other party by being clear and precise about what you can concede and what you absolutely cannot.

SETTING RULES
Sometimes negotiators make final concessions but then withdraw them or make them contingent on receiving a new concession. Set a clear rule that a concession cannot be withdrawn, unless it was explicitly offered as a tentative or conditional concession.

SPOTTING DEAL BREAKERS
Some concessions are deal breakers: if they are not offered, your counterpart will walk away from the negotiation table. Try to distinguish these from value-enhancing concessions, which are demands that are designed to get a better deal, but if not provided, would not result in the other party abandoning the negotiations.

A successful negotiation process requires effective persuasion. When attempting to influence your counterpart, it is crucial to identify your moments of power and take advantage of them. Seasoned negotiators understand how to use appropriate persuasion techniques to sell their ideas to the other party.

Influencing others

Effective negotiators use a range of persuasion techniques that take advantage of the natural responses of negotiators to certain types of information. For example, negotiators are generally more motivated to avoid losses than they are to obtain gains. A group of home-owners in California was given the advice that "if you insulate your home, you will gain 50 cents a day". Another group was told that "if you fail to insulate your home, you will lose 50 cents a day". More home owners under the second set of instructions insulated their homes than under the first set of instructions. Similarly, you are more likely to persuade the other party of the benefits of your deal if you emphasize what they would lose if they don't agree, not what they could gain if they do.

Making small unilateral concessions can be a successful way to influence your counterpart. Negotiators feel obligated to reciprocate, no matter how big or small the concessions are. Even a small concession on your part can help the other party to comply. The more beneficial your concession is to the other side, the more likely they are to feel obliged to return the favour.

USE SCARCITY
It is human nature for people to want more of what they cannot have. When you present your offer to the other party, inform them of the unique benefits you are offering that they would not be able to get elsewhere.

GAIN COMMITMENT
Encourage the other party to agree to an initially modest request. They are then more likely to follow up with their commitment by agreeing to your key demand to justify their past decision to say yes to you.

Strengthening your hand with persuasion techniques

GIVE "SOCIAL PROOF"

People often use "social proof" when making decisions – they think that if many people are doing things a certain way, it must be good. Demonstrate how your product or service has been successfully used by others.

LET THEM SAY "NO"

Give the other party the opportunity to say "no" by making an outrageous demand, before retreating immediately and putting forward a reasonable demand. This can also serve to make the other party feel obligated to make a concession.

GIVE A REASON

People are much more likely to agree to a demand if you have given legitimate justification for it. Try to give a reason that can be backed up with evidence, but using even a frivolous reason increases your chances of reaching agreement.

SET A BENCHMARK

Negotiators who are not fully informed tend to compare the cost of an item to a reference point or benchmark. You can influence the way they make their decision by setting a benchmark for them.

Managing impasses

Negotiations do not always conclude with an agreement. You may encounter an impasse or a deadlock during the process. How should you deal with a deadlock? Should you leave the negotiation table, concluding that the process has failed, or should you encourage yourself and your counterpart to remain at the table and keep the negotiations going?

Dealing with deadlock

Skilled and experienced negotiators expect there to be impasses in the negotiating process. They anticipate deadlocks and develop counteractions to deal with them when they occur. They view an impasse as a natural ingredient in negotiations and do not give up easily in their attempts to reach an agreement.

Impasses usually generate negative emotions and sometimes deep feelings of resentment. Prior to and during the negotiation process, you have to be sensitive to the other party's concerns, feelings, and, particularly, their self-image. Research has suggested that negotiators have an image to uphold and that negotiations are less likely to be successful when either or both parties are not sensitive enough to each other's dignity, or "face". You should always be mindful not to harm the self-image of your counterpart, and never more so than during critical moments of an impasse.

Oiling the wheels

If you are facing an impasse, experts suggest that, in the intensity of the moment, you should first take time out to cool down. This will help to defuse the emotional situation and you can resume the discussion at a later time.

Once you reconvene, start by trying to highlight any existing mutual benefits. Impasses usually occur after some progress has already been made. It can therefore be useful to frame the impasse in the context of what has already been achieved – the gains – and highlight the potential losses to both parties if agreement is not reached.

If you are still deadlocked, you may need to try expanding the pie. If you maintain a zero-sum, fixed-pie mentality towards the negotiation, this will restrain your creativity in negotiating for the best deal. Consider that the purpose of negotiation is not to win an argument, but to find satisfactory solutions that would maximize the benefits for both parties. Take the time to generate possible new ideas that could help you reach agreement. Expand the issues you are discussing, but avoid making concessions. In this way, you may be able to overcome the impasse on one critical issue by adding another issue that is attractive to the other party.

MANAGING DEADLOCK SITUATIONS

FAST TRACK

OFF TRACK

FAST TRACK	OFF TRACK
Anticipating potential impasses and planning in advance how to deal with them	Believing that you can just think on your feet if a problem arises
Being open-minded and flexible, and finding creative solutions	Thinking that deadlocks always lead to "no deal"
Reacting calmly and using your emotional intelligence, because you know that deadlock situations can be resolved	Leaving the negotiating table early because you are deadlocked with the other party

Avoiding decision traps

Most negotiators believe that they are rational. In reality, many negotiators systematically make errors of judgement and irrational choices. It is important for you to understand and try to avoid making these common errors, as they lead to poor decision-making.

WATCH YOUR TIMING

To avoid feeling that you have not made the best possible deal, never accept the first offer, even when it is a great offer. Always negotiate a little.

Making the right decisions

Understanding the decision traps that negotiators can fall into will help you avoid making the same mistakes yourself, and may allow you to use the other party's errors to leverage your own power. To avoid decision traps or to use them to your advantage:

• Do not hesitate to reverse your original decision and cut your losses; create an exit strategy even before you get involved in the negotiation process.

• Take the opportunity to set a benchmark that could give you an advantage when your counterpart is ill-informed, but be aware that they could do the same to you if you yourself are not fully informed.

• Engage a trusted expert who will challenge your overconfidence in your ability to negotiate and put pressure on you to do a reality check.

• Make sure that your offer is based on solid research. When buying, equip yourself with some security by demanding a performance guarantee of the product.

• Invest time and energy in looking for information that is not easily available. You will often find accessible information that can improve your position.

• Present information more or less vividly to influence others, but be wary of overvaluing information that is attractively presented to you.

• As a negotiator, be aware of how the other party frames the situation and presents its offers.

• Approach each negotiating event as a unique case. They are never identical.

UNDERSTANDING DECISION ERRORS

ERROR	DESCRIPTION
Non-rational escalation of commitment	• Acting contrary to your self-interest by increasing your commitment to an original decision, despite the fact that this decision produces negative outcomes ("throwing good money after bad").
Anchoring and adjustment	• Using a faulty anchor as a benchmark from which to make adjustments and decisions. An ill-informed home-buyer, for example, may use the seller's asking price as an anchor for their counteroffer, rather than solid due diligence on home values.
Overconfidence	• Believing that you are more correct and accurate than you actually are. This leads to an overestimation of your power within the negotiation, the options open to you, and the probability of your success.
The winner's curse	• If you settle quickly on a deal when selling, feeling that the "win" was too easy and that you could have got more from the deal. • If you settle quickly on a deal when buying, thinking "I could have got this for less" or "What is wrong with this item? I must have got a bad deal."
Information availability bias	• Making a decision based on limited information, even though information is readily available or would have been available if enough effort had been put in to finding it.
Vividness bias	• Recalling and assigning more weight to information that was delivered in a vivid fashion, and giving less weight to equally important, but dull, information.
Framing and risk	• Making decisions based on how the issues were framed (for example, a glass may be described as being half empty or half full). Risk-averse negotiators are more likely to respond positively to offers that are framed in terms of losses, for example, because they are afraid of losing out; risk-seeking negotiators, by contrast, will respond slowly, because they are willing to wait for a better offer.
Small numbers bias	• Drawing a conclusion based on a small number of events, cases, or experiences, believing that your limited experience allows you to generalize from it.

Managing emotions

In the heat of a negotiation, the emotions you display can significantly influence the emotions of the other party. Effective negotiators try to synchronize their behaviour with the other person's, developing an interpersonal rhythm that reflects a shared emotional state.

Understanding the approaches

There are three types of emotional approach in negotiations: rational (having a "poker face"), positive (being friendly and nice), and negative (ranting and raving). Some negotiators believe that exposing their emotions to the other party makes them vulnerable and will result in them giving away too much of the pie, and so try to always keep a "poker face" when they are negotiating. They also believe that emotional displays may result in an impasse or in defective decision-making, or cause negotiations to end.

Other negotiators believe that displaying positive emotions enhances the quality of the negotiated agreement, because a good mood promotes creative thinking, leads to innovative problem-solving, and smoothes out communication. Negotiators with a positive approach use more cooperative strategies, engage in more information exchange, generate more alternatives, use fewer hard tactics, and come to fewer impasses than negotiators with a negative or rational mood.

IN FOCUS...
STRATEGIC USE OF ANGER

Some negotiators successfully use displays of anger strategically to try to encourage the other party to agree to their demands. They aim to gain concessions from their opponent because the other party takes their anger as a sign that they are close to their reservation point. Inducing fear in their opponent pushes that person to cave in and agree. It sends the signal that they would rather walk away from the table without reaching an agreement than settle for less than what they want. The opponent may also wish to end the unpleasant interaction sooner by giving in.

Being negative

Negotiators who use the negative approach display anger, rage, and impatience in order to influence the other party. Anger is sometimes used strategically, but negotiators who are genuinely angry feel little compassion for the other party, and are less effective at expanding and slicing the pie than positive negotiators. They tend to achieve fewer win–win gains when angry than when they experience positive emotions. Angry negotiators are also less willing to cooperate and more likely to seek revenge.

Of the three emotional strategies, the positive and rational approaches are more effective than the negative approach in achieving targets in an ultimatum setting. The positive approach is more helpful in building a long-term, constructive relationship than the rational or negative methods.

Using emotional intelligence

When negotiators are emotionally overwhelmed, their mental capacity to negotiate effectively is impaired. To overcome this, you must manage your emotions intelligently. You need to be aware of the emotions you are experiencing and be able to monitor and regulate them, and you need to find ways to empathize with the other party. For example, when the US Secretary of State James Baker was negotiating with Hafez al-Assad, President of Syria, he had to make a conscious attempt to modulate his irritation. Although he was very angry when President Assad retracted from an earlier commitment, he used the term "misunderstanding" rather than openly displaying his anger.

ASK YOURSELF... DO I USE EMOTIONAL INTELLIGENCE WHEN NEGOTIATING?

- Am I able to make an emotional connection with my counterpart, even if I do not know them very well?
- Am I able to judge when my own emotions threaten to affect my ability to make rational decisions?
- Can I manage my emotions to ensure that I am always effective?
- Am I able to react in a measured way, keeping my emotions under control, even if the other party is using value-claiming tactics or behaving in a manner that I do not agree with?

Dealing with competitive tactics

In competitive win–lose position-based negotiations, negotiators use various manipulative tactics to maximize their interests while disregarding the interests of their counterparts. They usually believe that these tactics are quite effective. Often, however, these tactics can backfire, escalating the level of negotiation or even leading to an impasse. Skilled negotiators recognize these tactical traps and know how to avoid and neutralize them.

Competitive tactics and how to avoid them

MAKING A HIGHBALL OR LOWBALL OFFER
A negotiator assumes that you are not fully informed and tries to take advantage by making a very high offer as a seller, or a low offer as a buyer. Their objective is to replace the benchmark you have in your mind with one in their favour.
TO AVOID: Be confident in your benchmarks and try to see clearly through this ploy.

PLAYING GOOD GUY/BAD GUY
One negotiator plays tough and uses aggressive tactics, such as threats and ultimatums. Another empathizes to make you believe that he or she is on your side. Neither is on your side – both are trying to maximize their own interests.
TO AVOID: Focus squarely on protecting your own interests.

SEPARATING THE ISSUES
A negotiator insists on reaching an agreement on a single issue before moving on to the next issue. This prevents you from bundling issues together and creating opportunities for trade-offs.
TO AVOID: Negotiate multiple issues at once, stating that "nothing is agreed upon until everything is agreed upon".

NIBBLING
The deal is done, but at the last minute the negotiator asks for another small concession. Most negotiators concede, fearing that the last-minute demand might derail the deal if it is not fulfilled.
TO AVOID: Remember that refusing to budge on a small concession at the last minute is not usually a deal breaker.

APPLYING TIME PRESSURE
The other party uses the pressure of time to try to get you to concede by setting tight deadlines for an offer, or using delaying tactics to reduce the amount of time available for the negotiation.
TO AVOID: Use your judgement to decide whether a deadline is real or not.

USING EMOTIONAL BLACKMAIL
A negotiator tries to intimidate or influence you by fabricating anger, frustration, or despair. They try to emotionally shake you and make you feel responsible for the lack of progress.
TO AVOID: Use your emotional intelligence. Stay calm and centred, and try to steer the negotiations back on track.

Closing the deal

Closing the deal after reaching an agreement is the last but most critical part of any negotiation process. It is certainly not simple, and is not just about outcomes. It also has to do with building relationships and making sure that the negotiated agreements can be carried out smoothly. Closing the deal properly is especially important when negotiated agreements are complex and multi-dimensional.

Preparing to close

Before you close the deal, both you and your counterpart need to understand that the purpose of making the deal is not to sign the contract, but rather to accomplish what the contract specifies. What goals is each party pursuing through the deal and what will it take to accomplish them? As you depend on each other to accomplish your goals, it is important to make sure that both parties are signing the contract wholeheartedly. Review both parties' key interests and ensure that nothing has been neglected. It is quite possible for the other party to decide to overturn the entire deal if he or she feels pushed into an agreement without having their own needs taken care of.

✔ CHECKLIST CLOSING A DEAL

	YES	NO
• Have you considered all possible stakeholders?	☐	☐
• Have you clarified the purpose of the deal?	☐	☐
• Have you made sure that both parties understand what it takes to implement the agreement?	☐	☐
• Have you built a relationship with the other party, to pave the way for future collaboration?	☐	☐
• Have you made enough arrangements for another team to implement the agreement, if another team is taking over?	☐	☐

Considering implementation

Most negotiators underestimate the importance of implementation. If not considered, the intense process of negotiation can undermine your ability to achieve your goals after the deal has been signed. For example, if you have used hard negotiation tactics to push the other party to agree to the deal, the other party may feel, upon signing the contract, that they have been unfairly treated and sabotage the deal, or fail to deliver.

Before you put pen to paper, discuss the implementation of the deal with the other party. What you agree must fulfil the needs of both parties if you are to ensure successful implementation. Unless both parties have confidence that the deal can be successfully implemented, there is no point in continuing the discussion.

Reaching agreement

A written agreement usually marks the closure of a negotiation. The agreement, which includes solutions for both parties, may be summarized and you may ask the other party to sign this document. This is the most simple and natural way to conclude a negotiation.

HOW TO... ENSURE EFFECTIVE IMPLEMENTATION

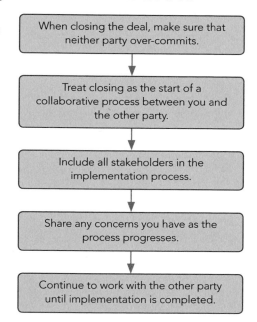

When closing the deal, make sure that neither party over-commits.

Treat closing as the start of a collaborative process between you and the other party.

Include all stakeholders in the implementation process.

Share any concerns you have as the process progresses.

Continue to work with the other party until implementation is completed.

Changes should be allowed after the agreement has been signed. In other words, if circumstances change, both parties should feel comfortable contacting the other party to discuss these changes. Upon mutual agreement, such changes can be incorporated into the new agreement. Make sure you include this last point in the agreement, as a deal is not done until it is done – it is better to allow for some flexibility than to force the other party to overthrow the entire deal, should the circumstances change.

Developing your technique

However experienced you are at negotiating, there are always ways to improve your technique. Negotiating in groups, in an international arena, and using your skills to mediate conflicts all require a tailored approach to achieve the best results.

Negotiating as a team

Many business situations are too complex for a solo negotiator to be fully informed about every aspect of the deal. In such cases, working in a team may give better results, though this requires a high degree of internal coordination and a smooth flow of information between members.

Deciding when to use a team

Some negotiations demand a diverse set of abilities. In addition to sound negotiation and psychosocial skills you may need specific technical expertise, for example, in areas of law, drafting joint ventures, or the planning system. You may need to exercise leverage on your opposite number through the use of PR, or require a keen appreciation of strategy and politics in order to identify the multiple stakeholders in the negotiation and figure out their interests. If you lack any of these abilities, you will probably benefit from the collective wisdom of a team.

Understanding the advantages

There are many benefits to negotiating as a team. Being part of a team provides for multiple creative trade-offs and options and has other advantages, too. Sheer "strength in numbers" makes a team feel secure and powerful and sends a clear message to the other party that you are serious about the deal. You are also likely to feel less pressured when negotiating as a team, and unlikely to make too many concessions too early in the process.

TIP

MAKE TIME TO PREPARE

Make sure that you have enough time to create a cohesive, trustworthy team, and allow time to prepare your strategy as a group before you enter into a team negotiation.

Avoiding the pitfalls

Working in a team can lead to a lack of focus and consistency, so appoint a chief negotiator to lead your team and agree in advance each member's role and responsibilities. Avoid falling into "groupthink", when team members feel pressured to conform to an existing group mindset and reluctant to present ideas that conflict with it. It can also be easy for a team to create a false sense of cohesiveness: "us", the good team, versus "them", the bad team. If this happens, genuine conciliatory attempts made by the other party can be dismissed as dishonest "tricks" and rejected, resulting in missed opportunities to make a deal.

 IN FOCUS... DECISION TIME

Negotiating as a team begs the question of how to decide on a course of action. Broadly, there are three ways to reach a decision: first is unanimity, in which all team members must agree on a given issue. This is a tough rule and not recommended for most situations. Second is the majority rule. The majority will decide and the minority comply with the decision. The hazard here is that the majority may impose a tough solution that the minority cannot live with. The third, and usually best, decision-making rule is consensus: making a decision that not all the team members agree with fully, but that all can live with.

Dealing with many parties

Many business partnerships or deals involve agreements between three or more different parties, each with their own positions, needs, and goals. Negotiating in this environment requires dexterity and a constant eye on the pitfalls, such as coalitions between the parties opposing you.

Balancing complex issues

Multiparty negotiations are in many ways similar to two-party situations but require a wider set of skills to deal with their additional complexities, which include:

• **Informational complexity** The number of parties involved produces multiple exchanges of information, proposals, and multiple trade-offs. You need to develop a solid information system that can record and recall all the information exchanged in the negotiation room.

• **Strategic complexity** Multiple parties have many interests, and often conflicts of interest, between them. Each party has its BATNA (Best Alternative to a Negotiated Agreement), which may change as alliances are formed. To be well prepared for a multiparty negotiation, you must constantly reassess your own and your counterparts' BATNAs.

CASE STUDY

Chairing multiparty talks
The central challenge for the Chair of a meeting is to gain the trust of the negotiating parties. Former Senator George J. Mitchell, US Senate Majority Leader, stated that in mediating the dispute in Northern Ireland, his ability to be effective ultimately depended more on gaining the delegates' trust and confidence than on his formal role and authority. The Chair should be clear about his or her role, introduce the agenda, introduce ground rules, provide parties with opportunities to express themselves, and distil common interests. The Chair should also regularly summarize the progress that has been made in the negotiation.

SUCCEEDING IN MULTIPARTY NEGOTIATIONS

FAST TRACK

OFF TRACK

FAST TRACK	OFF TRACK
Forming or joining coalitions	Insisting on acting independently
Resisting group pressure to modify your core interests	Settling too easily when faced by a coalition
Being clear when you disagree	Keeping quiet: silence may be interpreted as assent
Monitoring the positions of all the parties	Focusing on only one part of the negotiations

• **Procedural complexity** The design of the negotiation process may be fraught with difficulty. Its structure – the rules of engagement, the selection of the venue, the sequence of the issues, and how decisions will be made – must be perceived by all parties to be fair. In high-value negotiations, it is wise to employ a trained expert to facilitate the process more effectively.

• **Social complexity** With more negotiators involved, the social context becomes complex. In a two-party negotiation, your focus is on one individual, but multiparty negotiations require you to understand, analyze, and build relationships with each and every negotiator. You must learn to resist excessive social pressure and always protect your interests, even when faced by a coalition of parties in the negotiation.

• **Emotional complexity** Negotiating in a multiparty context can be very taxing. Make sure that your emotions are held in check; emotional distress often results in poor decisions.

GAIN POWER

Consider building a coalition if you think you hold a weaker hand than one of your opponents. Being part of a successful coalition may help you shift the balance of power.

Building winning coalitions

The moment there are more than two parties in a negotiation, there are opportunities to make coalitions. To protect your interests and remain in the negotiating game, one of your major objectives is to think well in advance about offence (how to build a winning coalition) as well as defence (how to put together a blocking coalition).

When attempting to build a stable coalition, there are three essential factors to consider. The first is the issue of agreement. Some parties will agree and others will disagree with your vision and the strategies and tactics you plan to use to achieve it. The second is influence. Some potential partners may be highly influential and can use their positions of power to assist you in moving your agenda forward, while others will be weak and unable to help much. The third factor to consider is trust. Coalitions are temporary entities driven by self-interest, so partners are easily seduced to defect once the pay-offs elsewhere become higher. Your main objective should be to recruit potential partners who are trustworthy and will remain loyal to the coalition.

DIVIDE THE PIE

Make it clear to your coalition partners how the benefits – the proverbial pie – will be divided if you achieve your goals. The division certainly must be fair, but fairness does not necessarily mean an equal share.

ASK YOURSELF... ABOUT FORMING A COALITION

- What is your agenda for the negotiation and what are you trying to achieve?
- What are the main factors that you need to consider in building your coalition?
- Can you identify potential coalition partners that are most likely to work with you to allow you to jointly fulfil your objectives?
- How should you sequence the recruitment of each potential coalition partner?
- What is the best way to approach potential partners?

Recruiting coalition partners

When building a coalition, start by identifying all stakeholders, both supporters and opponents of your objectives. Classify each one according to their level of agreement (high, medium, or low, on a scale from one to 10), the degree of influence they could bring to the coalition, and their level of perceived trustworthiness. First, approach your best potential allies – the parties who agree with your vision and agenda and are very influential and trustworthy. Next, focus on the allies who agree with your vision and are trustworthy, but who do not hold positions of power at the moment; they may gain influence as the negotiation proceeds. Ignore the weak adversaries: those who disagree with your agenda and have little influence. At the same time, think how you could block your powerful adversaries. Can you make a coalition with one of their potential partners?

Coalition partners are often motivated solely by gains. Once the gains elsewhere are higher, they may defect, so you should attempt to cement integrity within the coalition. One way to do this is to ask each partner to make a public commitment to the coalition, making it harder for them to defect.

Negotiating internationally

In today's global economy, ever more business deals are made across national borders. Negotiating international deals is a considerable challenge because you must be familiar with the complexities of the immediate negotiation context, such as the bargaining power of the parties and the relevant stakeholders, as well as the broader context, which may include currency fluctuations and government control.

Understanding the differences

You are likely to experience significant differences in several key areas when you engage in international negotiation:

• **Agreements** Western negotiators expect to conclude the process with a comprehensive bullet-proof legal contract. In other countries, and notably in Asia, memorandums of understanding (MOAs), which are broader but less substantial agreements, may be more common.

• **Time sensitivity** In countries in which a "doing" culture is prevalent, people believe in controlling events and managing time strictly. In some countries, time is not viewed as such a critical resource, and negotiations can be slow and lengthy.

• **Degree of formality** Negotiators from informal cultures tend to dress down, address one another by their first names, maintain less physical distance, and pay less attention to official titles. In contrast, negotiators from formal cultures tend to use formal titles and are mindful of seating arrangements.

POLITICAL RISK
While some countries have long traditions of an abundance of resources and political stability, others have scarce resources and are marked by volatile political changes.

IDEOLOGY
In individualistic cultures like the US, the purpose of the business is to serve the interests of its shareholders, but in collective cultures, the business has a larger purpose: to contribute to the common good of society.

Factors to consider in international negotiations

POLITICAL AND LEGAL SYSTEMS
Different countries have different tax codes, labour laws, legal philosophies and enforcement policies, laws that govern joint ventures, and financial incentives for attracting business investments.

BUREAUCRACY
Business practices and government regulations vary from country to country. In some countries, the government bureaucracy is deeply embedded in business affairs, and businesses are constantly required to secure government approval before they act.

INTERNATIONAL FINANCE
Currencies fluctuate and affect the balance of expenses and profits. The stability of the currency your investment is made in affects the risk to you. Many governments also control the flow of currency, limiting the amount of money that can cross their borders.

CULTURE
Different cultures have starkly different cultural beliefs about the role of individuals in society, the nature of relationships, and the ways in which people should communicate. These have a fundamental effect on how you need to approach a negotiation.

Negotiating in Asia

Succeeding in any international negotiation means taking the time to understand the complex negotiating environment, being sufficiently flexible to be able to change your ways if necessary, and learning to work within governmental bureaucracies. The cultural and business landscape in Asia is especially unfamiliar to Western organizations, and, with the region's rapid rise to economic prominence, every manager needs to be aware of how it differs.

Acknowledging differences

Asian culture is characterized by concern for people's feelings. It emphasizes interdependence, harmony, and cooperation, while Western culture tends to be more competitive and achievement-oriented, and rewards assertiveness.

Asian societies give a higher priority to collective goals; self-sacrifice for the good of the whole is a guiding principle. There is a greater acceptance of unequal power distribution, and relationships are built based on differences of stature, age, and gender.

Another cultural differentiator is the level of comfort of individuals in ambiguous situations. Business people in China and Japan like to avoid uncertainty, preferring structured and clear situations, in which they are able to make decisions after careful evaluation of a large amount of information. Contrast this with some Western societies, where people are more comfortable with ambiguous situations and are prepared to make quick decisions based on a limited amount of information.

Be aware too that there are differences in communication styles: Asians may be "high context" (indirect, implicit, and suggestive), while those from the West are "low context"– more direct and specific.

TIP

MAKE A CONNECTION

Present your partners with a long-term vision of the mutual benefits of a deal, stressing your personal relationship rather than legal obligations.

TIP

BE PATIENT

Indian negotiators are more concerned with getting good outcomes than with the efficiency of the negotiation process, and may negotiate for weeks or even months to get the best deal. Never put pressure on your counterpart to reach agreement more quickly or you may lose the deal.

The Asian style of negotiation

RELATIONSHIPS ("GUANXI")
Chinese business leaders invest heavily in making interpersonal connections and creating a dependable social network, known as "guanxi". They prefer to do business within their trusted network.

EMOTIONS
The Confucian teaching *xinping qihe*, meaning "being perfectly calm", makes it difficult for Western negotiators to "read" their counterparts and to know where they stand.

FAIRNESS
The concept of fairness is based on needs: those who have more should give to those with less.

TRUST FROM THE HEART
Asian businesses like to do business with trustworthy individuals rather than faceless organizations. The lengthy process of building trust is based on openness, mutual assistance, understanding, and the formation of emotional bonds.

FACE
Dignity and prestige are gained when individuals behave morally and achieve accomplishments. Face is a formidable force in the Asian psyche that negotiators in Western organizations must be particularly aware of.

LEGALISM
You risk insulting your Asian counterpart if you emphasize penalties for dishonouring commitments in detail. Contracts are short and merely a tangible expression of the relationships being created. They are not treated as "fixed" legal instruments.

DECISIONS
Although Chinese and Japanese societies are hierarchical, they use the consensus style of decision-making. Lead negotiators refrain from dictating a decision in order to preserve relationships and give face to others.

Examining the role of gender

Are women better negotiators than men? Research reveals real differences in negotiation styles between the genders, but there are also deep-seated gender stereotypes in many cultures. How these gender differences are handled, by both men and women, is critical in determining the quality of the agreement you reach through negotiation.

Being aware of perceptions

Enthusiastic and well-prepared negotiators, whether men or women, tend to perform better than less-interested and less-committed ones. In an ideal world, in which neither party is concerned about gender, female negotiators can perform just as well as their male counterparts. In the real world, it pays to be aware of the real and perceived differences between the sexes when approaching a negotiation.

Addressing stereotypes

Women are stereotypically portrayed as being at a disadvantage in the negotiating environment. The myths are that, while men behave rationally, women are emotional; where men are assertive, women are passive; and while men are competitive, women tend to prefer a collaborative approach.

As a woman, your attitude towards these stereotypes and how you choose to handle them when negotiating with men plays a critical role in determining the outcome of a negotiation. If you accept the stereotype and feel and appear anxious at the negotiating table, you may confirm the stereotype and trigger a self-fulfilling prophecy of expecting less and getting less. If you acknowledge the stereotype and try hard to overcome it, you will gain advantage; people are generally prompted to assert their freedom when they feel restricted by others, and using these feelings in a negotiation may serve to make you bolder and more assertive, and help you gain a bargaining surplus.

Men may also be affected by perceived or real gender differences in negotiations. When men negotiate with women, they may either choke under the pressure to over-perform, thus leading to a less favourable outcome; or they may feel guilty and fail to take advantage of their male traits, which would also lead to a less favourable outcome.

GENDER DIFFERENCES IN NEGOTIATION

AREA OF ACTIVITY	MALE CHARACTERISTICS	FEMALE CHARACTERISTICS
Setting goals	Tend to set high goals	Tend to set lower goals
Making concessions	Tend to make few concessions	Tend to make more concessions
Splitting the pie	Focus more on outcomes – getting a larger slice of the pie	Focus more on building and maintaining relationships than obtaining an outcome
Accepting offers	Tend to regret their decision later and feel they could have got more, especially after accepting a first offer	Tend to feel relieved after accepting an offer

Using a coach

Many negotiators have blind spots, hold false assumptions, and are prone to repeating their mistakes. Some continue to fail to fully understand the other party's perspective, are unable to convert positions to interests, or are unable to manage their emotions. Working with a coach is an excellent way to gain perspective on your weaknesses and strengths and develop your skills for greater success.

Understanding the benefits

Many negotiators do not realize that they could improve their techniques. They continue to make the same mistakes because they filter information, hearing only what they want to hear, rather than absorbing the complete information that is required to perform well. Another self-serving trap is attribution. Negotiators often attribute problems in negotiations to their counterpart negotiators. An objective coach who is willing to challenge you can help raise your awareness of your limitations and improve your performance.

WORKING WITH A COACH

FAST TRACK	OFF TRACK
Embracing coaching as a way to become more successful	Rejecting an offer of coaching, because you can't improve
Respecting your coach's assessment of your weaknesses	Believing that your coach doesn't understand your superior approach
Using the feedback your coach gives you to improve your skills	Dismissing your coach's advice, because you know better

Being assessed

When you first work with a coach, they will make an assessment of your performance. This often starts with a 360-degree feedback session, in which your coach collects data from people you negotiate with, in order to identify your strengths and weaknesses. The coach may also "shadow" you in actual negotiations, to take note of your performance. Witnessing you in action allows a coach to provide relevant and insightful suggestions for improvement. The key outcome from the diagnosis is for the coach to identify your patterns in beliefs and behaviours, so that you have a higher level of self-awareness.

Fine-tuning your style

The coach then works with you to identify the skill sets and attitudes you want to focus on throughout the coaching period. Coaches are experienced in diagnosing possible pitfalls in your negotiation styles, and can help you be proactive in preventing them from occurring. They can also help you to uncover issues and resolve them on your own. They can expand your repertoire of behaviours by trying out different approaches and styles with you. Coaches ask

IN FOCUS...
ROLE PLAY

Scenario role play can be an effective method of preparing for negotiations. A coach can help you rehearse your role and make sure there are no gaps or weaknesses in your case and in the negotiation process. For example, the coach can help identify your BATNA or make sure that you are not too enamoured with the potential deal to the extent that you are unable to walk away from it. Although it is impossible to perfectly script a negotiation process ahead of time, it is helpful to "know your destination and all the terrain" so that even if the other party takes the process off track, you can still find a way to achieve your goals.

a lot of questions. A good coach helps the negotiator to test his or her own assumptions, consider different perspectives, and reach a conclusion about how to proceed. Many will use scenario role play to help you practise new ways of doing things.

Once you have used the new approaches in a real negotiation, a coach can provide a non-threatening evaluation and help you learn from your mistakes, achievements, and missed opportunities. Your learning can then be applied in your next round of negotiations.

Being a mediator

As a manager, you will often have to negotiate directly with others within your organization, but will also sometimes be asked to get involved as a third party to try and help parties engaged in disputes to resolve their conflicts. You therefore need to understand the principles of effective mediation and how your role is different to that of other mediators.

Defining mediation

Mediation is a structured process in which an impartial third party facilitates the resolution of a conflict between two negotiating parties. For mediation to be successful, the person selected to mediate a dispute must be acceptable to both of the parties. They must be entirely happy that the mediator is unbiased and will assess the circumstances of the dispute objectively.

If you are asked to mediate a dispute, you need to be certain that you will be able to remain impartial and not let yourself get swept up in the emotional side of what is taking place. Your role will require you to look at the situation from the perspective of each of the disputing parties to find areas of common ground between them, and use this information to make recommendations that would be acceptable to both parties.

ENCOURAGE SELF-DETERMINATION
Ensure that the disputing parties recognize their differences and know that their participation in the mediation process is voluntary and they are free to leave at any time.

GIVE OWNERSHIP
Let the disputing parties know that they must take responsibility for the conflict and for its resolution, and are expected to identify the issues and engage creatively in solving the conflict.

REMAIN NEUTRAL
Ensure that you remain neutral and help to facilitate the mediation process, rather than actively trying to influence the outcomes of the conflict.

Principles of effective mediation

KEEP THE GOAL IN MIND
Always remember that the aim of mediation through integrative negotiation is not to achieve absolute justice, but to develop options and find the most workable and satisfactory option.

ADVOCATE CONFIDENTIALITY
Make it clear to all parties that the mediation process is confidential. Disputing parties are only likely to share important information if they believe that the mediator is neutral and trustworthy.

USE AN INTEGRATIVE APPROACH
Try to understand the interests of each of the disputing parties, and help them reach an integrative (win–win) resolution that they would both find acceptable.

Remaining impartial

The manager's role as a mediator is similar to that of other neutral third-party mediators. He or she is working to the same goal as other mediators: to help the disputing parties resolve their disputes. However, as the types of conflict a manager has to deal with often affect organizational goals and performance, he or she may sometimes find it difficult to remain neutral to its consequences. In order to protect the organization's interests, the manager may sometimes have to exercise more control over how the conflict is mediated and also over how the dispute will be resolved. In addition, managers will often have a shared history and possibly a future relationship with the disputing parties. Given these challenges, a manager must do his or her utmost to mediate the dispute in an unbiased manner.

Understanding the process

The mediation process is a step-by-step, structured process. However, unlike the rigid legal process used for mediation, the process used by managers is flexible. It involves five main steps:

• **Initial contact** Start by meeting with each party to identify the issues and provide general information about the mediation process and principles.
• **Assessment and preparation** Next, you need to introduce your role as the mediator, and talk to each disputing party to obtain information about the nature of the dispute. You should also make an assessment of your ability to mediate this dispute, by deciding whether the disputing parties are ready for mediation. You also need to get the parties to commit to engaging in constructive mediation, by asking them to sign a contract. Finally, make a list of the issues in dispute for later discussion.

• **Joint opening session** Once you are fully prepared, you then need to establish a psychologically safe environment in which the mediation can take place. Clarify the rules of engagement, such as mutual respect, taking notes and meeting privately with each disputing party. Educate the parties on the differences between each of their positions and interests and begin to work on the issues.

• **Joint sessions** Facilitate a productive joint problem-solving situation by continuing to move the disputing parties from positions to interests. Prioritize and narrow down the issues, identify areas of agreement and areas of disagreement, and encourage the disputing parties to make realistic proposals. This may take one or a number of sessions.

• **Agreement** Write down aspects of the agreement as the disputing parties begin to agree on more issues. Ensure that the final agreement is very precise, is owned by the disputants, and is forward-looking.

MEDIATING AS A MANAGER

FAST TRACK	OFF TRACK
Ensuring that the disputing parties reach an integrative agreement that is satisfactory to all	Failing to take the time to fully listen to and understand the interests of the disputing parties
Trying to resolve the conflict as quickly and efficiently as possible	Allowing the conflict to disrupt the organization's day-to-day business
Ensuring that the mediation process is fair to both parties	Introducing your own biases
Allowing disputing parties to express their feelings	Disregarding the emotions of the disputing parties

Learning from the masters

Irrespective of the field in which they ply their trade, be it business, law, diplomacy, labour, or sports, master negotiators possess a unique set of combined characteristics that clearly differentiate them from common negotiators, and define their success. Every negotiator can benefit by understanding the skills and attitudes of a master negotiator.

Becoming a winning negotiator

Master negotiators have superior negotiating capabilities in three major areas: the ability to understand and analyze issues (cognitive skills); the ability to manage emotions, especially negative ones (emotional skills); and the ability to connect with others by developing relationships and trust (social skills). These are the areas that you need to work on if you are to hone your negotiating skills and work towards becoming a master negotiator.

Defining key attributes

The following characteristics are common to all master negotiators:

• **Using masterful due diligence** Master negotiators understand the dangers of being poorly prepared, and invest ample resources in planning and gathering information.

• **Thinking strategically** Negotiations are rarely a one-on-one business, so master negotiators spend time analyzing the interests of the "players" who are not at the table, how the power balance lies, and what opportunities exist to increase their own power.

• **Being firm and flexible** Master negotiators are firm and clear about the issues they must have, and flexible on the issues they would like to have.

• **Seeing the other side** Master negotiators know that they can only present a good offer or trade-off if they know what their counterpart's interests are. They are able to easily shift from seeing things from their point of view to seeing things from that of the other party.

• **Investing in relationships** Master negotiators use all possible opportunities to nurture trust and develop relationships, and make sure that those connections remain intact over time.

• **Managing emotions** Master negotiators make an active choice to always monitor and control their emotions constructively.

• **Appreciating uniqueness** Master negotiators approach every situation afresh and are always ready to modify their practices and adapt to the specific conditions of the current negotiation.

 IN FOCUS... BAD DEALS

Master negotiators know that negotiations are not about making the deal and signing the contract, but rather about diligently pursuing their interests. No deal is better than a bad deal, so they condition themselves mentally to walk away from the table if and when their interests are not met. Inexperienced negotiators tend to be biased towards securing a deal and often tend to stay at the table and get a poor deal. There are two reasons for this: first, negotiators do not want to let go of the sunk costs (expenses) involved in attempting to make the deal. Second, they do not want to face the fact that it simply is not possible to make the deal and thus feel that they have failed to produce results. Master negotiators, in contrast, are willing to let go of the sunk costs and do not feel that they have failed in the negotiation task if the deal does not go through.

SELLING

Contents

Introduction

Selling is one of the world's oldest professions, and one that constantly moves with, and adapts to, broader changes in business practice, human interactions, and psychology. Selling is also – as every salesperson will tell you – at the cutting edge of every business. Without the eyes, ears, and intuition of a good salesperson, the business itself founders.

Every good salesperson knows their products inside-out – whether these are paper clips, aircraft engines, or consultancy services – and can present them capably to their customers. However, a great salesperson does much more. He or she understands their customers' needs, and brings a problem-solving mentality and real creativity to their interactions.

Selling is all about combining a set of attitudes, behaviours, and skills in a way that forges long-term relationships with customers – relationships that add value to the customer's business and that yield not just one agreed deal, but many.

Despite some bad press over the years, selling is an honourable profession. The aim of this book is to open your mind to help you approach selling in a very different way and to introduce the skills that you must demonstrate every day. Let the journey begin!

Chapter 1

Building meaningful relationships

People buy from people whom they like, respect, and trust, so selling is really about building and managing relationships. The first step is to find out what your customers expect and demand, and what you need to do to respond accordingly.

Adding value through selling

Offering good products at competitive prices just isn't enough to win sales in today's competitive market. You can bet that your best ideas will be emulated by others sooner or later. Today's customers expect you to add value to their business – to address their needs and deliver solutions.

The evolving selling mentality

Being a successful salesperson today involves you in collaboration, facilitation, and a sense of partnership with your customer. Long gone are the days of one-way persuasion – the canned pitch is considered the lowest level of selling. Ideas about selling have evolved rapidly as globalization and fast communication have produced more savvy and demanding buyers. Selling reflects wider changes in business and today goes far beyond pushing product, embracing an understanding of how organizations work, management structures, psychology, and self-awareness.

Understanding your role

THINK CREATIVE
Don't limit yourself to thinking only about your products and services – your customers need your creativity to help solve their problems.

In the past, a salesperson could get by through eloquently telling the customer everything he or she knew about their product, and explaining why their company was the best in its field. This approach may still win you business today in some areas, but most customers now demand much more from their salespeople. They expect them to add value to their business – to fully understand their needs and to offer up solutions to problems they didn't even realize they had. To succeed, you need to interpret what the client tells you, and often educate your customer about what's out there. Then you need to mesh together the abilities of your organization with that of the client for the benefit of both. You need a measure of curiosity and good listening skills to uncover what the client really needs. And you must be a brilliant innovator, with the ability to think creatively, and manage creative processes that find answers.

 IN FOCUS... SELLING PROFILE

There's no formula for great salespeople – they come from all walks of life and all levels of society. However, they share some characteristics that make them more likely to succeed:
• **Willingness to take risks** – putting their own necks on the line and entering unchartered ground to come up with unique ideas.
• **Generosity** – giving credit to others where deserved without reservation, and sharing credit without fear of diminishing individual contribution.
• **A thick skin** – knowing how to deal with failure, and understanding that even the best lose more often than

they win. With experience, salespeople learn how to deal with inevitable negative responses to their ideas, as well as their own innate emotional responses to knockbacks.
• **A methodical approach** – understanding that planning and follow-up are the keys to success.
• **Resourcefulness** – constantly innovating and challenging the existing approaches. Salespeople work well in groups and make the most of the talent around them.
• **Tenacity** – knowing that they need effort and determination to tackle daunting problems.

Addressing needs

Selling isn't a moment of inspiration; it is not about force of argument or the strength of your personality. It is a process. The process is fairly easy to understand, but – as you'll see – hard to do. The techniques in this book are centred around a process called needs-based selling, so let's examine its principles and set the scene.

TIP

REFRAME THE SALES VISIT

Think of every sales call as a problem-solving opportunity. You are selling more than products and services; you're selling ideas, perspectives, and insights.

Examining the process

The process of selling needs careful planning and management. Beginning a relationship with a new client is the first phase of the process: you can't just walk into a customer's office and kick off a sales meeting – it needs careful staging, and both you and your customer need to be prepared.

Next, you start the most important part of the sales process – determining the customer's needs. During this phase, you ask the key questions, listen to what the customer has to say, identify both the obvious and less obvious needs, enter into a meaningful dialogue, and review what you have learned. Needs determination drives everything in selling, and it is only once you have listened to your customer that you move on to the phase of the process that most salespeople enjoy the most: presenting their products and services. This is when you get to explain how you and your company can address your customer's needs. You know your products and services inside-out, and your customers want to hear how you can help them.

Once you have determined the needs and made recommendations, it is time to think about gaining commitment. But something almost always gets in the way – and you face resistance to commit. The customer needs to be allowed to object – even when they seem ready to buy – and you must resolve the client's objections if you are to close the sale.

Needs-based selling

Simply put, needs-based selling means determining a customer's needs before you start to propose solutions. Get to understand the customer by letting them speak – at length if necessary. When it's time to present, you'll do a better job than those who merely display their products and services and you'll be far better positioned to sustain a long-term relationship with your customer.

Solving problems

Success in selling is linked to effective problem solving. If you're good at one, the chances are that you'll excel at the other. The process of problem solving is also remarkably similar in its structure to that of selling (see below), further reinforcing the link.

COMPARING PROBLEM SOLVING WITH SELLING

STEP	PROBLEM SOLVING	NEEDS-BASED SELLING
1	Set the stage. Provide structure for the problem-solving session.	Open the meeting. Build rapport, confirm the agenda, prepare the customer.
2	Define the problem. Review background information and solutions already tried.	Determine needs. Engage with the client and tease out both their obvious and their hidden needs.
3	Generate ideas. Provide the climate where everyone can contribute creative perspectives without judgement.	Present products and services. Describe the features and benefits of what you have to sell. Impart your enthusiasm and belief in your products.
4	Evaluate the ideas and develop the best ones. Identify the appealing aspects of an idea, then list the concerns.	Resolve objections. Effectively and sensitively resolve the objections that customers inevitably raise.
5	Summarize the solution. Put together a specific action plan.	Close the deal. Agree how to move forward with fulfilment.

Appealing to buyers

Countless studies have addressed the central questions of sales – why do buyers buy? How do customers make decisions? What do they demand from salespeople? The answers come down to three discernible behaviours: believing in your position, empathy, and trust.

TIP

SET THE TONE
You don't have to be funny to be successful in sales, but it helps to be fun. Be the kind of person who brightens up a room when they enter, as opposed to the person who brightens up a room when they leave it.

Establishing your position

People buy from people who know their stuff. If the salesperson can't consistently demonstrate that he or she knows what they are talking about, it becomes almost impossible to buy from them.

Put yourself in the buying role. You want to buy a new refrigerator, but the salesperson just can't explain why model A is better for you than model B. Chances are that you'll shut down as a customer; in fact, you'll probably want to leave and go to a different store. Knowing what you sell inside-out is a given, but your credibility extends far beyond product knowledge. You must become familiar with your customer's business, competitors, industry, and marketplace. You need to be well prepared. It's not hard – almost everything you need to know about your customers and markets is readily available online.

✓ CHECKLIST GAINING RESPECT BY SHOWING RESPECT

	YES	NO
• Do you show respect for your client's space by, for example, avoiding placing objects on their desk?	☐	☐
• Do you show respect for their business by, for example, asking before you take notes?	☐	☐
• Do you show respect for your competitors? If you put down one of the client's existing suppliers, you are disrespecting the client.	☐	☐

Showing empathy

Empathy is the ability to connect with someone – to see things from their perspective. Several recent studies indicate that, for many buyers, a salesperson's ability to understand their situation is the single most compelling reason why they make the decision to buy.

Many people think that empathy depends on similarity of age, background, experience, or point of view. That's a myth. A young salesperson can connect with and relate to someone much more senior if they can identify areas of mutual interest. It's not hard to find common ground. For starters, both are already in the same business – even if they are on different sides of the desk. They may have similar interests and educations: if salespeople allow the customer to talk and genuinely show interest in what they say, the customer will appreciate the empathy they show.

Without understanding the customer and showing real interest in what he or she has to say, a key ingredient in the relationship will be missing and the salesperson will remain an order taker… at best.

GET IN TOUCH

Focus on empathy. Management guru David Maister famously said: "Customers don't care how much you know until they know how much you care."

Building trust

Trust takes a long time to build, but only a second to lose. To demonstrate that you can be trusted, you need to be responsive, direct, clear, reliable, and straightforward. Customers don't like to be manipulated and don't appreciate evasiveness. If you get caught being dishonest in any way, you'll not only lose that customer, but the ripple effect of your actions will spread far beyond the borders of that relationship.

Always assume that your customer is smart and give them due respect: don't play games, make sure to deliver on your promises, and avoid nasty surprises. Follow these simple rules and your customer's trust will follow in time.

Ways to mitigate risk and build trust

START SMALL
Don't ask for all the business; ask for a piece of it. Show the customer your capabilities and earn the business over time.

IDENTIFY PARALLEL SITUATIONS
Review a similar situation with the customer and demonstrate how it worked previously.

Managing risk

You know that you are trustworthy, and your customer thinks you are trustworthy. Good start. Being considered trustworthy and actually being trusted to fulfil a million-dollar contract are two different things. US consulting firm Synectics® Inc. carried out some inspired research that accounts for the difference between these two concepts – it is summarized in the trust formula:

$$trust = \frac{credibility \times intimacy}{risk}$$

The formula shows that your ability to demonstrate credibility and build relationships is directly proportional to trust. But trust is inversely proportional to the level of risk involved in making a decision – how much the client has to lose. The top of the equation is within your control. To be successful in sales, you need to demonstrate credibility (see above) and intimacy, which is comprised of behaviours such as empathy, affability, sensitivity, and likeability. Intimacy speaks to how safe and secure it is to work with you.

So it's the lower part of the equation – risk – that's less within your control and works against your ability to build relationships. To be successful, you must effectively learn to manage risk.

With that in mind, you as a salesperson must constantly ask yourself what you can do to make any commitments less risky for the customer. Remember the old adage: "Nobody ever got fired for hiring IBM." That's because the risk was much lower in hiring Big Blue than a less-established high-tech company.

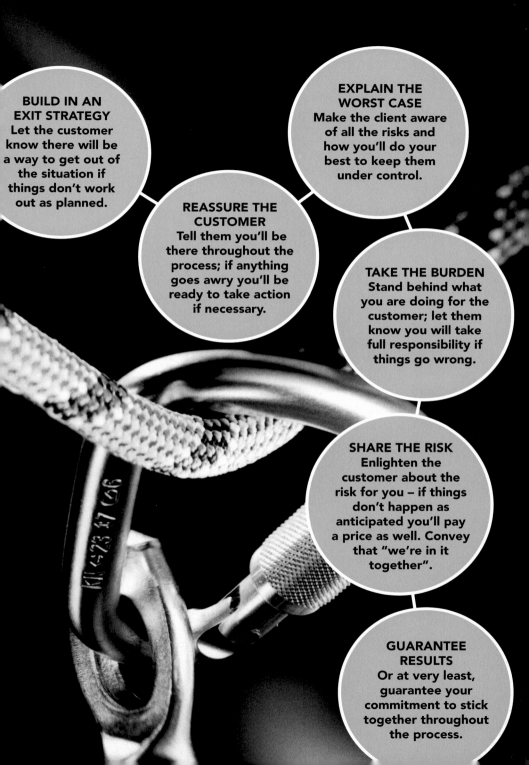

BUILD IN AN EXIT STRATEGY
Let the customer know there will be a way to get out of the situation if things don't work out as planned.

EXPLAIN THE WORST CASE
Make the client aware of all the risks and how you'll do your best to keep them under control.

REASSURE THE CUSTOMER
Tell them you'll be there throughout the process; if anything goes awry you'll be ready to take action if necessary.

TAKE THE BURDEN
Stand behind what you are doing for the customer; let them know you will take full responsibility if things go wrong.

SHARE THE RISK
Enlighten the customer about the risk for you – if things don't happen as anticipated you'll pay a price as well. Convey that "we're in it together".

GUARANTEE RESULTS
Or at very least, guarantee your commitment to stick together throughout the process.

Differentiating yourself

Whether you're selling computer support, pharmaceuticals, or plumbing supplies, chances are that your competitors offer similar products at equal or better prices with identical back-up. You need to do everything to set your product apart from the others, and there is no better way to differentiate your company than through your approach to your customer.

Providing more than the goods

To be a success in sales, you should constantly ask yourself what you can do to add value to the client relationship. If all you do is facilitate the supply of products and services, you are not adding value – just reacting. Even when you provide solutions to known problems, you are still in reactive mode and are not adding much value. This begins only when you help the customer to determine their needs.

The goal is to move up the value chain to become a strategic advisor to your customer – someone the customer calls for guidance, ideas, perspective, insights, and, quite simply, help. Once you rise to that level with a customer, your position is rock solid.

BE FIRST
Do whatever you can to keep yourself on the customer's mind, by emailing or sending personal notes and letters. Your customers don't think about you as much as you think about them, so ensure they think of you first when the opportunity arises. But beware – don't become annoying.

Achieving visibility

Make yourself visible to your customer. To rise to the level of a trusted advisor and differentiate yourself from your competition, visit your customers in person on a regular basis. This approach has many benefits: it strengthens the relationship with your customer; it gives you an opportunity to learn their needs directly and through non-verbal clues; and it enables you to see first hand who your customer regularly interacts with in their organization and the many facets of their work life that remain hidden on the phone.

Surprising your customers

Aim to give your customers something they did not ask for or expect. Let them know that you care a bit more than anyone else, that you are willing to do things others haven't even thought about, and that you are not just concerned about getting the sale. Tom Peters, the world-renowned customer-service guru, talks about "wowing and delighting customers". Showing them you are different can be what ultimately tips the scales in your favour when you and your competitor are running neck and neck.

❓ ASK YOURSELF... AM I "WOWING" MY CUSTOMER?

- Are there any relevant articles or pieces of research that you could send them?
- Can you put them in touch with a third party who can provide something you can't?
- Do you know of any suppliers who could help them reduce their costs?
- Can you help them solve a pressing problem?
- Is there a significant personal event that you could acknowledge?
- Do you know someone who is looking to change careers who they might like to meet?

Chapter 2

Understanding the needs of customers

Almost every sales professional worth his or her salt acknowledges the key importance of understanding their customers' needs. But what does this really mean, and how do you achieve it in the real world?

Implementing the model

The concept of needs-driven or needs-based selling is nothing new. Corporations have always boasted about their ability to develop products that address their customers' needs, and the concept has been incorporated into sales training programmes for decades. Why then, is needs-based selling often so poorly implemented?

PRACTISE YOUR SKILLS

When you are in non-business situations with friends or family, ask yourself what their needs are relative to your discussion. It helps you become better at identifying needs and can make you a better friend.

Breaking the 80/20 rule

"Do you understand all of your customers' needs?" In surveys, more that 80 per cent of salespeople answer "yes" to this question. Yet studies of their customers reveal that, seen from the client's side, only 20 per cent of salespeople are addressing needs. Some people call this startling discrepancy in perceptions the "80/20 rule". As a salesperson, you need to understand why this happens, and what you can do to make sure that you're part of the successful 20 per cent.

Taking your time

So why is it that so many salespeople respond in a way that their clients don't want? The answer is – in part – that they are too eager. Early in a sales meeting, they hear a need from a customer and, with the best of intentions, start to address it, start to provide a solution. "Isn't that what needs-driven selling is all about?", you ask. Not exactly: if you hear a need and respond to it immediately, it's a little like reading the first chapter of a book and drawing conclusions regarding the author's message. You know a bit – but just that; the whole story awaits. Any premature recommendation is likely to miss the mark, resulting in a disappointed customer.

It takes a lot of self-confidence to step back, and admit to yourself and your client that you're not yet prepared to make a recommendation. You need to acknowledge that you don't understand your customer as well as you thought and that you need to ask more questions. This level of humility doesn't come naturally to most salespeople.

? **ASK YOURSELF...**
HOW DO I TUNE IN TO A CLIENT'S NEEDS?

Each time you interact with a customer, ask yourself these types of questions to put yourself in the right mindset:

- What is this person trying to accomplish?
- What does he or she really want from me?
- What are their primary concerns?
- What's holding them back?
- What are they getting/not getting from their current supplier(s)?
- What gaps exist in their current relationship(s)?
- Why are they taking the time to see me?

Seeing the nature of needs

Before you start questioning your customer to uncover their needs, it helps to know what these needs might look like – and how they are likely to present themselves. You'd be surprised at how even the most seasoned sales professionals have difficulty recognizing needs.

Separating needs from solutions

The respected Harvard economist Theodore Levitt famously said: "Nobody needs a drill, they need a hole." In other words, people's real needs are sometimes hidden behind apparent solutions. A simple example may help illuminate what Levitt was getting at. Imagine you own a travel agency. A customer walks in days before the winter holidays; he's in a panic because he hasn't arranged that big holiday he promised his wife and children. You listen patiently. He says the family is so excited, but he's worrried that he's left the arrangements too late. He tells you that the holiday is hard to plan because his three children have such different interests – from going to museums to rock climbing – while his wife just needs to have some down time. He brags about how the cost issue is not a big deal to him.

CASE STUDY

New blood for Citibank

In the early 1980s, Citibank was one of the first major financial organizations to attempt the creation of a unique sales culture. The Consumer Banking Group interviewed many of the largest sales training companies, but – to the surprise of many – hired a young, small and virtually unknown firm to lead the charge. When the decision-maker was asked why she chose that firm, her response was simple: "Of all the firms we interviewed, they did the best job of demonstrating that they understood our needs. And if that's what we want to teach our people, let's go with people who practise what they preach." Enough said.

When salespeople hear stories like this, many immediately start thinking up solutions. "What can we offer him that will address all his issues? If he wants to spend more, let's help him – it's more more commission for us. 'What your family needs, sir, is a spa holiday in Dubai'".

This might indeed be a satisfactory solution, but the salesperson has done little to understand the customer's needs. A little analysis, and further questioning might reveal that the client has a need to impress and be respected by his family; to act quickly; to carve out some adult time on his vacation; to have a safe, supervised environment; and many other needs besides. Taking this longer approach has real benefits: the customer feels understood and valued; he'll buy this vacation from you, and come back for your guidance and advice, year after year.

"My family can't agree on what sort of holiday we should have."

"Katie and Mike love sports but Jack is much happier exploring, and Susan just wants to relax."

"I know I've left it late, but it has to be something that keeps both my kids and my wife happy."

"No problem. Let's start by exploring what you need a little further. What were the best things about your last holiday?"

TIP

BE SENSITIVE

After each meeting, ask yourself what the customer didn't say. You'll probably unearth some needs they did not consciously know they had.

Reading between the lines

Sometimes your customers will tell you exactly what they need. All you have to do is listen and respond. But if you address only these overt needs, you are not adding much value to the client, and you are doing no more than any of your competitors would do. Where you can differentiate yourself – and win the client's respect and trust – is by hearing and responding to implied needs. So your task is to look for the needs behind what the customer says. For example, if the client complains about his boss constantly second guessing him, he may be expressing a need to have a solid, tightly reasoned explanation for his buying decisions. Successful sales professionals know how to uncover these implicit needs – indeed, it is what drives their long-term success.

Selling would be a far easier task if customers could be relied on always to buy for sound business reasons – such as return on investment, quality, value, and competence. If the buyer always made his or her decision dispassionately, rather than based on how that decision made them feel, reading their requirements would be straightforward.

BUSINESS AND PERSONAL NEEDS

Business needs are measurable while personal needs are subjective. Below are some examples of each to illustrate the differences between the two.

BUSINESS NEEDS	PERSONAL NEEDS
Reduce cost	Look good in front of peers
Increase efficiency	Gain recognition
Shorten production time	Get that promotion
Become more effective	Minimize the risk
Increase profitability	Boost personal status
Improve turnaround time	Decrease stress

However, all customers – however company-focused they may be – are to some extent influenced by personal needs. These delve into areas that are harder to quantify – security, connecting with others, ego, and comfort. For this reason, showing empathy with the customer will bring you rich rewards.

Beginning the questioning

Before you begin to question your client to determine their needs, let them know why you need the information, how it will benefit them, and how it relates to the agenda. Explain that by answering your questions they will:
• Help you focus on the right issues
• Allow you to make better recommendations
• Get an opportunity to outline their concerns
• Ensure that you learn about them.
   They are more likely to be open and honest with their answers if they understand the structure of the needs determination process (see right).

Asking, and asking again

Many pieces of research on the selling process point to one simple conclusion: the more questions you ask of your client, the more success you'll enjoy – the person who learns the most needs is primed to win the business. But the corollary is that the longer you manage a relationship, the more likely you are to lose sales. That is because, over time, you become complacent, making assumptions about the customer rather than asking questions. That's why many salespeople report a falling share of sales, just when they thought the relationship was thriving. The bottom line is to keep asking questions consistently, methodically, and creatively.

HOW TO... FIND OUT CLIENT NEEDS

Introduce the questioning session

Ask the right questions

Listen for the needs

Review and check the needs

RECOGNIZE MOTIVES
Look out for customers who are risk averse, or who appear to worry about how they are going to appear; they tend to be driven more by personal needs.

Planning your approach

Most sales managers agree that the margins separating good, very good, and excellent salespeople are not dependent upon what happens face-to-face, but what happens before and after the sales process. You may feel energized and ready to jump straight into a sales meeting with a new customer, but if you spend time planning the content and thinking through the process, your chances of success will be greatly enhanced.

Doing your homework

The first stage of planning is getting your content right – ensuring that you have all the information you need for every stage of the sales process.

Start your preparation by determining the objectives of the meeting, both for you and the customer. Once these are established, ask yourself what you already know about the customer and what you still need to learn. There is no excuse for not knowing what is going on in your customer's industry and marketplace. There are many sources of data that you can tap to make sure you are prepared, including – but not limited to – annual reports, product brochures, articles, press clippings, industry magazines, and trade show summaries. Check out your customer's website

Questions to prepare you for the sales meeting

Who?
- Who makes the decisions?
- Who should I see?
- Who will do what from our side?

What?
- What questions will I ask?
- What drives this customer's decisions
- What ideas will I suggest?
- What objections do I anticipate?

and try to get a sense of what changes are on the horizon in their business. Find out about their competitors, key in on what the marketplace is saying, and understand what your customers are demanding.

If appropriate, think about what you want to recommend to the customer, and the corresponding features and benefits. Try to anticipate objections, and ask yourself what the real issues might be and what answers you may be able to provide.

Preparing the process

Getting the content right is important, but you also need to plan how to manage the selling process – the way you deliver the information. Consider all the stages of the selling process, from opening the meeting to closing the deal. Do you know what you will do and say in each one and how you will manage the transitions between the phases? Feeling relaxed and well prepared is crucial, so rehearse your presentation repeatedly, and ask for feedback from colleagues. Practise delivering your questions, resolving objections, and even closing. This will highlight any areas in which you are less than confident, and reveal any holes in the information you need to succeed.

Where and when?
- Where is the best place to conduct the meeting?
- When would be the most effective time?

Why?
- Why is this approach good for our business?
- Why are we targeting this specific customer?

How?
- How will I run the meeting?
- How can I differentiate us from our competitors?

Making your first move

It has lots of names – the initial contact, the cold call, the first call, the canvas, the exploratory call, and others. That first visit to a prospective customer can be a daunting, even scary, experience for most people early in their careers. The good news is that this does change over time.

HOW TO... MAKE INITIAL IMPACT

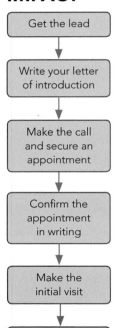

Get the lead

↓

Write your letter of introduction

↓

Make the call and secure an appointment

↓

Confirm the appointment in writing

↓

Make the initial visit

↓

Send a follow-up letter

Finding the way in

You can't set up a first meeting until you have a lead. Experiment with finding different sources of leads:
- Former customers
- Referrals from existing customers
- Newspaper articles and industry publications
- Trade shows/symposiums
- The "dead file" – prospects others have given up on
- Centres of influence (third parties).

Armed with leads, your key prospecting tool will be the letter. You can justify three of these in the prospecting process; one to introduce yourself, one to confirm an appointment to meet, and one to follow up the initial meeting. Emails are fine once you have a relationship, but send a traditional letter for the initial approach – it will set you apart from the competition.

Making an appointment

In some industries, it can be acceptable just to drop by, but regardless of the business you are in, you will be more successful if you obtain an appointment first. Send a confirmation letter, letting the customer know you are looking forward to meeting them and confirm the date, time, and time allocation. Review your own agenda and include some relevant material for the customer to look at. Encourage them to invite anyone who might benefit from attending.

Creating an impression

Your first meeting with a new prospect may have many purposes – from a simple introduction to a full-blown sales call. Whatever happens, stay calm and begin the process of understanding your potential customer's needs. You should try not to present anything specific (although you should be prepared to present your company's credentials, see overleaf). Instead, establish rapport, and let the customer do most of the talking.

Learn what you can about the individual and their business. Look for, and reinforce, common ground. Are they familiar with your company? Is there any relevant history between your organizations that could form a bond? Do you share interests or acquaintances in the industry?

TIP

HAVE FUN
Try thinking of cold calls as fun: you'll never know exactly what to expect, so be ready for anything and take pride in your ability to respond to the situation. It's a new beginning… so be sure to make it a memorable one.

MAKING THE FIRST VISIT

FAST TRACK	**OFF TRACK**
Confirming the meeting in writing to show interest	Just showing up without putting in the preparation time
Being humble – you haven't been there before	Showing unfounded familiarity – it's only the first meeting
Doing your homework and demonstrating what you have learned in preparation for the visit	Treating this meeting as if it were just another meeting
Showing appreciation for the customer taking the meeting	Acting like you are entitled to be there
Asking lots of questions of the customer and letting them talk	Presenting specific recommendations

Opening a sales meeting

When you make an appointment to see a client – whether it is your first or your fiftieth – you are effectively calling a meeting for that customer. For the meeting to run well, you need to take the initiative, while at the same time acknowledging that the meeting belongs to the customer – it must be focused on providing solutions to their problems.

Building rapport

What happens in the first few minutes of a sales visit sets the tone for the entire meeting. It helps to break the opening down into three critical steps: building rapport, confirming the agenda, and moving into the meeting itself.

At the start of the meeting, make sure everyone is comfortable, knows who is who, and has a chance to connect informally. Encourage small talk or a discussion of general business conditions. Use your intuition to decide when to move on – you need to work at your customer's comfort level, not your own. Here are a few ideas to help you get off to a good start:

• Look around the client's office for something to trigger conversation, such as a picture or trophy.
• Compliment the customer on their office or facility – but you must be sincere.
• Thank the customer for their time.
• Discuss something you know about their business – a relevant news event, for example – to show that you've done your homework.

⊗ IN FOCUS...
TALKING TO THE RIGHT PERSON

Surprisingly, two-thirds of all sales calls are made to people who do not make or implement decisions. Salespeople are often reluctant to ask a prospect whether they are speaking to the person who is responsible for calling the shots, for fear of sounding disrespectful. The following preamble can help you check if you're talking to the right person: "I visit many organizations like yours and everyone has their own way of making decisions. To ensure that I don't waste anyone's time or leave someone out of the loop, would you please share with me how the process works here?"

Setting the agenda

Next, ensure that everyone is clear about the objectives of the meeting. Even though this is a sales call, it requires a clear agenda, distributed in advance, that takes into account your needs and your client's (remember, it is their meeting). Give each person the opportunity to express their interest in the meeting and what they would like to get out of it. This is crucial: you may not realize the status or position of a participant in your meeting, and run the risk of missing out on a huge opportunity.

Finally, confirm the time available for the meeting, and stick to it. Customers resent people who overstay their welcome.

Guiding the meeting

Old-style salespeople were loath to lose control of a meeting, and so did all the talking and tried to force the customer on to their agenda. You can see now that this isn't consistent with a problem-solving approach to selling. Instead, you should acknowledge that the meeting belongs to the customer – you are there to solve their problems, after all. Your role is more as facilitator, to ensure that the meeting runs smoothly. Once you begin addressing issues on the agenda, ensure that the meeting stays focused on the stated purposes. Try to draw out ideas from all participants, then move the meeting towards an action plan, and schedule the follow-up.

Roles in the sales meeting

THE SALESPERSON
- **Facilitates the meeting**
- **May take minutes**
- **Participates in finding solutions**

THE CLIENT
- **Owns the problem**
- **May chair the meeting**
- **Participates in finding solutions**

OTHER PARTICIPANTS
- **Participate in finding solutions**
- **Contribute problem-solving resources**

Questioning for needs

Of all the skills demanded of a successful salesperson, questioning remains the most important. This is simply because you can't hope to understand a customer's needs without asking questions in a thoughtful, credible, and sensitive way.

Running the session

When you question a customer at a sales meeting, you need to keep the session light – think of it as an open discussion rather than an interrogation. Comfortable customers invariably reveal more – and more useful – information.

The questions you ask to determine needs fall into three broad categories – fact-finding questions, needs-oriented questions, and big-picture questions – each of which are considered below. There are no hard-and-fast rules about the types of question to ask

CASE STUDY

Asking the right questions

One of the classic stories in the sales business recalls how Pepsi Cola won the airline business from Coca Cola in the 1990s. At the time, Coca Cola owned the in-flight business and there was no way Pepsi could win the business in a price war. The new national sales manager was about to make his first call on one of the airlines and had prepared a lavish and thoughtful presentation. At the last minute, one of his internal resources suggested that they show up with only a pad and pen – no presentation at all.

Against his better instincts, he agreed. For two hours, all they did was ask questions and learn about the airline. They hardly mentioned Pepsi. They learned that beyond ensuring safety, the biggest need the airline had was to sell more tickets. They had uncovered a critical need that they had to meet if they were to be successful in their bid for the business.

They developed a plan to give retailers coupons that allowed them to buy airline tickets at a discount: at the time, this was a unique approach that departed from the pattern of typical promotions. The airlines loved the idea, awarded Pepsi the business, and in the first year alone were able to sell more than $2 million in additional tickets. A legendary result.

your customer, but experience suggests that a ratio of around five fact-finding questions, to three needs-oriented-questions, and one big-picture question is comfortable for the client and achievable for you.

Finding the facts

To scope out an account or manage a relationship, you need some fundamental pieces of information about the client – their customers, partners, suppliers; their company structure; number of employees; and so on. These questions may seem obvious, but it's surprising how often they are overlooked. These are usually closed questions that can be answered "yes" or "no" or with a fact. Their job is to elicit information, so they tend not to be all that imaginative (virtually everybody asks them), but can be surprisingly provocative (for example, "Who makes the decisions here?"). They are essential but won't do a whole lot to differentiate you from your competition.

Probing the needs

Needs-oriented questions get the customer talking and are far more open-ended. They can be quite imaginative – "If you could change one thing about the way you do business today, what would that be?" – or even provocative. Typically, these questions do not have "right" or "wrong" answers; they open up new areas of discussion, and will absolutely help differentiate you from your competition.

Responses from the customer will encompass everything from their objectives, goals, hopes, expectations, and aspirations to their problems, concerns, worries, and fears. As your relationship with the client evolves, you can ask progressively deeper questions that will help reinforce trust.

TIP

LEARN FROM THE PROS

Watch the great interviewers on television. They ask short questions and don't give the person being interviewed possible answers. They ask a question and stop talking; try the same technique.

Learning about the big picture

Big-picture questions position you to uncover needs that the customer does not necessarily know he or she has. They are strategic in nature, in essence asking the customer to think about things that they may not like to consider – the future of the business, difficulties to be overcome, the need to plan, contingencies, and long-term goals. Big-picture questions require planning on your part because they can lead to uncomfortable – albeit valuable – discussions. They are necessarily thought-provoking, and will stay in the customer's mind for a long time. They elevate the conversation, and will eventually result in your being perceived as an advisor or consultant – much more than a salesperson.

TIP

BEWARE OF THE WHY?
Be careful of questions that begin with a "why" – they can appear judgemental and condescending and can put people on the defensive. It helps to introduce these types of questions with a preamble.

Planning the ask

Most people are naturally suspicious of questions. When determining needs, you should be as sensitive as possible during the process of questioning your client.
• Give a preamble: let the customer know that questions are coming, why you are asking, and how it is in their interests to answer.
• Cluster questions into categories, focusing on strategy, finance, inventory, and so on, each with its own preamble.
• Be straightforward in your questions.
• Don't shy away from the tough questions.

Questions to investigate the client's needs

FACT FINDING
- What are your annual sales?
- Who are your current suppliers?
- How often do you purchase?
- How much do you have with this account?
- Who makes the decisions?

NEEDS ORIENTED
- What are your expectations of someone like me?
- What changes are you initiating to stay competitive?
- How has globalization impacted your business?
- What are some of the biggest challenges you face today?
- How has your customer base changed?

BIG PICTURE
- What is your vision for the company?
- Where would you like the company to be in five years?
- What obstacles could prevent that from happening?
- How do you see yourself leveraging your strengths in the long term?
- How will you ensure that you benefit from globalization?

Listening to your client

You can ask your client brilliantly incisive questions to determine their needs. But these are worth little if you don't listen to their responses. Listening isn't easy – studies reveal that we retain a tiny percentage of what we hear – but it is a critical skill for any salesperson.

ASK FIRST
Always ask if it's OK to make notes and show respect for confidentiality. Clients will rarely decline and will probably be flattered that you want to record what they say.

Keeping tuned in

As a salesperson, you are the eyes and ears of your organization; what you learn about your client in a sales meeting will make your company stand or fall. You should be listening at a high level all the time – collecting facts, information, and business-related concepts – but most of all, listening for needs. Of course, this is the ideal scenario, and in reality your ability to listen is jeopardized by many factors. Instead of listening, you may start anticipating the next question, planning your response, or trying to understand what the customer meant. You may get distracted thinking about your route home or tomorrow's meetings; and there are biological reasons why attentive listening is harder than it seems – we think much faster than we can talk. But whatever your reason for tuning out, you can be sure that when you do, you're missing vital information.

CASE STUDY

Showing interest
Four out of five clients think that when you don't make notes, you aren't fully engaged. This research is borne out by a story related by a sales manager, who, along with a colleague, began a sales meeting with a prospective client. Neither was taking notes. After a few awkward minutes, the client called his assistant on the phone and said: "Please bring two pads and two pens for our guests as I would like to have the impression that they are at least somewhat interested in what I have to say." This is a true story – don't let this happen to you!

Making notes

There are many ways to enhance your listening skills, of which one of the best known is Active Listening* – a concept that has been around more than half a century and is explored in dozens of courses and books. A simple, and arguably more effective technique can be set out in just two words – Take Notes, or more accurately, Make Notes. From the minute the customer starts talking, you should put pen to paper. The distinction between "making" and "taking" notes is important because you are doing more than just recording the client's words – you are jotting down any connections you make, and capturing on paper the need, the concern, the issue, the opportunity. Don't analyze too much – there will be plenty of time for that later.

   The discipline of making notes has further benefits – it stops you from trying to respond too early, and it ensures that you listen to the customer throughout the meeting – it's a fact that many people "save the best for last", revealing their deepest needs towards the end of a conversation. If you present too early, chances are you'll miss hearing vital information.

*Active Listening — *a structured form of listening that focuses attention on the speaker. A listener consciously attends fully to the speaker and then repeats in their own words what he or she thinks the speaker has said, often interpreting the speaker's words in terms of feelings.*

Approaching a problem

Bringing a problem-solving approach into your dealings with customers has clear benefits. But how do you put it into practice? Problem-solving seems intangible and difficult, but following a structured process, such as the technique of brainstorming, will bring focus to your interactions with customers and increase your chances of sales success.

TIP

MAKE SPACE FOR INNOVATION
Don't overdefine a problem. Usually, if people learn too much about a problem, they will become less willing to speculate and will find themselves putting on the same blinkers that the problem owner already has.

Setting the scene

Problem solving requires creativity – but that doesn't mean chaos. When you bring together a group to develop creative solutions, you need to give the meeting structure. Be sure to define the task, decide what approach you will use and how much time is available, and establish who is chairing, facilitating, and minuting the meeting.

Next, the group should identify the problem and set it into a proper context of background information. Why is the problem a problem? Could it be turned into an opportunity? Has the problem been addressed before, and how? Who is responsible for results? Once the meeting has been staged and the problem defined, the group is ideally positioned to generate ideas through brainstorming.

IN FOCUS... BRAINSTORMING

When it is done right, the technique of brainstorming taps people's capacity for lateral thinking and free association and boosts creative output. The concept was conceived in the 1920s by Alex Osborn, partner in international advertising agency BBDO (he was the "O" in the company). Osborn summarized the technique in the statement: "It is easier to tone down a wild idea than to think up a new one." Many precede their brainstorming sessions with creativity or relaxation exercises to help participants move into a more creative state.

Encouraging creative solutions

When you begin a brainstorming session, invite ideas, perspectives, recommendations, and insights. Encourage participants to be speculative and open – the meeting should be energetic, exciting, and fun. Resist any temptation to evaluate ideas as soon as they are put forward – anything goes. The opportunity to be innovative invariably yields richer results than if individuals feel constrained by rules or limitations.

Evaluating results

Brainstorming is a great way to spend the first half of a problem-solving session. The second part must be devoted to selecting the most exciting ideas and evaluating them diligently to develop solutions.

The evaluation process doesn't have to be complex, but it does have to be managed with care. Once an idea has been selected, the challenge becomes how to turn it into a solution.

One of the most common approaches suggests first identifying the appealing aspects of an idea and then listing concerns. Identifying the positives ensures that the parts of the idea that you want to save are captured and preserved. Then address each concern, beginning with the most troubling, until the idea becomes acceptable. At this point, when the idea has been transformed into a solution, carefully summarize your conclusions and put together a specific action plan that includes the next steps to implement the results.

Reviewing needs

The perfect way to complete the needs assessment and move into the presentation phase is to demonstrate to the customer that you have been listening, that you understand what they have been saying, and that you're in tune with what they hope to accomplish.

TIP

SEEK CONFIRMATION

If there are several people in the room, check with each of them that your understanding of the needs matches theirs. Just because one person agrees with you doesn't mean they all do.

Selling before presenting

Everything you have done up to this point has been focused on learning the needs of your customer. But before you start to present your solutions, you should demonstrate a clear understanding of his or her situation. If you review the needs well, you'll demonstate credibility, empathy, sensitivity, and trustworthiness – and many buyers will make their decision to buy at this point, even before you have presented your goods and services. Conversely, without thoroughly reviewing the needs, you risk misunderstanding your client and missing the mark with your recommendations.

CHOOSING YOUR WORDS

FAST TRACK

OFF TRACK

FAST TRACK	OFF TRACK
"Here's my understanding of what you said…"	"What you need is…"
"I may be reading too much into this, but it appears that…"	"You said that…"
"How I interpreted X's statement was that you had a desire to…"	"X told us that you wanted…"

IN FOCUS...
THE PSYCHOLOGY OF LISTENING

Carl Rogers (1902–1987) was one of the world's greatest psychologists and students of human communication. He famously said that the "greatest compliment one human being can pay another is to demonstrate that he was listening." When a sales professional takes the time to review with a customer his or her understanding of that customer's needs, they are indeed paying a great compliment and differentiating themselves – yet again – from the competition in an emphatic manner.

Ensuring a close match

When you begin the review, choose your words carefully: tell the client what you heard as opposed to what they said. The distinction is subtle, but avoids putting words in the client's mouth (see box, opposite). Start by summarizing the client's overt needs and move to those you need to infer. Ask the client to confirm that your review is correct, and request that they prioritize their needs. Ask if you missed anything, if there's anything they'd like to add, or if your understanding is flawed. You just might pick up another need along the way.

Timing the review

The best time to review needs is either at the end of a needs-determination meeting or at the beginning of a meeting in which you are presenting (especially if new people are present, or a lot of time has passed since the last meeting). Concluding a meeting by reviewing needs ends it on a positive note and sets the stage for the next meeting when you will present. If you have done everything right, the client will already have a strong inclination to buy from you.

Selling with others

Bringing a colleague with you – whether it's your manager, a subject expert, another member of the team, or the new salesperson who just joined the company – can potentially make your sales meeting much more effective. However, joint sales meetings need to be managed carefully if they are to live up to their potential.

TALK UP YOUR COLLEAGUES
When you introduce your colleagues on a joint call, emphasize why it is important that they have been able to come along. For example: "I'm delighted Susan could join us – she has been working on these kinds of problems for 15 years."

Being prepared

Preparation is the key to effective joint sales meetings. Firstly, anyone you bring with you to the meeting needs to have a full understanding of its objective. At the very least, they need to know who the customer is, what they do, where you are in the relationship, and what you hope to accomplish. Equally importantly, your colleagues need to be clear about what their role in the meeting will be, or you run the risk that they will be unprepared. Are they there to ask questions, make recommendations, help deal with objections, or just to show support and interest?

Managing a joint meeting

In a joint sales meeting, it is even more important that you act as the facilitator, managing the process and trying to ensure that the meeting fulfils both your own objectives and your customer's. Get the meeting off to a positive start by inviting introductions: make sure that everyone knows who everyone else is, and that they are clear about what each party hopes to accomplish. During the meeting, it is important that every member of your team makes a contribution, so call on your colleagues when their expertise is needed, and explain why: "I would like John to answer that question as it falls within his area of expertise".

Benefits of joint sales meetings

SPECIALIST KNOWLEDGE
Inviting colleagues from different functional areas of your organization to join you at the meeting allows you to offer a greater range of expertise to the customer.

LOOKING GOOD
Bringing a team – especially if it includes senior members of your organization – may impress the customer, and make them feel that they are important to you.

TWO PAIRS OF EARS
Sales meetings can be fast paced, especially if you are acting as the facilitator. If you have a colleague with you, they can pick up on small details that you may miss.

DIFFERENT PERSPECTIVES
With more than one of you interpreting what the customer is saying, you may get a fuller understanding of the customer's needs.

IMPROVING PERFORMANCE
Your colleagues can give you feedback on your performance, enabling you to be even more effective at your next sales meeting.

Chapter 3

Making your recommendations

Providing solutions and making recommendations is the part of the selling process that most salespeople like best. It's time to demonstrate how you can help the customer, to tell your story, and present your products and services.

Using features and benefits

Client presentations take many forms; they range from informal one-to-one meetings to formal expositions to a conference room full of potential clients. Surprisingly, regardless of the situation, your approach will not vary that much: your presentation will focus on features and benefits.

Defining the terms

Salespeople have used features and benefits to describe their products and services for many decades. This approach has stood the test of time for one reason – it works!

Features tell customers how products or services work. They are characteristics, descriptions, attributes, specifications, and explanations. Benefits explain how the product helps – why it is important to the client and how it addresses their needs. Benefits set out to the customer the value of the item being discussed and why it is in their interests to purchase it.

Selling the benefits

People make the decision to buy things because of their benefits rather than their features. However, most salespeople are more comfortable talking about features than benefits. It's not hard to see why. Features are facts and hard to debate. You will rarely be challenged when you explain the features of a product or service – they are tangible and objectively notable.

Benefits, on the other hand, are educated guesses. They are subjective – what might be a benefit for one person may not be a benefit for another. Talking benefits makes some people uncomfortable because it feels like a "hard sell". It shouldn't. Benefits do no more than explain why a recommendation makes sense.

When you make your presentation, think in terms of benefit statements, and always try to link your features to the benefits. If you don't, you're only telling half the story. The example below – where a salesperson presents a new design of conference chair – shows the types of connections to make.

Linking features and benefits

FEATURE OF CHAIR	BENEFIT OF CHAIR
Neat, stackable design	Saves space, making it ideal for even the smallest venues
Metal legs	Durable – has a lifespan twice as long as close competitors, saving money
Stiffened back	Enhanced comfort and better sitting position – ideal for longer conferences
Discreet handle	Easy to carry and reposition – gives more flexibility at the venue.

Targeting the pitch

Features and benefits are the trusted selling tools that address the client's questions "What?" and "So what?" But if you can answer one further question – "What's in it for me?" – you'll set yourself apart from the competition. This question addresses the specific benefit – the particular needs of an individual customer.

TIP

HOLD BACK THE BROCHURE

Try using your sales brochure only after you have presented, not before. Highlight the areas where your products meet the client's needs.

Focusing on specifics

Your ability to express the features and benefits of your products is vital, but there's one more conceptual step to take – understanding and presenting specific benefits. Every customer buys for slightly different reasons: some base their decisions on quality, convenience, and price; others on the level of service, or personal reasons that reflect how they feel about themselves. Specific benefits speak to the confirmed, most important, needs of a particular client; they differ from generic benefits, which make broader statements about the value of a product or service.

Prioritizing your messages

Information about your products and services and their corresponding features and benefits is fixed information – it's what you might include in your brochure, spec sheet, or catalogue. In contrast, the needs of each customer and the specific benefits you present are variable. This variable information is at the heart of the needs-driven selling process – it's what elevates your presentation far above the canned pitch.

So, when the time comes to present, deliver the variable information first. Start by succinctly reviewing the customer's needs; next, make recommendations and demonstrate how they address the customer's needs – the specific benefits. Only when this is done should you move on to presenting the generic features and benefits. At first glance, this ordering of the information appears back-to-front – going from the specific to the general. However, it addresses the reality of your audience's attention span. High-level listening efficiency lasts a frighteningly short time – up to 90 seconds – before dipping precipitously. Specific benefits are what close deals, so be sure to get them in early, before your client's attention wanders.

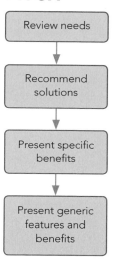

**HOW TO...
ORDER
YOUR
PITCH**

Review needs

Recommend solutions

Present specific benefits

Present generic features and benefits

 IN FOCUS... THE HUMAN TOUCH

Back in the 1960s, social forecasters were predicting that salespeople would be made obsolete by the turn of the century through advances in computing and revolutionary marketing vehicles, such as direct mail and telemarketing. They could not have been more wrong. More people are selling today than ever before, and even professions that never considered using the "s" word in the past, such as banking, accounting, law, and medicine, find themselves soliciting business on a day-to-day basis. That's because the consumer does not want to buy from a catalogue, a piece of mail, or a voice on the telephone. They want to buy from a person who listens to them, understands their needs, and responds with appropriate products and services.

Offering your ideas

Many sales professionals think that all they have to offer is their products and services. But it's not just what's in your bag that's important – it's what's in your head. When you present your customer with an idea that helps them do their job a bit better, teaches them something new, or addresses a personal issue, you are building value in your relationship that lets you leapfrog way ahead of your competitors.

Giving to receive

When a sales professional presents a customer with an idea that has no revenue attached to it, it's called an uncompensated idea. This is a great misnomer because surprising your customers with novel and unexpected thinking accumulates great value and brings long-term financial reward. If you're prepared to give, you will receive.

ASK YOURSELF... ABOUT OFFERING NEW IDEAS

Before each client meeting, think of areas in which you could help the client by offering uncompensated ideas.

- Are they doing something that we know they could do better with better technology or software?
- What problems do they consistently raise – how hard is it for me to research them?
- Is there something in the client's non-working life where I could offer an idea – for example, suggesting a venue for their child's party?
- Is there something about the client's facility that could be improved – a lack of signage, for example?
- Can I enhance the client's industry knowledge – by recommending a good seminar or training programme?

Salespeople are reluctant to present uncompensated ideas for fear that they will come across as inappropriate or embarrassing. So is it really worth taking the risk of crossing established boundaries? The answer is an emphatic "yes". When the customer sees that you have put in effort to offer a new perspective they will know that you value the relationship – even if they're not keen on the idea itself.

Adding value

The idea you offer up doesn't have to be related to business and it doesn't need to be Earth-shattering; however, it must add value – don't present an idea just for the sake of doing so. Your customer doesn't know that you're about to offer an uncompensated idea, so before starting, get their permission. Let them know you have been thinking about their situation and that you have an idea for them. Ask if they think it's appropriate for you to present it. Most customers will be intrigued. Next, express what you think their need is, present the idea, and explain its specific benefits. Be humble when you offer the idea and give credit to others whenever you can; there's nothing to be gained by trying to make the customer think that you're smarter than they are.

TIME YOUR TIPS
Uncompensated ideas are best unveiled at the end of the meeting, not the beginning. They offer a great way to end any meeting on a high note.

CASE STUDY

Going the extra mile
A US training company was seeking bids for a new video system. They spoke to three potential suppliers, each of whom made good recommendations. There was little to choose between the three on price, quality, capabilities, and service agreements. While they were in the decision-making process, the salesperson from one of the three suppliers emailed an article that appeared in *The Wall Street Journal* that day about one of the training company's clients. The email was accompanied by a short note: "I'm sure you saw this, but just in case...". Without other differentiators, the salesperson who took the extra step won the contract.

Asking for feedback

You have delivered your presentation. Your customers nodded enthusiastically throughout, so your recommendations must have been spot on. Or so you think. The only way to be sure and to move to the next stage of the selling process is to ask your client for feedback. It's time to hear from them.

TIP

GET YOUR TIMING RIGHT

You can ask for feedback at any time in your presentation. It's best to wait until you are finished so you don't get derailed, but if you suspect that the customer has a strong concern, ask for feedback earlier.

Facing the music

Even seasoned salespeople will hesitate before asking the customer to respond to their recommendations. A lot of time went into getting to this point and the fear of rejection can be paralyzing. No matter how many times you tell yourself that it's not you that's being rejected but your product or idea, it's hard not to take it personally. But don't make the mistake of delivering your recommendations and then saying… nothing, and just waiting to hear from the customer. If you don't ask, you don't learn. Even if the answer may not be what you were hoping for, ask the question and move on.

Welcoming objections

When you ask for feedback, the response you get is usually an objection; you should accept now that people almost always object even when they are convinced they want to buy. There are complex reasons for this, and techniques for resolving objections will be explored in the next chapter. But for now, you should welcome the objection. If you had not given an opportunity for the objection to surface, it would have still existed in the customer's mind, and you would never have closed the deal. With the objection out in the open, you have a chance to work with the customer to resolve it.

Asking open questions

You will get better feedback if you ask the right questions. It's hard to rebound from a blunt "No" so use open-ended questions to elicit responses from the customer that you can work with. Your questions should be non-manipulative and straightforward: slippery sales patter like "Sounds pretty good doesn't it?" may antagonize the customer, so frame questions in a way that maintains the high level of dialogue that got you to this point.

"What do you think about our recommendation?"

"I've been talking for a while; now I'd love to hear from you."

"I would appreciate some feedback."

"I'd love to hear your reaction."

"So, what are your thoughts?"

"How does that sound?"

"Any questions?"

Chapter 4

Resolving objections and closing the sale

Resolving objections is often the most challenging part of the sales process – it can be uncomfortable and unpredictable. But understanding the situation and practising your responses will help you perform well when you encounter resistance.

Understanding objections

Up to this point in the needs-driven selling model, your role has been that of facilitator and advisor. Now, when you start to encounter objections from the client, the role can feel a lot more like selling. However, there's no reason to freeze and miss the opportunity.

Making buying decisions

Most people object to a selling proposal even though they are interested in buying. It's human nature. The lesson to learn is that not all objections are as bad as they first appear, and most can be resolved.

So why do buyers object when they're ready to buy? Most are simply looking for reassurance from the salesperson; they want to feel like they are making good, thoughtful, reasonable decisions, and they don't want to think that they are being hasty or foolish. They know that they will start questioning themselves soon after they make the purchase.

You may have heard some of the terms associated with this phenomenon, such as buyer's remorse and cognitive dissonance*. When you make a decision to buy, especially when spending a lot of money, you may experience a sense of disequilibrium. Part of you feels good about the purchase, but part isn't so sure. It's not a comfortable feeling. Professional buyers are also subject to these feelings, so to protect themselves and feel like they are doing the right thing, they object – even when they may be ready to buy.

*Cognitive dissonance — *a feeling of tension that arises when you keep two conflicting thoughts in mind simultaneously.*

Reacting to resistance

Most salespeople react in one of three ways when faced with objections – becoming defensive, aggressive, or simply giving up. None of these is constructive, and none is likely to help you close the deal. To stop falling into one of these traps, do what you do best – problem solve with the customer.

The three common responses to resistance

BECOMING AGGRESSIVE
This suggests that you must convince the customer you're right – and by implication that they are wrong. This doesn't encourage discussion.

GETTING DEFENSIVE
This sends out the message that the process is more about you than the client.

BECOMING PASSIVE
Giving up is worst of all. For all you know there may be considerable interest.

TIP

GET EXPERT HELP
Use all your resources when you encounter difficult objections. Consult with your colleagues, and invite experts to the presentation if you need support in specific areas.

Approaching conflict

Dealing with customers' objections is less daunting when you stick to a process derived from proven conflict-management techniques. This helps you focus on the objective, maintain your professionalism, and curbs your tendency to react too quickly.

Before introducing the objection-resolution model, there are two assumptions that you need to accept. Firstly, many, if not most, objections are unfulfilled needs. Needs are motivational in nature and when you don't meet them to the customer's satisfaction, they usually appear later as objections. Put another way, if you don't discover all the needs, you risk being blindsided later by an objection.

The second assumption – which may seem counterintuitive – is that most objections indicate interest at some level. Indifference and apathy are the reactions you want to see least in response to your recommendations. When the client complains about something, at least they care about the outcome. Taking the customer's objection as a good sign will encourage you to work to resolve it. It's a healthy way to approach conflict.

You don't have to accept these assumptions at face value, but work with them and decide later whether or not you agree.

 IN FOCUS...
JUSTIFYING DECISIONS

People's desire to resolve the cognitive dissonance that accompanies buying decisions is illuminated by an observation from the advertising industry. A person is more likely to read an ad for a major purchase – such as an automobile – after they have bought the product than before the purchase. Reading the ad reinforces the correctness of the decision made in the buyer's mind.

Introducing the process

When you encounter resistance, start by acknowledging what the customer has said without responding to it with offence or defence. Next, ask questions to learn the totality of the objection. Make sure that you have heard and understood the entire issue. Review your understanding with the customer of what is troubling them. Sometimes, you will simply need to paraphrase the objection in order to clarify it; at other times, you will have to reframe the objection and transform it into a need that you can address. Next, address the concern as effectively as you can in order to resolve it. If the customer accepts your response, you should determine if there are other concerns. If there are, repeat the process. If there are none, close the sale.

Resolving objections is a linear process, similar in many ways to the needs-driven selling model as a whole. As with any other linear process, you don't have to use every step to succeed, but having a well-defined process to which to refer will help you deal with what most people find to be the hardest component of the sales process.

TIP

STEER TOWARDS A SOLUTION

Think of yourself as a facilitator when you resolve objections. It's your job to lead the way as you navigate towards resolution.

ASK YOURSELF... ABOUT YOUR BUYING BEHAVIOUR

You can learn about your client's attitudes by reviewing how you react when you make a significant purchase.

- What reasons do I come up with to delay or prevent a buying decision?
- How much is my behaviour shaped by the salesperson?
- Do I object because it helps me feel more confident about my purchase?
- Do I object because I want to test the salesperson?
- How do I react to an aggressive sell?

Collecting the data

The first two steps in the objection resolution process are acknowledging the client's objections and asking them to elaborate on their concerns. Posing the right questions helps you collect the critical data you need to understand and deal with the customer's objection.

TIP

TRANSFER YOUR SKILLS

Acknowledging is more than just a tool for use in the selling process – it is a life skill. Use it with your significant others, colleagues, children, even strangers. When you acknowledge how someone may feel, good things usually follow.

Acknowledging objections

Your aim at this point is to encourage your customer to open up about their objections. To begin this process, you should acknowledge their concerns: this doesn't mean agreeing with their objections (which would suggest a lack of conviction on your part) or implying that you disagree (which would set the scene for confrontation). Instead, simply recognize their right to object, demonstrate empathy, and show that you are amenable to discussing the situation. They will see that you are willing, and hopefully able, to solve the problem.

A good technique for acknowledging objections is to reflect the customer's own language in your response. Aim to paraphrase their objection, without being patronizing. For example, if they bring up the objection that your product is far too expensive, you could reply "I recognize that expense is a big concern for you."

Below are some examples of the types of phrases you can use to acknowledge objections:
• "I can see why…"
• "I appreciate that investing in our system may seem daunting…"
• "That's a fair question…"
• "I think I understand why you might feel that way based on what you've heard so far…"
• "I appreciate your candour…"
• "I guess I wasn't as clear as I wanted to be…"

Questioning the client

The customer's stated objections are often just the tip of the iceberg. They may not be expressing all their concerns, or may be masking their true objections. To get to the bottom of their concerns, you need to start asking questions. Keep these questions crisp, open-ended, and void of content so that you don't "lead the witness". For example, if a client voices a general objection, don't ask, "Is it the price?" This will succeed only in making them suspicious of price – you will have given them another reason not to buy! Instead, try something like: "Could you be more specific?" This will encourage the customer to elaborate without giving them new reasons to object. Similar question phrasings include:

- "Would you please elaborate?"
- "Can you say a little more about that?"
- "How come?"
- "I'm not sure I understand. Could you clarify?"

BE RESTRAINED
Don't go too far in expressing your desire to work with a prospect – it can work against you.

ASKING QUESTIONS

FAST TRACK	**OFF TRACK**
Being objective	Appearing judgemental
Staying in control	Displaying emotion
Asking open-ended questions	Asking leading questions or patronizing the client
Being straightforward	Being perceived as manipulative
Using appreciative phrases	Being an interrogator

Being sensitive

When you deal with the client's objections, don't forget that you are in conflict resolution mode and sensitivity on your part is not only desirable but critical. The questioning process must not seem like an interrogation – it needs to be a comfortable experience for the customer so he or she will explain their concerns and continue the dialogue. Like so much of what impacts the sales process, it's how you do it that matters most.

Accepting objections

Of course, there are times when you should agree with what the customer is saying, but without closing off the conversation. For example, if your product is more expensive than the competition's and you are unable to shift on price, your reply could be: "Yes, it is expensive, but I hope you think it's worth discussing its cost in respect of what it can do for you."

 IN FOCUS...
CROSSING THE LINE

Almost any positive behaviour can become a negative one when used in excess. It's great to be curious until you become nosy. You should be assertive but not aggressive. By all means be pleasant; but stay away from obsequious. Be empathetic and customer focused, but don't appear patronizing. Take a position, but don't become dogmatic. And of course be tenacious, just don't get stubborn. These distinctions become particularly important when resolving conflict, but if you trust your instincts and build on them with experience, you'll be right a lot more than you'll be wrong.

BE POSITIVE
Let your customer know that you appreciate their insights by interspersing your questions with appreciative phrases such as: "Thank you" and "That's very helpful".

BE DIRECT
Clearly signal your intentions using phrases such as: "I'd like to ask another question or two in order to..." to make the climate more conducive to problem solving.

Encouraging the customer to open up

INTRODUCE YOUR QUESTIONS
Give reasons for why you need the information to help to diffuse suspicion and put the customer at ease. If your customer raises the objection that your solution is complicated, respond with: "Yes, it is complex – but it's also very manageable. Can we discuss this further...?"

MIRROR THE CLIENT
If the client becomes obstructive and puts you on the back foot, try mirroring his or her objections. For example, counter "Your suggestion is ridiculous" with "Why do you think this seems ridiculous?" Do this in a non-judgemental way that conveys your real curiosity about the answer.

BE SILENT
Sometimes, and especially when a client reacts in an inappropriately strong manner, being silent is the best option. Silence can defuse the situation and give the client time to realize that his or her behaviour is not contributing to a resolution.

Reframing objections

By this time, you have heard the customer's objections to your proposal. Most – but not all – objections that you will hear from clients are really disguised, unfulfilled needs. So the next step of the selling process is reframing* the objections as needs.

Translating into needs

*Reframing — *the art of turning a negative into a positive, changing the apparently unresolvable into the possible.*

Objections from customers are barriers to progress, whereas needs are aspirational, so it follows that turning objections into needs makes them easier to discuss and resolve. These examples illustrate how objections in fact mask needs:

• A client complains about the high complexity of your proposal: what he may need is a clearer explanation of how it works pitched at his own level.
• A client recounts a bad experience of a purchase similar to the one you are proposing: what she may need is reassurance that it won't happen again.
• A client laments the difficulty of changing their in-house systems: he may need to understand that you can help to facilitate the process.

CUSTOMER We've used our existing suppliers for eight years

SALESPERSON Naturally, you need to know that the work is secure in our hands

CUSTOMER It's not workable – you're based too far from our offices

SALESPERSON There's a need to identify tasks that demand close collaboration

You can reframe almost any objection into an invitational question that asks how something can be done as opposed to why it can't. An objection like "My manager will never go for this" becomes "It appears to me that there's a need to establish a rock-solid business case for this purchase."

When you reframe a client's objection you are changing the tone of what they said, and you should avoid putting words into their mouth – note the use of "it appears to me" in the example above.

TIP

KEEP TRYING
Don't worry if the way you reframe the objection is off target. Ask the customer to correct you and keep trying until you get it right.

Setting objectives

When you reframe the concern as a need, make sure it is a need that you are able to address. For example, don't say something like "It seems like you need to get a lower price" if you can't move on price. Instead, try "As I understand, you need to see more clearly the cost/value equation here."

After you have reframed the objection, confirm with the customer that they agree with your interpretation. You have now converted their objection into a new objective – with the client's agreement you can now move towards meeting the objective and edge closer to closing the deal.

CASE STUDY

Reframing for success
Reframing is not restricted to selling situations. A multi-billion dollar company was in the process of selecting a new CEO: during the interviews, one of the leading candidates was challenged by the chairman. The candidate had a reputation for risk taking, and the chairman expressed his worries about his judgement in financial decisions. The candidate's reframe went something like this: "My impression is that you're concerned about my reputation for trying new things and need to feel comfortable that when it comes to financial decisions I will demonstrate the fiduciary responsibility that the job demands. Is that correct?" He gave a great response and two days later he got the job.

Discussing price

Customers will always complain about price. Indeed, price resistance is the most common objection salespeople will encounter, and can be the hardest to resolve. However, as with other types of objection, understanding why the customer is objecting and turning that objection into a need can be an effective way of managing the resistance.

BE CLEAR ABOUT THE VALUE

Don't confuse price with value: people are always willing to pay more if they understand the value they are getting for their money.

Understanding price resistance

Everyone wants to find a good deal and feel like they are getting a keen price. However, objections about price are sometimes used as a convenient and acceptable reason to object, but are a smokescreen to mask other issues. In these situations, it is important that you question your customer to determine what the underlying issue really is. At other times, however, the objection truly is all about price. In instances where the buyer is making his or her decision on price alone, there may be little leeway for negotiation, and you may choose to walk away from the relationship.

Pre-empting the objection

If you have undergone a thorough needs determination, when you make a recommendation your customer should not be surprised or shocked about the price. Needs determination should include a discussion of what the customer is currently paying or expects to pay. Questioning the customer about their budget or pricing guidelines will help you recommend a price that is close to what is expected. If the customer won't answer your questions, give them a "sense of" cost: "Just so you know, a programme like this typically costs £100. How does that sound?" You will quickly find out whether this is a long way from what they expect to pay.

Resolving price objections

The objection-resolution process is your best tool in dealing with price objections. Firstly, acknowledge the objection as you would any other, for example: "I know you are trying to keep costs down." Next, get the customer talking. Ask questions, and find out about any other offers they have had from your competitors – how do they compare to yours? Are the deals comparable with yours in terms of the value delivered? Learn as much as you can regarding how far off you are in price from other offers.

When resolving price objections, reframing the objection is critical. Do everything you can to turn your customer's objection into need, using phrases such as: "So if I understand you correctly, you need to know what you will get for the additional 10 per cent", "My understanding is that you need to understand why we charge a bit more than X and why it's still in your interest to buy from us...", or "It appears to me that you need to feel comfortable with your decision to pay us more than some of our competitors..."

If the customer agrees with your reframe, go ahead and address the need. Give it your best shot, and see if they will accept your point of view. You will be surprised how an objection often turns out to be less significant than it originally appeared to be.

TIP

CHOOSE YOUR QUESTIONS CAREFULLY

Getting a customer to elaborate about price or cost issues is a delicate matter. Be sensitive in your approach, using questions such as "How far off are we?" or "Can you tell us a bit more?"

 IN FOCUS... LOWERING YOUR PRICE

The last thing you should do is lower your price without taking something off the table. If you provide a quote and a customer objects and you then subsequently drop your price, the message is clear – you were charging too much originally. This sentiment can have serious negative impact on further business and how you are perceived. If you do have to lower your price (which happens), let the customer know what you have to remove or reduce from the original proposal. As a last resort, let them know you are lowering the price to earn your way in, but that the original price was fair and this is a short-term offer that you will not repeat.

Responding to objections

Once you have reformulated your customer's objection into a need, it's time to respond. Usually, this is straightforward – the answers lie in what you have already proposed and in knowledge you already have – but sometimes you will need to be creative to lead your client to a solution.

Playing to your strengths

Before you can move to the final stage of the selling process – closing – you need to deal definitively with the customer's objections (or unfulfilled needs, as we know them) by using all means at your disposal (see opposite). If you still cannot not resolve the objections, you need to revert to problem-solving mode. If you still draw a blank, call time out and ask to come back in a day or two with fresh ideas to move forward. Your customer will respect you for it in the long run.

BE RELAXED
Remember that some questions customers ask are not objections – simply plain questions. Just because someone asks you about inventory issues doesn't necessarily mean they are worried about them.

Mopping up the concerns

Your final act in the objection-resolution process is to learn if there are other objections. This may sound like opening Pandora's Box, but it's critical. If other objections do exist, you need to learn about them because if you fail to uncover them now, they will certainly spoil the deal later. So ask the question. Keep your enquiry neutral and use expressions like: "Is there anything else we need to discuss?" Try to stay away from negative language and terms such as "objections" or "issues" or "concerns". If you use words like these, you can give the customer the impression that you know something that they don't. Keep it simple. If objections remain, re-loop and repeat the process until you have removed all the obstacles that stand in the way of closing.

CREATE CONFIDENCE IN YOUR SOLUTIONS Review similar problems that you have solved for other clients.

Closing in on closing

HIGHLIGHT THE SPECIFIC BENEFITS
Repeat or rephrase a benefit the client has forgotten or did not fully appreciate during the earlier presentation phase.

REVIEW THE FEATURES AND BENEFITS
Go back over these trusted selling tools.

SELL YOURSELF
Make your customer feel confident in your ability. Explain why you're so well placed to address their concerns about service, quality, or specification.

SELL YOUR COLLEAGUES
Make sure that the customer knows that you're part of a dedicated and responsive team.

GET CREATIVE
Generate ideas together with your client to modify the strategy: use inclusive language when describing how to overcome objections: "*we* have to figure out why..." or "*our* priority is now to...".

SELL YOUR COMPANY
Talk about your company's history, successes, and commitment to excellence.

Closing the sale

Over the years, salespeople's ingenuity has given life to scores of "sure-fire" closing techniques. Going by names such as the Puppy-dog Close, the Distraction Close, and the Treat Close, some are just gimmicky, while others border on the manipulative. Their faults lie in the fact that they all see closing as a special technique, rather than the natural outcome of a problem-solving dialogue with the client.

BE GRACIOUS
Always thank the customer for their business – it is the classy thing to do.

Approaching the close

You have built the relationship, determined the needs, made great recommendations, and resolved the customer's objections. It's time to close – to ask for the business. So why do so many sales professionals find this step so difficult? The answer is simple – it is that fear of rejection rearing its ugly head once again. This fear pushes many experienced salespeople towards canned "closes", like the Specific Terms Close, where the idea is to present the customer with a prearranged buying scenario, and then ask them to agree to it. For example, "We can deliver 10 palettes on 12 May for $1,000 – is that OK?" Of course, on occasion, this approach – and others in a similar vein – may bring about a sale, but often the customer will think you presumptive and rude. It's canned selling at its lowest.

Assuming the best

To close a deal you shouldn't need to rely on corny closing tactics. You need simply to demonstrate the same credibility, integrity, and degree of interaction with the customer that you showed throughout the selling process. Don't change the basis of your hard-won relationship at this point.

Assume that if the customer does not have a reason not to buy, he or she is ready to buy. This is called the Assumptive Close. In this Assumptive Close, the dialogue with the customer is direct, and goes something like this:

SALESPERSON: "Anything else we need to discuss?"

CUSTOMER: "No, not that I can think of."

SALESPERSON: "So everything seems OK?"

CUSTOMER: "Yes, I believe so."

The point is clear even though the words you choose may vary: you ask the customer if there are other concerns. If they say no, you double check. If everything seems OK, just ask for the business.

SALESPERSON: "Great, then how do we get started?"

Asking and getting

If you've done your job well up to this point, the customer will know that you have something valuable to offer and will want to buy from you; moreover they'll want you to ask for their business. If you don't, you're expecting the customer to do your job. It seems obvious, but if you don't ask for the business, you're much less likely to get it.

Planning for completion

Once there has been a commitment to buy, close the sale by beginning to pin down the specifics. A good way to cover all the key variables is to answer the "four Ws" – who will do what by when with help from whom? When you have the answers to these questions, you are ready to execute.

If you don't close the deal – and of course you won't always – it is vital to keep the momentum of the selling process going. Set objectives for resolving issues and be clear about what has to be done before the next meeting. Experienced salespeople will tell you that the only time you fail in a sales call is when you don't get a next step.

Consolidating the close

Everyone needs reassurance after making a large purchase – to silence the nagging voice asking if they did the right thing (discussed earlier in this chapter). With this in mind, it is important to make sure you are highly visible to the customer after you have closed the deal. Some salespeople say that "the real selling starts after you get the business", and it's hard to argue with that sentiment. With hard work, anyone can get the first order; it's the ones who get the second, third, and fourth who are most successful. Whatever you do, don't fall into the stereotypical image of a "love 'em and leave 'em" salesperson. If you do, your relationship will be a short one. Guaranteed!

To be successful repeatedly, you need to acknowledge the transfer of power that occurs when the deal is closed. When a customer is a prospect, they hold all the cards, but once they commit to the deal, they lose some of that power because they are dependent upon you to deliver. It's uncomfortable for them, and it is a good reason for you to show humility after closing the deal – it's not the time to whoop and punch the air.

Collecting for success

There is a distasteful acronym out there in the world of selling – ABC, Always Be Closing – that reflects the strong emphasis placed on closing by many sales managers. Of course, closing is important, but it shouldn't be viewed as an isolated aim. Transform this unhealthy acronym into an ABC that will help you – Always Be Collecting: only when you consistently question, understand, and resolve issues together with your customer will you be on the road to success.

TIP

JUST ASK

Ask for the business, even if it feels uncomfortable. Research has revealed that customers rank asking for their business as the sixth most important reason for doing the deal.

CASE STUDY

Using a "closer"
A young salesman had called on the same client twice a month for two years. Sensing he was close to his first order, he brought his boss with him. The junior salesman reviewed price agreements, credit terms, and product specifications with the client. He kept asking the customer if everything was approved, whether they were satisfied, and if there were any other questions. All the answers were positive, but the salesman just couldn't pull the trigger. Finally, the manager lost patience and blurted out

"Well then, how about an order?" The customer's response was "What took you so long to ask?"

The customer was obviously ready to buy and the young salesman's reluctance to close was only raising suspicions in the client's mind. If the manager hadn't stepped in, the sale could have been lost.

However, using a more senior person as a "closer" is a poor selling model: the salesperson should feel adequately equipped, trained, and empowered to ask for the business.

Moving beyond the close

After you have closed, you earn yet another great opportunity to differentiate yourself from the competition. Following through goes beyond just following up on your promises – doing what you said you would do professionally and on time. Following through means exceeding what's expected of you and so sending the clear message to your customers that you are consistently thinking about them.

Following up

Follow-up is doing whatever you committed to do at the end of the sales meeting with your customer. It is a process that you initiate to ensure that objectives are accomplished and commitments are fulfilled. It is your responsibility to make sure that all of your organization's resources are doing what is needed to move the relationship to the next level. Will the samples be there on time? Is everyone aware of and able to meet the agreed delivery dates? Is the team committed to participate in the next meeting?

Every single sales call you make – from a brief catch-up meeting to a formal presentation – deserves a follow-up letter. This can be a letter, an email, or even a hand-written note – whatever suits both your style and the occasion – but must follow every call.

IN FOCUS... TRACKING CONTACT

Time speeds by. It's not hard for 90 days to pass before you realize that you haven't made any contact with a customer. "Out of sight... out of mind" may be a cliché, but it's true: and if you haven't been in touch with a client, it's a safe bet that your competitor has. To prevent long silences, track how often you make contact with your customers. Use a spreadsheet, graph paper, or whatever suits your style to record every face-to-face meeting, as well as phone calls, letters, and emails.

The letter should thank the customer for their time, review what was discussed, and define the next steps. It can also serve as a reminder of who committed to do what by when.

Following through

When you follow through, you do more than you need to. Here are some ways you can surprise your customers with your level of commitment:
• Regularly check how things are progressing internally, and communicate effectively to everybody involved on a day-to-day basis.
• Send your customers a list of follow-up activities and deliverables, including dates; make sure you meet them consistently.
• Let your customer know well in advance if for some reason you can't meet a deliverable.
• Send emails updating your customers without requesting a response. This instils confidence that you have their interests in mind all the time.

MAKING THE MARK

FAST TRACK	OFF TRACK
Promising and delivering	Overpromising and underdelivering
Putting it in writing	Assuming the customer understands
Being visible	Being a nuisance
Being consistently professional	Forgetting details
Showing interest in doing business	Appearing desperate or over anxious

WORKING WITH DIFFICULT PEOPLE

Contents

Introduction

The skill of an effective manager is measured not only by how well they manage their motivated employees, but also by how well they work with the difficult people on their team. A difficult employee can have a negative impact on the performance of the entire group, and yet very few managers have the necessary skills to manage the difficult team member.

To harness the strengths of the difficult person and secure their co-operation, you need to develop the relevant skills, refine your technique, and apply disciplined processes. This book introduces the key techniques and skills that are essential to working with difficult people.

As you build competency, you will become capable of successfully transforming a potentially frustrating experience into a satisfying and productive one. *Working with Difficult People* provides you with the tools and processes which will allow you to effectively manage the difficult employee.

This book also touches on the reasons behind difficult behaviour and how to respond to them. You will learn skills that will make you a better communicator, and this will change the way you approach conflict and allow you to forge strong working relationships. Your managerial skills will improve as you use this book to navigate the human dynamics of the workplace.

Chapter 1

Understanding difficult people

People are often difficult because you allow them to be so. If you uncover the cause for their difficult behaviour, take responsibility for it, and apply steps to manage it, you can turn even the most difficult person into a productive, happy, and loyal employee.

Changing your mindset

When faced with difficult people you might throw up your hands in despair and attribute the problem to their aggravating personality. Although you can sometimes walk away, mostly you need to work with them. Realize that you can influence their behaviour by vigilantly managing your own.

TIP

RESPOND THOUGHTFULLY

Try not to react impulsively when dealing with a difficult person. Think before you respond: it will advance the interaction and make the other person feel they are being taken seriously.

Focusing on behaviour

While you cannot change people, you can influence their behaviour. It is therefore useful to see the *behaviour* as difficult rather than the *people*. When you perceive *people* to be difficult, you see yourself as a victim and allow them to hold power over you. This can make you frustrated, angry, and defensive, and cause you to react negatively. Separating the two will make it easier for you to achieve perspective. It will help you manage your emotions, be objective, and respond with thoughtfulness and purpose. This change in mindset is the first step in dealing with difficult behaviour.

Using influence

When faced with difficult behaviour, we tend to assert our own demands, thus generating resistance in the other person. However, we can influence their behaviour by engaging and working with them rather than against them. This involves a careful application of processes, techniques, and skills that can achieve collaboration.

Taking responsibility

To manage people who show difficult behaviour, you must first take responsibility for your contribution to their behaviour. You may be enabling them to behave difficultly without realizing it. For example, you may be passive, thereby telling them their behaviour is acceptable. Or you may react aggressively and engage them in further battle. You may talk *at* them rather than *to* them, making them defensive. It could also be a seemingly minor issue, such as your body language, tone of voice, or facial expression.

TIP

MENDING RELATIONSHIPS

If a relationship is becoming strained because of the other person's behaviour, analyze what you might be doing to contribute to that behaviour, and how you might change it.

TAKING CONTROL

FAST TRACK

OFF TRACK

FAST TRACK	OFF TRACK
Thinking I can alter their behaviour	Thinking they will never change
Thinking maybe I am to blame too	Thinking it is all their fault
Understanding their motives	Thinking they are unreasonable
Thinking I can resolve this with them	Thinking there is nothing I can do
Refusing to be a passive victim	Getting angry and frustrated

Creating a useful framework

When you are working with difficult people, a useful framework to apply is one that is made of three fundamental components: managing the relationship, engaging the other person in dialogue, and negotiating* a working solution. Each of these involves skills that, when mastered, will enhance your effectiveness as a leader.

*Negotiating — *working together to design a solution that meets the needs of all parties involved.*

Managing the relationship

By the time a person has become difficult with you in the workplace, you can assume that your relationship with them is also in distress. This can be caused by an underlying resentment, anger, mistrust, or any other relationship stressor that they feel. It is common for managers to ignore the relationship issue and attempt to address the problem at hand directly. This seldom works because a stressed relationship does not lead to constructive dialogue. You cannot resolve the problem at hand without first repairing the relationship, at least to the extent that effective dialogue can take place.

Engaging in dialogue

A crucial component of the "working with difficult people" framework is engaging in productive dialogue. When faced with a difficult person, avoid presenting them with a monologue about your demands. If one or both parties talk but neither listens, communication is ineffective and does little to advance understanding. Productive dialogue expands the scope of discussion and digs out relevant information. It reveals deeper concerns without which you cannot work towards resolution. Also, as information is exchanged and understanding is achieved, dialogue lays the foundation for lasting resolution.

Negotiating a working solution

The final key component in the framework is negotiating a working solution. After restoring the relationship and understanding one another's needs through dialogue, you will be ready to search for a workable solution. You should strive to construct a solution that addresses everyone's needs, and involve all parties in the process by inviting them to contribute ideas. This is important as it will give them a stake in the outcome. Remain open to creative solutions, and do not be limited to preconceived ideas and old ways of doing things. Your negotiation process should be innovative and collaborative, not restrictive and threatening. This approach will help achieve amicable and durable solutions.

HOW TO...
USE THE FRAMEWORK

Listen to the other person with sympathy and without defending your position.

Then summarize your understanding of their position and check this with them.

Next, inquire by asking clarifying questions to expand dialogue.

Encourage the other person to discuss their needs, and show interest in them.

Share your needs and concerns with them in a composed and friendly way.

Jointly explore options that could potentially satisfy both your needs.

Be creative and open-minded when you look for solutions, and invite others' ideas.

CHECKLIST APPLYING THE FRAMEWORK

	YES	NO
• Have you acknowledged emotions and discussed feelings?	☐	☐
• Have you engaged in a constructive two-way dialogue?	☐	☐
• Are you understanding the other person's needs and concerns?	☐	☐
• Are you inviting the contribution of ideas for a solution?	☐	☐
• Are you building and carrying forward on others' ideas?	☐	☐
• Are you remaining open-minded to creative and innovative ideas?	☐	☐

Building competency

Encountering difficult people in the workplace is inevitable, yet most of us do not have the competency to deal with them. It is not taught in business schools, but is an invaluable asset in the manager's repertoire. Competency results from disciplined processes, refined techniques, and strong skills.

HOW TO... UNCOVER HIDDEN FEELINGS

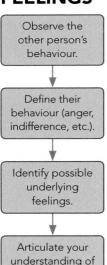

Observe the other person's behaviour.

↓

Define their behaviour (anger, indifference, etc.).

↓

Identify possible underlying feelings.

↓

Articulate your understanding of the issue.

↓

Confirm your understanding, but be open.

↓

Engage them in further discussion.

Having a process

A process is a series of steps or actions that, when implemented properly, achieves a desired result. Just as a process is necessary in any complex operation, it is also essential to the success of any difficult human interaction. When facing a difficult person, you probably react impulsively, and at times confrontationally. This is because you have no roadmap to show you the way; in short, you lack a process. The more learned processes you have at your disposal, the better equipped you will be to deal with difficult behaviour. An example of such a process is the six-step model (see left) for analyzing difficult behaviour to uncover the underlying deeper feeelings.

Refining your technique

As you learn to implement the processes, you will find that you develop techniques of your own that sit well with you and fit your unique personality. Techniques here refer to the methods you use to best apply the steps of a process. It may be the phraseology you choose, the way you ask questions, or how you use body language to put the other person at ease. The process, however, will always provide the framework within which to apply the technique. As you learn to implement

these processes* and techniques there will
be a period of initial awkwardness, as with any
learning. Make sure that you persevere, and
within a short time you will find your competency
improving. As you become more comfortable,
be prepared to experiment with some of your
own techniques, too, and before long they
will feel very much a part of you.

*Process —
*A process is a
framework which
provides a
manageable and
repeatable system
to successfully
accomplish a
complex operation
or interaction.*

Developing strong skills

The final part of achieving competency is developing
skills. You can strengthen your competency
by extensively practising the processes and
techniques. The more you practise, the better
you will get, and, in time, you will notice that you
are able to deal with challenging situations with
composure and grace, even while optimizing
results. Use every opportunity to practise dealing
with difficult behaviour and strive to become
a master at working with difficult people.
This will enhance your managerial
capacity and provide you with a
competitive edge in today's
challenging workplace.

**HIGH
LEVEL OF
COMPETENCY**

**PRACTISED
SKILL**

=

**REFINED
TECHNIQUE**

+

**DISCIPLINED
PROCESS**

+

Addressing root causes

When dealing with a difficult person, you may be trying to deal only with their behaviour, rather than uncovering the behaviour's cause. This is like a doctor treating a patient's symptoms instead of the disease. To deal with difficult behaviour, you must learn to uncover and articulate its root causes.

Recognizing the symptoms

The key to dealing with difficult behaviour is to recognize that the behaviour is a symptom that usually has an underlying emotional cause. People may get defensive (behaviour) when they are unjustly blamed (cause), or get angry (behaviour) when they feel unfairly treated (cause). The underlying causes need to be discussed. Once made explicit, they will lead to understanding and productive discussion. It is important to broach this topic in a non-judgmental way. This will engage the difficult person, rather than causing them to close up and become even more difficult.

INDIFFERENCE

Loss of interest or motiva too much work, or too routine work; uncomfortable with co-workers; lack of recognition for previous efforts.

Understanding the causes

When a person exhibits difficult behaviour, try to understand what fear, concern, or need is driving it. Say you are in a meeting discussing a project delay and a team member angrily says "If she had sent us the information we requested on time, we would have been on schedule". This anger is driven by the team member's frustration at not receiving the requested information on time. Expose the *cause*, and not the symptom, by checking your understanding with them: "So your frustration comes from not getting the important information on time?". This will then lead to discussion of ways to streamline information flow in the future.

Root causes underlying difficult behaviours

ASSERTING BLAME

NON-COMPLIANCE

ANGER

DEFENSIVENESS

Desire for more autonomy and say; doesn't trust, understand, or agree with management; vague and unclear objectives.

Unjustly blamed; threat from co-workers; fear of tarnished image; feeling attacked.

Frustration; feeling of being exploited or unfairly treated at work; not being respected; needs not being met.

Insecure; wants to appear strong; concerned about others' perceptions; worried about career.

Transforming confrontation

Difficult people can draw you into playing their confrontational "game" without you even realizing it. When they raise their voice, you raise yours; when they assert demands, you assert counter-demands; and when they threaten you, you threaten them back. To work productively with difficult people, it is crucial that you change their game by changing your own.

RESIST ASSERTING YOUR DEMANDS
When you are confronted with demands from the other party, resist the urge to counter-demand. Instead, ask questions that will help you understand the other side's needs better.

Understanding their game

Difficult people like to engage in confrontation rather than collaboration. They try to engage you in a battle of wills with the intent of dominating you. They perceive you as an adversary rather than a co-operative problem solver, and their objective is to "win" as opposed to meeting everyone's needs. Unless you have a process of your own, you are likely to be drawn into playing the game their way. This results in distressed relationships, erosion of trust, and sub-optimal outcomes.

Changing their game

To work better with difficult people, you must change their game of war and tactics to your game of diplomacy and authenticity. Any time your interests are being threatened, it is quite normal to immediately want to defend them. However, when you become defensive, you will cause the other party to become defensive too, so that the opportunity for productive exchange is obstructed. To change the game, resist the urge to immediately defend your position. Instead, adopt an attitude of inquiry, a mindset of learning, and an open mind. Suspend your views and positions and make every effort to probe, learn, and understand the other person's views. This will advance productive dialogue dramatically as understanding and trust builds.

BEING COLLABORATIVE

FAST TRACK

OFF TRACK

FAST TRACK	OFF TRACK
Resisting the urge to defend	Interrupting and talking at them
Keeping an open mind	Imposing your views
Suspending your judgment	Matching their negative behaviour tit-for-tat
Asking relevant questions	Becoming defensive
Maintaining an atmosphere of respect	Showing disinterest

Using collaboration

To build collaboration, you must cultivate a collaborative mindset as opposed to an adversarial one. The adversarial mindset says that if they win, you lose, whereas the collaborator understands that you can work out a creative solution that meets both your needs. An adversarial mindset does not trust the other party, whereas the collaborative mindset seeks ways to build trust and relationships. An adversarial mindset thinks that you have to assert your demands relentlessly, but a collaborative one tries to understand what the other party's concerns and needs are.

CASE STUDY

Altering the game plan

During negotiations with the labour union, the president of a large South African steel company demanded that the man-hours per ton be cut down. When the union representative heard this, he assumed it meant some steel workers would lose their jobs and became angry. He was on the verge of turning defensive and threatening to stage a strike if a single worker lost his job. Instead, he altered the game. He resisted the urge to defend his position and adopted an attitude of inquiry. He asked the president why he believed a cut in man-hours was necessary. The president explained his concern about their competitors' plants being more efficient. This then led to productive brainstorming for other ways to become more competitive.

Chapter 2
Communicating with excellence

Effective communication drives all successful human interaction. You can develop and refine your communication skills so that you can communicate with persuasion and influence at all times, especially when faced with difficult behaviour.

Overcoming barriers

To become an effective communicator, you first need to know about communication barriers and ways to avoid them. Overcoming these barriers requires the ability to negotiate cultural differences, an environment suitable for interaction, and an appreciation of the other person's viewpoint.

TIP

RESPECT OTHER CULTURES

If you do or say something that causes offence in another culture, point out politely that it was in no way intentional, but rather due to your lack of familiarity with their culture.

Understanding differences

Ambiguous communication or misunderstandings can crop up in today's globalized world where intercultural workforces are common. To prevent this, if something sounds ambiguous or makes little sense be prepared to ask questions and clarify. When dealing with other nationalities, explain to them that misunderstandings are possible due to cultural differences and invite them to question anything that does not make sense or is not clear. Although this may not eliminate misunderstandings altogether, it will go a long way towards minimizing them.

Preventing distractions

Sometimes two people may appear to be talking to one another when they are, in fact, not. Take, for example, a union representative negotiating with management in the presence of the media. The representative may be more interested in impressing their rank and file than communicating effectively with management. If you need to confer with a person you know can be difficult, create a secure environment: a time and place without distractions that could inhibit both of you from having an honest and productive discussion.

Acknowledging perceptions

An interaction is unlikely to be productive unless each side makes an effort to understand the other side's viewpoint. Try to understand how they see the situation even though you may disagree with them. Listen carefully, ask clarifying questions, and put yourself into their shoes. Acknowledge and articulate the different perceptions without trying to convince each other which is right. This will allow the other party to feel heard and understood, and advance productive communication.

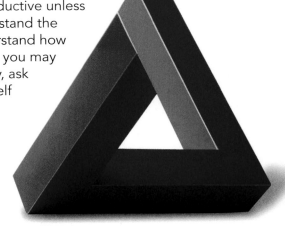

CASE STUDY

Creating a safe environment

When US President Ronald Reagan met Soviet leader Mikhail Gorbachev for the 1986 Reykjavik Summit on ballistic missiles in Iceland, he stipulated that only essential personnel, such as interpreters and national security advisors, would be present, and the media would not attend. Reagan understood the importance of creating a secure environment. By doing so he was able to conduct open and honest talks, and this also led to a close and productive friendship between the two leaders.

Listening in both directions

Listening lies at the heart of effective communication, especially when dealing with difficult people. Remember that listening works in two ways: being a good listener, and being effectively listened to. Attentive listening is a competency made up of three skills: paraphrasing, clarifying, and observing. To get listened to, you can use a similar three-step process.

TIP

LISTEN, THEN SHARE YOUR THOUGHTS

People will be much more likely to listen to you when they feel you have paid attention to them.

Paraphrasing

In a meaningful exchange, you need to understand the other party, and they need to know that you have understood them. Paraphrasing what you have understood helps you check with them for accuracy. Suppose your colleague is complaining about team members not delivering assignments on time and how this is delaying a project. To paraphrase you might say: "So when assignments are not delivered on time, you become concerned about delaying the project and disappointing our customers. Is that correct?". Here you are allowing them to clarify misunderstandings, and, more importantly, you are letting them know that they have been understood.

✓ CHECKLIST LISTENING WITH ATTENTIVENESS

	YES	NO
• Am I listening carefully to what the other party is saying?	☐	☐
• Am I checking my understanding by summarizing and paraphrasing?	☐	☐
• Am I asking clarifying questions to discover missing information?	☐	☐
• Am I sure our communication is purposeful and productive?	☐	☐
• Am I observing their non-verbal cues and matching those with their verbal messages?	☐	☐
• Am I listening more than I am talking?	☐	☐

Clarifying

Use clarifying questions to keep the interaction focused. Often while communicating it may seem that information is missing. People may say they feel overwhelmed but not explain why, or that they feel unfairly treated but not provide a reason. Clarifying questions can uncover missing information. Suppose an employee says: "She always makes me angry", then your clarifying question could be: "When did she make you angry, and what did she do that upset you?". This expands the discussion, bringing to it a new context.

Observing

Listening attentively also includes being aware of and carefully observing non-verbal cues such as body language, voice intonation, and facial expressions. Look out for any inconsistencies between what is being said and the non-verbal cues. If you spot something like this you should point it out in a non-judgmental way. Training yourself to observe non-verbal cues and then matching them with verbal cues will improve your ability to work with difficult people.

summarize

body language

clarify

observe

understand

converse

intonation

listen

uncover

OFFER IDEAS
Always offer your ideas, never impose them. People do not like to have things imposed upon them and they will often resist.

Demonstrating understanding

To be listened to, show you understand the other person. Suppose development and marketing are discussing a new accounting software. Development believes the software will revolutionize the way businesses share financial data, and boost revenues. But marketing think its features and price are more than most companies would need or pay for. You could then paraphrase: "Development sees great potential in terms of our bottom-line, but marketing are concerned it is too much for our typical user. Is that correct?". Both sides will then feel validated and relinquish the urge to continue asserting their positions.

Offering your idea

When both development and marketing know you have understood them, they will be more receptive to your ideas. Do not impose your ideas, rather offer them. You may say: "One option for us is to design a base system with add-on features for specific customers". Bring your idea full circle by explaining how it addresses the concerns of both parties. You should also acknowledge that both sides have helped devise the solution.

validate   address

collaborate

exchange   focus

consider

question   offer

uncover

Asking questions

After offering your idea, engage both sides in further discussion and invite them to refine it and offer ideas of their own. An effective way to do this is by asking focused questions. For example: "What concerns might not be addressed by this idea, or are there any new concerns that it raises?", "What variations could further develop this idea?", or "Can you think of ideas we haven't yet considered?". By doing this you are turning potential confrontation into collaboration, generating more creative thinking, and involving both sides in the solution. When you are fluent in this three-step process and use it in your repertoire, you will find it easier to get your ideas heard and accepted.

HOW TO...
GET LISTENED TO

> Show the other side you have understood them by paraphrasing them.

> Once they are receptive, offer your own ideas; never impose your idea.

> Explain how your idea addresses their concerns and needs too.

> Close the discussion with a focused question that engages them further.

LISTENING EFFECTIVELY

FAST TRACK

OFF TRACK

FAST TRACK	OFF TRACK
Assuming the other side has a legitimate perspective of their own	Insisting you are right and know all the answers
Putting genuine effort into understanding them	Interrupting, contradicting, and trying to enforce your will
Making sure you listen in order to be listened to	Disparaging the other side or their ideas in any way

Avoiding confrontation

Sometimes a colleague consistently fails to do what is required of them. This can be frustrating and cost the company significantly. Blaming the person is not the way to fix this. You need to avoid confronting the person and instead apply the Action, Feeling, Impact, and Request (AFIR) model.

TIP

ALWAYS USE THE AFIR MODEL

Always use the AFIR model to reframe blame even if the other party really is at fault. You will get a lot further in engaging them in problem-solving because they will not feel the need to defend themselves.

Reframing the problem

When dealing with a difficult colleague it is crucial that you choose a process which encourages dialogue and joint problem-solving. You can do this by reframing the problem. Suppose a co-worker is not returning your phone calls. You could either blame him by saying: "He never returns my phone calls", or you could reframe the problem: "When my calls are not returned I feel anxious as I am unable to get the information I need". Instead of looking to blame someone, focus on what is happening, the impact it has, and what is actually needed.

Preparing the message

To prepare a non-confrontational message you need to ask the AFIR questions: what is happening? (Action), how do I feel about it? (Feeling), what impact is this having? (Impact), and, what would I like? (Request). For example, a co-worker comes in late and leaves early, disrupting everyone's schedule. You decide to confront them. First ask yourself the four questions: What is happening? (Your co-worker does not respect office timings.) How do you feel about it? (You feel exploited.) What impact is this having? (You have to pick up the slack.) What would you like? (You would like the workload to be shared fairly.) By breaking the message into AFIR steps, you have moved from assigning blame to a more productive view of the problem and its solution.

Transmitting the message

To reframe the message, put the four elements in this format: "When... (put in action), I feel... (put in feeling) because... (put in impact). Would you be willing to... (put in request)?". For example: "When you are absent from work (Action), I feel exploited (Feeling) because I have to pick up the slack (Impact). Could we find a way to deal with this (Request)?". This formula avoids putting the other party on the defensive, leaving the door open for further dialogue.

TIP

PRACTISE!
These are skills like any other so practise, practise, and practise!

AVOIDING BLAME STATEMENTS USING AFIR

BLAMING STATEMENT	(A) ACTION, (F) FEELING, (I) IMPACT, (R) REQUEST	AFIR (STATEMENT AND QUESTIONS)
You are never available when needed.	**A.** Not being available. **F.** Frustrated. **I.** I cannot get feedback on the project. **R.** Regular feedback on the project.	When you are unavailable I feel frustrated because I cannot get the feedback I need. Would you be willing to talk about a set time that we could meet once a week?
You are always late with your reports.	**A.** Not receiving reports on time. **F.** Concern. **I.** Delays and customer disappointment. **R.** Receiving reports on time.	When we do not get the reports on time, I get concerned because it causes delays and ultimately customer disappointment. Would you be willing to talk about ways in which we might streamline this?
You are always interrupting me.	**A.** Not being able to express my thoughts. **F.** Frustration. **I.** Not getting a fair hearing. **R.** Listening to each other adequately.	When I am unable to finish my thoughts, I get frustrated because I am not getting a fair hearing. Could we agree to listen to each other first without interrupting and then allowing for rebuttals?
You are spending too much time on just one thing.	**A.** A lot of time being spent. **F.** Anxious. **I.** More important things may not get done. **R.** Focus on the more important things.	When I see so much time being spent on this I become anxious about whether the other important things will be achieved. Would you be willing to prioritize with me what needs to get done?

Building trust

In any working relationship, trust is essential. When you are working with difficult people, it is most likely that trust has already been impaired, and the relationship has to be rebuilt. Trust is achieved not only by *what* we communicate but also by *how* we communicate it.

Communicating with authenticity

To build trust, your communication should be authentic at all times. Be genuinely interested in what the other person is saying and listen attentively. When you speak, make sure that you are clear and purposeful, and that you say what you mean. Avoid vague and ambiguous language. Ask questions to understand better, and not just to challenge. When engaged in an interaction, ask yourself if you are communicating with authenticity. This will make you understand what might be missing and allow you to make the necessary adjustments.

Being consistent

Another aspect of building trust through communication is ensuring that your non-verbal cues are consistent with your verbal ones. Imagine telling someone you are interested in what they have to say, and then checking your e-mail when they are talking to you. This sends out an inconsistent message and undermines trust. When you engage with another person make sure your non-verbal cues send the right message. Lean forward and make eye contact. Show them you care with your body language and tone of voice. Being consistent means that your actions and your words must be consistent over time.

Taking concerns seriously

When you are working with difficult people, their perception will most likely be that you are trying to impose your interests at the expense of theirs. They will feel threatened and will not trust you. To build trust you need to change that perception. In order to achieve this you need to set a positive tone. You have to indicate that the other person's concerns are important to you, and that you wish to work to protect not just your interests but theirs too. You could say, for example, to someone who feels threatened by you: "We have had our differences, perhaps, but this relationship is important to me. I would like to reconcile our interests and to do that I would really like to know more about what you truly care about.". By saying so you have set a positive tone and started to change the other person's untrusting perception.

TIP

UNDERSTAND INTERESTS AND CONCERNS
The more you learn about other people, the better equipped you will be to create specific solutions that address their concerns.

USING AUTHENTIC COMMUNICATION

NON–AUTHENTIC COMMUNICATION	WHAT YOU REALLY MEAN	AUTHENTIC COMMUNICATION
Don't you think you should talk to your boss?	I think you should talk to your boss.	What do you think you should do about your boss?
You certainly are quiet.	You are too quiet and it bothers me.	I notice that you seem quiet – is my observation correct and if so would you be willing to share with me why?
You should expect me back by noon.	I cannot make a promise to you and will not commit.	My hope is to be back by noon but I really cannot promise you. Would you like me to call you if I am running behind schedule?
I guess she is ok.	I am not sure about her.	She seems ok overall, although I have some reservations.

Using questions skilfully

Strong questioning skills are crucial to effective communication. They are used to advance dialogue, focus debate, obtain information, and redirect discussion. To master questioning techniques you need to be familiar with different kinds of questions and when to use them.

Asking open-ended questions

An open-ended question is one to which there is no yes-or-no answer, but which provokes a thoughtful response. It makes the other party actively participate, expands the scope of discussion, and encourages further dialogue. Words that commonly introduce an open-ended question are: "what", "how", and "why". As in: "What led you to that conclusion?", "How will you implement the plan?", and "Why do you feel unfairly treated?". They are used when there is a need to uncover missing information, and to keep the discussion focused.

Asking closed-ended questions

A closed-ended question is one with a yes-or-no or other short answer. The closed-ended question limits further discussion. Examples of such questions are: "Did you tell him?" (allows only a yes-or-no answer). "When did this happen?" (has a limited day, date, and time answer). "Who did it?" or "Where did they go?" are other examples. Closed-ended questions are useful to interrupt a person who is rambling and to obtain specific information. Suppose an irate customer is complaining about the lack of service he has received from your company. A closed-ended question you can ask him is: "Have you spoken to the manager yet?". This limits him to a yes/no answer and allows you to take control.

Avoiding loaded questions

We sometimes use questions as a means to lead the other person to what we want them to do or say. These are statements, accusations, or advice disguised in the form of loaded questions. An example would be: "What did you expect?". The intent here is not inquiry but rather a statement: "How incompetent of you not to realize this". Loaded questions with agendas will make the other person defensive and obstruct communication. When using questions to advance dialogue, ask them with true curiosity and a desire to understand.

TIP

ASKING YOURSELF FIRST

Before asking a question, ask yourself: "Is this a true question of enquiry or a loaded question with an agenda?".

WHEN TO USE OPEN-ENDED QUESTIONS:

- To clarify missing information
- To keep the discussion focused
- To achieve a deeper level of understanding
- To help the other side clarify their own thoughts, concerns, and interests
- To expand the scope of discussion

WHEN TO USE CLOSED-ENDED QUESTIONS:

- To get answers to very specific questions
- To interrupt a person who is in endless monologue, in order to regain control of the conversation

WHEN TO USE LOADED QUESTIONS:

- Never. They have no purpose in effective communication

Tackling negative emotions

When strong negative emotions are present, you might tend to ignore them and hope that they will just go away. But when someone is angry or upset, you cannot have productive discussions. You need to deal first with the emotions and then guide the conversation back to the substantive issues.

Responding to emotions

Suppose you are meeting with a difficult colleague to discuss their repeated tardiness. They respond with an emotional outburst, and complain how they are always picked on unfairly. Before you can resolve the tardiness issue, you must address their emotions. Acknowledge the way they feel and show them that you understand (even though you may not agree). Allow them to let off some steam, then follow up with a clarifying question. Once the emotional level has diminished, lead them back to the issue at hand.

ACKNOWLEDGING
Acknowledge their feelings, and show them you understand. ("When you were passed over for a promotion you felt you deserved, you were hurt ... correct?")

Controlling your emotions

When you lose control of your emotions, you may say things you regret later, and also risk losing your credibility. Conduct yourself with grace and composure with your colleagues. If you feel overwhelmed at times, it is crucial you control your emotions. A useful technique is to mentally detach yourself from the situation and become an objective observer. A small degree of mental detachment can go a long way in regaining control over your emotions. Another technique is silence. Resist the urge to respond immediately, and sit silently for a while to regain your composure.

TIP

MONITOR YOUR OWN EMOTIONS
Ask yourself periodically: "How am I feeling?", and "What is the emotional temperature in the room?". This awareness will help you to better control your emotions.

Ways to manage others' emotions

MONITORING
Watch for cues that their emotions have calmed, before continuing discussions on the substantive issues. Cues include body language and tone of voice.

LISTENING
Listen actively while allowing them to let off steam, and do not interrupt or defend your position. They need to express themselves before emotions can subside.

LEADING
Guide them back to the substantive issues after dealing with their emotions. ("I respect how you feel. But we need to discuss the matter, now or at a later date.")

ASKING
Ask clarifying questions to show your engagement, and to generate dialogue.

Avoiding e-mail conflict

Most communication today takes place through e-mail. It is fast and efficient, but it also creates opportunities for misunderstandings to crop up. You can avoid them by making sure that your mails are accurate and convey the right "mood", and aren't written on the spur of the moment.

TIP

AVOID CAPITALS
Resist the temptation to use capital letters in e-mails (except where required by grammatical rules). They are the e-mail equivalent of shouting.

Steering clear of vagueness

Since most people at the workplace are overloaded with e-mails, it is important your message stands out by being accurate and concise. It must be simple and easy to understand. Do not put your thoughts in one long unstructured paragraph. Sort out your ideas and put them into a logical order in short paragraphs or bullet points. Avoid vague comments which can cause confusion, particularly where multiple issues are being discussed. Instead, write to the point, as in: "I agree that we meet every Wednesday at noon to discuss progress". When you receive an e-mail that is confusing, reply at once and ask for clarification. Be specific about your point of confusion, such as: "Is the scheduled meeting intended for all team members or just project leads?", rather than "Who did you mean?".

**? ASK YOURSELF...
BEFORE SENDING
AN E-MAIL**

- Is it clear and concise?
- Does it convey the tone I wish to communicate?
- Is it professional?
- Have I put across all my points?
- Have I replied to all the queries?

Conveying the right mood

Studies have shown that in face-to-face communication almost 65 per cent of your message is communicated non-verbally. This means through your tone, pitch, volume of voice, and body language. In e-mail, with no visual or auditory communication, as much as 65 per cent of your message could be missed. Messages may be misinterpreted as being terse, irate, sarcastic, or impatient due to the absence of visual cues. When writing an e-mail, consider the tone you wish to convey and then read through your mail before you send it to see if it conveys what you mean.

TIP

BEING PRE-EMPTIVE

Any time a misunderstanding seems to be developing via e-mail, pick up the phone and call the other person.

Establishing e-mail guidelines

Using e-mail in complex issues that require face-to-face conversation can create serious conflict and emotional responses. Establish a set of guidelines for e-mail usage, for instance: if an e-mail is very lengthy it should not be sent, rather an agenda should be sent and a phone call scheduled; e-mail should be used only for sharing data and information or to schedule live conversations; anything of an emotional nature should be discussed over the phone or in person. Such an e-mail protocol will contribute to a more productive work environment.

 IN FOCUS... APPLYING THE 24-HOUR RULE

The 24-hour rule means waiting 24 hours before sending an e-mail written in a moment of emotion, so that your response is driven by reason alone. High pressure at work can cause you to become stressed. You might want to send an angry e-mail, but this can hurt feelings and raise legal issues. You could write a mail to calm your feelings, but wait a whole day to send it. By then you will have calmed down and be able to write a more constructive e-mail.

Chapter 3

Negotiating conflict

The key to creating successful working relationships is the ability to deal with differences. Imposing your will seldom produces results. Knowing how to negotiate effectively will help you cultivate strong working relationships, even with difficult workers.

Negotiating true needs

If you are negotiating with a difficult person, do not use your authority to make demands, as this will result in low-quality work and diminished morale. Instead, try to uncover your employees' true or personal needs, and then present yours. This will lead to real collaboration and solutions.

*Position —
Your initial presenting demand, or what you want, as in: "You must be available when I need you!".

*True need —
Why you want it, the need, concern, or fear driving the position, as in: "When I need information you have access to, I would like to be able to get it in a timely manner".

Avoiding positions

When faced with a position*, do not counter with your own position. Rather, find out why that position is important to the other side and what needs of theirs would be met were that position accepted. This helps uncover their true needs*, as opposed to their negotiating positions. Many people negotiate by asserting demands or positions. Consider a manager who says to an employee: "I insist that you hand me that report by 5 p.m.", and the employee retorts with: "That's impossible!". Both sides have dug in their heels, leading to impasse and limited solution options.

Uncovering true needs

You can only reach effective solutions when true needs have been addressed. Say a union representative demands higher wages for his membership. He has presented a position, but not a true need. A good negotiator will not counter the union's position, but try to uncover its members' true needs. He might discover that they would like to pay for the occasional vacation or save for a child's college fund. So their true need is more disposable income, and not necessarily higher wages. With this new understanding in mind, an alternative option could be restructuring the healthcare plan to lower membership contributions, thereby increasing disposable income without increasing wages. Some questions to ask when uncovering true needs are:
- Why is that important to you?
- In what way would that help you?
- What concerns do you have?
- What needs of yours would be met if we did that?
- What needs of yours would not be met if we did not do that?

Sharing true needs

After uncovering and understanding the other side's true needs, you are now ready to share yours. Share your true needs as opposed to your positions, because the other side will perceive a position as a demand. Suppose a co-worker likes the window open, which is causing a draft to blow your papers off your desk. Instead of telling the person to close the window (your position), it would be less threatening and more productive to share your true need: "I am concerned about my papers blowing off my desk". You have not imposed a solution but defined the problem: how can the papers be stopped from blowing off the desk? This will then open the door to problem-solving.

Being aware of personal needs

At the workplace, you must consider both the professional and personal needs of employees. Their professional needs will relate to their job: skilled co-workers, a high-performing team, good management, or a manageable workload. They will be forthcoming about these issues. Below the surface lie personal needs, such as job security, career advancement, and recognition. These personal issues often lie at the core of problems, and are crucial in resolving conflicts.

*Self-disclosure —
*Exposing a
vulnerability of your
own to the other
party as a means to
make it comfortable
and safe for them
to talk about their
needs and concerns.

Using self-disclosure

Self-disclosure* is a useful technique for uncovering employees' personal needs. If you suspect they feel unrecognized for their work, which is a personal need, you could make them feel comfortable by saying: "Part of my satisfaction comes from my work being recognized by my colleagues. Is this a concern with you too?". By telling them that this is important to you as well, you have created a safe environment for them to talk about their personal needs.

Discussing personal needs

An employee's hidden personal concerns are more important than the obvious ones. Employees are usually reluctant to talk about these issues, which makes them difficult to address. But they do exist, so listen carefully for clues that may help you uncover them. After uncovering personal needs it is important to generate further dialogue around them to gather as much information as possible. Useful questions to ask would be in the following vein: "Tell me more about the events that caused you to feel unrecognized", or "What was it specifically that made you feel unfairly treated?", or "Describe how you would like things to be". These kinds of questions will bring relevant information to the surface that can help you deal with the problem. Often you will notice that, as constructive dialogue occurs and these issues are brought to the surface, your employees will find solutions themselves while you do nothing more than listen.

TIP

RECOGNIZE THE IMPORTANCE OF PERSONAL NEEDS

When all efforts at resolving an issue have been unsuccessful, consider whether there are personal needs which remain unresolved and attempt to address them.

UNCOVERING PERSONAL NEEDS

FAST TRACK	**OFF TRACK**
Recognizing that there are personal needs beyond work-related issues that may not be surfacing	Working to resolve work-related issues while neglecting personal needs
Listening between the lines for clues to the personal needs of emplyees	Implying that the work environment is no place to air personal issues
Using the self-disclosure technique to create a safe place to talk about personal needs	Jumping to conclusions as to what the real issues are without really trying to listen and understand

Using collaboration

Working with difficult people will frequently give rise to conflict situations. When you are working on resolving a conflict, involve the other party in designing the solution. This will give them ownership of the agreement, making them more committed and more likely to comply with it.

*Bridging question — The key question that defines the problem by bridging both sets of needs. For example: "What ideas can we think of that will satisfy both your needs and ours at the same time?"

Defining the problem

You cannot negotiate conflict until you have a clear definition of the problem you wish to solve. To define the problem you need to communicate all the needs that must be satisfied in order for both parties to agree. Before attempting to find a solution, take time to explore the other party's needs, and then communicate yours. It is a good idea to put these needs up on a white board in two columns. This will help objectify the problem and separate it from personalities. Use the "bridging question"* to define the problem This will allow you to focus on finding a mutually acceptable solution.

Brainstorming creative options

Brainstorming is a way of listing potential solutions. Invite the other person to join you as this will engage them in the process of designing the solution. Encourage creative ideas, and assure them that all ideas are welcome no matter how unrealistic, because even unworkable ideas can help to trigger more realistic ones. Capture the ideas on the white board in full view. Some ground rules for brainstorming are:

• Separate coming up with options from deciding upon solutions.
• Do not allow judgment or criticism, just generate ideas.
• Welcome all ideas.
• Do not commit to any ideas that are suggested.
• Record ideas in full view.

Evaluating the options

After you have generated and captured a good list of options, you can begin to evaluate them. You can jointly identify which of the options you both agree have potential and are willing to discuss further. These options can then be cultivated, developed, and refined as you work towards an agreement that both of you can feel satisfied with. By using this method for collaborative problem-solving you greatly enhance the chances of reaching an optimal and mutually agreeable solution. In addition, this method also allows the commitment to build incrementally so that neither party feels that they are being rushed or pressured into commitment.

✓ CHECKLIST SOLVING PROBLEMS

	YES	NO
• Are you using questions to understand the other party's needs?	☐	☐
• Are you checking your understanding of their needs with them?	☐	☐
• Have you asserted your needs in a friendly and composed way?	☐	☐
• Have you used the "bridging question" to define the problem?	☐	☐
• Are you engaging them in brainstorming for mutual solutions?	☐	☐
• Have you generated a range of options?	☐	☐
• Have you reached consensus on the most promising options?	☐	☐
• Have you formalized an agreement?	☐	☐

Breaking impasse

When parties in conflict dig in their heels over their demands, impasse can develop rapidly. It takes skill, patience, and persistence to guide the negotiation back towards resolution while maintaining the relationship. Reframing and questioning are good tools to break impasse.

Reframing

Impasse is reached when people are inflexible. If someone presents a rigid position to you, do not counter with an equally rigid position, but reframe the position in question. For example, a customer might say: "We do not trust you to deliver the product on time". Respond with the reframing technique by saying: "So you like the product and terms, but would like assurance of timely delivery?". You have translated their rigid declaration into a flexible statement of need, and averted potential impasse.

**PARTIES TALKING
AT ONE ANOTHER**
Listen attentively to the other party; summarize their position before presenting your thoughts.

Questioning

Impasse can also be reached when solutions are proposed too early. The more information you obtain about the other side's concerns and needs, the better equipped you are to offer solutions. Question and probe to loosen their positions and understand their needs and concerns better. If, for example, they say the slides will not be ready on time for the meeting, rather than insisting, ask (non-threatening) questions such as: "What is preventing you from having them ready on time?". By getting more information you can think of possible solutions, and steer clear of impasse.

HOW TO...
REFRAME

Listen to the other party's position.

Ask yourself what their needs and concerns are.

Translate them into more flexible need statements.

Causes and resolutions to impasse situations

RIGID POSITIONS ON BOTH SIDES
Reframe and translate rigid positions into more general and flexible statements of need.

SOLUTIONS PUT FORWARD TOO EARLY AND REJECTED
Question the other party and probe to obtain further information about their concerns and needs.

OPTIONS NOT SUFFICIENTLY EXPLORED OR EXHAUSTED
Look to change strength and/or scope of a proposal so that other options are opened up to you.

Getting past resistance

Occasionally, you might be faced with a stubborn person who refuses to engage in negotiation or problem-solving. Before throwing up your hands in utter frustration, remember that there are skills and techniques you can use to get past the resistance and guide the negotiation forward productively.

Understanding resistance

When someone refuses to engage, consider it an expression of a concern they have. You need to uncover that concern and address it appropriately. Instead of trying to engage the person in the issue at hand, talk about why they do not wish to engage. You might ask them: "What is the worst outcome that could happen if we discussed this?". They might say they are concerned about being pressured into a commitment they regret. Having understood their concerns, you could suggest an initial meeting with no expectations of commitment, thereby alleviating their fears.

Having alternatives

Before negotiating, it is crucial you consider your alternatives. What would be the best option in case the other person refuses to engage? It may be getting HR to send a warning to the individual about his performance. This can be used as leverage if absolutely necessary. For example, you could say: "I am hoping we come to an understanding because it wouldn't be good for either of us if this were to escalate further – so how should we proceed?". The purpose of alternatives is to steer the discussion back towards negotiation.

Responding to threats

Think carefully too about ways in which the other person might try to threaten you. Then consider how you can make it harder for them to do so, or ways to persuade them that such an action would be unwise. You should do this before you start to negotiate. Let's say that they try to intimidate you by threatening to tell your manager about your ineffective management skills. You could make it harder for them to pursue by briefing your manager beforehand. Then when they make their threat, you can calmly and gracefully tell them that although they are welcome to do so, you have already briefed your manager, who is fully aware of the situation. By doing this you have neutralized the threat from the difficult person, and they can no longer hold you hostage. A little thought and preparation beforehand can make a big difference later.

❓ ASK YOURSELF... BEFORE ENTERING A NEGOTIATION

- What could I do independently of the other person in the event that they are unwilling to engage?
- How can I use that as leverage to engage them?
- How might they try to threaten and intimidate me?
- What can I do or say to neutralize their threat?

CASE STUDY

Dealing with threats

The pilots' union of a major supply chain company was not pleased with how they were being compensated by management. They attempted to engage management to discuss this on several occasions, but were met each time with resistance, defiance, and refusal. Management knew that the union was in no position financially to stage a strike and therefore felt they had the upper hand. The union considered all alternatives carefully, and then decided to strengthen their option of a strike by securing a line of credit from the bank. Armed with this very real and serious alternative they approached management again and suggested that perhaps they should sit down and talk before matters escalated to a costly strike. This time around management sat down to discuss things with the union and together they were able to resolve the issues and reach an agreement.

Defusing turf wars

It is not uncommon for internal competition to exist within the organization, either between individuals or between teams. These struggles could revolve around resources, funding, project ownership, recognition, and visibility. When people are concerned about protecting their turf, this leads to performance, productivity, and morale being undermined.

Diagnosing turf wars

When teams exhibit diminished performance and productivity, one possible cause is internal competition, either within the team or between teams. Talk to the team or individuals and listen very carefully for clues that turf wars are the problem. These can be destructive if ignored, but a source of creative collaboration when resolved. Consider two competing product teams in a large corporation. Each team believes that the product on which it is working will be a key product for the company and will boost revenue and market share. Each is therefore convinced that they should have priority with regards to budget and resources. As a result each team expends enormous effort to achieve visibility for their project as they vie for the limited funds and resources. This misdirected energy causes the teams to miss deadlines, delay deliverables, and use resources inefficiently, leading ultimately to customers being left disappointed.

Reviewing objectives

The first step in resolving turf wars is facilitating dialogue between the relevant teams or individuals. Each must have an understanding of their own objectives, and be able to share it. As the dialogue evolves, record the objectives of each party in full view. This allows each side to absorb what the other's concerns are. It is important to encourage them to discuss not only business objectives such as revenues and growth, but personal concerns such as recognition and career advances too. Besides being an important step in resolving internal competition, this process will also help build trust and collaboration.

Aligning objectives

When dialogue takes place, both sides should look for ways to align objectives so as to maximize resources and optimize efficiency. They could integrate their products and add value for customers, or collaborate on features common to both products. They could jointly market both products. They could even negotiate for both sides to achieve more visibility for their work, rather than competing for attention. Once the teams or individuals have reached an agreement, it is good practice to document the points of agreement into a charter of collaboration, to act as a roadmap for the future.

FOSTERING CO-OPERATION

FAST TRACK	OFF TRACK
Creating an environment that rewards collaboration	Deliberately undermining others for the purpose of competing
Engaging other teams or individuals in communication and dialogue	Reacting to competitive tactics used by other people
Looking for creative ways of working together	Tolerating destructive internal competition
Taking the initiative to lead the other team into collaboration	Trying to control others rather than collaborating

Managing the agreement

You might assume that once an acceptable resolution has been reached, the negotiation is complete. This might be true where there is no ongoing working relationship. In the average work environment, however, you usually need to continue to work together, and the agreement you reach needs to stand the test of time.

TIP

ANTICIPATE PROBLEMS

Look ahead, and try to see what problems might occur with the agreement. If you try to deal with a problem after it occurs, you will already be emotionally embroiled and may find it harder to deal with the issue objectively.

Asking insightful questions

A few careful questions before you leave the negotiating table could prevent emotional distress, frustration, and financial loss later. Reaching an agreement is only part of the negotiation. How that agreement will be managed and maintained is equally important. Disputes may arise, commitments may be missed, and circumstances may change, calling for renegotiation. You need to agree on a plan to address such issues. Ask some "what if" and "worst-case scenario" questions, for example: "What is there that we could possibly imagine that might go wrong with this arrangement?", and "What circumstance would trigger a need to renegotiate?". These questions should generate some very productive discussions.

Planning for contingencies

Having identified potential problem areas in the agreement through questioning, both parties should jointly prepare for contingencies by designing systems to address them. Both parties will then feel responsible for managing the agreement. Plans may include a mutually acceptable dispute-resolution system, or perhaps a communication plan that allows for open discussions on a regular basis, or identifying potential triggers that would make re-negotiation necessary.

Putting it in writing

People generally comply with written agreements more readily than verbal ones. Putting it in writing also clarifies the points of agreement and makes it harder for the other party to deny later. Once you have decided on contingency plans, put them in writing along with the primary agreement. Your agreement will now address not only what you agreed to, but also how it will be implemented and managed in the long term. Involve the other party in this and make sure that you both feel comfortable, and that the language of the agreement accurately reflects your intent.

MANAGING THE AGREEMENT QUESTIONS

ISSUE	QUESTIONS
Miscommunication	• What kind of communication plan do we need to have in place to maintain this agreement? • What foreseeable gaps might occur in our communication? • What should be the frequency of our communication? • Which methods should we use for our communication?
Misunderstandings	• What misunderstandings could potentially occur around this agreement? • What can we do to decrease chances of these misunderstandings occuring? • What is our plan for dealing with these misunderstandings, if and when they do occur?
Missed deadlines and commitments	• What potential reasons may cause missed deadlines and commitments? • What can we do to decrease the chances of deadlines and commitments being missed? • What is our plan for dealing with missed deadlines and commitments when they do occur?
Breakdown in the agreement	• What potential situations might occur that would trigger the need for renegotiation? • Within how many days will we agree to communicate should such a situation become evident to one or both of us? • What is our plan for re-negotiation should the need arise?

Saying "no"

Many of us avoid saying "no" even when we know we should. We are afraid of the defensiveness and anger it may cause, especially in a difficult person. But knowing how to say "no" constructively and positively is a skill we need in order to manage our relationships with authenticity and effectiveness.

Saying "no" constructively

Never agree to anything which is unacceptable to you just out of a fear of saying "no". John F. Kennedy's statement: "Don't fear to negotiate but don't negotiate out of fear" is a good rule to remember when working with difficult people. However, assertiveness heightens the potential for confrontation. To say "no" constructively, first explain your needs and constraints, invite them to suggest solutions, and conclude by telling them what you *can* do.

DON'T CONCEDE
If you feel uncomfortable saying yes, ask yourself why. If the reason is legitimate then resist the urge to say yes just to avoid an adverse reaction.

Replenishing the relationship

Even though the other party may comply with your constructive "no", the relationship could be affected. Also, in a long-term working relationship, there may be other times you need to say "no". You therefore have to balance your "no" with replenishing the relationship. Look for opportunities to nurture the relationship. Get together with the person for coffee or lunch and include them in events. Show them your "no" was not personal.

EXPLAIN YOUR CONSTRAINTS
Explain to the other person in a firm but friendly way what your constraints are and why you are unable to comply with their request.

LISTEN TO THEIR REQUEST
Make sure that the other person feels that their request has been heard, by summarizing and then checking your understanding with them.

Saying "no" constructively

TELL THEM WHAT YOU *ARE* WILLING TO DO
Let them know what you are willing to do for them which would not conflict with your needs or constraints.

BRAINSTORMING ALTERNATIVES
Invite them to jointly brainstorm alternative ways of satisfying their needs and requests.

REPLENISH THE RELATIONSHIP
Go out of your way to nurture the relationship and demonstrate that despite your declining their request, you still wish to be friends.

Making requests

When you want a difficult person to change their behaviour, you will usually tell them what you *do not* want them to do. However, unless you request positive action that is specific, doable, and framed positively, their behaviour is unlikely to change.

TIP

FRAME YOUR REQUEST BEFOREHAND

Always think about how to frame your request in advance. You will then be able to design a request that is more likely be well received and accepted.

Being specific

When making requests, you should be as specific as possible. Suppose you have a team member who you would like to participate more in team meetings. You could tell them that you would like them to be less passive, or that you'd like them to participate more in meetings. This is ineffective because you will have communicated what you don't want rather than what you do want. An optimal request would be that you want at least two meaningful comments from them in every project meeting. By being specific and framing your request positively in terms of what you do want, you have communicated a clear directive that the other person can implement.

Making it doable

When you make a request, be sure it is realistic, and that it does not conflict with the other party's needs, authority, or ability. For example, suppose you decide to reduce the use of paper in your office, as part of an environmental initiative. Asking your staff to do everything electronically is not practical because there are times when hard copies may be necessary. A more suitable request would be to ask them to develop a policy for when to use electronic copies only. You have now made your request realistic and doable.

Requesting respectfully

Even difficult people need to feel respected. When that happens they tend to be a little less difficult, and when it does not, they will be even more difficult. When making a request, present it as a respectful request and not as a command, demand, or ultimatum. This will allow the other party to accept it without losing face. Let's say a co-worker habitually stops by your office to chat and interrupts your work. If you say: "Stop barging in here unannounced and wasting my time", it will make them feel disrespected, rejected, and defensive. Even if they cease their behaviour they will not do so gladly and will continue to be difficult. A more respectful way would be to say: "I would love to chat more but I must complete these assignments. Would you like to continue after work?". The content is similar but the phraseology makes all the difference.

ASK YOURSELF... ABOUT YOUR REQUEST

- Do I clearly understand what I need?
- Am I making a specific request?
- Is it framed positively (what I *do* want, and not what I *do not* want)?
- Is it doable from their perspective?
- Have I thought about how to phrase it so that it is respectful?

INTERPRETING PHRASEOLOGY

DISRESPECTFUL	RESPECTFUL
Do not interrupt me!	I would be happy to hear your thoughts once I have finished what I would like to say.
Do not be so angry!	Would you please talk to me about what is causing your anger?
You better get that done or else... !	Would you be willing to do that for us?
You are never around to help!	Could you be available on Monday afternoon to help with the office move?

Dealing with dishonesty

When confronted with dishonesty, you might feel betrayed, angry, anxious, or disappointed. You might be confused as to whether to confront it or ignore it, or how to confront it. There isn't a single answer for all situations, but there are guidelines you can apply to any given situation.

TIP

RESIST ACTING IMMEDIATELY

Take some time to consider whether the other person's actions were intentional. If they were, carefully decide what course of action to pursue.

Evaluating your options

When faced with dishonesty, do not immediately accuse the other person, as they will deny the allegation and become defensive. If you are not sure whether the other party is intentionally dishonest, or if the issue is unimportant, you may give them the benefit of the doubt. Where you find an established pattern of dishonesty and you need to continue the working relationship, you will need to address the dishonesty constructively. If a pattern of dishonesty appears, and the working relationship is not crucial, it may be time to disengage. When disengagement is not an option, consider taking the issue to higher management.

TIP

LET THE OTHER SAVE FACE

After confronting dishonesty, you could say something like: "I would like to hear more about your perspective, and discuss how we might overcome my feelings of uneasiness so that we can continue a successful working relationship".

Confronting dishonesty

If you have decided that confronting the dishonest person is the right course of action, provide specific instances of their deceitfulness, while at the same time allowing them to save face. For example, after telling them what led you to believe they were being dishonest, you could say: "I feel mislead at best and deceived at worst, and am uneasy about working with you further. What can you do that might overcome my anxiety?". This response confronts the dishonesty directly, even while allowing them to save face and negotiate a solution. Raising the issue explicitly will also discourage them from being dishonest with you in the future.

Disengaging
with dishonesty

If someone demonstrates a pattern of deliberate dishonesty, and your working relationship with them is not essential, you have the option of walking away. This option may also be appropriate if you have confronted them about their dishonesty with no effect. However, before disengaging, carefully weigh the costs, benefits, and practicality of terminating the working relationship. Once you decide to disengage it is a good idea to let them know what you intend to do and why. For example, after clearly explaining instances of how they deceived you, you might say: "Having felt misled and deceived on several occasions while working with you, I would feel more comfortable if we did not work together in the future. I hope you can respect my feelings". This lets them know in simple and unambiguous terms about where you stand with them.

Chapter 4

Managing the difficult person

Managing the difficult person can be a taxing and frustrating experience. The more techniques and skills you have in your repertoire, the better equipped you will be to work with them in a way that is fulfilling and rewarding for the both of you.

Starting with yourself

At times, when other people appear to be difficult, you will find that if you examine yourself it is you who is being difficult. They are merely reacting to your negative attitudes. Attitudes are contagious, so if you show leadership and set the right examples, these will help others behave appropriately.

USE COLOURFUL POSTERS

Post colourful laminated posters of the desired attitudes and values you wish to reinforce around your department, so that your employees are constantly being reminded of them.

Setting an example

As a manager, you are the leader, and your example will be adopted by your group. If your employees are not working productively, perhaps they do not see you as a role model. If they are not accepting responsibility for their actions, be prepared to show more responsibility yourself. Acknowledge your mistakes, and you will notice their attitude improving. If your employees are not giving each other credit for good ideas and exceptional work, you should set an example and be generous with praise where it is deserved. Look at your employees to diagnose your own management attitude.

Seeking feedback

Your employees are a valuable source of feedback for improving your management attitude. You can find out how others perceive you, and create an environment where self-improvement is valued. When you ask for feedback, reassure them that constructive criticism is important and will not have negative consequences. Explain that you want to understand what it is like working for you. Ask them what they feel you do well, and where you could improve. Resist the urge to become defensive, and consider how you can use their feedback to improve your management attitude.

Being positive

There are some general positive attitudes that managers need to possess and demonstrate. A sense of humour is important: studies show that humour in the workplace promotes productivity and creativity. Remember not to take yourself too seriously. Do take an interest in the personal lives of your employees. Ask after the health of a spouse who was unwell or how their summer vacation was. Do not just give praise for a job well done, but also provide encouragement when your employees are finding things difficult. Being honest, transparent, and ethical are other positive traits.

TAKING RESPONSIBILITY

FAST TRACK

OFF TRACK

FAST TRACK	OFF TRACK
Understanding that your employees' behaviour may be a reflection of yours	Being out of touch with your employees
Setting examples and being a role model for the way you want your employees to behave	Paying little attention to your employees' needs and concerns
Seeking feedback from your employees	Discouraging frequent, open, and honest communication
Taking an interest in their personal lives	Behaving in underhanded and unethical ways

Tackling difficult behaviour

Your effectiveness as a manager is measured not only by how you manage your motivated people, but also by how you handle your difficult people. Awareness of common difficult behaviours and how to respond to them will give you the expertise to manage the less common ones too.

TIP

CHANNELLING BEHAVIOUR

Manage others' difficult behaviour by channelling it towards a productive resolution If you find yourself at a loss, ask them: "What would you do in my situation when faced with (describe their behaviour)?".

Neutralizing the antagonist

The antagonist will always blame others for failures and seldom take responsibility for their own actions. To manage this behaviour, redirect their attention back to themselves, and encourage them to take responsibility. Guide them in coming up with positive ideas, rather than getting drawn into their blame-game.

Defeating the defeatist

The defeatist is the perpetual pessimist in the group. Whenever an idea is presented, they throw up their arms and cry out that it will never work. This kills the idea even before it has been explored. In responding to the defeatist, ask them what specifically it is about the idea that they find unrealistic. This technique engages the defeatist constructively.

Interrupting the rambler

The rambler brings group productivity to a halt with their endless monologues. To regain control, use summarizing plus a closed-ended question. If the rambler is holding forth about some new product feature they are promoting, summarize their key points for them, then ask a closed-ended question. This interrupts their counter-productive behaviour and gives you control.

Dealing with common difficult behaviours

THE ANTAGONIST
Always blames others and does not take responsibility.

→

Redirect their attention back to themselves: ask them to suggest ways they can contribute positively to the project.

→

Example: "If you feel that the new person is not being supportive in the project, what could you do to improve that?".

THE DEFEATIST
Cynical and pessimistic; believes no idea will ever work out.

→

Ask them what specifically they think will not work, and why. Ask them how the idea could be improved to make it work.

→

Example: "What exactly about the marketing plan is concerning you? What ideas could you suggest to improve it?".

THE RAMBLER
Interrupts proceedings with endless, pointless monologues.

→

Interrupt them, and summarize their relevant points, then ask a closed-ended question to regain control.

→

Example: "Have you discussed this with marketing yet?" (closed-ended question). "Let's discuss that off-line".

TIP

Aligning tasks with competencies

**MAKE IT SAFE
WHEN ASKING
QUESTIONS**

When questioning
employees about
job satisfaction and
challenges, explain
that you want them
to perform better –
not dismiss them –
and only honesty
and openness
will facilitate this.

If an employee is given a job for which they are
not trained or which they do not find satisfying, it
can cause loss of motivation and difficult behaviour.
If a highly creative person is put into the accounting
department to crunch numbers, they will be
unmotivated and will underperform. When you
notice an unmotivated employee, try to find out
how they feel about their job. Ask questions such as:
"What do you particularly enjoy about your job?",
and "What do you find most challenging?". Another
useful question to ask is: "If you could describe
your ideal job, what might that look like?". These
questions will give you a sense of whether their
tasks are aligned with their skills. If not, you will
either need to give them training in the skills that
they are lacking, or perhaps move them to a position
that is more aligned with their abilities. Before you
can determine the alignment between tasks and
competencies, however, be sure that the task
and its desired results have been clearly defined
and that the employee understands exactly
what is required of them. Otherwise, the problem
could just be a lack of clear understanding
instead of a loss of necessary skills.

CASE STUDY

Fitting competencies to roles

A manufacturing company adopted a
new pay-for-performance scheme which
would be benchmarked by standards of
efficiency. One particular employee was
resistant to this because her strength
was quality. Realizing that her ability
to work to high standards was no longer
aligned with the company's new focus
on efficiency made her feel dejected.
Her manager realized the problem and
did not wish to lose a valuable and
hard-working employee. He created
a new position in which she was to
oversee quality so as to ensure that it
would not be compromised in the
name of efficiency. By making sure
that her tasks were aligned with her
competencies, he was able to retain
a satisfied and motivated employee
who would advance the interests of
the company significantly.

Meeting employees' needs

Besides obvious needs such as a suitable work environment, safety, and respect, employees are motivated by a sense of being valued. They should feel recognized for good work. Find things you can acknowledge them for, even if it is something small. Responsibility is another way of motivating people. Look for opportunities to give your employees responsibility in line with their capability. Suppose in a meeting on increasing sales someone suggests the development of a new distribution channel. You could say: "That sounds interesting. Could you research feasibility using our SWOT analysis method and suggest an implementation plan at the next meeting?". Giving them a specific task and added responsibility will motivate them.

TIP

RECOGNIZE SINCERELY

Any contrived acknowledgement on your part will be transparent to employees and will not motivate.

Using incentives and rewards

An incentive-and-reward programme is a good way to keep your employees motivated and performing well. Airlines do this with their customers through frequent-flier rewards and large retailers encourage buyers with special discount coupons. A similar system can be used to drive your employees' performance. An incentive-and-reward programme can include paid time off, trips, profit sharing, free merchandise, and employee-of-the-month contests with associated perks. Involve your employees in designing such a programme. Also consult with HR, accounting, and legal on the plan. Make sure the plan is clearly communicated and well understood.

Analyzing performance

The process of reviewing performance and setting goals often generates anxiousness among managers regarding their employees' reactions. This robs them of the opportunities that performance reviews and goal-setting offer to improve team management. Knowing how to conduct reviews and set objectives is essential in leading the difficult person.

Understanding the purpose

The term "performance review" is slightly misleading, as it implies an emphasis on past performance. The purpose of such as review is to set objectives for the future: to analyze the employee's strengths and weaknesses and provide constructive feedback. It should be positive and objective at all times. When the employee leaves the review, they should feel like a valuable member of the team with the skill to contribute positively. See yourself as a mentor and not as a judge.

Involving the employee

A performance review should be collaborative. Engage the employee so that they participate and feel involved in the process. As points of departure for further discussion, ask them about their accomplishments over the past year and what they want to change about their job. When giving feedback, avoid vagueness and ambiguity. Be specific and provide detailed observations that illustrate the issue at hand. This will let your employee know exactly what they need to do to improve.

Setting achievable goals for your employees

COLLABORATIVE
Make sure you involve your employees in goal setting by seeking their input, ideas, and suggestions. Aim for mutual agreement.

MANAGEABLE
Articulate goals in specific and realistic terms. "Reducing time to market from 12 to nine weeks" is more helpful than "Reducing time to market".

MEASURABLE
Establish agreed-upon benchmarks to measure whether goals have been met. Document goals and benchmarks and share the results with employees.

TIME-BOUND
Jointly determine timeframes within which results can realistically be expected. Definitive timeframes create a sense of urgency.

MONITORED
Set up regular communication for monitoring and feedback. This will ensure employees stay on course, and allow for mid-course corrections.

Spotting the symptoms

When an employee is performing poorly, look for symptoms of demotivation such as lethargy, lack of enthusiasm, lateness, frequent health problems, anger, depression, or any other sign that all is not well. If such symptoms are present, view their poor performance as a call for help rather than as incompetence or a refusal to cooperate. Look for what might be causing their demotivation and how you can help. Consider causes such as objectives not being clearly defined, insufficient feedback, tasks being too challenging, or a lack of confidence in their own ability. There could also be personal reasons, such as an ailing parent or marital problems. Make sure you try to uncover any underlying problem that may be present.

Talking about poor performance

Once you have identified poor performance and spotted behaviour patterns that suggest an underlying problem, you need to address the problem with the employee. Talk to them in a supportive way and try to jointly figure out what the problem is. You might say: "Your performance of late has been below par. Last week you were not ready with the presentation. The previous week, accounting found several mistakes in your financial report. I have also noticed a general lack of enthusiasm in you and am concerned. I think you are going through a difficult time, and I would like to help you.". With this approach you have sent a message of understanding, sympathy, and support, allowing your employee to explain the situation to you.

TIP

ASK YOUR EMPLOYEES FOR INPUT

Always try to elicit input from your employees when resolving problems. People do not like to have solutions imposed upon them.

Knowing your limitations

There will be times when, after listening, careful questioning, suggesting ideas, and engaging the employee in designing possible solutions, you still fail to resolve their behaviour. This is the time to recognize your limitations and seek help elsewhere. Do not see this as a failure on your part. Just as a doctor sometimes needs to refer a patient to a specialist, you might at times need to refer an employee to someone who has more expertise or experience in handling the issue. Use all the resources available to you. Get advice from other managers. Get help from executives. Speak to the appropriate people at HR and where necessary get help through your company's employee assistance programme. Don't try to solve a problem that is beyond your competency and expertise. Accept that you can help others realize their potential, but that you cannot change others or mould them in your own image. Even if you feel that you have been unsuccessful, use the opportunity to improve your skills by asking yourself what lessons you can learn from the experience.

TIP

DISCUSS YOUR IDEAS

Talk to your managers, colleagues, and mentors about how best to tackle the difficult employee. Besides helping you with the problem, it will also expand your learning experience.

✔ CHECKLIST EXAMINING POOR PERFORMANCE:

	YES	NO
• Does the employee have a clear understanding of their goals and are they realistic?	☐	☐
• Are they receiving adequate and timely feedback?	☐	☐
• Do they have the ability, training, and resources to perform the required tasks?	☐	☐
• Are they bored with too little challenge, or overwhelmed with too much challenge?	☐	☐
• Are there personal issues that they are dealing with?	☐	☐

Coaching your employee

Coaching* is a useful, though under-utilized, means to drive your employee to higher levels of self-awareness, discovery, action, and productivity. As a manager, it is important that you have the coaching skills to draw out the best from your employees, even diffficult ones, for their benefit and for the benefit of your organization.

Understanding coaching

*Coaching —
*Engaging the
employee in a
thought-provoking,
creative process that
inspires them
to maximize
their personal
and professional
potential.*

Coaching is a process that pushes your employee into recognizing professional obstacles, creatively devising action plans to overcome those obstacles, and evaluating the results. It is not the coach who develops the solutions but the employee. The coach is the facilitator who inspires the employee to go ahead and fix the problems. The coaching objective is to help your employee gain greater clarity, new insights and perspectives, organized thoughts, and the ability to arrive at their own solutions.

TIP

**GIVE THE
EMPLOYEE TIME**

When you are coaching and have asked a question, wait patiently and quietly for the employee to answer. Don't try to avoid the discomfort of silence by offering your own answer.

Questioning

The management guru Peter Drucker once said of leadership: "The leader of the past knew how to tell; the leader of the future will know how to ask". Asking questions that lead to deep thinking is the coach's most important skill. Not all questions generate deep thinking. The question "What is on your to-do list today?" does not inspire thought. The revision: "Which three tasks on your list will have the greatest impact?" will force the employee to think. When coaching, look for questions that inspire deeper thought and unlock new ideas. It is those questions from which your employee will learn and benefit the most.

Balancing encouragement

When your employee is working hard in a coaching session, give encouragement as far as posssible. For example: "I really appreciated your rigorous self-analysis and am impressed by the insight it produced". This recognizes their effort and motivates them further. Make sure your encouragement is genuine. Balance encouragement measure-for-measure with challenge. Be aware that challenges need to stretch your employee beyond their current thinking and actions, but not so far that it goes beyond their abilities. You will need to assess this based on your knowledge of your employee.

USE BODY LANGUAGE EFFECTIVELY

When interacting with the employee, make sure to maintain eye contact and lean in towards them. This will indicate genuine interest, attention, honesty, and trust on your part.

COACHING: THE FOUR PHASES

PHASE	USEFUL QUESTIONS TO ASK
Identifying Helping the employee identify the core issue that needs to be addressed. If there are multiple issues, use this phase to break down the issues into manageable tasks.	• Where are you stuck? • What is the most important thing you need to do today? • What topics would give you the greatest return for this investment of time?
Discovering Helping the employee discover their needs, wants, options, resources, assets – anything that could make an immediate difference to their performance.	• What are your initial thoughts in approaching this problem? • What have you already tried? And what were the results? • What are some options to deal with this?
Planning for action Helping the employee design a specific action plan that is realistic and practical. This plan is driven by the information gathered in the discovering phase.	• What action do you plan to take? By when? • Of all the options we listed in the discovery phase, which would be the best action? • What resources do you need to implement this plan? • How could you mitigate the risks?
Evaluating Helping the employee put systems into place to measure the success of their action plan.	• What systems do you need to put into place to hold yourself accountable? • What criteria will you use to measure your success?

Dealing with difficult teams

As a manager, you may find yourself challenged not just by difficult persons, but also by difficult and unco-operative teams. Being able to resolve issues between teams is a critical managerial skill. It involves creating the right conditions for dialogue, developing collaboration, and maintaining relationships.

TIP

ESTABLISH ROLES AND RULES
When facilitating dialogue, establish roles and agree on ground rules. Roles might include someone to chair the discussion. An example of a ground rule could be only one person speaking at a time. This will keep the discussion productive.

Facilitating dialogue

Consider two competing teams in your organization. Each team is certain that it is working on a product that will boost revenue. Each fights for budgets, resources, and visibility, believing that their product deserves priority. This conflict results in reduced productivity, missed deadlines, increased costs, inefficient use of resources, and eroded morale. In this situation, your first step is to facilitate dialogue between the teams. You need a rigorous appraisal of each team's goals, objectives, needs, and concerns. Make each team feel heard and understood, and a collaborative atmosphere will soon develop.

Working towards collaboration

Once you have an understanding of the needs and concerns of each team, look for creative ways to meet those needs. In a case of competing product development teams, for example, you may find ways of integrating products that will add value, or perhaps ways of collaborating on some specific component common to both products, or even a joint marketing campaign. Seeking creative ways of aligning teams' objectives can turn potential conflict into collaboration.

Going forward

Even after a working relationship has been developed between the two teams, effort is still needed to maintain and manage the relationship going forward. It is useful to document the agreement reached between the teams in a memorandum of understanding. This helps build compliance and pre-empts misunderstandings. Open communication between the teams should be encouraged, as problems usually arise when effective communication is absent.

CASE STUDY

Using feedback

An American company used customer feedback to improve its products. The marketing department contacted customers to obtain feedback, which they passed on to product development. Product development was to act on the information and produce new and improved products. Marketing accused product development of not fulfilling the company's promise to use customer feedback to improve products. Product development accused marketing of not appreciating the resources and manpower required to design and develop the new products that customers suggested. Tensions between the two teams grew. Then both teams worked towards collaboration. They created a joint work group with representatives from both marketing and product development, which would interface with customers and mediate issues between marketing and product development. The company's products improved as a result.

Including the difficult person

A team is greater than the sum of its members. When faced with a difficult team member, you may be tempted to insulate yourself from them. However, including them as a valued member of the team will help alleviate their difficult behaviour. Frequent interaction, encouragement, and delegation are effective ways of including the difficult employee.

LET EMPLOYEES DEVISE THEIR OWN SOLUTIONS

When delegating, give your employees space to find their own solutions. By trying to impose your own thinking, you will defeat the purpose of delegation.

Interacting frequently

Frequent personal interaction with your employees will make them feel connected to you and the team. A few moments of talking to an employee will promote satisfaction in them about the work they are doing. Greeting them by name adds meaningfulness to the interaction. Show an interest in their personal lives: ask them how their weekend was, or about their outside interests. This will build the relationship and provide you with information. For example, if they talk about their art lessons, you will learn they have a creative side – a resource that you may not have accessed. Ask them work-related questions too. A sense of self-worth is needed for people to perform at their best.

BE GENUINE

When offering encouragement, be genuine, authentic, and sincere at all times. Lacking sincerity, patronizing, and pretending will be transparent and will backfire on you.

Providing encouragement

To make people feel they are valued team members acknowledge jobs well done and give encouragement for challenges not yet met. This does not mean that constructive criticism is not important, but it will be better received if it is balanced with acknowledgment and encouragement where appropriate. Bear in mind that you can find words of praise even with difficult people. When offering encouragement, be specific. It shows you know what was involved, and helps your praise seem authentic.

Delegating

A good way to demonstrate belief and trust in an employee, and make them feel valued and included, is to delegate tasks and responsibilities to them. Besides showing your team that you trust and respect the person, this will also demonstrate that you are helping the person grow professionally. That person in turn will trust and respect you. Do not just delegate to your best workers, as this will breed resentment among others. Make sure to include everyone according to their capability, including the difficult employee. They may surprise you by how well they rise to the challenge. When delegating, start with smaller tasks and allow your employees' confidence to build before assigning larger projects. An employee who feels you trust them will reciprocate with a desire to please, and even the difficult person may make an effort at being reasonable.

HOW TO...
DELEGATE

> Communication: Explain accurately what it is you need done, by whom and by when, and the expected results.

> Context: Explain how the task links to the overall project and who is in charge of the other components of the project.

> Standards: Set realistic and achievable standards to measure the success of the task.

> Authority: Assign to your employee the authority that is required to get the task done.

> Support: Provide resources, funding, training, and access to the employee as needed for the task.

> Commitment: Make sure the employee knows the task to be accomplished, and that you have answered their questions.

IN FOCUS... CONSTRUCTIVE CRITICISM

People can be resistant to criticism, even the constructive kind. They become more resistant when the only time their manager communicates with them is to provide negative feedback. Ongoing interaction with an employee will allow criticism to be better received. A manager who interacts with an employee frequently can congratulate them on a successful project and also provide constructive criticism. Because of the regular communication between them, this will be received positively.

Implementing the last resort

When all your efforts at resolving an employee's attitude and performance are fruitless, it shows that there are irreconcilable differences between them and the organization. The only remaining option then might be termination of their employment. Knowing how to communicate this, and how to tackle its emotional and legal aspects, helps minimize associated damage.

*Dismissal —
To terminate
employment due to
unacceptable levels
of performance
or behaviour.

Being familiar with legalities

A carelessly handled dismissal* can lead to a costly wrongful-termination or discrimination lawsuit. It is therefore important you are familiar with company procedures and legal requirements with regard to terminating an employee. Consult HR for specific policies and procedures. These will often include: how to document poor performance or problematic behaviour, necessary steps for the termination process, and potential union issues. Be vigilant in following these procedures and consult with your legal counsel.

Communicating the bad news

When communicating the dismissal, look to preserve the employee's dignity and respect. Deliver the bad news in private to avoid humiliating the person. When dismissing them, speak in objective, non-judgmental terms. For example: "The improvement standards we both agreed on last quarter have not been met. We have made a decision to dismiss you." as opposed to: "You disappointed us by not meeting the standards we agreed upon – you're fired". If you are feeling anger towards the employee, postpone this discussion until you have calmed down. Show them sympathy, and give them an opportunity to vent any resentment they may feel towards you or the organization.

Helping employee transition

A disgruntled employee who talks about how badly they were treated can give your organization a poor reputation and make it hard for you to hire in the future. They might also talk to other employees and erode morale. Help the fired employee with the transition to another organization so that they feel well treated and are less likely to spread negative reports. Allow them, where possible, time to use the office to look for a new job. If HR offers career counselling services, help your employee access them. Offer to provide references, and try to arrange the best possible severance package. Showing compassion and goodwill will help soften the blow, and preserve your organization's integrity.

ASK HUMAN RESOURCES TO BE PRESENT

HR can help answer questions, serve as a witness to the discussion, and be a neutral voice in assisting with any adverse emotional or physical reactions.

DECIDING WHEN TO TERMINATE

DISMISS IMMEDIATELY	WARN AND PROCEED WITH DOCUMENTATION	NO CAUSE TO DISMISS
Carrying a weapon to work.	Persistently underperforming.	Taking a day off work that was legitimate under law or civic duty.
Revealing trade secrets.	Abusing sick leave or any privilege.	Blowing the whistle on something illegal.
Being blatantly dishonest.	Being consistently tardy or absent.	Filing for worker's compensation.
Endangering co-workers.	Being insubordinate.	Reporting health and safety code violations.
Being involved in sexual harassment.	Having a destructive attitude and being a negative influence.	Electing to belong or not to belong to a union.
Engaging in criminal activity, including involvement with illegal drugs.	Refusing to follow instructions.	Being a particular race, gender, age, sexual orientation, or marital status, or being pregnant.

Index

Author Biographies

MANAGING PEOPLE

Johanna Hunsaker is Professor of
Management and Organizational
Behaviour, and Team Leader of the
Management, Leadership, and Ethics
Group in the School of Business
Administration at the University of
San Diego. She has been on the
faculty at San Diego State University,
the University of Wisconsin,
Milwaukee, and has taught in France,
Germany, Spain, Hong Kong, and
Saipan. Dr Hunsaker has published
over 50 articles on management and
organization topics, and a book on
gender issues in the workplace,
*Strategies and Skills for Managerial
Women*. Her consultancy work
focuses on gender-related issues
in the workforce, especially with
reference to sexual harassment and
gender discrimination. Her clients
include Security Pacific Finance
Corporation, San Diego Community
College District, the United States
Border Patrol, the Australian and New
Zealand Institutes of Management,
Episcopal Community Services, the
San Diego Zoological Society, Naval
Personnel Command, the Brooktree
Corporation, several law firms, and
General Dynamics.

Phillip L. Hunsaker is Professor of
Management in the School of
Business Administration at the
University of San Diego. He has been
a faculty member at Bond University,

University of Wisconsin Milwaukee,
California State University Northridge,
University of Southern California,
University of California San Diego,
and Ahlers Center for International
Business in Paris, Rome, Munich,
Barcelona, and Prague. He consults
for many international organizations
including Coca-Cola, Qualcomm,
Atlantic Richfield, General Dynamics,
J.I. Case Co, Mead-Johnson, Boston
Scientific, and American Honda.
Dr Hunsaker has authored over
100 articles on management and
organization behaviour. He has so
far written 14 books including *The
New Art of Managing People*;
Management: A Skills Approach;
Training in Interpersonal Skills;
Communication at Work; *Training
in Management Skills*; *The Dynamic
Decision Maker*; *Management and
Organizational Behaviour* (European
edition); *You Can Make It Happen: A
Guide to Personal and Organizational
Change*; and *Strategies and Skills for
Managerial Women*.

**MOTIVATING PEOPLE AND
ACHIEVING HIGH PERFORMANCE**

Mike Bourne is Professor of Business
Performance and Director of the
Centre for Business Performance at
Cranfield School of Management in
the UK. After spending 15 years in
industry, Mike gained his PhD at
Cambridge University and has spent

the last 15 years helping companies design, develop, and use balanced scorecards and performance-management systems. He has worked with and consulted for companies including Accenture, Amadeus, BAe Systems, European Central Bank, Lloyds TSB, McCormick Europe, NHBC, Oki Europe, PWC, Schering, Thales, Tube Lines, Unilever, and Wolseley. He has authored over 100 publications and is a regular conference presenter and workshop leader. Mike is also a Chartered Management Accountant and a Chartered Engineer.

Pippa Bourne is Regional Director, East England, for the Institute of Chartered Accountants in England and Wales. She gained her MBA from Aston Business School and her early career was in marketing. She then moved into management development, running profit-making training businesses over many years at the Chartered Institute of Management Accountants, City University Business School, and the Chartered Institute of Management. Her recent interest has been in developing strategic processes for measuring and managing business sustainability. She has authored five books and co-edited the journal *Measuring Business Excellence.* Pippa is a Chartered Marketer.

PROJECT MANAGEMENT
Peter Hobbs has been training and consulting with project managers in a variety of industries for the past 15 years, and is a twice-published author on the subject. His particular passion is introducing project approach to those who would not traditionally have thought of their work in this way, giving them practical skills with which to scope, plan, and manage initiatives of all kinds. Peter is Managing Director of Vondel Professional Development, a consultancy specializing in project management, team leadership, and commercial skills. The company's core offerings of "Team Planning"™ and "Profitable Projects" have become part of many of their clients' core management programmes.

EFFECTIVE COMMUNICATION
James S. O'Rourke teaches management and corporate communication at the University of Notre Dame, where he is a Professor of Management and the Arthur F. and Mary J. O'Neil Director of the Eugene D. Fanning Center for Business Communication. Dr O'Rourke (PhD, Syracuse) is the author of numerous books, including *Management Communication: A Case Analysis Approach,* now in its 4th edition, as well as *The Truth About Confident Presenting,* published by the *Financial*

Times, and *Effective Communication,* published by Dorling Kindersley. He is principal author or directing editor of more than 200 published case studies in management and corporate communication, and a trustee of both The Arthur W Page Society and the Institute for Public Relations. He is a member of the Reputation Institute, and the Management Communication Association, and a regular consultant to Fortune 500 and mid-size businesses throughout North America.

INTERVIEWING PEOPLE

DeeDee Doke is the editor of fortnightly business-to-business magazine and leading UK recruitment industry title *Recruiter,* and its online sister *recruiter.co.uk.* She launched related title *Resourcing* and has written on human resources and recruitment issues for numerous magazines and daily newspapers.

PRESENTING

Aileen Pincus is the president and founder of the media and communications skills consultancy The Pincus Group, providing training in presentation, media, and crisis communications from offices in Washington DC to clients around the world. She is a former television reporter, having reported at both the local and national levels, a communications director for a US Senator, and a senior executive trainer for a global public relations firm. She is a sought-after speaker on effective executive communication. She lives with her husband Scot and two children, Benjamin and Anna, in Silver Spring, Maryland, USA.

NEGOTIATING

Michael Benoliel is the Director of the Center for Negotiation (www. centerfornegotiation.com). He has provided negotiation training for multinational corporations including Shell Oil, Prudential, British Petroleum, Applied Micro Devices, and PTT Chemicals, in the USA, UK, Switzerland, Singapore, Malaysia, Thailand, India, and Hong Kong. Some of his media interviews include: Bloomberg Television; CAN TV Channel 21, Chicago; *BusinessWeek; Straits Times; The Deal; The Washington Diplomat;* The Wall Street Radio Network; WXRK New York; and Reuter. Dr Benoliel is currently Associate Professor of Organizational Behaviour and Human Resources Practice at Singapore Management University. His more than 20 years of academic experience includes teaching effective negotiation in the MBA and Graduate Executive programmes at The Johns Hopkins University, University of Maryland University College, and Singapore Management University. He received his doctorate degree in Human Resource Development from The George Washington University and his doctoral dissertation was selected as a finalist in the Donald Bullock Award. He was trained in the Participant-Centered Learning method at the Harvard Business School. He is also a certified mediator and a certified trainer in Herrmann Brain-Dominance Instrument (HBDI). In 1991 he received the Special Achievement Award from The American Society for Training and Development. Currently, Dr Benoliel is serving on the editorial board of two academic journals.

Wei Hua is the founder of the management consulting firm International Perspectives (www.international-perspectives.com), and has extensive international experience in research, consulting, training, and teaching in mainland China, Japan, the USA, and Singapore.

SELLING

Eric Baron is the founder of The Baron Group, an international sales and sales management consulting firm. The Baron Group has been training sales professionals and sales managers around the world for almost 30 years, and the concepts included in the selling section of this book reflect much of what is covered in their programmes. Eric is an adjunct professor at Columbia University Business School. In 2008 he received the highly prestigious Deans Teaching Excellence Award for his popular course, Entrepreneurial Selling Skills.

His first book, *Selling Is a Team Sport,* was published in 2000 and is considered by many to be the definitive book about team selling. The Baron Group's client list includes many international companies including American Express, Research International, Pfizer Inc, JPMorgan Chase, BNP Paribas, BNY Mellon, Deutsche Bank, Prudential, Cadbury, Ogilvy, and Publicis. He lives in Westport, Connecticut, USA, with his wife of 40 years, Lois. His two grown daughters, Andrea and Deborah, have blessed him with three grandchildren.

WORKING WITH DIFFICULT PEOPLE

Raphael Lapin is a Harvard-trained negotiation specialist who advises corporations and governments around the world. He is a principal of the consultancy Conflict Management, Negotiation, and Mediation, and founding principal of Lapin Negotiation Strategies.

Acknowledgements

Original editions produced for DK by

cobaltid

The Stables, Wood Farm, Deopham Road,
Attleborough, Norfolk NR17 1AJ
www.cobaltid.co.uk
Editors: Louise Abbott, Kati Dye,
Maddy King, Sarh Tomley, Marek Walisiewicz
Designers: Darren Bland, Claire Dale,
Paul Reid, Annika Skoog, Lloyd Tilbury,
Shane Whiting

and

DK India
Editors: Ankush Saikia, Saloni Talwar
Designers: Ivy Roy
Design Manager: Arunesh Talapatra

The publisher would also like to thank
the following for their work at DK on the
original editions:
Peter Jones (Senior Editor), Daniel Mills
(Project Editor), Helen Spencer (Senior Art
Editor), Adèle Hayward (Executive Managing
Editor), Kat Mead (Managing Art Editor),
Ben Marcus (Production Editor),
Sonia Charbonnier (Creative Technical
Support), Stephanie Jackson (Publisher),
Peter Luff (Art Director).

The publisher would like to thank Yvonne
Dixon for indexing.

Picture credits

The publisher would like to thank the
following for their kind permission to
reproduce their photographs:
10 **Getty images:** Stephen Swintek;
12–13 **Getty Images:** Mike Powell; 19
Alamy Images: Jose Luis Stephens; 25
Alamy Images: artpartner-images.com;
33 **Alamy Images:** Horizon International
Images Limited; 36–37 **Getty Images:** Jetta
Productions; 42–43 **iStockphoto.com:**
Stefanie Timmermann; 47 **iStockphoto.com:**
Todd Harrison; 48–49 **Alamy Images:** Sarah
Weston; 52 **iStockphoto.com:** Jasmin Awad;
62 **Getty Images:** Chad Baker; 66–67 **Alamy
Images:** David Wall; 68 **Alamy Images:**
Steve Bloom Images; 70–71 **iStockphoto.
com:** imagedepotpro; 75 **iStockphoto.
com:** Jamie Otterstetter; 76 **iStockphoto.
com:** Evgeny Kuklev; 78 **Corbis: James W.
Porter;** 80–81 **Getty Images:** Zia Soleil; 83
iStockphoto.com: Ethan Myerson; 86–87
Corbis: Frédérik Astier; 88–89 **Getty Images:**
Werner Dieterich; 90–91 **Getty Images:**
Digital Vision; 92 **Corbis:** Cultura/Corbis
(cl); **Getty Images:** Susan Vogel (fbl); Brad
Wilson (clb); 93 **Corbis:** Cultura Limited (c);
Harry Vorsteher (ca); Getty Images: Rainer
Elstermann (cra); Frank van Groen (crb); Jed
Share/Kaoru Share (tr); Anthony Strack (tc);
Chev Wilkinson (cr); Hideki Yoshihara (cb). 94
iStockphoto.com: Kanstantsin Shcharbinski;
100–101 **Getty Images:** Scott Kleinman; 101
Corbis: William Whitehurst (ftr); 104–105
Corbis: Steve Allen; 109 **Getty Images:**
David Sacks; 111 **Corbis:** Solus-Veer; 115
iStockphoto.com: Sebastiaan de Stigter;
117 **Getty Images:** Medioimages/Photodisc;
120–121 **Getty Images:** Tanya Zouev; 124
Getty Images: Kevin Summers; 128–129
Getty Images: Hans Neleman; 134–135
 Corbis: So Hing-Keung; 140–141 **Corbis:**
Bruce Benedict; 142–143 **Corbis:** Tony
Kurdzuk/Star Ledger; 146 **iStockphoto.com:**
Robert Hadfield; 148–149 **iStockphoto.com:**
Alexandr Tovstenko; 155 **Alamy Images:**
FoodPhotography Eising/Bon Appetit; 161
iStockphoto.com: Vasiliki Varvaki; 164–165
Alamy Images: Redmond Durrell; 168–169

iStockphoto.com: Dmitry Kutlayev; 173 iStockphoto.com: Igor Smichkov; 174–175 **Alamy Images:** Tim Graham; 176–179 iStockphoto.com: Julien Grondin; 181 iStockphoto.com: Florea Marius Catalin; 187 **Corbis:** Leo Mason; 190 **Getty Images:** Michael Dunning; 196–197 **iStockphoto.com:** Emrah Turudu; 201 **Alamy Images:** Lenscap; 205 **iStockphoto.com:** Christian Pound; 208–209 **iStockphoto.com:** Chan Pak Kei; 210 **iStockphoto.com:** Kanstantsin Shcharbinski; 214 **Corbis:** Pete Saloutos (photo); 214 **iStockphoto.com:** Dar Yang Yan (icon); 216–217 **Getty Images:** Jacobs Stock Photography; 220 **iStockphoto.com:** mevans; 228–229 **iStockphoto.com:** Denis Babenko; 233 **Getty Images:** David Madison; 236 **iStockphoto.com:** bora ucak; 239 **Getty Images:** Coneyl Jay; 245 **iStockphoto.com:** james steidl; 246–247 **iStockphoto.com:** David Joyner; 250–251 **iStockphoto.com:** Denis Vorob'yev; 259 **iStockphoto.com:** tioloco; 262–263 **iStockphoto.com:** sandsun; 264 **iStockphoto.com:** mustafa deliormanli; 269 **iStockphoto.com:** dra_schwartz; 276 **Getty Images:** Joe Drivas; 280–281 **Getty Images:** Timothy Allen; 282 **Alamy:** Herbert Kehrer/imagebroker; 284–285 **Alamy:** artpartner-images.com; 288–289 **Getty Images:** Justin Pumfrey; 291 **iStockphoto.com:** Eric Isselée/Global Photographers; 293 iStockphoto.com: PeterNunes_Photography; 299 **iStockphoto.com:** Guillermo Perales Gonzalez; 302–303 (background) **Alamy:** Dan Atkin; 302–303 (sticky notes) **iStockphoto.com:** Julien Grondin; 308–309 **iStockphoto.com:** Kevin Russ; 312–313 **iStockphoto.com:** Robert Kohlhuber; 314 **iStockphoto.com:** blackred; 324–325 **Alamy:** David Osborn; 331 **Getty Images:** Darrin Klimek; 335 **Getty Images:** David Gould; 338 **iStockphoto.com:** Hanquan Chen; 340–341 **iStockphoto.com:** Susan Trigg; 347 **Getty Images:** Peter Dazeley; 350 Constantine Chagin; 352–353 IMAGEMORE Co., Ltd.; 357 Ravi Tahilramani; 359–359 **Getty Images:** George Diebold; 365cb Zac Macaulay; 365bc **Corbis:** Randy Faris; 366 **iStockphoto.com;** 372 Image Source; 374–375 Marc Dietrichc; 378–379 Ted Horowitz; 383 George Cairns; 390–391 Mads Abildgaard; 391 Vasiliy Yakobchuk; 395bl, br, tl Yunus Arakon; 395cl, cr, tr Sergejs Cunkevics; 399 Paul Taylor; 404–405 Thom Lang; 408–409 Coneyl Jay; 412–413 Darren Robb; 414–415 Luis Pedrosa; 418 **iStockphoto.com:** Emilia Kun; 420–421 **Alamy images:** Swerve; 428–429 **iStockphoto.com:** bluestocking; 430–431 **iStockphoto.com:** Rafa Irusta; 436 **iStockphoto.com:** Tammy Bryngelson; 439 (background bottom left and right) **iStockphoto.com:** Valerie Loiseleux; 439 (foreground bottom left) **iStockphoto.com:** Irina Tischenko; 439 (foreground bottom right) **iStockphoto.com:** Alexey Khlobystov; 443 **iStockphoto.com:** Mustafa Deliormanli; 444–445 **iStockphoto.com:** Alexandra Draghici; 445 **iStockphoto.com:** Oktay Ortakcioglu; 450 **iStockphoto.com:** Clint Scholz; 454 **iStockphoto.com:** Matjaz Boncina; 456–457 **iStockphoto.com:** Hsinli Wang; 460 **iStockphoto.com:** bluestocking; 461 (full page) **iStockphoto.com:** Robyn Mackenzie; 461 (centre) **iStockphoto.com:** Jennifer Johnson; 465 **iStockphoto.com:** Cristian Ardelean; 468–469 **iStockphoto.com:** Mustafa Deliormanli; 470–471 iStockphoto.com: Leon Bonaventura; 473 Alamy images: Judith Collins; 475 **Alamy Images:** bobo; 478 **iStockphoto.com:** eon Bonaventura; 480–481 **iStockphoto.com:** Kristian Stensoenes; 486 **Getty Images:** Tipp Howell (photo); 486 **iStockphoto.com:** Marc Brown (icon); 488–489 **Getty Images:** Neil Emmerson; 492–493 (background) Alamy: Ken Welsh; 492–493 **iStockphoto.com:** Clint Scholz; 496 **Getty Images:** artpartner-images; 498–499 **iStockphoto.com:** Aliaksandr Stsiazhyn; 501 **iStockphoto.com:** Floortje; 504–505 **iStockphoto.com:**

Joshua Blake; 510 **iStockphoto.com:** Luca di Filippo; 513 **iStockphoto.com:** Andrew Lilley; 514–515 **Alamy Images:** Food drink and diet/Mark Sykes; 518 **iStockphoto. com:** Chris Scredon; 521 **iStockphoto. com:** 7nuit; 522–523 **iStockphoto.com:** Lisa Thornberg; 524–525 **iStockphoto. com:** Olena Druzhynina; 530–531 **Getty Images:** Betsie Van der Meer; 537 **Corbis:** Patti Sapone/Star Ledger; 539 **iStockphoto. com:** Gary Woodard; 540–541 **iStockphoto. com:** Perry Kroll; 542–543 **iStockphoto. com:** blackred; 544 **iStockphoto.com:** Lise Gagne; 548–549 **Getty Images:** Ryan McVay; 552 **iStockphoto.com:** blackred; 554 **iStockphoto.com:** Steve Dibblee (photo); 554 **iStockphoto.com:** Bubaone; 556–557 (icon); **iStockphoto.com:** John Boylan; 564–565 **Alamy Images:** Pokorny/f1 online; 566–567 **iStockphoto.com:** Suprijono Suharjoto; 574–575 **iStockphoto.com:** Julien Grondin; 578–579 **iStockphoto.com:** Eliza Snow; 581 **iStockphoto.com:** Jennifer Borton; 584–585 **iStockphoto.com:** Mark Evans; 587 **iStockphoto.com:** Terry Wilson; 589 **Corbis:** Klaus Hackenberg/zefa; 593 **Corbis:** Joel W. Rogers; 595 **iStockphoto. com:** Adam Derwis; 596 **iStockphoto.com:** Roberta Casaliggi; 601 **Corbis:** Guntmar Fritz/zefa; 603 **iStockphoto.com:** Paul Kline; 609 **Science Photo Library:** Michael Clutson; 610 **iStockphoto.com:** Mehmet Ali Cida; 615 **Corbis:** David Madison; 618 **iStockphoto. com:** Cyrop; 624–625 **Corbis:** W. Perry Conway; 631 **Getty Images:** BLOOMimage; 631 **iStockphoto.com:** Kun Jiang; 632–633 Matthias Kulka; 639–640 Jeff Metzger; 644–645 Jeffrey Coolidge; 646–647 Gary S Chapman; 648–649 Luca Trovato; 650 Gregor Schuster; 656 UpperCut Images; 658–659 Ryan McVay; 660 Matthias Clamer; 662–663 Frans Lanting; 666–667 Shannon Fagan; 671 Buero Monaco; 675 George Diebold; 677 Alexander Vasilyev; 678–679 Joseph Sohm; 680 Image Source; 684 Jeppe Wikstrom; 688 DAJ; 688 Image Source.

All other images © Dorling Kindersley
For further information see:
www.dkimages.com